Japanese Capitalism and Entrepreneurship

Japanese Capitalism and Entrepreneurship

A History of Business from the Tokugawa Era to the Present

Pierre-Yves Donzé
and
Julia S. Yongue

OXFORD
UNIVERSITY PRESS

Great Clarendon Street, Oxford, OX2 6DP,
United Kingdom

Oxford University Press is a department of the University of Oxford.
It furthers the University's objective of excellence in research, scholarship,
and education by publishing worldwide. Oxford is a registered trade mark of
Oxford University Press in the UK and in certain other countries

© Pierre-Yves Donzé and Julia S. Yongue 2024

The moral rights of the authors have been asserted

All rights reserved. No part of this publication may be reproduced, stored in
a retrieval system, or transmitted, in any form or by any means, without the
prior permission in writing of Oxford University Press, or as expressly permitted
by law, by licence or under terms agreed with the appropriate reprographics
rights organization. Enquiries concerning reproduction outside the scope of the
above should be sent to the Rights Department, Oxford University Press, at the
address above

You must not circulate this work in any other form
and you must impose this same condition on any acquirer

Published in the United States of America by Oxford University Press
198 Madison Avenue, New York, NY 10016, United States of America

British Library Cataloguing in Publication Data

Data available

Library of Congress Control Number: 2024932040

ISBN 9780192887474

DOI: 10.1093/oso/9780192887474.001.0001

Printed and bound by
CPI Group (UK) Ltd, Croydon, CR0 4YY

Links to third party websites are provided by Oxford in good faith and
for information only. Oxford disclaims any responsibility for the materials
contained in any third party website referenced in this work.

Foreword

The idea for this book grew out of discussions and exchanges between the co-authors, who over the course of living and working in Japan for many years, have witnessed firsthand a transformation in the academic environment, one that in many ways reflects the broader changes in society. The demographic decline, which is affecting the choices of young people in particular (the number of undergraduate students in social sciences in Japanese universities decreased from 241,275 in 2000 to 203,351 in 2018) and the growing ambivalence toward pursuing studies in graduate school (the continuation rate fell from 4.16 per cent in 2000 to 3.3 per cent in 2018) have necessitated a profound rethink in the way courses are taught. Despite much initial resistance at every level, Japanese universities are showing a greater openness to foreign students and a switch to English-language education, two encouraging illustrations that positive change is underway. These programmes are generally very successful, as Japan retains its strong appeal to younger generations of students from all over the world. However, it is often difficult to find high quality textbooks, based on recent research findings, to explain the historical evolution of Japanese business and society. This is the reason why the co-authors of this book, who both teach business history at Japanese universities to overseas and Japanese students, decided to write this book. While our focus is on Japan, the book is intended for all students and scholars of business history, history of capitalism, social and cultural history, management, and other social sciences. As it is aimed primarily at a non-Japanese audience, we have tried to make maximum usage of works published in English, so that these readers can easily deepen their knowledge through further reading. Though there are omissions, the reader should find references to many of the major works on Japanese business and economic history in this volume.

Finally, we would like to express our sincere thanks to our colleagues, friends, and teachers at the Business History Society of Japan, who encouraged us to produce this book. Special thanks go out to Kurosawa Takafumi, who enabled the two authors to meet regularly as part of his research project, 'Competitive Advantage of Regions: Europe and East Asia in Comparative Studies on Industries', launched in 2011. We would also like to thank Yuzawa

Takeshi, Professor Emeritus at Gakushuin University, for his comments on parts of the manuscript. Finally, we would like to express our gratitude to Adam Swallow and Ryan Morris of Oxford University Press, who assisted us throughout the process of preparing the manuscript for publication.

Osaka and Tokyo, August 2023

Contents

List of Figures — viii
List of Tables — ix
Note to the Reader — x

Introduction — 1

1. **Continuity, Discontinuity, and Change: Tracing the roots of capitalism and entrepreneurship in the Tokugawa Period** — 7

2. **Capitalism and Entrepreneurship in the Meiji Period (1868–1912): Public sector** — 29

3. **Capitalism and Entrepreneurship in the Meiji Period (1868–1912): Private entrepreneurs** — 50

4. **Industrial Capitalism in a Changing Social and Geopolitical Environment (1895–1930)** — 66

5. **The Role of Foreign Companies (1895–1930)** — 88

6. **Empire, War, and Business** — 106

7. **Business during the Occupation Period: Continuity and change** — 124

8. **The 'Japanese Miracle'** — 143

9. **Business and Consumerism in the High and Stable Growth Periods** — 165

10. **The Bubble Economy and its Aftermath** — 186

11. **Global Competition during the Lost Decades** — 203

12. **Rebooting Global Competitiveness in Post-3.11 Japan** — 224

    Conclusion — 248

References — 255
Index — 272

List of Figures

0.1	'Japanese Business' in Google Books, 1900–2019	2
1.1	Echigoya Drapery Shop in Surugachō during the New Year by Torii Kiyonaga (1752–1815)	8
1.2	Founding of 'old firms' by period (%)	15
5.1	Percentages of gross sales by the origin of products at Fuji Electric, 1925–1934	94
5.2	Ownership and control structure of Nestlé Japan and ARKK, 1934	103
8.1	Toyota *keiretsu*, simplified organization and cross-shareholding structure, 1981	158
10.1	Nikkei Index, 1949–2019	187
10.2	Japanese outward FDI, flows in million USD, and exchange rate with the US dollar, 1971–2000	190
10.3	Waves of mergers and formation of mega banks in Japan, simplified chart	200
12.1	Abe dressed as Super Mario at Rio Olympics closing ceremony, 2016	225
12.2	Ratio of Japan's energy mix, fiscal years 2010 and 2019 in %	229
12.3	Regular and non-regular workers, 10,000 persons, 1984–2017	236
12.4	Inbound visitors to Japan by year, 1965–2021	244

List of Tables

1.1	Japanese enterprises founded before 1200	16
2.1	Meiji government foreign employees, 1868–1900	37
2.2	Beer production and market share by company in 1900	43
3.1	Cotton market shares in Japan, as a %, 1861–1900	60
3.2	Ratio of industrial production in Tokyo and Osaka, 1909	63
4.1	Changes in adjusted real GDP, 1918–1936	69
4.2	Growth ratios of real GDP in selected countries, 1913–1938	71
4.3	Summary of changes in the Japanese economy, 1914 to 1940	73
4.4	Comparison of the number of male and female workers (%) in the textile and mining industries in 1909	83
5.1	Number of companies with foreign capital in Japan, 1931	89
5.2	Market for electric light bulbs in Japan, values in yen, 1898–1908	93
5.3	Japanese car market, 1916–1935	100
6.1	Dependency of the trade between the colonies and their mainland, 1937	107
6.2	Direct investments from Japan to its colonies, 1926–1936	108
6.3	Private companies employing more than two DAP graduates, 1942	114
6.4	Japanese employees that moved from Ford and GM to Nissan and Toyota	120
8.1	Japanese chemical companies with American capital, 1950–1977	151
8.2	Japanese companies with overseas production worth more than 150 million US dollars, 1977	160
9.1	Japan's 'worst four' environmental disasters caused by pollution (*yondai kōgai*)	166
9.2	Early start-ups of the 1970s and 1980s	171
9.3	Westernization of the Japanese diet: daily caloric intake per capita (%)	174
9.4	Ranking by sales of retailers by year (1962–1972)	176
10.1	Evolution of housing prices in major Japanese cities, as a percentage, 1985–1992	188
11.1	Tokyo Stock Exchange, shareholding ratio by investor category, as a percentage, 1990–2019	205
11.2	Largest companies of the world, electronics and electrical appliances, revenues in million US dollars, 1995–2010	208
11.3	FDI stocks, inward, as a percentage of GDP, 2005–2019	213
12.1	Effects of Abenomics on profits, labour costs, cash equivalents, and capital investments in FY2009 and FY2018 in trillion yen	232
12.2	Amendments to the Labor Standards Law	238

Note to the Reader

Except for personal, business establishment, and location names, all Japanese words have been italicized. Following the Japanese convention, Japanese surnames precede the given name, except in cases where the Japanese author publishes mainly or exclusively in English. Macrons are used for long vowel sounds in names, terms, and places, except for well-known cities and islands, which generally appear without macrons, such as Tokyo and Hokkaido.

Introduction

In the 1960s, while he was a professor at Harvard University, Simon Kuznets, who would receive the 1971 Nobel Prize in Economics for his works on growth, used to tell his students, 'There are four sorts of countries: underdeveloped, developed, Japan and Argentina.'[1] While Argentina experienced a dramatic decline from one of the world's wealthiest to a poor country during the first decades of the twentieth century, Japan followed exactly the opposite path. When it was forced to open to world trade in 1853 by US special envoy, Commodore Matthew Perry, it was the last country on the globe to still be closed to free trade. About one century later, at the end of the 1960s, Japan had become the world's second largest economy, just behind the United States. Although its seclusion policy during the Edo period (1603–1868) did not signify poverty nor the absence of economic development, as we will see in this book, the shift from being the last country to open to global trade to becoming the second largest economy is impressive. How can we explain this success story?

The fast economic development of Japan and the strong competitiveness achieved by its firms during the postwar decades attracted the attention of numerous scholars who explored the sources of this power. Data from Google Books clearly shows that the popularity of 'Japanese business' grew quickly between 1960 and 1990 (see Figure 0.1). There was a need to understand what had made Japan become so strong. Books such as James Abegglen's *Kaisha: The Japanese Corporation* (1973), Ezra Vogel's *Japan as Number One* (1979), and Chalmers Johnson's *MITI and the Japanese Miracle* (1982), were best-sellers. In the 1980s in particular, the term 'Japan, Inc.' was widely used not only in books on Japan's political economy. It was likely first employed in works published by the US Department of Commerce to designate the relationship between politics and business that had emerged in Japan at the end of the occupation and was, according to the views of US trade negotiators, posing a threat to market expansion (Pempel, 1987). This literature offered different yet complementary views to explain the development of the Japanese economy, but they all shared one basic understanding: Japan

---

[1] Quoted in *Financial Times*, 22 January 2011.

Japanese Capitalism and Entrepreneurship. Pierre-Yves Donzé and Julia S. Yongue, Oxford University Press.
© Pierre-Yves Donzé and Julia S. Yongue (2024). DOI: 10.1093/oso/9780192887474.003.0001

was different. Authors in this period argued that Japan would become the new dominant nation in the world because it did not follow the common rules of capitalism seen in the United States and Western Europe. Japanese culture, which places more importance on the group than the individual, values long-term thinking, and is guided by a strongly interventionist state that did not let market mechanisms rule the economy, were seen as the main factors for the dramatic growth of the Japanese economy (Dore, 2000).

Since the early 1990s, however, Japan entered a long period of economic stagnation which still lingers on today. It never became the new dominant nation and was surpassed by China as the world's second largest economy in 2010. Most Japanese companies have disappeared from the global rankings of the most competitive firms. Thus, in recent years 'Japanese business' has lost the attention of the public (see Figure 0.1), and a new generation of scholars maintains that Japan is not different and never was. The government has always been weak (Callon, 1995, Garside, 2012) and unable to improve the competitiveness of private companies (Porter et al., 2000). Japanese firms were strong during the high-growth period because they had adopted practices to fulfil their needs, following market mechanisms, not because of the specificities of a national culture (Miwa and Ramseyer, 2006). However, this decline of the Japanese economy and loss of competitiveness of many of its once high-performing firms should actually reinforce the interest in studying modern Japanese history in depth in order to understand why. The dynamics of Japanese capitalism is much more complex than the simplistic view of the successful development proposed by Kuznets in the 1960s.

New approaches and methods for the study of the history of capitalism offer excellent tools for reconsidering the evolution of Japanese economy and society over the last two centuries. The study of capitalism as an academic approach emerged in the United States during the 2000s as a new way to look

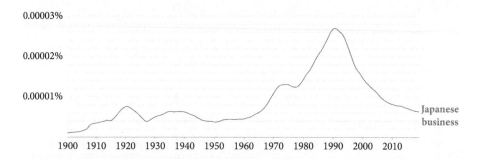

Figure 0.1 'Japanese Business' in Google Books, 1900–2019
Source: https://books.google.com/ngrams (accessed 10 June 2021)

at the historical development of the modern world, characterized by the integration of various academic perspectives that had developed autonomously and without much correlation during the final decades of the twentieth century. The history-of-capitalism approach argues that economic policy is at the core of the formation and transformation of the modern world. However, it does not look at the economy as an abstract system through mathematical models and equations. Rather it brings back social and cultural factors into the discussion to help make sense of the evolution of societies driven by the quest for profits and enrichment (Beckert and Desan, 2018). Despite its immense success, the history of capitalism as an academic field is still largely based on examples from the United States and Western Europe. However, this offers an excellent opportunity to reconsider the modern history of other parts of the world, particularly outside the West, and we focus in this book on Japan. As many US historians have emphasized, capitalism is the result of actions embedded in specific social and cultural contexts, meaning that its nature varies across countries.

This position is close to that of scholars of economic policy who have also discussed the nature of capitalism over the last two decades. In their seminal book, Hall and Soskice (2001) have emphasized that capitalism was not a unique economic system. They argued that a market economy could take various forms, and stressed the existence of two different kinds of capitalism: liberal market economies (LMEs), like in the United States and the United Kingdom, where economic activities result from market mechanisms; and coordinated market economies (CMEs), like in continental Europe, where coordination between firms, the state, and other organizations contribute to regulating economic activities. According to this model, Japan belongs to the category of CMEs, mostly because large companies have 'demonstrated a greater capacity for coordination, especially in wage-bargaining, than that in the UK and the USA' (p. 100), and developed industrial standards based on cooperation between them and with the government. The basis of their narrative can be traced to the Meiji Restoration, characterized by an interventionist government and large family-owned business groups (*zaibatsu*) to emphasize the coordinated nature of Japanese capitalism over time.

Hall and Soskice (2001)'s model has been criticized for its oversimplification by other scholars who refined the varieties-of-capitalism approach. Amable (2003) maintained for example that there were five major types of capitalism, among which there is an Asian model that includes Japan, while Yamamura and Streeck (2005) argued that Germany and Japan shared a similar non-liberal model of capitalism. However, these studies in economic policy lack a proper historical contextualization. They develop a conceptual model and apply it to various countries without considering changes in the organization of economic life over time. Dutch business historians have persuasively shown that a single country—the Netherlands—could move from a model close to LMEs at the end of the nineteenth and early twentieth centuries, to CMEs during the interwar years, and back to LMEs since the 1980s–1990s (Sluyterman, 2015). The nature of capitalism changes over time. Hence, one of the objectives of this book is to discuss how and why it transformed in Japan from the Edo era to the present.

Although Japan was largely isolated from the world economy from the seventeenth to the mid-nineteenth century, this does not mean that capitalism did not exist there. In his history of the world economy and material culture, Braudel (1979) has shown that a local market economy and international trade developed relatively independently from each other, although there were some relations between both, such as foreign commodities sold locally through a dense network of merchants. In the case of Western Europe, merchant capitalism or mercantilism, that is, wealth accumulated from international trade, was a major source of economic growth and led to the Industrial Revolution (Kocka, 2016). The seclusion of Japan gives different local conditions for the emergence of capitalism. Rather than international trade as the impetus, domestic trade represented the major source of profits and capital accumulation before the mid-nineteenth century. Hence, instead of *merchant capitalism*, which strongly connotes a Western European model, we use the expression *rural capitalism* for Japanese early modern history. This term expresses a mode of development relying on purely domestic factors in which manufacturing and trading activities were strongly anchored in the countryside.

The opening of Japan and the influence of Western powers marked a major break which deeply impacted society and the economy. The adoption of foreign technology and knowledge enabled the formation of a modern state and industrialization. Like in Western countries, manufacturing became the core economic activity and the new way to generate profits. *Industrial capitalism* emerged and became the dominant force of economic development. After World War II, when reaching the technological and economic level of the United States became a major political goal, Japan followed a model of *communitarian capitalism*. This form dominated until the 1980s, when *financial capitalism*—where profits and capital accumulation derived directly from financial investments—became the new paradigm. The shift from trade to manufacturing to finance is however a general model that can be observed in most countries. In order to discuss the specificities of Japan in a global perspective, the focus in this book is on the role of entrepreneurship which came in many forms, including not only individuals but also organizations like the state and the military. *Entrepreneurship* is a way to bring the actors back into the history of the economic development of Japan, in contrast to the most recent textbooks which focus on macroeconomic dynamics and economic policy (Francks, 2015; Ohno, 2017). The image chosen for the cover of this book perfectly expresses the fact that Japan's strong economic growth in the decades following World War II cannot be understood solely through statistics and mathematical equations. It was in large part the result of entrepreneurs making choices and opening up new markets. In this photograph taken in 1972, Morita Akio, co-founder and CEO of Sony, presents a new television set to Laudo Natel, governor of Sao Paulo. Morita decided that year to invest directly in Brazil, because its protectionist policies made imports from Japan uncompetitive. Sony do Brasil Ltda. was founded as a wholly owned subsidiary for the manufacture of electronic consumer goods. Hence, we follow an approach inspired by Wadhwani and Lubinski (2017) who argued that historians should focus more on what they called the 'intersection of entrepreneurial processes and historical change'. Entrepreneurship is not merely the result of an individual actor who seizes opportunities and takes risks. The understanding of historical change by entrepreneurs—including government officials and the state—led them to take specific actions to propel this change (Kikkawa, 2023). The new entrepreneurial history approach proposed by Wadhwani and Lubinski (2017) applies particularly to an individual—or a small group of—firms (e.g. Xia and Donzé, 2022). As this book focuses on more than two centuries of entrepreneurship in a single country, it was not possible to strictly follow their approach, but we have derived inspiration from it.

The transformation of corporate governance and the common career path in Japanese enterprises since the mid-nineteenth century also had a strong influence on entrepreneurship. For example, during the Meiji period (1868–1912), numerous young Japanese seized the opportunities offered by social and political changes to found their own businesses. However, after World War II, the situation had crucially changed. In the context of in-house training and gradual promotion before retirement within large companies, the rate of firm creation per capita in Japan became one the world's lowest (Katz, 2016). The entrepreneur is a major actor in the history of capitalism, but the scope of their action was shaped by institutions—which will be discussed in detail in this book.

Consequently, this book offers a history of the development of capitalism and entrepreneurship in Japan since the Edo era by following both a chronological and a thematic perspective. Some periods are covered in two chapters which focus on different yet complementary themes. Chapter 1 starts with a discussion of capitalism during the Edo period, emphasizing how private entrepreneurs carried out business and accumulated wealth in the context of seclusion. Going back to the seventeenth and eighteenth centuries was necessary to explain the roots of a specific form of economic development. The opening of the country and the end of *shogunate* marked a major departure in Japanese history. The Western impact deeply affected trade and manufacturing. Industrialization was realized by a broad range of actors who seized the opportunities offered by social and political change. The birth of *industrial capitalism* during the late Meiji and Taishō periods resulted from the actions of the state and private entrepreneurs, analysed in Chapters 2 and 3, respectively. The social effects of industrial capitalism and the emergence of a labour movement are presented in Chapter 4. Chapter 5 focuses on the role of foreign firms during the first third of the twentieth century. The industrial development of Japan was hence not merely the result of domestic entrepreneurs. Foreign companies introduced new technology and invested in Japan, cooperating with local enterprises and individuals. During the interwar years, imperialism became a major driving force of economic development. It gave birth to a new form of capitalism, which is referred to as *wartime capitalism*—discussed in Chapter 6. The occupation of Japan by US military forces in 1945–1952 was a short period, but had a deep impact on social and economic institutions. Major reforms, such as the anti-monopoly law, were introduced with the objective of democratizing business practices and dismantling the *zaibatsu* (Chapter 7). This led to the foundation of the so-called 'Japanese Business System', which often embodied *communitarian capitalism* in the workings of economic policy. The development of capitalism and entrepreneurship during the high-growth years is presented in Chapter 8, while social change in the domestic market, resulting from economic expansion and new business opportunities, is discussed in Chapter 9. Although finance had been mostly an instrument to support trade and industrial development since the Edo period, a paradigm shift occurred in the 1980s in the context of the price asset bubble. *Financial capitalism* emerged as a new feature in the Japanese economy, with dramatic effects after the collapse in the value of securities and land prices in the early 1990s. Chapter 10 tackles this major watershed. Finally, the last two chapters focus on the decades after 2000 from different perspectives. Chapter 11 discusses the impact of global competition and the subsequent transformation of the 'Japanese Business System', while Chapter 12 focuses on some major institutional and political changes enacted in response to mounting global competition, specifically through the lens of Abenomics and its impact on Japanese employment practices and society more broadly.

1
Continuity, Discontinuity, and Change

Tracing the roots of capitalism and entrepreneurship in the Tokugawa Period

One of the first forms of Japanese artwork to enter Western collections was the *ukiyo-e* or woodblock print. In the late nineteenth century, their popularity helped to inspire a movement known as *Japonisme*, which strongly influenced the paintings of impressionists such as Vincent Van Gogh and Édouard Manet, and spawned new trends in architecture, design, fashion, and even gardening. Many of the early purchases of these prints depicted everyday life in the bustling capital of Edo (Tokyo). Through these images, early Japanese art enthusiasts caught a glimpse of Japan's pastoral landscapes as well as its urban business environment. Among the places of commerce that were often featured, the Echigoya drapery (*kimono* fabric) shop in Nihonbashi, founded in 1673 by Mitsui Takatoshi (1622–1694), was perhaps the most common theme (see Figure 1.1). Echigoya can be easily identified even by those who are not art collectors thanks to its size and distinctive Mitsui family logo, shown in the shop's curtains or *noren*. Echigoya would later become the Mitsukoshi Department Store (Mitsukoshi Isetan Holdings today). This chapter explores Mitsui Takatoshi's early entrepreneurial activities (see Box 1.1) and the changing environment in which he lived, as well as some of the most salient features of Japanese business development in the Tokugawa or Edo period.

This period is referred to as Japan's feudal or proto-industrial era. While it did not yet have a market economy in the true sense, one can find the tiny buds of both capitalism and entrepreneurship, particularly during the second half of the Genroku period (1688–1704). Evidence of some early capitalistic development can be witnessed in the form of cross-regional competition, a point that is explored in section 1.4 (Howell, 1992). As argued in this chapter and by other scholars, the changes that took place during the Tokugawa period were vital to the foundations of economic and business development in Japan (Hauser, 1983; Hanley and Yamamura, 1971). Thus,

8 Japanese Capitalism and Entrepreneurship

Figure 1.1 Echigoya Drapery Shop in Surugachō during the New Year by Torii Kiyonaga (1752–1815)
Source: Courtesy of Mitsui Memorial Museum

Box 1.1 The House of Mitsui: Tracing the roots of modern management

Today, one of Japan's leading companies is Mitsui and Company Ltd., a general trading company or *sōgō shōsha*, whose roots can be traced to the Edo period. The purpose of this box is to offer some perspectives on the most salient and innovative features of the House of Mitsui's management system and its early leaders.

Hachirōbe Takatoshi and the establishment of the House of Mitsui

The founder of the House of Mitsui, Mitsui Hachirōbe Takatoshi (1622–1694), who would later take the inherited first name of Hachirōemon, was born in the town of Matsuzaka in Kii province, near Ise. Takatoshi's father is thought to have been a descendant of the Fujiwaras, making him a member of the warrior class, while his mother was the daughter of a merchant. His family opened a shop in Matsuzaka where they sold *miso* and *sake* and ran a pawn brokerage. Takatoshi spent his youth in Edo with one of his brothers before briefly returning to Matsuzaka. He then returned to live in Edo in 1672 with his six sons. There, he ran a wholesale and retail shop or *gofukuya* called Echigoya, which sold *kimono* fabric procured from Kyoto. As his business grew, he opened a second shop, where Mitsukoshi Department Store in Nihonbashi still stands today.

Novel business practices at the House of Mitsui

According to established Edo business customs, merchants sent their employees on visits to the homes of their regular clientele. Customers would be shown cloth and other wares that they could buy on credit. One of Takatoshi's innovations was to do away with the inefficient practice of home visits by employees, who would remain instead in the shop to attend to customers. He also discontinued the business custom of selling on credit and replaced it with 'cash pay; low prices; no markups'. Another innovation was the introduction of a new marketing technique. In those days, fabric was sold by the roll, which meant that customers often had to buy in excess of their needs. According to the new practice, customers were able to purchase the exact amount they desired. In addition, he succeeded in accelerating the delivery of orders thanks to the introduction of division of labour among the various artisans involved in the *kimono*-making process. Such new business practices not only contributed to Echigoya's financial success, they earned Takatoshi a favourable reputation both among his customers and government officials, resulting in his being selected as a purveyor to the *bakufu* (*seishō*).

The 1680s was a period of business expansion and diversification for Echigoya. In 1683, Takatoshi entered the financial sector as moneychanger (*ryōgaeya*) and established a shop in Kyoto, shortly after which he opened a second branch in Osaka. The opening of a *ryōgaeya* in Kyoto was an important strategic move that greatly contributed to business development. As a purveyor to the *bakufu*, he was entrusted with handling government transactions in Osaka, a privilege he returned by offering his exchange services without charging any interest. Having control over the *bakufu*'s financial transactions allowed him to take advantage of the delay period in the transfer of the government's funds to Edo. During this period, he could use the large sums he held to make purchases of fabric from wholesale suppliers in Kyoto, which could in turn be sold in retail shops at a sizeable profit. His success in this venture made him a wealthy merchant in Edo as well as in the other two major capitals of Kyoto and Osaka.

In 1674, Takatoshi died leaving his business and his name, Hachirōemon to his first son. Before Takatoshi's death, he drew up a family precept for future generations to follow, according to which the House of Mitsui would remain a single, jointly owned, family business, comprised of nine families (six sons, and three sons-in-law). At the core of the business was the headquarters or *ōmotokata*, which was invested with

(continued)

> **Box 1.1 Continued**
>
> the authority to control all the other branches. Although the branches were obliged to remit a portion of their earnings to the ōmotokata on a regular basis to support its activities, they were relatively autonomous in the governance of daily operations (Miyamoto, 1996, 105, 111).
>
> ### Innovations and new approaches to governance
>
> The House of Mitsui continued to evolve. Under the Hachirōemon IV, the Echigoya shop in Edo faced greater competition. He responded by introducing advertisements, an example of which was to distribute umbrellas with the Mitsui logo free of charge to customers. The use of marketing in this way was a novel idea at the time given the existence of guilds, which prohibited competition among their members through such practices.
>
> On the eve of the Meiji restoration in 1835, another Mitsui, Hachirōemon VIII, appointed Minomura Rizaemon as his chief bantō. This was a decisive move that enabled the House of Mitsui to make a smooth transition to a new era and gradually become the nation's largest zaibatsu (discussed in later chapters). Minomura introduced various reforms to modernize the core governance structure or ōmotokata by introducing a clear separation of the management of operations from the ownership. Henceforth, salaried managers as opposed to family members oversaw the business of the House of Mitsui, while the Mitsui family exercised little influence over the management of their daily operations. However, from the perspective of corporate growth, perhaps his most successful long-term reform was the transformation of the financial division (ryōgaeya) of the house into Mitsui Bank (Yonekura, 1985, 65–67). Thanks to Minomura's modernization of the business operations and the close political connections he helped to forge with the key leaders in the new Meiji government, the House of Mitsui was well positioned to face the crises caused by the collapse of the bakufu and the opening of the nation to the West.

one should avoid misinterpretations of this period as being 'medieval' in the negative sense of the term, a point that is succinctly underscored by Miyamoto (1996, 97):

> The Edo period in Japanese history tends to evoke the image of an age of "pure feudalism," and thus of a fairly dark age. People conjure up visions of peasants forced to eke out a bare subsistence that left them forever suspended precariously between life and death; of infanticide and trafficking in human bondage being practiced on a large scale; of a country being cut off from overseas civilizations

by the seclusion of the country and of being left in cultural backwaters while the rest of the world marched forward in economic development and scientific and technological progress. Even where there may have been development in the cities and commerce, these have been considered as having benefited only a few privileged wealthy merchants. The Edo Period has tended to be thought of, in extreme assessments, as a "stagnant society", a "zero-growth society".

The origins of this image of the Edo period as one of stagnation are in part derived from its seclusion policy (*sakoku seisaku*) enacted in the mid-1630s which were designed to limit contacts with the outside world. According to most histories of this period, government officials believed that the Spanish and Portuguese missionaries, who they had initially tolerated, were planting the seeds of dissent among the growing numbers of Japanese converts, and that this would lead to the destabilization and eventual overthrow of the *Tokugawa Shogunate*. Faced with this perceived threat, the Tokugawa government decided to restrict the nation's contact with the Western world to a tiny enclave, the artificial island of Dejima (sometimes appearing as Deshima) in today's Nagasaki prefecture, which was open to Dutch traders.

According to Arano Yasunori, while Western histories often portray Japan as a nation that was completely isolated from the outside world, this image is not entirely accurate. He argues that there were indeed 'maritime restrictions' (*kaikin*); however, the nation was anything but closed. He identifies 'four portals' through which diplomatic contacts as well as trade relations took place. Trade occurred with Japan's East Asian neighbours of China and Korea, the Northeast Asian coastal peoples or Santan, the Ainu traders in Ezo (today's island of Hokkaido), and the Kingdom of Ryūkyū (today's Okinawa prefecture) (Arano, 1989, 3–28; Arano, 2005).

Through the Dutch trading outpost at Dejima, foreign consumer goods flowed into the country along with books and other sources of knowledge and innovation. The Chinese, who were also allowed to conduct business, brought in products such as sugar and medicines. Through these early contacts, scientific and technological progress could be witnessed in a variety of forms and gradually spread throughout Japan on a wide scale (Morris Suzuki, 1994). Though the process was often piecemeal, learned Japanese were able to procure, disseminate, and build upon the information they collected most often via the Dutch on the recent developments in Western medicine and other sciences.

Although trade took place in this way on a limited scale due to the government's seclusion policy, this situation did not prevent Japan's economy from experiencing economic booms and busts, which according to Mark Metzler, closely mirrored those that were occurring over the same period in Europe (Metzler, 1994). Of note is that a market economy also began to develop, growing out of the tax collection system based on payments in rice, known as the *kokudaka-sei*.

This chapter is divided into three sections on the sources of economic development and the underlying system of values upon which it was built. The first section examines the *context* for business development and entrepreneurship and how it influenced early commercial activities. The second, exploring some of the *fundamental features of Japanese firms*, serves to deepen the reader's understanding of the themes discussed in the chapters that follow. The third provides an analysis of the various *types of business in operation and their role in Tokugawa society*.

1.1 Historical context and its implications for business development

At the core of the Tokugawa regime was the *shōgun* and his entourage of bureaucrats, known as the *bafuku*. The central government was supported by a network of domains or *han*, led by feudal lords or *daimyō*, who governed their lands with relative autonomy. Unlike the Meiji period, when knowledge would be derived from Western nations, during the Tokugawa era China was the main source of cultural, social, and scientific inspiration. One feature of Tokugawa society is that it was structured on a rigid class system, based on Confucianism. According to Confucian philosophy, one's status in society and station in life were determined by birth, and thus, in principle were immutable, though class lines began to blur towards the end of period due to the rise in the living standards of commoners (Hanley, 1987). On the whole Tokugawa society could be characterized as orderly, conservative, and peaceful.

For the government to ensure stability and centralized control, society was hierarchical and divided into four main classes: the samurai warriors (*shi*) at the top, followed by the farmers (*nō*), artisans (*kō*), and at the bottom of the social stratum, the merchants (*shō*). The merchants were referred to as *shōnin* (*shō* meaning 'commerce' and *nin* 'person', which can also be read as *akindo*) or by using a more pejorative moniker, *chōnin* or *o-chōnin-san*, which literally signifies *townsman*. As reflected in the term, *chōnin*, the merchants, could be found in the three major cities of Edo (today's Tokyo), the nation's political capital, Osaka, the centre of finance and business, and Kyoto, the capital of culture and imperial tradition. Merchants also conducted commercial activities in the castle towns (*jyōka-machi*) found in the various domains.

As shown in the third section, however, class lines were often blurred, as were the locations where merchants conducted business. Though officially prohibited, some peasants (farmers) residing in the provinces also engaged in commercial and production activities. Moreover, while merchants were officially barred from conducting business in these areas, they could sell specific goods such as pipes or candy (Sheldon, 1958, 25, 27).

A second important feature of the Tokugawa period was the system of alternative residence or *sankin kōtai*, which served as one means for the *bakufu* to retain control over their semi-autonomous domains. Under this regime, the head of the domain or *daimyo* was obliged to maintain a residence in Edo for his wife and children. In this way, the close family members of the *daimyo* were in a sense held hostage in the capital in order to prevent any threat of subversion. Maintaining a separate residence and travelling across the country to visit Edo were a considerable expense for the *daimyo* households. However, this system was highly conducive to the economic development of the many Edo businesses, some of which are portrayed in the *ukiyo-e* prints mentioned above, which catered to the domain of family members and their retainers. Moreover, it also benefited the local domain economies, whose products were procured and brought as gifts to the capital. Visits to and from the domains also encouraged improvements of the five main transportation networks (*gokaidō*), the most important one being the *Tōkaidō*, which linked Edo to the other two major capitals. Transportation networks by land and sea to carry both goods and people contributed to the foundations of an early monetary system, market economy, and regional development. The government's decision to standardize the weights and measures, which were overseen by designated merchants, contributed to some extent to the standardization of the coinage in circulation and the development of a money-based economy (Sheldon, 1958, 6).

In addition to infrastructural expansion, the *Doshima* Rice Exchange market in Osaka is an important financial institution that developed during the Edo period. Since the seventeenth century, Osaka was the principal market for the trade in rice collected from the feudal domains as taxes paid to the *shogun*. By the end of the century, merchants not only took part in the rice trade; rice bills were also issued by the *daimyō*. In 1730, the *shogunate* authorized an early form of spot market for these bills as well as a futures market for rice. This financial market is considered as one of the oldest in the world, and contributed to the wealth of merchants (Takatsuki, 2018).

Along with economic development, promoted thanks to the alternative residence system and subsequent movement of people and goods, were demographic changes. According to Susan B. Hanley's study on population trends and economic development, pre-modern population statistics were not only collected; they were 'far better than those of most other countries'. She concludes that the Japanese population nearly doubled during the Edo period from 18 million to approximately 35 million. Edo thus transformed from a small, sparsely populated fishing village to the nation's capital, and by the eighteenth and nineteenth centuries had become what was perhaps the largest city in the world with an estimated population of between 500,000 and one million (Hanley, 1968, 622).

1.2 Connecting present and past: distinctive characteristics of Japanese firms

To broaden the reader's understanding of the roots of capitalism and entrepreneurship in Edo Japan, it is useful to consider three general features of Japanese firms and their connections to this period. The first feature is the large number of '*old firms*', known as *chōju kigyō* or *shinise kigyō*. *Chōju* literally means 'longevity' while *kigyō* can be translated as 'firm'. The term, *shinise*, connotes an old, well-established enterprise, particularly one having earned a high degree of customer trust. Teikoku Databank (TDB), founded 1900, is one such firm, whose large database contains information on these old Japanese companies. TDB publishes an annual analysis, comprised of *chōju* or *shinise kigyō*, which they define as firms having a history of a hundred years or more (Teikoku Databank, 2019). Given the large number and importance of these firms to the Japanese economy, there are numerous specialists, some of whom publish regularly on the subject. One of the most prominent is Goto Toshio, who co-edits a white paper on *chōju* or *shinise kigyō*, which he refers to in English as '*century-old, long-lived family businesses*' or LLFBs (Goto, 2006). This section explores the findings of both TDB and Goto, while considering some connections between these firms and the development of Japanese capitalism and entrepreneurship.

According to the 2019 TDB report, based on a total of approximately 1.47 million firms listed in their database, some 33,258 (2.27 per cent) have a history of a hundred years or more. Among these century-old companies, a relatively small number, 532 firms, are listed. Two of the three oldest listed firms registered in their database were founded around the time of the Tokugawa period: Yōmeishu Seizō Company (founded in 1602), a medicinal wine producer, and Sumitomo Forestry Company (1691), a builder and wood products manufacturer whose origins can be traced to the House of Sumitomo. The oldest listed company in their database is Matsui Construction

Company (established in 1586), a temple builder (Teikoku Databank, 2019). According to TDB's 2016 survey, firms with a century or more history are for the most part small in scale. Among them 47.1 per cent have fewer than four employees; only a relatively small ratio (1.7 per cent) has a workforce exceeding five hundred (Teikoku Databank 2016).

As shown in Figure 1.2, roughly half of the companies registered (14,032 firms or 48.4 per cent) were founded in the late Meiji period (1891–1912). The fact that a significant number began their operations from this time suggests that for entrepreneurs, starting and sustaining a business in the late Meiji period was a more feasible aspiration than in the periods that preceded it. This is, however, not to say that the number founded in the early Meiji Period (7,255 firms or 25.0 per cent) or before was in any way insignificant, particularly when viewed from a global perspective. An appreciable number (3,186 firms or 11 per cent) can be traced to the Tokugawa period. Of note in this chapter on the Tokugawa period is that among the types of businesses that were founded before the start of the Meiji period, the most prominent sectors are *sake* brewing, traditional inns (*ryokan*), and kimono/clothing retailers.

The geographical locations with the largest number of companies founded before 1867 include Kyoto with 312 companies, followed by the Tokyo (283 firms), Aichi (165), and Osaka (145). Some 3,343 enterprises were set up across Japan before 1867; however, when the firms established in or before 1916 are added the total comes to 28,972, of which those founded in Tokyo (2,656) top the list, followed by Osaka (1,532) (Teikoku Databank 2016, 1 and 7). These figures illustrate the rising prominence of Tokyo as a rival to Osaka, Japan's preeminent business centre throughout the Tokugawa period

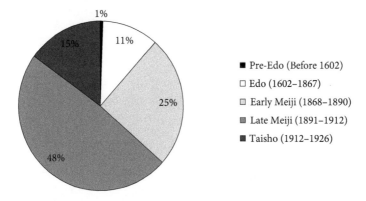

Figure 1.2 Founding of 'old firms' by period (%)
Source: Teikoku Database, 2016

and beyond. Kyoto's importance as a commercial capital began to wane towards the end of the Tokugawa period (Miyamoto and Kasuya, 2009).

The second feature is a large number of firms with a history of over two hundred years of operation. As shown in Table 1.1, the location of these firms extends across Japan. Among them, the significant number of inns demonstrates that the flow of travellers along the nation's transportation network began well before the Tokugawa period. The birth of Japan's early hospitality industry may be credited to the many temple and shrine worshippers who patronized these inns during their pilgrimages.

According to TBD, the ratio of Japanese firms in their database that were established prior to the start of the Edo period and remain in business at the time of the report's publication is relatively low (0.6 per cent) (Teikoku Databank 2016). However, when Japan is compared to other countries, the number of firms with a 200-year or more history is high. As in Japan, among the oldest European businesses one can also find a significant number of establishments offering food and beverages. Saint Peter Stiftakulinarium

Table 1.1 Japanese enterprises founded before 1200

Firm	Founding year	Location	Business sector
Nishiyama Onsen Keiunkan	705	Yamanashi	Hot springs inn
Sen'nen no yu koman	717	Hyogo	Hot springs inn
Hōshi Ryokan	718	Ishikawa	Hot springs inn
Tanaka Buguten	885	Kyoto	Buddhist goods
Nakamura Shaji	970	Aichi	Temple and shrine construction
Ichimonjiya Wasuke	1000	Kyoto	Confectionery
Shūmiya Shinbutsuguten	1024	Yamanashi	Buddhist goods
Takahan Ryokan	1075	Niigata	Hot springs inn
Getō Onsen	1134	Iwate	Hot springs inn
Sudō Honke	1141	Ibaraki	*Sake* distillery
Tsuen	1160	Kyoto	Tea producer
Fujito	1184	Okayama	Confectionery
Kikuoka	1184	Nara	Medicinal herbs shop
Sakan Ryokan	1184	Sendai	Hot springs inn
Itō Tekko	1189	Yamagata	Metalwork
Shirasagiyu Tawaraya	1190	Ishikawa	Hot springs inn
Kotabe Foundry	1190	Ibaraki	Foundry (temple bells, etc.)
Tosen Goshobo	1191	Hyogo	Hot springs inn
Arima Onsen Okunobo	1191	Hyogo	Hot springs inn
Yoshinoya Irokuen	1192	Ishikawa	Hot springs inn

Source: Data compiled from the websites of the establishments listed above

(Austria, founded in 803), Stafelter Hof (Germany, 862), and Sean's Bar (Ireland, 900) are Europe's oldest business establishments. Other firms with a long history of operations include two mints: Monnaie de Paris (France, 864) and Royal Mint (United Kingdom, 866).

The third, and perhaps the most prominent feature of Japanese business development is that among the one-century- or even two-centuries-old companies, many remain family-owned and operated. While having a significant number of such firms is a distinctive feature, Japan is not the only nation that possesses old, family-owned enterprises, as the website of the Hénokiens, a French association of such enterprises proves. As of 2020, the Hénokiens was comprised of forty-nine mainly European firms, all of which have a history of at least 200 years. Age, however, is not the sole criterion for joining this exclusive group. To be considered for admission, the original founder's descendants must also currently manage and control a majority stake in the company.[1] Of note is that Japanese firms are well represented in the Hénokiens with nine member firms. Hoshi Ryokan (inn), founded in 718 and family-run for forty-six generations, is currently the oldest member.[2]

Firms such as Hoshi Ryokan have survived in large part due to their capacity to adapt to changing circumstances. However, in some cases, these changes are too great for even for the most well-established firms to surmount. While many of Japan's *old firms* have shown themselves capable of adjusting to numerous crises, they are not immune to decline and in some cases failure. According to a July 2022 survey by TDB, the pandemic has caused a rise in bankruptcies among Japanese firms—both old and new.[3] Fluctuations in the economy, poor strategy choices, technological change, new competition, and other factors can cause even the oldest of businesses to falter. Such was the fate of one former Hénokien, *Kongo-gumi*, founded in the year 578. This family-owned and managed builder of temples and shrines was once the world's oldest firm; however, circumstances arose that forced the family of the company to file for bankruptcy in 2006. Today it has become a subsidiary of another construction company, *Takamatsu Kensetsu*.[4]

Japan's oldest family-owned companies are reputed for their resilience, especially in times of crisis. As shown below, this can be credited to various factors including the institution of *adult adoption* in many cases by adopting a son-in-law or *mukoyōshi*, through an arranged marriage with the firm owner's daughter. This demonstrates Japanese family businesses'

---

[1] https://www.henokiens.com/content.php?id=4&lg=en
[2] https://www.henokiens.com/content.php?id=5&lg=en
[3] https://www.tdb.co.jp/tosan/covid19/index.html
[4] https://www.takamatsu-cg.co.jp/eng/about/group/takamatsu/kongogumi.html

prioritization of competence over blood ties and a culture that strives to be pragmatic and adaptive to new circumstances—from global competition to global pandemics—without relinquishing core values. The preservation of traditions, particularly those supporting firm longevity, as well as the foundation of vibrant indigenous industries continued to play an important role in the distinctive type of industrialization that Japan experienced during as well as long after the fall of the Tokugawa regime (Tanimoto, 2006, 36; Kasuya, 2012, 33–35). Such features have enabled these family companies to survive over centuries and generations.

International comparisons bring to light the novel ways that old firms have dealt with both a variety of crises, periods of decline, and temporary closures, and their specificities. According to Olejniczak et al. (2019), past studies, however, have tended to emphasize 'continuity' in business without sufficiently considering 'discontinuity': that is, interruptions in their operations and the causes. The authors' case study explores the 'continuity and discontinuity' of one family-owned firm, Jablkowski Brothers Department Store, specifically how the company's management was able to cope with political regime change. Their results reveal *discontinuity* in their operations caused by the firm's forced nationalization in postwar Poland. At the same time, they demonstrate *continuity* as seen in the restoration of original property rights to the founders' descendants in 1996 following the successful filing of a legal claim (Olejniczak et al., 2019). The notions of 'continuity and discontinuity', particularly in terms of ownership are pertinent to Japanese business development during the Tokugawa period, in part—as was in the Polish case—because they illustrate the significance of a changing political environment and the various ways that families have coped with crises.

1.3 Institutions of longevity and their Tokugawa roots

This section discusses the development of some of the major institutions of business, particularly those formed in the early eighteenth century. At the same time, it provides an overview of the types of businesses, business practices, and the philosophy on which these businesses were built. By exploring institutions and norms, this section should provide further perspectives needed to explain why Japan possesses an especially large number of *old, well-established firms* (*chōju* or *shinise kigyō*).

The emergence of business institutions occurred in direct response to two major changes in Japan's social context. The first change was economic. Sudden fluctuations in the economy produced a volatile business environment

(Metzler, 1994). The merchants dealt with the sharp economic downturns by introducing practices to curtail expenditures. The second change was political. In the early eighteenth century, particularly during the Kyōhō period (1717–1736), the Tokugawa government began to view the merchants and their growing wealth as a destabilizing factor for the regime. To counter this perceived threat, the government introduced repressive policies. One of the most drastic measures was the seizure of the assets of one of the wealthiest merchant houses to serve as a warning to others (Goto, 2006). The merchants responded to this inhospitable climate and threat of expropriation by implementing, strengthening, and adapting their business practices to shield their operations from future crises.

Institutions of business

The central institution of business during the Tokugawa period was the *ie*, meaning merchant 'house' or 'household'. The largest houses were concentrated in the commercial capitals of Osaka, Edo, and Kyoto, often in clusters or areas according to the type of trade in which they engaged. In Japan, as in many European nations, 'house' signified both the *business operation* and the *family* that owned it. Unlike the commercial houses of Europe, however, the philosophical foundations of the merchants' management practices rested on the values of Confucianism, particularly its core notion of filial piety. The insightful work of Miyamoto (1996, 122) on the Tokugawa merchant houses succinctly summarizes their philosophy through the case of one well-known merchant house, Kōnoike:

> The headship of the family and the family estate were not conceived of as things that belonged to the head individually, but as "something given in trust" by the ancestors that was meant to be passed on to the succeeding generations in other words, as things that jointly belonged to the multigenerational, consanguineal group known as the *ie* (house). Also, the role of the current head was stipulated as being no more than of "a caretaker" in other words, someone whose turn it is to be on duty until he hands things over to the next person.

This passage while not only encapsulating the governance practices of the merchant houses, is also illustrative of the individual merchant's perception of his duties to the household as the standard-bearer for all his ancestors as opposed to simply being a business owner.

To ensure their preservation, many merchant houses introduced a strict set of rules called *kakun*, often translated as precept or constitution. This was a written document that served as the basis by which the owner-families oversaw their operations. Under the reign of Yoshimune (1684–1751) the use of precepts gained popularity among the merchant houses and can be seen as a response to the climate of government repression described above. Inspired by Confucian doctrine as well as other ethical teachings of the times, these precepts—similar in some ways to a modern-day mission statement—reflected a strong desire on the part of the merchant class to counter criticisms of their wealth accumulation by legitimizing the moral elements of their activities while also justifying the important role they felt they were fulfilling in society. These precepts were devised and passed down through the generations for all the future descendants to follow with the utmost meticulousness. Common to them was an enumeration of the duties of the head of the household, which consisted of rules to ensure the prosperity of the house and perpetuate stability in its management for the generations to come.

To uphold these obligations, numerous supporting institutions were put in place. The first was a system of succession (*seshūsei*). Although succession was generally determined by primogeniture, it was not always the case: the head of the household could make an exception if he deemed that the eldest son was unsuitable. In such cases, adult adoption of a non-family member such as a loyal and capable clerk or fellow guildsman was not uncommon. According to adult adoption customs, the adopted son would take the family surname, and, if one existed, the hereditary first name of the household head. Adult adoption was a feasible option when the family had no children or in cases where there was no male heir. In the latter case, a marriage would be arranged whereby the daughter's spouse (*mukō-yoshi*) would be officially adopted and take her family's surname. Arranged marriages involving two households within the same guild were not only pragmatic, they were also advantageous as they resulted in the formation of a type of strategic alliance, with the potential of bringing greater prosperity and a stronger political voice in guild affairs for both houses. At the same time, such practices ensured the continuity and longevity of the business as an institution.

One can find some variations in these practices according to the customs of the house in question and/or its geographical location. For example, Osaka merchant houses did not generally practice primogeniture, and instead adopted an heir from outside the family (Yui and Hirschmeier, 1975, 38). Achieving stability through the selection of a suitable heir was key, as Takemura (1997, 80) wrote of the Kyoto merchant houses: 'The stable succession of the household business, and the household itself in an ultimate sense, were of the highest priority in the trading houses of Kyoto in the second half of the eighteenth century, especially in large houses.' These examples reiterate that pragmatism—preserving the house by whatever means available—prevailed over kinship.

It should be noted that adult adoption of a non-family member could provide a small window of opportunity for exceptionally talented male clerks, even those of humble origin. Through institutions such as adoption, it was thus feasible, at least in principle, for the son of a peasant to begin an apprenticeship at a large merchant house and to one day rise to the position of chief of operations (*shihainin*). Through marriage, he could even become the household heir. The practice of adult adoption runs counter to the image of a rigid Tokugawa society, one where one's station in life was determined by birth, and shows a certain degree of flexibility. Moreover, it also provides evidence that mobility at least within one's class system was possible. Interestingly the practice of adult adoption is still permitted under current Japanese law and is not uncommon, especially at the old firms mentioned above.

The existence of adult adoption has wider implications for the meaning of 'family-owned' in Japanese business. Adult adoption helps to explain why Japan has such an impressive number of family businesses with a history of over a hundred years. Nonetheless, while adult adoption is still witnessed today among many family-owned firms, having adult adoption as an option does not necessarily guarantee or even facilitate the process of selecting a suitable heir (Morikawa, 2001). On the contrary having more choices could complicate the succession rather than simplify it.

The second supporting institution is the house employment system, characterized by an apprenticeship (*kogai hōkōnin*) of a non-family member (Miyamoto, 1996, 136–140). According to this system, a young apprentice or *detchi* joins the house, usually through an introduction, at the age of 12 or 13, and then works for the household in exchange for room, board, and educational training in reading, writing, and using the abacus. These young apprentices also receive instruction in the 'merchant's philosophy', discussed below. By the age of 17 or 18, he becomes eligible for promotion to the position of clerk or *tedai*. As such, he is allowed to wear a formal dress or *hakama* and receive a salary based on the number of years of service. Around the age of 30, *tedai* who are deemed suitable for promotion can advance to the position of chief clerk or *bantō*. According to Miyamoto, only a small percentage of those who entered the house as a young apprentice would ever attain the level of *bantō* for reasons ranging from illness and dismissal to adult adoption (Miyamoto, 1996, 140).

Large households, such as the House of Mitsui, discussed in Box 1.1, often had more than one chief clerk or *bantō* as well as numerous intermediary ranks between those of *detchi*, *tedai*, and *bantō* (Yui and Hirschmeier,

1975, 39). Over time, the role of the *bantō* grew to resemble in many ways that of a salaried manager in the modern sense. He oversaw the accounts of both the family and its business operations, which in smaller households were not separated (Yui and Hirschmeier, 1975, 42). Towards the middle of the Tokugawa period, there was a tendency among the large houses to separate the roles of ownership from the management of the daily affairs of the house. As Goto (2006, 575) emphasizes, however, there were other notable features: 'The difference between a *bantō* and a professional manager in family firms in Western countries is that the former is in a sense like a teacher who carefully checks as well as rectifies any acts of misconduct that the young head of household might commit.' Thus, in addition to his role of overseeing the house's current business, the *bantō* was also entrusted with its long-term planning in a more personal way than the modern-day professional manager due to his responsibility to instruct and prepare the house's successor for a new generation of operations.

Another similarity with salaried managers is that the *bantō* was permitted to reside outside the merchant house in his own residence, and if the house so allowed it, to establish his own house-affiliated branch business or *bekke*. A *bekke* is similar to a subsidiary today in the sense that it continued to provide financial support and loyalty to the main house from a different location, and in some cases, from a different region. Another type of branch business was called *noren-wake*. This type of branch engaged in a form of commerce that was unrelated to that of the main house in order to avoid becoming a competitor. *Noren-wake* resembled a franchise in that the owner was allowed to use the main house's name (Goto, 2006, 562). The following section delves further into Tokugawa business practices through their philosophical roots.

The role of merchant houses: values and implications for modern business development

The merchants' philosophy or *shingaku*, whose founder was Ishida Baigan (1685–1744), had a profound impact on the business practices and values held at the merchant houses. Indeed, according to the work of Robert Bellah, 'Many Japanese scholars consider it to have been one of the greatest influences on morality of the common people of the Tokugawa Period' (Bellah, 1985, 133). Ishida Baigan, the son of a farmer, was born in a village called Higashi Agata. He left in 1896 to work as an apprentice in Kyoto. After joining a merchant house, he might have risen to the rank of *bantō* and been allowed to open his own shop. However, instead of remaining under the merchant house's charge, Baigan left Kyoto and began studying Shintoism, the Chinese classics, and Buddhism with great fervour. By 1729, he had started giving lectures free of charge in Kyoto and Osaka, which were attended by large audiences, including a growing number of merchants (Bellah, 1985, 134–137). Baigan authored several works during his lifetime, including *Seikamon* (Essay on Household Management) and *Toi-mondo* (City and Country Dialogues). One of his disciples, Tejima Tōan, formed a movement and penned new works that were published after Baigan's death.

The writings of Baigan were widely read by members of the merchant class and served as an inspiration for their work ethic. His teachings emphasized respect towards customers, fellow merchants, and oneself as well as frugality, obedience, humility, and honest behaviour (Goto, 2006, 570). Baigan's ideals of virtue were reflected in the merchant house's business practices and were laid down in writing in the form of the house's set of rules found in the family precepts, many of which were drawn up in the eighteenth century. As is clear from Bellah's translation below, Baigan's work kindled the merchant's interest in engaging in ethical business practices. Moreover, it gave their profession, or to borrow Bellah's words, their 'Way' (*Dō*) as merchants a greater purpose and meaning by justifying their role in society—one that had been viewed with distain by the samurai class in particular—within the Confucian doctrine of the times:

> Obtaining profit from the sale is the Way of the merchant. I have not heard selling at cost called the Way... The merchant's profit from sale is like the samurai's stipend. No profit from sale would be like the samurai serving without a stipend. (Bellah, 1985, 161)

Baigan's teachings held special appeal to the merchant class, as it did not conflict with the Tokugawa value system they strove to uphold. At the same time, they helped to instil a greater sense of pride in their work at a time when the merchants were under attack for alleged excessive profit-making and extravagance.

Rural networks and the roots of commercial capitalism in feudal Japan

Studies on European economies have referred to the stage of development that emerges just before the rise of capitalism as *proto-industrialization*, a term first coined by Mendels (1972). According to Ogilvie and Cerman (1996, 1), proto-industrialization is 'the expansion of domestic industries producing goods for non-local markets which took place in many parts of Europe between the sixteenth and nineteenth centuries. Often, although not always, such industries arose in the countryside, where they were practiced alongside agriculture; usually, they expanded without adopting advanced technology or centralizing production into factories.' As shown below, Japan's development shares similarities with that which took place in Europe. A significant difference is, however, the absence of international trade as a source of profit. Due to the circumstances imposed by the Tokugawa regime, domestic economic development was largely disconnected from the world economy. Thus, we use the expression of *rural capitalism*, rather than *merchant capitalism*, to characterize a form of early growth which relied mostly on domestic commerce. This sub-section explores two groups that contributed to economic development during this period: the first, rural traders, wholesalers, moneychangers, and warehouse merchants and the second, wealthy farmers. Though 'capitalism' in its modern sense had not fully formed, evidence of its early roots could be found in this period.

In the first group is a category of rural traders who made a living as itinerant merchants (*gyōshōnin*), and whose roots often originated in the provinces of Omi and Ise (Shiga and Mie prefectures). The foundations of two of the Japan's largest trading companies, Marubeni and Itochū, can be traced to one itinerant merchant, Itō Chūbei, who first founded a linens business in Omi. Such merchants peddled their wares in villages scattered along the Tokaidō route, but also set up shops, as was the case for Itō Chūbei, whose business was established in Osaka.

These merchants travelled and traded throughout the country, some as far as the hinterlands of Ezo (Hokkaido), carrying mainly lightweight goods to ensure easy transport. Some of the items they commonly sold were medicines, *tatami* mats, and cloth. Among the rural traders, the medicine peddlers of Echizen (Toyama prefecture) are perhaps the most well known (Futaya and Blaikie, 2021). However, Toyama was not the only area where commerce in medicines prospered; a significant trade could also be witnessed along different routes in areas near today's Nara and Saga prefectures. Another company that has its roots in this type of business model is the Hisamitsu Pharmaceutical Company, whose operations developed in the Tashiro area in Kyushu.

It is noteworthy that itinerant medicinal peddlers, like the other rural tradesmen, served several different functions in Tokugawa society. First and foremost they facilitated the circulation of goods outside the three major cities. However, in the process, they played a vital role in the collection and dissemination of information. Moreover, some of these merchants contributed to the early roots of capitalism. One example is the Omi merchant, Nakai Mitsutake, who began his career as an itinerant medicine peddler with a small shop in Hino. Thanks to Nakai's success in the medicines trade, he was able to accumulate enough capital to expand the scope of his operations geographically. By allowing his employees to establish shops in the form of limited partnerships, he succeeded in setting up branches in various parts of the country from Kyoto and Osaka to Odawara and Sendai (Miyamoto, 1996, 118–121).

The second category, wholesalers (*ton'ya*), often established their businesses in port cities. From these trading hubs, they were able to make a living by shipping goods on a large scale via a complex web of local intermediaries. The use of wholesaling (distribution) networks would become an important feature of Japanese business development, which is revisited in other chapters in this volume. The third and fourth categories are moneychanger (*ryōgaiya*) and warehouse merchant (*kuramoto*). Both types of business were based largely in Osaka, the financial capital, and formed in response to the gradual emergence of an early monetary system.

According to the monetary system in place at that time, only the central government could issue specie money in gold, silver, and copper. The domain or *han* governments, on the other hand, were permitted to print their own paper money in their own currencies, while the *ryōgaiya* could issue their own checks, giving rise to a system of credit. The *ryōgaiya* functioned not only as moneychangers; they also engaged in deposit banking. In response to the need for loans, the large Osaka *ryōgaiya* formed a group, which operated in a similar way as a modern central bank. By expanding the scope of their deposit-banking functions, they succeeded in establishing an early form of a money market (Yui and Hirschmeier, 1975, 29–30).

The fourth category, warehouse merchant (*kuramoto*), earned a living by renting and overseeing warehouse space for the *daimyō*, who needed a convenient means of housing their tax payments in rice. In addition to rice, they were also able to store gifts for their visits to pay respect to the *bafuku* in Edo (*sankin kōtai*). Warehouse merchants thus benefited from this system by collecting storage fees and issuing interest-bearing loans. They also engaged in finance through a form of trading, based on mortgaging future rice crop yields (Yui and Hirschmeier, 1975, 30–31, Miyamoto, 1996).

The second group were *gōnō*, which can be literally translated as 'wealthy farmers', though other translations exist. For example, Thomas Smith refers to this group as *wealthy peasants* as well as *rural capitalists* (Smith, 1989). In his work devoted to their emergence in the late Tokugawa and early Meiji periods, Edward E. Pratt, translates *gōnō* as 'Japan's proto-industrial elite', but mentions other possible translations including *rural entrepreneurs* (Pratt, 1999). This group of merchants, who were mainly of farmer (peasant) origin are important as they made a considerable contribution to the early roots of capitalism and entrepreneurship in the late Tokugawa and Meiji periods. Indeed, one of the most well-known rural capitalists is Shibusawa Eiichi, often referred to as the father of Japanese capitalism. Such early entrepreneurs also illustrate that the class lines between the merchants and peasants were sometimes blurred.

The accumulated wealth of this important group can be tied to the *kokudaka* system whereby the government determined in advance the amount of rice owed by each domain in taxes. Because the amount was fixed, farmers could boost their earnings by producing a surplus of rice and finding new ways to use it such as *sake-* or confection-making or by growing and selling other crops. One clever 'rural capitalist' was able to increase his yields by procuring fertilizers from Ezo (Hokkaido). Others developed their own agri-based technologies by experimenting with ways to turn out new, more productive plant varieties. Additional opportunities for profit-making could be found in the production of handicrafts, which was well suited to the lifestyle of the farming families, who were idle during the winter months due to inclement weather conditions. As the growth of profits was tied to the increase of inputs of labour as opposed to other factors such as improved productivity, some scholars have referred to the characteristics of the economic and social changes that took place in regions as a Japanese version of the 'industrious revolution' put forth by De Vries (1994) as opposed to the commonly used term 'industrial revolution', which emphasizes the role of technological change (Hayami, 2015). However, unlike the Northern European experience used by De Vries (1994) to develop his argument, where household consumption is related to the growth of international trade, the increasing income of households in Japan led instead to the extension of the consumption of domestic goods.

Japanese business history is replete with examples of successes in regional industry development. Some include silk production and sericulture in today's Fukushima, Gunma, and Nagano prefectures, and the innovations that yielded them. The Nambu region, in what is now Iwate prefecture, was and still is known for its ironworks. Other examples include Awa (Tokushima) province's renowned indigo dyeing industry and the districts of Kawachi and Sesshu, near Osaka, where cotton and cotton products as well as vegetable oil were produced. The domains of Satsuma and Sanuki in Kyushu were celebrated for their sugar, while those of Tosa (Kochi), Shinano

(Nagano), and Echigo (Niigata) were known for their paper production (Smith, 1989, 166–168; Ravina, for Awa dyeing Pratt, 1999).

Opportunities for the growth of rural economies resulted in part from the weaknesses in the Tokugawa regime. While the Tokugawa government did succeed in establishing its hegemony over certain strategically important cities, the fact that its rulers were unable to gain full control over the country's some 250 domains, meant that the latter could enjoy a certain degree of political and economic autonomy. This situation helped to carve out a *division of the country into competing economic units*, which brought positive spillovers to the regions not only in economic terms, but also, and perhaps more importantly in technological terms, since [inter-regional] competition helped to promote the spread of new ideas. (Morris Suzuki, 1994, 21, 27).

From an early date, the 'rural capitalists' became leaders in the local economies, in some cases gaining considerable political clout. Through their connections, they engaged in development projects to improve rural life and support commerce. The capital they derived from their early business activities facilitated investments in necessary infrastructure. New irrigation systems were built, which in turn contributed to an increase in agricultural yields, making it possible to fund improvements in roads and bridges that would be vital to the expansion of inter-regional trade. Through money-lending (usury) activities, the rural capitalists—not unlike their large *ryōgaiya* (money-changer) counterparts in Osaka—were able to increase their land holdings and wealth.

1.4 Conclusions

With some notable exceptions (see Box 1.1), it was not the merchant houses, but the 'rural capitalists', who would sow the seeds for the early roots of Japanese capitalism and entrepreneurship. These seeds would germinate and bloom particularly in the latter half of the Meiji period (see Chapters 2 and 3). Rural capitalists would contribute to regional development in three ways. First, they fostered a complex organization of production, based on a division of labour, which encouraged specialization in certain goods. Second, this cross-regional trade in turn generated cross-regional competition among the producers of a variety of products. Third, the development of rural commerce helped to erect a strong foundation for producing certain goods, which could be scaled up relatively quickly in the Meiji period. The process of scaling up, which was already underway in the Tokugawa period, hastened the transition from a cottage to a manufacturing industry, which was followed by the emergence of factories. Some rural capitalists became important change-makers in their towns or regions, and for this reason could be considered early entrepreneurs. They differed significantly from their city-dwelling merchant counterparts, who often valued both stability and continuity in their operations and harmony with the political regime. Furthermore, some rural capitalists searched for new business opportunities, and embodied a central feature of Japanese capitalism by generating regional and inter-regional competition.

Thanks to a surplus of rice in some areas of the country, some 'rural capitalists' began producing goods such as *sake* and confections as ancillary occupations to their profession and social status of farmer (peasant). In later periods, some of them would abandon rice production altogether and specialize instead in the manufacturing and sale of these products—one reason why producers of *sake* and confections are among Japan's oldest firms. The transition that took place in this environment of relative stability—but not stagnation—provides one example of 'continuity and discontinuity', and sheds light on the dynamics of Japanese capitalism and entrepreneurship.

2
Capitalism and Entrepreneurship in the Meiji Period (1868–1912)

Public sector

The signing of diplomatic treaties with Western nations marked the official opening of the country to the outside world and the end of the Tokugawa *shogunate*. The momentous shift from a largely 'closed nation' (*sakoku*) to a full-fledged player in the global economy offered Japan new opportunities for international trade while at the same time also exposed it to new risks in the form of sudden and unpredictable fluctuations in world markets. Signs of an impending transition from a system of feudalism and proto-industrialization could already be witnessed in the late Genroku period. The start of the Meiji period, however, signalled a true beginning for Japanese capitalism in the fullest sense of the term. One symbol of the rise of capitalism and entrepreneurship was the growing number of new firms. While many of the new firms failed, some would continue to thrive thus providing the foundations of Japanese business in the periods to follow.

The emergence of what can be referred to as *industrial capitalism* transformed the Japanese economy and society in the late Meiji period. Entrepreneurship flourished on a scale that would not again be observed until the early postwar period. Over the course of the Meiji period some 32,000 new factories were built, providing jobs to some 800,000 workers (Morris Suzuki, 1994, 72). With the founding of new businesses came great changes in the Japanese lifestyle as witnessed by new work and leisure patterns as well as styles of dress. Given the sheer significance of the Meiji period to the development of Japanese capitalism and entrepreneurship, the central concepts in this volume, we decided to include two chapters covering two different phases and themes.

This first of the two chapters considers the role of the state as an entrepreneur. More specifically, it examines the ways that government bureaucrats aided in the establishment of modern businesses and by so doing fostered the development of what might be considered a form of *state capitalism*. In the first phase of the Meiji period (1868–1890), the state served as the key actor in the formation of new businesses, while in the second (1891–1912), the private sector assumed the central role. One of the major turning points in this transition was the government's decision to sell off (*haraisage*) most of the state-owned firms that it had founded in the first phase of the Meiji period to the private sector. As a result, many public-sector businesses—with the exception of firms whose activities were connected to the military and communications networks—pivoted over to the private sector, thus allowing entrepreneurial individuals, motivated by a combination of profit-making aspirations and economic nationalism, as opposed to bureaucrats, to take a leading role in the development of the domestic economy.

This chapter is divided into five sections: (2.1) Contextual factors for the development of Japanese capitalism and entrepreneurship; (2.2) Key players in the transition from proto-industrial to capitalistic development; (2.3) International relations and the brewing of beer; (2.4) Symbols of culture and enlightenment: the case of Tomioka Silk Filature; followed by (2.5) Conclusions. The first sections provide general information on the period, while the remaining sections offer specific examples to demonstrate some of the characteristics of the government-supported firms. Following these sections is a box devoted to the creation and significance of Japan Post to the foundations of the nation's transportation and communications infrastructure (see Box 2.1).

Box 2.1 The creation and development of a postal service in Meiji Japan

---

While forms of a delivery service existed during the Tokugawa period, a modern mail and communications system would not begin in earnest until the establishment of a national postal system. The Japanese postal system was introduced in the 1870s and fulfilled a variety of functions ranging from mail delivery to insurance and financial services (Westney, 1987). The long-term impact of Japan's postal system was more than just economic; its social implications were equally profound: 'Before the introduction of the telephone, the telegraph, and the steam engine, the post was often the sole means of communication . . . it hastened the expansion of commerce and trade, and introduced ordinary citizens to the world of modern finance' (Maclachlan, 2011, 2). Following the introduction of mail delivery came the birth of other systems for sending telegraphs (1870s), postal money orders (1875), and telephone operations (1890s). These systems, like the railways, would advance the formation of modern businesses in the decades to follow.

Features of the postal system as a business

Many features distinguish Japan's modern communications industry, particularly its postal system, from the others covered in this chapter. The first is that it is comprised of sectors that remained state monopolies for a much longer time, a characteristic that shielded them from competition and protected their interests. One reason for their longevity as public entities was that the state's interests closely coincided with those of private business, a point that is clearly illustrated in the case of the postal system. In the Meiji period, for example, the state supported the growth of the manufacturing and agriculture sectors through the introduction of reduced postal rates for sending commercial samples and promotional information (Hunter, 2005, 13–14). Compared to the railroads, the postal system served as a stronger vector by which the state could stimulate economic growth, although the government also engaged massively in fostering the railway industry (Ericson, 1996).

The postal system offered new opportunities for the spread of technology within and across industries. As Hunter (2005, 5) asserts, 'Postal systems were . . . in themselves a form of new technology. They made use of other technologies, such as railways, in effect piggybacking on their development, they also developed their own techniques particularly in relation to the interconnections between different modes of transport utilized. Developing mechanisms for the transfer of mail from the postbox to the post carriage, and then to the railway wagon was key to efficiency. Post systems also entailed new organizational technologies and fundamentally influenced other new forms of organization, management, and institutions.' Thus, the interconnections between technology and business fostered synergies that were vital to Japan's economic development as a nation in the short and long term.

Finally, the geographical interconnections that the provision of postal services conferred facilitated new commercial relationships between the urban and regional economies. For the regional economies especially, the integration of local markets with urban ones sparked economic growth and new business opportunities, the implications of which were significant. The Tomioka Silk Filature, mentioned above, encouraged growth of regional economies and the expansion of trade beyond the borders of Japan. The rapidity and distance by which goods and people circulated not only strengthened commerce; it also facilitated the flow of information and new ideas.

(continued)

Box 2.1 Continued

Maejima Hisoka, founder of the Japan's postal system

First introduced to Japan by Maejima Hisoka (1835–1919), the postal system was inspired by the British model, though many of its fundamental characteristics can be tied to the ideas and goals of its founder. Born in what is today Niigata prefecture, Maejima studied *Rangaku* (Dutch learning), medicine, and English before joining the Meiji government. In 1870, he was sent on a mission to Britain to observe the workings of its postal service. According to Hunter, 'For Maejima the provision of an efficient and comprehensive communications system was a prerequisite for the establishment of a great nation' (Hunter, 1976, 79) His endeavours to introduce a modern postal system contributed to Japan's gaining sovereignty in the realm of communications, as illustrated by the fact that Japan became a member of the Universal Postal Union in 1877. The nation's speed in introducing and expanding the postal system is impressive: by the late 1800s, Japan's postal system was one of the largest in the world in terms of the number of financial transactions and volume of letters. Over time, it would also garner considerable political influence (Maclachlan, 2004; 2011).

Maejima played a key role in forging an alliance between the mail service and the nascent shipping industry, which he accomplished through negotiations with the Mitsubishi Trading Company. He also instigated some of the services one now takes for granted in today's postal system, including the shipment of mail, money orders, and banking. Under Maejima, Japan's postal system was comprised of two networks: large state-owned bureaus staffed by civil servants and small post offices operated by small shop-owners. Maejima also implemented a central feature of Japan's postal system, one that would have consequences for the political economy in the long term: its network of commissioned post offices (*tokutei yūbinkyoku*), managed by individuals with a high status in their communities who initially received no remuneration for their services. Finally, Maejima was also an entrepreneur, as his achievements clearly demonstrate. During his career, he founded a newspaper, which would later become the *Yomiuri*, and established two railroads, the Kansai railway (Osaka) in 1886 and the Hokuetsu (Niigata) railway in 1894.

By 1873, the government had gained a monopoly on the carriage of mail, one that would remain unchallenged until the election of Prime Minister Koizumi Jun'ichiro (Chapter 12). During the high-growth period, Prime Minister Tanaka Kakuei (see Chapter 11) was able to seal the lasting business–government relationship with the nationwide postal system, thus providing one means of ensuring the long-term

> dominance of the Liberal Democratic Party (LDP). The postal system remains, even today, an impressive institution, which is relevant to the study of Japanese business history, not only for its influence on business development and infrastructure, but also for the sheer scale of its operation. Before the official establishment of Japan Post Holdings in 2007 as a publicly traded company, Japan possessed the world's largest postal savings system in terms of financial assets.

2.1 Contextual factors for the development of Japanese capitalism and entrepreneurship

The year 1868 marks the fall of the Tokugawa *bakufu* and the restoration of the Meiji emperor to the imperial throne. To avert the threat of Western imperialism, the *han* (domain) governments agreed to surrender their autonomy and to unify the country under a single, centralized regime. This change was momentous, as it ended a period of Japanese history that had endured for over two hundred years. Though its impact on politics, the economy, and society, was nothing short of a revolution, this turning point is referred to by most historians as the *Meiji Restoration* to mark the restoring of imperial rule. Along with the ascension of the new Meiji emperor to the throne came the transfer of the nation's capital from Kyoto to Edo, which was given a new name, Tokyo. On 6 April 1868, the Meiji government promulgated the Five-Article Charter Oath. Of the five articles this document contained, the fifth one: 'Knowledge shall be sought throughout the world so as to strengthen the foundations of imperial rule', would be particularly significant to Japan's political economy and its choice of a course of development in the short and long term.

Though not explicitly stated, in the Meiji context, 'seeking knowledge' invariably signified *Western* knowledge, an objective that was also synonymous with modernization. Against a backdrop of the spread of Western imperialism, the government's commitment to 'pursue knowledge throughout the world' was not just a goal; it was a means of survival. Japanese policymakers believed that the only way for the nation to preserve its sovereignty was for it to stand as an equal alongside Western powers by embracing the same high aspirations for scientific, technological, and even cultural attainment. The factories that Meiji bureaucrats built employed the latest Western technologies, and produced the most advanced goods for an increasingly Westernized lifestyle. They were erected across Japan not only as tangible embodiments of modernity and progress, but also, as argued below, symbolic ones.

As mentioned in the previous chapter, even before the Charter Oath was issued, Western traders and missionaries had penetrated Japan's waters and even its inner territories. However, as Catholicism and the powerful nations from which it was propagated were perceived as threats to political stability, the government introduced the national seclusion policy (*sakoku seisaku*) to limit foreign exchanges. In the mid-1850s, however, with Western powers' growing desire to open new trading routes in Asia, the nature and purpose of types of foreign contacts evolved substantially. Sometimes referred to as *gunboat diplomacy*, exchanges with Westerners became increasingly aggressive and, in some cases, openly hostile.

One visit would change the course of Japanese history. In 1853, US Admiral Matthew C. Perry arrived at Uraga, the gateway to Edo Bay, aboard his 'black ships' (*kuro-bune*), a term that is used metaphorically even today to describe an unwelcome foreign intrusion particularly one that upsets the status quo by forcing change, often in the form of political concessions. Perry delivered a letter addressed to the Japanese emperor that was signed by US president, Millard Fillmore, requesting the opening of diplomatic ties. Perry promised to return one year later, which he did, at which time he concluded the Convention of Kanagawa, also known as the Japan–US Treaty of Peace and Amity, the first in a series of such bilateral treaties with Western nations.

These bilateral treaties were collectively known as the *unequal treaty system* (*fubyōdō jōyaku seido*), and as the name denotes, placed Japan at a disadvantage vis-à-vis Western nations in significant ways. First, from an economic perspective they hampered the country's efforts to establish and protect its nascent industries from foreign competition by depriving it of the right to impose tariffs on foreign goods. Second, from a political standpoint, though the treaties did not result in colonization, they prevented Japan from enjoying full national sovereignty. According to the terms of the treaty, Japan was obliged to open the port of Yokohama to commerce with the West, followed by Kobe, Nagasaki, Osaka, and Niigata. While foreigners were permitted to reside and trade freely at these ports, as shown below in the example of the beer industry, they were barred from venturing into areas located beyond the port cities to conduct business. The treaties also granted foreigners the right to extraterritoriality, meaning that they did not have to comply with what foreign authorities perceived as 'inferior' Japanese laws and were thus exempt from being tried and/or prosecuted for crimes they had committed on Japanese soil. Another related point is that the treaties also prevented the creation of businesses between foreigners and Japanese. These restrictions would be particularly detrimental to domestic businesses, as they hindered the formation of new modern industries. Furthermore, they would also ironically prove to be a formidable barrier even to foreigners who sought to expand their business activities in Japan.

In 1871, a group of government officials sailed out of Japan on a three-year journey, known as the Iwakura Mission, during which time they visited the major capitals of Europe and the United States. During their sojourn, their goal was above all to renegotiate the unequal treaties, an endeavour that was left largely unrewarded. As prescribed in the Charter Oath, they would also seek 'knowledge throughout the world' through the observation, study, and introduction of a variety of Western institutions and models. While taking part in the Iwakura Mission, the participants selected what they perceived to be the most advanced institutions and models for Japan's development. Their goal was to rapidly modernize the nation, and by so doing, 'catch up' with the West. Some of the systems and institutions that were already in place in Western nations—ranging from medical practices to mail delivery—were in many cases initially adopted wholesale then improved upon through a process of imitation and innovation (Westney, 1987).

In 1875, one of the Meiji period's most prolific and outspoken leaders, Fukuzawa Yukichi, penned *An Outline of a Theory of Civilization*. In this work he employed the phrase 'civilization and enlightenment' (*bunmei kaika*), which became a slogan that in many ways set the tone for the first phase of the Meiji period (Dilworth and Hurst, 2008). Fukazawa, like many of the other builders of Meiji Japan, believed that only through Westernization could the nation ever be recognized as an equal among its more technologically advanced Western peers. Other slogans that served as guiding principles for policymakers during this period and beyond were 'out with Asia; in with Europe' (*datsu-a-nyū-ō*), 'foster and develop industries' (*shokusan kōgyō*), and 'enrich the nation and strengthen the army' (*fukoku kyōhei*).

2.2 Key players in the transition from proto-industrial to capitalistic development

The Ministry of Industry (*Kōbushō*) was established in 1870 to oversee the industrial development process, launch pilot enterprises, and provide technical and financial support. The government was the main source of entrepreneurship in the first phase of the Meiji period (1868–1890); however, this is not to say that the private sector was completely uninvolved. Innovation had long flourished across Japan thanks to aspiring entrepreneurs residing in the provincial domains or *han* whose experimentation had yielded a variety of novel inventions and technologies (Morris Suzuki, 1994).

Western books and other objects that these entrepreneurial individuals had procured, in many cases through the Dutch residing in Nagasaki, often served as sources for their creative inspirations.

However, what has been called the '*han* model' of industrial development, combining tinkering with foreign objects acquired from abroad, studying blueprints found in Western books, and engaging in experimentation with ample trial and error, was neither a practical nor a speedy way for a nation to catch up with its Western rivals. One could argue that the inherent inefficiencies of such a model serve as one explanation of why so many private-sector businesses failed. Other more practical explanations for their failure include insufficient capital, limited technical expertise, sudden market fluctuations, and unforeseeable changes in the competitive environment (Yui and Hirschmeier, 1975). Given the insurmountable obstacles faced by the private sector, particularly in the early Meiji period, the state stepped in to assume the central role as entrepreneur.

Foreign sources of business creation

Having the state, as opposed to the private sector to guide the industrialization process in the early Meiji period was advantageous for various reasons. The government was best suited to (1) provide a model for the private sector to follow and imitate, (2) absorb the significant start-up costs and losses that private entrepreneurs were unable to bear, and (3) facilitate transfers of technology in order to enable nascent industries to overcome technical barriers more quickly. State-of-the-art, government-backed factories would promote the development of commerce and provide symbols to the outside world of Japan's strong determination to create a modern state.

Of note regarding this approach are the major differences between Japan's development process and those of other latecomer Asian economies, particularly in South East Asia. Whereas some Asian nations relied on foreign direct investment (FDI) as the quickest and most effective means of industrialization, the Japanese state invested heavily in the transfer of advanced technologies while also strictly curtailing the activities of foreign companies. From 1870 to 1885 the Ministry of Industry directly oversaw the importation and application of Western technologies, some of which would be used to construct modern railway, telegraph, and shipping lines. Another characteristic of Japanese development during the early Meiji period was the importance that the state placed on direct forms of technology transfer via human capital in the form of foreign experts or *oyatoi gaikokujin* (Uchida,

1991, 265–272). Foreign experts travelled to Japan to provide onsite advice to Japanese regarding the most appropriate technology options. They also directly supervised these transfers to ensure the proper operation of the state's purchases of foreign equipment. This mode of technology transfer proved to be more efficient than the trial-and-error *han model*, mentioned above. While the state model did have a high success rate, it had one significant drawback, its sizeable economic burden. In 1872 and 1875–1878, the Ministry of Industry employed some five hundred foreigners, the cost of which exceeded 50 per cent of the total annual budget. The total number as of 1900 amounted to 825, of whom more than five hundred were dispatched from the United Kingdom. The Ministry of Industry was by far the largest employer, with more than one-third of all *oyatoi gaikokujin* hires (see Table 2.1).

In the first phase of the Meiji period, policymakers prioritized the light industries particularly those that would increase opportunities for export and promote economic growth. According to Ohno Ken-ichi Japan experienced a 'light industrial revolution' in the early Meiji period, though as David Wittner asserts, the heavy industries were also undergoing a transformation. Ohno posits that by prioritizing the light industries, namely spinning, Japan was

Table 2.1 Meiji government foreign employees, 1868–1900

Ministry	United Kingdom	France	United States	Germany	Other	Total
Industry	553	90	13	24	145	825
Education	86	39	105	93	44	367
Prefectures	119	27	94	38	37	315
Navy	118	69	12	8	8	215
Home	26	2	15	43	31	117
Army	2	75	–	16	15	108
Hokkaido development	4	1	56	5	22	88
Finance	38	20	13	6	11	88
Council of State	11	59	3	1	9	83
Government shipping	29	1	15	1	8	54
Justice	6	14	2	5	3	30
Agriculture and commerce	4	–	8	15	1	28
Foreign	4	1	6	12	4	27
Cabinet	19	1	1	5	–	26
Communications	14	–	1	3	3	21
Imperial household	1	2	2	2	1	8
Total	1,034	401	351	279	335	2400

Source: Jones (1985), p. 226

striving to redress the problem of the nation's dependence on Great Britain, which Japan relied upon for nearly half of its cotton and woollen goods and cotton yarn (Ohno, 2006, 2017, 52; Wittner, 2000). From the second phase of the Meiji period through World War I, one can see a notable shift in emphasis towards the heavy industries. As prescribed in the slogan, 'enrich the nation; strengthen the army', two of the government's objectives in later years were to secure a formidable national defence while continuing to fortify its communications network (Yui and Hirschmeier, 1975).

In addition to foreign technology transfers in the first phase of the Meiji period, the government also sent Japanese overseas on scholarships to study at the most advanced universities of Europe, in many cases in the United Kingdom and Germany (Donzé, 2010). The government's aim was to create a bastion of academic elite comprised of specialists in the most advanced fields of Western science. Of the fields selected, the study of medicine was a top priority; however, some government-sponsored scholars pursued engineering, chemistry, and other fields that were vital to Japan's scientific and technological development. Once their studies were completed, these scholars were summoned to return to Japan to replace the many foreign experts that the government had hired to provide advice and direct supervision on factory floors. The efforts of these Japanese scholars would contribute to the founding of new industries, one being pharmaceuticals (Yongue, 2016). They would also fill positions in the nation's new imperial universities, which emulated the overseas institutions where they had studied. Their influence on education was profound and enduring (Bartholomew, 1989). Classes at Kobu Daigakkō, the forerunner of the Faculty of Engineering of the University of Tokyo, were taught in English and German using textbooks procured in England and Germany (Oqubay and Ohno, 2019).

Domestic sources of entrepreneurship

In the early Meiji period, the social order and system of values that the merchant class had grown accustomed to for over two centuries fell into disarray. In 1872, the government dissolved all the guilds (*kabu nakama*), a change that led to the disintegration of the merchants' competitive advantages, namely their well-established networks and business relationships. Re-establishing new institutions of business in the Meiji period would take time. According to Yui and Hirschmeier (1975), faced with this overwhelming new situation many of the merchant houses were passive and slow to respond. Underpinning these tendencies was the rigid Tokugawa class system, which had bred conservatism and instilled a psychology that was averse to risk-taking—a mindset that was difficult to amend. Consequently, as they assert, many lacked a spirit of entrepreneurship, were reluctant to create new business ventures, and were generally slow to embrace the new system of capitalism.

While this may be to some extent an accurate portrayal of some of the merchant houses, their reticence to embrace the ideas of the new regime and engage in new business creation is understandable given the circumstances in which they found themselves at the start of the Meiji period. Immediately after the fall of the Tokugawa regime, the merchants were heavily indebted, due to the outstanding loans that many had been forced to provide to the *bakufu* in its waning days. These debts would never be repaid, leading in some cases to insolvency. Some large merchant houses, even ones as prominent as the House of Sumitomo, found themselves on the brink of bankruptcy. Many merchant houses failed. Not all the merchants faced the same circumstances, however. Thanks to their strong connections to the new Meiji government, the Houses of Mitsui, Ono, and Shimada safely weathered the crisis. The House of Mitsui had particularly large operations in Edo and was able to anticipate and prepare for the fall of the Tokugawa regime. It was also, at least to some extent, sheltered from going into debt as the Mitsui family precept prohibited the provision of loans to the *bafuku*.

Some of the early literature on this period concludes that the merchants had little interest or involvement in the early development of capitalism in the Meiji period. However, work on specific sectors of the economy calls into question this long-held assumption. One example is a study by Yamamura on the Meiji banking sector. He asserts that the merchants were proactive, and played a much more important role in business development than was previous assumed. Using primary sources, he emphasizes that although the samurai technocrats and the government officials have often been credited for their role in enabling the formation of an early banking sector, it was 'chōnin [merchant] entrepreneurs and capitalists who began the industrialization of Japan' (Yamamura, 1969, 107). As demonstrated in the example below on the beer industry and in the previous chapter, the 'rural capitalists' (*gōnō*), were especially entrepreneurial and made notable contributions to business creation and the development of Meiji period capitalism.

Thanks to the transfer of technology, the Meiji bureaucrats were able to begin the long process of putting in place a modern, Western-style factory system (Fruin, 1994). This would, in the years to follow, provide new opportunities for private-sector entrepreneurship. The goal of these bureaucrats was clear: the wholesale importation of a system of production. This was seen as the quickest means of catching up with Western nations, one that would help Japan to regain its political and economic sovereignty. It is interesting to note that this process often did not conflict with or replace existing production systems, nor did it hinder the growth of indigenous industries. While new businesses and systems of production were being introduced, tradition would continue to play an important role both in Japan's industrialization and modernization. Thus, the process by which Japan industrialized can be characterized by its duality, or the simultaneous development of traditional indigenous businesses and a modern factory system (Tanimoto, 2006, 8–11).

2.3 International relations and the brewing of beer

The beer and silk industries were selected as case studies for this section for two reasons. First, the cases of Snow Country Breweries and Tomioka Silk Filature shed light on the Meiji government's state-led model of development whereby new industries were initiated by bureaucrats, who put in place the necessary industrial infrastructure, followed in most cases by the transfer of ownership and governance to the private sector at a later stage. Second, the industries selected help to illustrate multiple themes witnessed in the first phase of the Meiji period: the problems posed by the unequal treaties, the imitation-innovation dynamic, the Westernization of Japanese society, and the role of public-sector entrepreneurship in the early development of business. The first half of this section traces the evolution of the early beer industry by comparing the cases of a public-sector firm, Snow Country (Sapporo) Breweries, and a private-sector enterprise, Japan Brewery (Kirin). The second case on the development of the silk industry provides an example of a public-sector firm whose infrastructure was put in place by bureaucrats, then sold to the private sector.

As mentioned above, the government sought to construct pilot plants to provide models for aspiring entrepreneurs while also decreasing the nation's dependence on imports of certain foreign goods such as textiles. However, these were not the only goals. Its support of pilot plant construction was also based on the desire to produce symbols of 'civilization and enlightenment' (*bunmei kaika*).

According to Jeffrey Alexander, 'The encouragement of Western eating and drinking habits during the Meiji era was part of a determined effort by Japan's government to convince the Great Powers both to accept Japanese as peers and renegotiate the "unequal treaties"' (Alexander, 2013, 17). Beer, a beverage that is undeniably of Western provenance, was first brewed and consumed exclusively by Westerners in Yokohama (Kirin, 1957, 1–11). As the frequency of the Japanese contacts with Westerners increased in the 1870s, however, the notion of beer as a symbol of modernity intensified due to its use of imported ingredients such hops and malt, incorporation of German brewing technologies, and association with new forms of leisure. Beers were served in a new type of Western establishment, the beer hall, where Meiji elites, bedecked not in kimono but in suits, hats, and other Western attire, could gather to socialize. The formation of an early brewing industry, while a symbol of modernity, also illustrates a key theme of the Meiji period, 'imitation and innovation' (Westney, 1987). Although the brewers of domestically manufactured beer strove to make their products as authentic as possible by meticulously following imported brewing techniques, it would one day evolve into a uniquely Japanese beverage of equal sophistication as its German precedents.

Founding a beer industry: Snow Country brand

Snow Country, known today in Japanese as Sapporo Beer, was founded in 1876 on the northern island of Hokkaido, known as Ezo until 1869. The emergence of Japan's early beer industry in Hokkaido coincided with two mutually reinforcing policy aims promoted by the home minister, Ōkubo Toshimitsu, of developing industries (*shokusan kōgyō*) and promoting economic activities to build up a national defence against the threat of a Russian attack. To realize these objectives, the government founded the Hokkaido Colonization Office in 1869. As was the case for many of the government's projects, foreign experts or *oyatoi gaikokujin* were appointed to assist in finding ways to enhance the region's potential for business development, particularly in the area of agriculture. In their capacity as advisors to the Meiji government, Americans made significant contributions to the economic growth of Hokkaido and more specifically to the beer industry. One such advisor was Horace Capron. After carrying out a survey, Capron recommended that the Japanese government cultivate hops in order to alleviate the country's dependence on imports (Alexander, 2013, 32–33). Another American, Edwin Dun, provided assistance in the construction of the brewery.

Though foreign expertise was vital to the development of an early beer industry, Japanese would also play an important role. Nakagawa Seibei, who had studied beer brewing in Germany, was key in the establishment of Japan's first domestic beer enterprise. In the 1870s, many promising young Japanese were sent to Europe, often to Germany, on government scholarships. These scholars left Japan to study medicine as well as other fields of science and engineering, which would prove to be essential to the development of businesses during the Meiji period and beyond. Nakagawa, who left Japan in 1872 for Berlin, was not one of the elite government scholars, and initially sought work as a domestic servant. However, en route to Germany he had the good fortune of meeting Aoki Shūzō, who had been dispatched by the Meiji government to study medicine. Thanks to the political connections and financial support of Aoki, who would later be appointed as a Japanese diplomat in Berlin, Nakagawa was able to secure a scholarship from the Japanese government and earn a certificate in beer brewing. Upon completion of his studies, thanks again to Aoki's introductions, Nakagawa gained employment as a *beer brewer* in the agriculture section of the Hokkaido Colonization Bureau (Alexander, 2013, 34).

The Meiji government envisioned erecting a beer production facility in Tokyo, however, these plans were revised, due in part to climatic conditions. It was felt that Hokkaido provided a more suitable location due to an abundance of ice which could be used to keep the beer refrigerated during its transport by ship to Tokyo. Nakagawa received official approval to produce beer in Hokkaido in 1876, and while working at the Hokkaido Colonization Bureau he began drawing up plans for the construction of a factory. In preparation for its opening, he ordered the factory's equipment and most of the ingredients directly from Germany to ensure the beer's authenticity as a German-style brew.

Though the factory construction was completed, an insufficient supply of raw materials and a general lack of preparation delayed the starting date of production. By May 1877, the first beer was at last produced; however, its delivery fell behind schedule, in part because there were no glass bottles in which to ship it. In June the first shipment of beer, whose brand name was Sapporo Cold-Brewed Beer (*hiyazei bakushu*), left the Port of Otaru, arrived in Tokyo the same month, and was then presented to top-ranking officials in the Meiji government and members of the imperial family. A second shipment was expedited from Tokyo and delivered to the senior Imperial Japanese Army staff, who had been dispatched to southwestern Japan to counter the insurgents in Satsuma (Kyushu). Thus, Nakagawa succeeded in manufacturing and delivering beer to a select group of Japanese elites but had given little if any thought to how to market it on a larger scale (Alexander, 2013, 37–38, 40).

The year 1886 marked a turning point for the company: the shift from state to private-sector ownership. At the that time, the Ōkura Trading Company had developed a keen interest in investing in the beer-brewing industry, and decided to buy the Hokkaido Colonization Bureau as well as purchase shares

Table 2.2 Beer production and market share by company in 1900

Brand name	Manufacturer	Production (koku)	Market share (%)
Ebisu	Nippon Beer	37,452	31.1
Asahi	Osaka Beer	28,370	23.6
Kirin	The Japan Brewery	18,379	15.3
Sapporo	Sapporo Beer	14,300	11.9
Kabuto	Marusan Beer	5,226	4.3
Tokyo	Tokyo Beer	2,300	1.9
Others		14,344	11.9
Total		120,371	100.0

Source: Sapporo Biiru KK, *Sapporo Biiru 120 nenshi* (120-year history of Sapporo Breweries Ltd.), Sapporo Biiru KK, 1996 Note: 1 koku = 180 litres.

in Japan Brewery. In 1888, Shibusawa Eiichi, often referred to as the father of Japanese capitalism (see Chapter 3), joined by other investors including Asano Sōichirō, a wealthy industrialist who made his fortune in the cement industry, acquired the brewery from the Ōkura Trading Company and established Sapporo Breweries Company, Ltd. Under the direction of this new group of investors, Sapporo Breweries would continue in its tradition of producing German-style beer. To guarantee the beer's authenticity and improve its taste, the company solicited advice from another foreign expert, Max Portmann, who would not only provide the company with the necessary technical assistance to improve the beer's quality; he would also play an important role in the establishment of another brewing company, Osaka Beer (later Asahi Breweries) in 1889 (Alexander, 2013, 41–42) (see Table 2.2).

From Japan Brewery to Kirin Brand Beer: early private-sector initiatives

Snow Country was not the only producer of beer in Meiji period Japan. Foreigners began to brew the beverage in the treaty ports, one being Yokohama, for the local market. As succinctly summarized by Alexander (2013, 16), the complicated—at least from a legal perspective—development of what would first become Japan Brewery and later Kirin 'is the story of Japanese investors purchasing, reincorporating, and managing a foreign-owned business during an era when Japanese and foreigners were legally forbidden to do business with one another'.

One of the oldest producers was Spring Valley Brewery (*Izumi no tani*), founded around 1870 in Yokohama by Danish-born William Copeland. At a time when most of the beer consumed in Japan was imported, Copeland succeeded in domestically producing three German-style brews: Lager Beer, Bavarian Beer, and Bavarian Bock Beer. Copeland's early success in this industry can in part be tied to the unequal treaty system. This provided him with an advantage over local producers, who before the introduction of an alcohol tax in 1905 joined the market in large numbers. As a foreign producer, not only was he exempt from the burden of paying any alcohol taxes; it was not even necessary for him to procure a production license from the local authorities (Alexander, 2013, 13–14).

Though some Japanese did not initially appreciate the taste of beer, its popularity steadily grew, thus attracting numerous local entrants. Many of them were 'rural capitalists', mentioned in the previous chapter, who perceived beer brewing as a potentially profitable means of carving out a new niche in the alcohol market, which consisted primarily of *sake*. Another attraction of brewing was its low entry barriers, as beer was not yet subject to taxation at the time of their entry. While the quality of the local beers was inferior to imports, early brewers enjoyed a competitive advantage in terms of price. Though at the outset promising, most would not, however, survive in the long term. This was not because of fierce foreign competition but because of the government's decision to impose a beer excise tax in 1905—a pivotal moment in the industry's early history. Other challenges the brewers faced were logistical in nature, namely the problem of transporting beer across long distances over rough terrain. What this meant for the Meiji-period beer industry was that the beverage would remain essentially a locally produced and consumed commodity (Alexander, 2013, 11).

An opportunity arose for the development of a Japanese brewing industry when Copeland decided to sell his factory in 1885. With the steady rise in beer sales, Thomas B. Glover, a special advisor to the Mitsubishi Company and an employee of the already highly globalized British firm, Jardine Matheson & Co. (Jardine Matheson Holdings today), convinced a group of Japanese investors to purchase it. However, the unequal treaties, which clearly prohibited Japanese nationals from doing business with foreigners, presented a major obstacle to its acquisition. Aided by legal expert, M. Kirkland, who had been hired by of the Japanese Ministry of Justice, Glover found a clever solution that enabled them to circumvent the treaties' strict clauses: Kirkland called upon British and European investors in Hong Kong to register the company there as a British firm.

Thus in 1885, the company was officially registered as a British Hong Kong firm, and following a series of meetings, a public offering (IPO) was issued. As the company, Japan Brewery, was legally registered *outside* Japan, investment by Japanese was therefore legal. Consequently, both Japanese and foreign investors could buy shares in the company. Having registered the company outside Japan meant that the problem of Japanese doing business with foreigners *inside* Japan was overcome, at least in the short term. Japanese investors would, however, not be able to purchase the shares owned by foreigners nor be allowed to take full control of the firm's operations until after the treaties were fully renegotiated in 1894.

The first opportunity to purchase and re-register the company in Japan came in 1894 when Makoshi Kyōhei of Mitsui Trading Company, made an offer, which was refused. A second offer followed, which was negotiated by Kōmei Genjirō of Meidi-ya, the company's local distributor, who was able to convince the head of what would become the Mitsubishi *zaibatsu*, Iwasaki Yatarō, to offer to purchase Japan Brewery. The offer was accepted, and in 1907, the company would finally become fully 'Japanese' when a group of Japanese investors joined with Iwasaki to buy up all the foreign-owned shares in the company. Among them was the leading private-sector entrepreneur, Shibusawa Eiichi.

The Japanese beer industry is currently comprised of four main producers: Sapporo, Kirin, Asahi, and Suntory. Though Japanese beer is sold in overseas markets, it is still largely a domestic industry, one where the major players compete fiercely for market share. Today, Japan's largest beer brewery is Asahi, which grew out of Osaka Beer, founded in 1892, while Suntory, whose Suntory Beer brand was launched in 1963, would follow a different development trajectory.

2.4 Symbols of culture and enlightenment: the case of Tomioka Silk Filature

Since the Tokugawa times, farmers in rural parts of the country were involved in silk production through sericulture and spinning. In some areas a sophisticated cottage industry had begun to take shape as early as the late 1600s (Morris Suzuki, 1994, 29). By the mid-1850s, however, regional economies would begin to embark on a transition, one that would gradually integrate local silk producers into the global economy. One catalyst for the change was a sudden rise in the French demand for raw silk, stemming from the spread of the pébrine virus, a parasitic disease that attacked their silkworms and had begun to wreak havoc on the nation's key industries. The misfortunes of the two main players in the world silk industry, France and Italy, however, provided a new business opportunity for Japan. The

Meiji government's decision in 1870 to erect a modern silk filature came in response to rising foreign demand for high quality raw silk that this situation created.

Japanese shipments of raw silk were expedited to Europe from the Port or Yokohama, a trade that would quickly grow to become Japan's first major export. As European demand for Japanese raw silk rose, however, its quality declined in equal measure. As a result, the British and French governments began negotiating with Meiji government officials to suggest ways to improve the quality of the wares produced in Japan for export.

In 1869, F. Geisenheimer, head of a Lyon-based silk operation, Lilienthal, Hècht and Company, approached Itō Hirobumi, who would later become the nation's prime minister, regarding the possibility of establishing a modern silk filature. Geisenheimer offered to put up the necessary capital for the operation and provide French technology. Following their discussions, Itō brought the French proposal up with other government ministries. After further deliberations, it was decided that a Japanese mill would be constructed and that Shibusawa Eiichi would be placed in charge of setting up its operations. Upon the recommendation of Geisenheimer and his associate Dubousquet, Paul Brunat was named as the company's foreign advisor. Brunat, who was already working for the company at the Port of Yokohama, possessed extensive experience in silk production and was also abreast of the situation in Japan (Wittner, 2000, 56–57).

Image over technological appropriateness

In response to the Meiji government's request, Brunat presented a conventional, yet reasonable recommendation for Japan's first modern silk filature. He proposed a hybrid model, which combined existing and new technologies to avoid uprooting the long-standing spinning traditions, which he thought might incite resistance from local weavers. Brunat believed that local reelers would be more likely to cooperate if they had at least some familiarity with the technologies they would be employing, and felt that such an approach would have a greater likelihood of success in the long term.

Despite Brunat's reasonable advice on the adoption of a hybrid model and technologies—an approach that would also have been more appropriate to Japan's circumstances as a developing industrial nation—the Meiji government went ahead with its plans to build a state-of-the-art factory, one that would rival those in France and surpass those in Italy. By so doing, the Meiji government flatly rejected Brunat's proposals and sent him to France to purchase the necessary machinery and implements for the new mill. All the items found in the factory embodied the Meiji government's notion of modernity. The Tomioka Silk Mill was French in every respect, from its design down to the imported coal used to power the French steam engines and boilers (Wittner, 2000, 65–66).

Why were the Japanese reluctant to adopt a more appropriate yet less prestigious Italian or even a hybrid model, combining both indigenous and foreign elements? According to Wittner (2000, 6), the government's aims were both pedagogic and symbolic. The purpose of the factory was 'to serve as a national model of modern industry ... and to disseminate the latest silk reeling technologies to the people'. Symbols of Tomioka's modernity could be seen in every aspect of the filature from its architecture and building materials to the machinery placed therein:

> Icons of the first Industrial Revolution, cast iron and brick, steam engines and coal were materials that symbolized "modernity" and "progress." Described by such works as "permanent" and "sturdy," a society that had brick buildings and iron bridges, railroad and telegraph networks was "modern" and "civilized." Conversely wood was considered impermanent and flexible; it was the material of traditional crafts and was presumed to lack the precision of iron and industry. Any society that relied on wood for its buildings was traditional, and that was "uncivilized." In selecting the technologies with which to build a nation, the new Meiji government placed almost exclusive reliance on these "modern" materials and the values they embedded. (Wittner, 2000, 43)

The Tomioka Mill serves in some ways as a highly successful model of technology transfer. Of note is that the late nineteenth century was a period of international fairs, which were portrayed as venues for nations to showcase their industrial and technological achievements (Daykin, 2015). It is thus significant that Tomioka was recognized at the 1873 International Exhibition in Vienna for the quality of its silks. As Wittner (2000, 54–55, 100) writes of Tomioka silk, such accolades 'became the yardstick by which the government measured itself against other European and Asian nations'. To increase Japan's international prestige even further, Meiji policymakers encouraged Japanese participation in such expositions. Similar events were organized in Japan on a large scale, which served the important function of celebrating the achievements and promoting innovation among local producers.

From state entrepreneurship to the birth of the *zaibatsu* capitalism

The quality of the silk produced at Tomioka Silk Filature would eventually reach a level that was on a par with factories in Europe. Yet as a business operation its performance was far less stellar. Despite all the expert technical guidance and financial backing it had received from the Meiji government, Tomioka Silk Filature never became a profitable under state management (Wittner, 2000). The period from 1881 to 1885 was a turning point in business creation, as it was marked by a transition from public to private ownership. Tomioka represents but one example of the many firms that would change hands.

The decision can be traced to the financial policies introduced by Finance Minister Matsukata Matsuyoshi as a means of redressing the domestic economy and other issues (Ericson, 2014). Matsukata sold off (*haraisage*) state-owned enterprises, with the notable exception of the military-related firms, to a select group of private investors who had shown their loyalty to the government since the early days of the Meiji Restoration. The new owners of these enterprises would give birth to Japan's early 'big-business' or *zaibatsu* (see Chapters 3 and 4). Tomioka Silk Filature was purchased in 1893 by what would grow to become Japan's largest *zaibatsu*, Mitsui. Another state-owned company, Nagasaki Shipyards, whose roots as a foundry can be traced to the Tokugawa period, was also privatized. The new owner was the Iwasaki family, whose business empire would soon constitute Japan's second largest *zaibatsu*, Mitsubishi.

2.5 Conclusions

As illustrated through the examples of two light industries, beer brewing and silk production, the state played a crucial role as entrepreneur in the first phase of the Meiji period. Even in the case study of the private-sector firm, Kirin, public policy directly impacted its strategies. The state was able to channel the necessary financial and technical resources in order to create new companies at a critical juncture; that is, when private investment capital and technical know-how were extremely limited. Without government assistance, the development process would have occurred at a much slower pace or perhaps not at all.

These two examples show that bureaucrats were successful as new business creators but were often far less effective as business operators. Nonetheless, the central government would continue to provide direct support to the private sector through financial assistance, protective legislation, and technical guidance, when it was needed. Many of these state-sponsored companies would not begin to earn profits until they had been transferred to the private sector in the second half of the Meiji period, namely from the 1890s, while some, as shown in Chapter 4, would require further assistance due to unforeseen circumstances.

Thanks to the state's endeavours, key industries were established that would serve as the foundations for economic development in later periods. Reliance on human capital—foreign experts—as the main vectors of technology transfer proved to be an especially effective approach for Japan as a latecomer economy. However, as the example of Tomioka illustrates, the advice of foreign experts was not always heeded. Moreover, as both the brewing and silk industry cases showed, the government's choice to develop certain sectors was not always rational. Providing *symbols of modernity* in the form of authentic German-style beer and French-style factories was a central consideration in Meiji-period policy formulation, perhaps another factor for a lower short-term success rate of the government-backed firms. While firms founded by the state were often unprofitable, the importance of the state's role as an entrepreneur during the early Meiji period should not be underestimated. At this difficult point in history—when Japan was thrust into the global economy as a full-fledged player with no legal means to enact measures to protect its nascent industries—private-sector entrepreneurs in need of basic infrastructure and industrial models to emulate greatly benefited from the assistance and guidance that the state strove to provide.

3
Capitalism and Entrepreneurship in the Meiji Period (1868–1912)

Private entrepreneurs

Although the state played a major role in providing infrastructure and introducing new technologies, as explored in the previous chapter, the industrialization of Japan also relied heavily on the actions of private entrepreneurs. Between the mid-1880s and World War I, the stabilization of public finances and the monetary system following the Matsukata Deflation (1881–1885), as well as the fast growth of foreign trade, offered nearly unlimited opportunities to a new generation of businessmen who took charge of the development of the country.

The latter half of the 1880s is usually considered as the first boom in enterprise creation, particularly in the manufacturing industries and maritime transportation. In 1890, there were more than 2,200 private companies in the industrial sector, while five years earlier, there were less than 500. Moreover, this trend accelerated after the First Sino-Japanese War (1894–1895). The total number of corporations reached 2,458 in 1895 and grew to 12,308 in 1910 (Miwa and Hara, 2007, 68 and 85). Despite this impressive development, Japan, however, still fell behind Western countries in terms of the number of public corporations. The corporate stock value as a share of GDP was 32 per cent in Japan in 1910, against 173 per cent in the United States, 162 per cent in the United Kingdom and 44 per cent in Germany (Hannah, 2015, 558).

This boom in the creation of private enterprises was facilitated by a new legal environment. In the context of free trade and global competition, it was necessary to facilitate the formation of companies as new kinds of organizations, with a limited responsibility of partners, especially to develop firms in capital-intensive industries (e.g. railways, cotton spinning, and maritime transportation). The first modern commercial code, adopted in 1890, was based on the German model. It gave a legal definition of three kinds of companies: unlimited partnership (*gōmei gaisha*), limited partnership (*gōshi gaisha*), and joint-stock company (*kabushiki kaisha*). The revision in 1899 introduced the principle of a free transfer of shares, giving birth to the modern joint stock corporation (Okazaki, 1997).

Yet the creation of thousands of private companies between 1885 and 1914 was not merely the result of a favourable economic context and new legal framework. It required seizing opportunities and taking risks. A major challenge was producing in Japan rather than importing from abroad. Economic nationalism was also an important driving force of entrepreneurship. Hence, who were the private entrepreneurs who engaged in the creation of firms and the transformation of Japanese economy and society during the Meiji era? The answer to this question is multiple. There was not a single type of entrepreneur, but a broad variety of them. We can identify four major private-sector actors, who are explored in detail in the following sections: the founders and owners of *zaibatsu*, the financiers, the founders of large joint-stock companies, and the owners of small- and medium-sized enterprises (SMEs) in urban areas. All these actors played a significant role in supporting economic development during the boom that occurred in second half of the Meiji period. Before embarking on this overview, we should start with one specific entrepreneur, Eiichi Shibusawa, the father of Japanese capitalism.

3.1 Shibusawa Eiichi, the father of Japanese capitalism

The life and career of Eiichi Shibusawa (1840–1931) embodies the profound mutation in Japanese business, society, and culture that occurred from the end of the Edo to the early Showa periods (Shimada, 2017; Fridenson and Kikkawa 2017; Udagawa, 2002a). All of his activities can be summarized in the idea of connecting people and organizations. He developed the concept of *gapponshugi* as a specific form of capitalism where the quest for profits was not the only goal of entrepreneurship, but linked to human development through education and to the general economic development of catching up with the West. Shibusawa hence engaged in the transfer of knowledge from the West, worked for both the government and for private firms, and contributed to the foundations of hundreds of joint-stock companies throughout Japan (Miyamoto, 2016).

Shibusawa grew up in the margins of Edo society which was still largely based on a division between social classes. His social origin was ambiguous given his unusual upbringing (Miyamoto, 2016, 210–212). He was born in today's Saitama prefecture to a family of wealthy farmers or rural capitalists, discussed in Chapter 1, received the education of a young samurai, and spent his adult life engaging in manufacturing and commercial ventures. Miyamoto (2016) has demonstrated that his marginal position in society played a major role in making Shibusawa a modern entrepreneur. It helped him to free himself from a social origin which would have restricted his actions and allowed him to launch innovative projects in the context of the changing world of the Meiji period. He is hence a perfect embodiment of the Schumpeterian entrepreneur; that is, a businessman driven by innovation, whose actions result in a social transformation (what Schumpeter referred to as 'creative destruction') (Schumpeter, 1994 [1942]).

He was schooled in Confucianism, worked in the family business, and was employed in 1863 by Hitotsubashi Yoshinobu (1837–1913), a member of Tokugawa family. Shibusawa was placed in charge of the household finances and stood out for his outstanding ability. Hence when Hitotsubashi was appointed *shogun* in 1866, Shibusawa became an important member of the bureaucracy. In 1867, he joined the official Japanese delegation that visited the Paris Exposition and toured European countries. This was an opportunity for him to observe the economic and social achievements in Western Europe and to become more acutely conscious of the need to transform Japanese society and economy. Returning to Japan the following year, he set up residence in Shizuoka, where his former master had retired after he lost power following the Meiji Restoration. Shibusawa founded a commercial association and encouraged local farmers and merchants to pool their resources to found joint-stock companies, a new kind of business association Shibusawa learned about in France. His idea was to show that enterprises could be created without the assistance of large operations like the Houses of Mitsui and Konoike which dominated the Japanese economy in the Edo period and continued to do so as trading companies in the Meiji period. In 1869, he was summoned by the new government to join the central bureaucracy, which provided him with a great opportunity to contribute to modernizing the country.

Between 1869 and 1873, Shibusawa worked as head of the Reform Office of the Ministry of Finance. His main task was to introduce and implement the new institutions needed to transform the country and to support its economic development. In particular, he introduced a centralized system for granting monopolies over inventions in 1871 and 1872, based on the idea of the patent laws in force in Europe. The system was suspended in 1873–1884 but led to the adoption of a first patent law in Japan in 1885. Moreover, Shibusawa promoted the foundation of First National Bank in 1873, the first joint-stock company in Japan. This was a private company controlled by the Mitsui and

Ono merchants, whose business, until the foundation of the Bank of Japan (BOJ), was the printing of yen.

In 1873, Shibusawa resigned from public service and thereafter engaged only in private-sector activities. He started by founding two industries that would provide the basic infrastructure necessary to modernize Japan's economy and society: banking and papermaking. Banks were extremely important, as they offered financial support to numerous entrepreneurs. Shibusawa took the helm of First National Bank in 1875, after one of the major shareholders, the Ono group, withdrew. His position as a financier helped him to found numerous firms in a broad range of industries, one being papermaking. Although Japan had a long tradition of manufacturing its own traditional paper (*washi*), the adoption of Western techniques would enable the mass production of cheap paper which would support the development of education (printed books and newspapers). Hence Shibusawa engaged in the foundation of Oji Paper in 1872. These two decisions clearly express the fundamental objective of Shibusawa: supporting the economic and social development of Japan.

Shibusawa's approach to economic development was to create large and competitive private firms, which used the best technology imported from Western countries, to take charge of the modernization process. He did not create a specific firm that would tend to dominate the economy as the *zaibatsu* did. The specificity of his approach was his ability to bring together investors and entrepreneurs with a common vision to create joint-stock companies in many industries. He invested directly, through his position in Daiichi Bank, but he especially served as an 'organizer' of companies. He was involved in the foundation of more than two hundred firms, including Tokyo Marine Insurance (1878), Osaka Spinning (1879), Bank of Japan (1882), Asano Cement (1883), Japan Railways (1884), Sapporo Beer (1887), and Imperial Hotel (1887); that is, all major firms in their respective industries (Udagawa, 2002a, 23). Moreover, he contributed to the foundation of the Tokyo Stock Exchange in 1873. His will to build business networks and give business leaders a voice in society led him to found the Tokyo Chamber of Commerce in 1878. He also engaged in connecting industrialists in Tokyo to local entrepreneurs in the countryside, for the purpose of providing the financial means necessary for local economic development through the creation of railway companies, banks, and textile firms. In addition to his business activities, Shibusawa actively engaged in philanthropy to support education and the development of hospitals and the Red Cross. His success as a major industrialist with a social conscience made him a hero in Japanese society—not so much during his lifetime—but in the early twenty-first century at a time when large firms were having to scale back their welfare activities. Shibusawa was chosen in 2019 to replace Fukuzawa Yukichi, mentioned in the previous chapter and below, in 2024 as the new image on the 10,000-yen banknote.

3.2 The development of the financial system and private banks

Economic development and industrialization required the implementation of a new financial system in order to provide capital to entrepreneurs. The traditional financial system, based on transactions through private merchant houses, was sophisticated, with rice exchanges for futures trading and other financial products. Its scope was, however, inadequate for supporting the fast development of thousands of manufacturing companies. The introduction of banks as a new kind of financial institution was thus an urgent matter during the early Meiji period.

Japanese authorities adopted the National Bank Act in 1872, based on the American system. This law did not include the foundation of a central bank to control the creation of money and the printing of banknotes. The system entrusted private national banks to print their own notes and provide financial means to entrepreneurs to found new businesses. The First National Bank opened in 1873 and was followed by several others. By 1879, there was a total of 153 national banks throughout Japan. The activities of these banks were not limited to the issuing of money. They were commercial banks offering a broad range of services to private customers, from credit and loans to investment in private enterprises. Private banks—that is commercial banks which did not print their own notes—also appeared during the 1870s, Mitsui Bank being one of the oldest (1876) (Hoshi and Kashyap, 2001, 18–24).

The lack of coordination between the national banks and the absence of oversight led to a quick increase of the money in circulation and inflation. The total value of banknotes increased from 1.4 million yen in 1873 to 34.4 million in 1879 (Miwa and Hara, 2007, 59). The Meiji government intervened in the early 1880s to stabilize prices, a policy often called *Matsukata deflation*, after the name of the finance minister who implemented it (see Chapter 2). This policy was characterized by the privatization of a large number of state-owned enterprises (mostly taken over by *zaibatsu*) and the foundation of the Bank of Japan (BOJ) in 1882. BOJ was a joint-stock corporation whose main shareholders were the government and the major *zaibatsu* (Mitsui, Sumitomo, Yasuda, etc.). In 1884, it was granted the privilege of issuing notes, while private national banks were forced to withdraw from the printing of currency within twenty years after being granted a charter. The number of national banks decreased to fifty-eight in 1897 and to four in 1898. By the early twentieth century, BOJ had gained full control over the printing of money. Most national banks were converted to private commercial banks, and increased in number from thirty-nine in 1880 to 217 in 1890 and to more than 1,600 in 1911 (Miwa and Hara, 2007, 59 and 89). Most of them were small with a low level of capital. They supported the economic development of Japan until World War I but were severely weakened by the crises occurring during the interwar years.

For entrepreneurs, the banks were not the only way to procure the capital they needed to found and develop their firms. The market to exchange securities was organized during the 1870s, with the opening of the Tokyo Stock Exchange and Osaka Stock Exchange in 1878, followed by similar organizations in Yokohama (1879), Kyoto (1884), and Nagoya (1886) (Hoshi and Kashyap, 2001, 25–27). Public companies could find investors to purchase their shares and envisage growth on a large scale. Businesses were allowed to issue corporate bonds starting in 1890. The number of firms listed on the Tokyo Stock Exchange rose from twenty-six in 1885 to 130 in 1900. Most of them were railway and maritime transportation companies (Okazaki, 1997, 65–67).

The Matsukata deflation caused a change that would affect Japan's integration into the international financial system. While silver and gold were in practice both used for international transactions, the government adopted the silver standard in 1885. Thus, it became easier to devalue the yen in international markets to support exports. Between 1885 and 1897, the yen lost 41 per cent of its value against the US dollar and the British pound (Okazaki, 1997, p. 62). In 1897, Japan converted to the gold standard in an attempt to align its currency with those of Western countries and to enable inward FDI (see Chapter 5).

The Yokohama Specie Bank (YSB) played a major role in financing foreign trade, which relied mostly on foreign banks, essentially British, that had branches in the treaty ports until the 1880s. In order to gain control over their foreign trade, Japanese elites founded YSB, a financial institution specializing in foreign exchange. It supported trade through the purchase of import and export bills, and established several branches and agencies abroad, including London, New York, China, and India (Nishimura, 2012). Consequently, the formation and growth of a modern financial system in Meiji Japan resulted not only from the actions of private bankers, but also from the intervention of the state through regulation and the creation of state-controlled institutions.

3.3 The development of *zaibatsu* and their transformation into modern corporations

Among the numerous private companies that were founded and developed from the beginning of Meiji period, a distinctive form emerged and grew quickly to become as a major player in Japan's industrialization and economic development: *zaibatsu*. *Zaibatsu* are large family-owned firms engaged in a broad and diverse range of industries. They embody the Japanese variety of business groups; that is, family conglomerates as also observed in numerous countries, particularly in Asia and Latin America (Colpan et al., 2010). The reason for their emergence and specific characteristics relates to what economists call 'market imperfections' or the inability of market mechanisms to allocate resources properly. This includes difficulties in accessing capital and material resources, such as raw materials. The importance of the relationship with government to secure contracts also led some entrepreneurs to internalize some of their activities and diversify. This process can be explained by the 'transaction cost theory' (Williamson, 1981), which argues that firms tend to do some business activities by themselves when it is too costly to rely on the market.

Zaibatsu can be classified in two major ways. First, one can divide them according to their size and scope of activities. In this case, scholars generally distinguish the four largest *zaibatsu* (Mitsubishi, Mitsui, Sumitomo, and Yasuda) from a large number of smaller *zaibatsu* with a regional (e.g. Itochu in Osaka) or sectorial (e.g. Furukawa in mining) focus. However, most regional and sectorial *zaibatsu* did not remain small; many enlarged the scope of their activities, especially during the interwar years. Second, they can be distinguished by their historical roots as *zaibatsu* founded during the Edo period (Mitsui and Sumitomo) or as those founded after the opening of Japan (Mitsubishi and Yasuda). Until the 1860s, the former was active essentially in trading and finance, but diversified into new businesses, by seizing the opportunities offered by economic and social changes (see Chapter 2). The development of Mitsubishi *zaibatsu* is an excellent illustration of how family conglomerates were able to experience fast growth after the Meiji Restoration.

Despite its opening to global trade, Japan relied completely on foreign shipping companies for its foreign trade in the 1850s and 1860s. This was politically and militarily risky, as a change of international politics could threaten Japan's economic development. Hence the foundation of a national shipping company was a major concern for Japanese elites. In 1870, Iwasaki Yatarō (1835–1885) was a former employee of Taso Clan's office in Nagasaki. His task was to import weapons, ammunitions, and steamships in the late 1860s, and founded a maritime transportation company that was renamed Mitsubishi in 1873. Its main competitor was a semi-public company founded in 1872 by the government and merchant houses, but which stopped operations in 1875. This resulted in Mitsubishi's rise to becoming the largest domestic maritime company, which gained the support of the government as a means of competing with foreign shipping firms. The government's efforts paid off: Mitsubishi succeeded in establishing foreign shipping routes to Shanghai (1875) and was able to compete against American and European shipping firms for this route. However, Mitsubishi not only succeeded in overtaking its foreign competitors; it also gained a monopoly on domestic shipping and greater profitability by raising its fees. The dominance of one company led to the intervention of Shibusawa, who was joined by other investors. In 1882, a new large shipping company was founded through the merger of three smaller firms, called Kyōdō Unyu Company, which was financially supported by both the government and Mitsui *zaibatsu*. Fierce price competition followed, threating the sustainability of both firms. Shibusawa and Iwasaki's philosophy regarding business differed deeply, the first targeting a prosperous society through economic development, while the second aimed more at self-enrichment through monopoly. This difference emphasizes the need to avoid a simplistic narrative when discussing Japanese capitalism, and demonstrates that the opportunities offered by social and political change during the Meiji period led to the emergence of various types of entrepreneurs.

After the death of Iwasaki, the government intervened and encouraged a merger of the two firms. Nippon Yusen was hence founded in 1885, with the majority stake held by Mitsubishi. Mitsui had in the meantime founded its own shipping company, Osaka Shōsen (1884). Nippon Yusen pursued its expansion, dominating Japanese shipping industry and opening new routes such as Mumbai (1893) and London (1899) (Yamazaki, 2004, 38–39). In 1907, it was ranked as the eleventh largest shipping company in the world and number one outside Europe (Headrick, 1988, 39).

However, Mitsubishi was not merely a shipping firm. Iwasaki reinvested his profits in related businesses, gradually integrating a wide range of activities linked to shipping. The privatization of public firms was a major step in the diversification process. Iwasaki took over Takashima coal mines (1881) and Nagasaki shipyard (1884). The latter gave birth to Mitsubishi Shipbuilding, a company that led Mitsubishi to becoming a leading player in the machine industry. The hiring of foreign engineers and the importation of foreign technology allowed Mitsubishi Shipbuilding to experience fast growth. Production increased from 252 ships in the 1880s to 1,776 in the 1910s (Fukasaku, 1992, 29). The knowledge acquired to design and produce modern ships was used to diversify into related activities, a feature of all the major *zaibatsu*. In 1920, the company's diesel engine workshop transformed into a new company specializing in the development of cars and aircrafts, Mitsubishi Engine. It was renamed Mitsubishi Aircraft in 1928 and merged with Mitsubishi Shipbuilding in 1934 into Mitsubishi Heavy Industries, Japan's seventh largest company in 1937, with thirty thousand workers. The need to acquire new technology led to cooperation with foreign firms (see Chapter 5). The joint ventures, Mitsubishi Electric and Mitsubishi Oil were founded respectively in 1921 with Westinghouse Electric (USA) and in 1931 with Associated Oil (1931), which boosted its growth and procurement of new technologies.

Outside the manufacturing sector, Iwasaki introduced a financial services business related to shipping, and developed them as autonomous activities. He opened a currency exchange office (1876), which became Mitsubishi Bank, and created Tokyo Marine Insurance Company (1878), followed by Meiji Life Insurance (1881). Mitsubishi Bank became the financial arm of the *zaibatsu*. During the interwar years, it invested in a broad range of new businesses, thus strengthening the position of Mitsubishi in the Japanese economy.

The high-growth and diversification process of *zaibatsu* made it necessary to adopt a new organizational structure in order to oversee a broad range of businesses. In the early twentieth century, *zaibatsu* adopted a holding company structure (see Box 1.1 Chapter 1 for its precedents). Mitsui was the first to do so in 1909, followed by Sumitomo (1912), Yasuda (1912), and Mitsubishi (1918). Ownership of the holding company was held by the family members, while the management of both the holding and the various operating companies were transferred to professional managers, most of whom had graduated from the first business schools founded in Japan (see Box 3.1). These large groups and the domination they exerted on the Japanese economy made their owners as well as their managers a new class of social elite in Meiji Japan. In 1916, the top ten wealthiest families in Japan included eight owners of *zaibatsu*, among whom were Iwasaki (ranked first), Mitsui (second), Sumitomo (third), and Yasuda (fourth) (Yamazaki, 2004). Japanese *zaibatsu* continued their expansion during the interwar years, achieving a dominant position in most sectors of the economy, until their dismantlement after 1945, as shown in the following chapters.

Box 3.1 The foundation and development of business schools

The entrepreneurs of Meiji Japan were not simply self-made men who created hundreds of firms. The development of companies, particularly for the largest, required skilled managers at the helm. A broad variety of specialized knowledge, from accounting and legal affairs to the management of technology and labour, was necessary to achieve successful growth. Universities and business schools were opened throughout Japan by various actors as early as the end of *shogunate*. Based on American and European models, most of them were founded by entrepreneurial individuals who had visited Western countries.

Private entrepreneurs and statesmen opened the first business schools in Japan. One of the oldest was *Keio Gijuku* (today, Keio University), established in 1858 by Fukuzawa Yukichi (1835–1901), a young intellectual from Nakatsu in present-day Oita who engaged in Dutch studies (*rangaku*) to explore Western knowledge and visited the United States and Europe in the early 1860s. He was a promoter of a modern education system, and his school earned a high reputation for its instruction in finance, law, and literature at the end of the nineteenth century. Other private schools providing business education in the early twentieth century include Doshisha (1875), Meiji (1881), Waseda (1882), and Kansai (1886).

The central government intervened to support higher education in business. In 1883, it took over a school of commerce founded eight years prior in Tokyo, and made it a national school for the study of business-related matters (today, Hitotsubashi University). It would gradually expand thanks to backing from influential industrialists such as Shibusawa and Masuda Takashi, who was behind the transformation of Mitsui into a *zaibatsu*. In 1902, it founded a second national school of commerce in Kobe (today, Kobe University). Small-scale public business schools were also founded in Yamaguchi (1905), Nagasaki (1905), and Hokkaido (1910). This network expanded during the interwar years.

These institutions trained the professional managers who took charge of large firms during the Meiji era, particularly joint-stock companies and enterprises belonging to *zaibatsu*. One example is Mitsui Bank whose top managers in the 1890s were almost exclusively graduates of *Keio Gijuku* (Yamazaki, 2004, 137).

3.4 Private large firms: the example of Osaka Cotton Spinning Co.

The *zaibatsu* were not the only form of 'big business' in Meiji Japan. Modern joint-stock companies were created in industries that required a large amount of capital and foreign technology, examples of which include principally railways, electric power, and cotton spinning. Private companies in these sectors dominated the stock exchanges after the nationalization of the railways (1906), which was initially the most capital-intensive industry. In 1912, textile companies represented 22.2 per cent of capital transactions on the Tokyo Stock Exchange (Miwa and Hara, 2007, 86). Cotton spinning is an excellent illustration of a traditional industry that succeeded in strengthening its international competitiveness through the adoption of a modern form of incorporation and technological innovations.

Cotton cultivation was introduced in Japan in the sixteenth century. The production of fabric and clothing was realized by the end of Edo period in the context of a putting-out system (household manufacturing of cotton thread and fabrics in the countryside, collected and sold in cities by merchants). Western imports of machine-made cheap foreign cotton cloth caused a major shock that threatened local production. Table 3.1 shows that the share of domestic handmade cloth dropped from 100 per cent to 31.1 per cent between 1858 and 1874 and disappeared entirely in the 1890s. Japanese merchants started importing foreign cloth, especially in the 1860s, peaking in 1874 with 40.3 per cent of market share. They then shifted their focus to foreign cotton thread, used to produce cloth in Japan with 40.5 per cent of market share in 1880. As clothing is related to fashion and customer tastes, it was important to manufacture cloth domestically. However, after 1880, the

Table 3.1 Cotton market shares in Japan, as a %, 1861–1900

	Imported cloth	Domestic cloth, with imported thread	Domestic cloth, with Japanese handmade thread	Domestic cloth, with Japanese machine-made thread
Before 1858	–	–	100	–
1861	10.0	1.0	89.0	–
1867	31.7	9.4	57.9	1.0
1874	40.3	26.9	31.1	1.7
1880	23.4	40.5	34.9	1.2
1891	11.4	18.6	19.3	50.7
1900	18.6	5.9	–	75.5

Source: Miwa and Hara (2007), 63

production of cloth with imported thread started to decline precipitously. It dropped to just 5.9 per cent of the market in 1900. In the meantime, the development of a cotton-spinning industry enabled the manufacture of domestic cotton cloth with Japanese machine-made thread, which exceeded the volume of imported cloth in the 1880s. This change is the result of a successful transfer of production technology in the cotton-spinning industry.

As cotton manufacturing was a leading sector for industrialization and economic development, Japanese elites could not afford to rely on imports of foreign thread. However, developing a modern cotton-spinning industry was a major challenge after the opening of the country. The first initiatives came from the local domain governments of Kagoshima (1867) and Sakai (1870) where spinning factories were opened thanks to cooperation with British engineers, who installed modern British machinery. Despite this support, both firms went bankrupt because investment was too costly and because Japanese raw cotton was unsuitable (short and weak thread) for spinning with British machinery. Other unsuccessful attempts were made in the 1870s throughout the country. These examples illustrate the failure of the so-called 'han model' discussed in the previous chapter and were one of the reasons that the government had to step in to support the industry. In cotton spinning, the Meiji government intervened, opening two factories using imported British machinery in Aichi and Hiroshima prefectures in 1881. The objective was, as seen in the case of the Tomioka Silk Mill, to introduce modern technology to private entrepreneurs and encourage them to invest in this new industry. The government provided access to foreign machinery and loans to private entrepreneurs to encourage them to import additional equipment.

To be competitive in the cotton-spinning industry a private company had to be large. Economies of scale were the only means of coping with a global market dominated by cheap cotton thread manufactured in modern factories. Shibusawa Eiichi was conscious of the need to build a large-scale private spinning company. He collected the capital from investors and textile merchants necessary to found a joint-stock company in 1882: Osaka Cotton Spinning Company (OCS). It was equipped with the best and most modern technology. Power was provided from steam engines imported from the United Kingdom, and the spinning machines were supplied by Platt Brothers & Co., the British textile machinery manufacturer that dominated world markets at that time. British engineers also cooperated with the organization of the production site. Electric lighting was introduced in 1886. The owners of OCS wanted to make it a perfect copy of a Manchester factory: even the red bricks of the plant built in Osaka were imported from Lancashire (Saxonhouse, 1974).

The management of the firm was entrusted to Yamabe Takeo (1851–1920), trained in economics at the University of London and King's College. While he was studying in the United Kingdom, Shibusawa sent him to Manchester to study the management of spinning companies. He became the technical superintendent of OCS in 1882 and general director in 1898. He was a leading entrepreneur of the Japanese textile industry, and in 1901 was appointed president of the Japan Cotton Spinners Association.

Production started in 1883 with raw cotton imported from China and India. OCS experienced successful growth which led to the foundation of numerous other spinning companies based on the same business model (joint-stock corporation, foreign technology, and industrial production). Mitsui Bussan, the trading company of the eponymous *zaibatsu*, played an important role in this process. As the exclusive representative of Platt Brothers & Co. in Japan, it imported the machinery that equipped most of Japan's cotton-spinning companies. Their number reached twenty-one in 1887 and seventy-seven in 1898 (Odagiri and Gotō, 1996, 116–117). Cotton spinning was a leading industrial sector in Japan which grew to become competitive in world markets. Exports overtook imports of cotton yarn in 1897 and for cotton cloth in 1909 (Robinson, 1979). What is most impressive, however, is that this achievement was realized in the context of a free-trade policy, as the Japanese cotton-spinning industry did not benefit from any protectionist policy until 1911.

Competition between Japanese companies led entrepreneurs to adopt essentially two kinds of actions: mergers and acquisitions (M&A) and diversification into related businesses. One example is OCS, which was losing its dominant position in domestic cotton yarn. While it had a share of more than 20 per cent in the second half of the 1880s, the ratio dropped to about 5 per cent in 1900 (Miyamoto, 1989, 119). Hence, in 1906, OCS acquired Kanakin Cotton Weaving (founded in 1888). This move strengthened its position in the cotton cloth market (more than 20 per cent of national production in the 1900s). In 1914, OCS merged with Mie Cotton Spinning (founded in 1886). The new firm was named Tōyōbō. It merged in 1931 with Osaka Joint Spinning and became the world's largest spinning manufacturer.

3.5 Hundreds of SMEs in the cities of Osaka and Tokyo

In addition to the large private enterprises that played a leading role in cotton spinning and other capital-intensive industries (railways, maritime transportation, electric power, chemicals, large machinery, etc.), hundreds of small- and medium-size enterprises (SMEs) were founded by private entrepreneurs in the light machinery as well as low-tech sectors. Economic and social changes that occurred during the Meiji era provided an opportunity to launch businesses to manufacture a broad range of new products.

These SMEs played a major role in Japanese industrialization. In 1907, firms with less than a hundred workers employed a total of 21 million Japanese, the equivalent of 97.7 per cent of the total workforce in the manufacturing industry (Abe, 2002, 58–59). Tanimoto (2006) has demonstrated that these small companies were not backward and focused on the domestic market. Small-scale manufacturing and cheap labour enabled Japanese SMEs to produce and export a wide variety of simple consumer goods, from brushes and buttons to bicycles and clocks. The demand for such goods was high but fluctuated significantly over time, so that the flexibility and low production costs of Japanese SMEs made them competitive in the early twentieth century in foreign markets, mostly in Asia, where they challenged the domination of trade by Western firms.

Another major feature of these SMEs is their concentration in the two largest urban centres of Japan, Tokyo and Osaka. While both cities represented respectively only 4 per cent and 2 per cent of the national population in 1909, their cumulative share of industrial production amounted to about 30 per cent (see Table 3.2). It was particularly high for machinery and instruments (46.7 per cent). These SMEs clustered in specific areas of these two cities and developed in a context of urban industrial districts characterized by a high degree of specialization and a division of labour. Some of them such as Tokyo Electric (1890), Lion (1891), Morinaga (1899), and NSK (1914) in Tokyo, and Kubota (1890) and Matsushita (1918; Panasonic as of 2008) in Osaka would become large modern enterprises during the interwar years.

Table 3.2 Ratio of industrial production in Tokyo and Osaka, 1909

	Tokyo	Osaka	Japan
Industrial production, total (1,000 yen)	97,566	139,209	796,349
Ratio (%)	12.3	17.5	100.0
Dyeing and weaving	7.9	15.6	100.0
Machinery and instruments	23.8	22.9	100.0
Chemicals	18.6	22.6	100.0
Food and beverage	9.2	10.7	100.0
Metal smelting	3.8	82.0	100.0
Various	24.3	19.5	100.0

Source: Sawai (2013), p. 3

The case of the clock and watch company Hattori & Co., better known under its brand name Seiko, is an excellent illustration of the beginnings of these small firms and their transformation into large companies (Donzé, 2017). The roots of this enterprise go back to the early Meiji period, when a young man, Hattori Kintarō (1860–1930), opened a store in Ginza, Tokyo, in 1877, to repair and sell clocks and watches. He was a retailer and got his supplies from Swiss merchants based in Yokohama. Western timepieces were new products whose consumption started to develop steadily at that time, as the Japanese authorities had decided to adopt the Western calendar and way to measure time in 1873. Hattori founded his own company in 1881, then transformed it into a joint-stock company (Hattori & Co.) in 1917.

About ten years after founding his company, in 1892, Hattori decided to start the production of clocks. He bought a small plant in the Honjō district of Tokyo and engaged around ten workers to manufacture clocks, before diversifying into watch cases (1893), pocket watches (1895), and alarm clocks (1899). This expansion required the construction of a new factory, equipped with electric engines. It was opened in 1894 with ninety workers. Honjō was one of Tokyo's major industrial districts, specializing in small machinery. In 1909, Honjō had a total of 166 factories in this sector, mostly very small workshops (Imaizumi, 2008). Hattori benefited from their presence. For example, in the 1900s, he ordered pinions for clocks from an umbrella factory (Uchida, 1985, 323). He also cooperated with the machine-tool company Wachigai, founded in 1887. Until 1900, Hattori was a small company that employed less than two hundred employees. However, it grew fast at the beginning of the twentieth century thanks to the production of clocks, which made Hattori the largest manufacturer in the country in the late 1890s and an early globalizer. He started exporting wall clocks to China in 1895 through the trading company Mitsui & Co. The transformation to a large enterprise occurred during the interwar period with the production of watches in a large modern factory rebuilt after Great Kantō Earthquake of 1923. Hattori & Co. launched the Seiko wristwatch in 1924 and benefited from customs protectionism in the domestic market. It became the world's largest manufacturer of watches in the 1930s.

3.6 Conclusions

Private entrepreneurs were major actors in the economic and technological development of Japan, particularly during the latter half of the Meiji period. Their actions contributed to making Japan independent of foreign domination. Social and economic changes after 1868 offered a broad range of opportunities for entrepreneurs to create manufacturing and service-sector companies. The general trends of importing and then producing manufactured goods explain the development of numerous enterprises. The volume of domestic production exceeded that of imports for many goods such as beer (1886), cotton cloth (1886), hats (1892), medical instruments (1898), cheese and butter (1907), cameras (1907), bicycles (1911), and combustion engines (1914) (Shimano, 1980). Success in import substitution required the organization of companies that could turn a profit—not just produce goods. Entrepreneurs also needed access to capital to hire workers and to find some outlets for their products. They were, however, not alone in their endeavours. The government, through various policies and the implementation of different economic and legal institutions, supported the growth of private enterprises.

Japanese industrialization was not a process driven merely by the aspiration of achieving the objective of import substitution. Becoming competitive abroad, especially in Asian markets, was also a major goal—as Japanese authorities did not have full control of their customs policy until the renegotiation of the unequal treaties in the late 1890s. Exports started with commodities like silk and tea, giving birth to transportation and trading companies. Cotton yarn was important in this perspective because it was the first major manufactured good to be widely exported, leading the way for other goods during the interwar years. The share of manufactured goods to total Japanese exports grew appreciably from 12 per cent in 1873–1877 to 80 per cent in 1914. This increase relied essentially on textiles, which accounted for 47 per cent of exports in 1914 (Howe, 1996, 93 and 129). Cotton textile production was also one of the very few industries that carried out foreign direct investment during the Meiji period, thanks to the opening of spinning factories in Shanghai in the early twentieth century (Duus, 1989).

4
Industrial Capitalism in a Changing Social and Geopolitical Environment (1895–1930)

The rise of *industrial capitalism*, which coincided with the rapid growth of a factory system, took place in Western nations between the 1860s and World War I (Hobsbawn, 1975; 1987). For Japan too, this period was vital to the development of business in both quantitative and qualitative terms. Ample entrepreneurship combined with the channelling of resources by policymakers into specific areas led to the creation of new businesses at an unprecedented rate. Of the 8,612 companies in operation in 1902, some 84 per cent were established in a few years following the Sino-Japanese War of 1894–1895 (Garon, 1987, 10).

Growing numbers of men and women left their agrarian lives in the countryside to seek employment in factories. By 1930 more than 50 per cent of the workforce was employed in the manufacturing sector (Taira 1970, 84–85). For business, the downsides of this rapid industrial growth were the frequent labour shortages and strikes that characterize this period. However, for workers, the problems for employers provided opportunities to demand better working conditions, a development that would sow the seeds of a labour movement as well as the foundations of Japanese-style management, which is emblematic of the Japanese Business System, discussed in the chapters that follow. The growth of both business and demand for new manufactured goods sparked changes in Japanese society that would shape the way both men and women worked, consumed, and spent their leisure time. Firms responded to this rapidly changing business climate by adjusting their output and/or adapting their labour practices. The different approaches introduced to deal with the changing circumstances would strongly impact the formation and features of Japanese capitalism and entrepreneurship in this period and beyond. This chapter focuses on the internal influences on the development of Japanese business and entrepreneurship from the latter half of the Meiji period to the build-up for war in the 1930s, a period of great market

Japanese Capitalism and Entrepreneurship. Pierre-Yves Donzé and Julia S. Yongue, Oxford University Press.
© Pierre-Yves Donzé and Julia S. Yongue (2024). DOI: 10.1093/oso/9780192887474.003.0005

volatility and instability, while Chapter 5 tackles the role of foreign business during the same time span.

Thanks to the endeavours of Meiji-period bureaucrats to modernize selected industries, by the mid-1890s tangible evidence of genuine progress could be seen in the form of new, well-equipped factories. The development of modern businesses had broad implications for the nation's standing in the world. By the late 1890s Japan's economic achievements placed it on a stronger footing vis-à-vis Western powers, allowing policymakers to re-negotiate the many unequal treaties that had forced the nation to relinquish its tariff autonomy. In 1899, the bilateral treaty with Great Britain was revised, and by 1910, government officials had succeeded in re-negotiating all its bilateral treaties. As a result, Japan was no longer forced to pay low duties on imported Western goods and raw materials, making it possible to impose its own tariff regime, something the policymakers wasted no time in doing. Duties were levied on imports of such goods as raw cotton, textiles, electric equipment, watches, glass, sugar, and others, which ranged from 5 to 40 per cent (Yui and Hirschmeier, 1975, 147). Thanks to such protective legislation, Japan, as a latecomer nation to industrialization, was able to use the tariff policymaking mechanism to promote and guide its economic development. This particularly benefited the infant industries it wished to protect from foreign competition and fostered import substitution.

In addition to the rise of industrial capitalism, this chapter examines three interconnected themes that dominated Japanese business during this period. The first is dualities, which began to emerge in various contexts and forms, and were a major cause of the uneven growth of Japanese businesses in this period and beyond. Examples can be seen in various guises: the large (mainly *zaibatsu*) enterprises versus the small- and medium-sized businesses; the modern versus the traditional industries; the wealthy industrialists versus the factory and farm labourers, and so on. The winners in this period were the *zaibatsu* enterprises and those who owned and/or managed them. Collectively the *zaibatsu* groups controlled all of Japan's major industries and would reach their zenith during World War II. The *zaibatsu* benefited disproportionally from economic booms, and for the most part weathered the sharp economic downturns that characterized this period with relative ease, often even profiting from crises. The losers were most often the small- and medium-sized enterprises and especially their workforce—the men, women, and sometimes even children—who supported the nation's rapid economic growth through their labour. The workers employed by these firms spent long hours toiling under harsh conditions, performing their jobs in what were exploitative, sweatshop-like conditions. The unequal distribution of the rewards of economic growth, a result of 'big business' domination or *zaibatsu* capitalism, caused rifts that engulfed and divided society and created new tensions across class and gender lines. Though related to the notion of *zaibatsu* capitalism, in this chapter, the more general term of *industrial capitalism* is used.

One conspicuous consequence of the situation that these dualities produced was the formation of a labour movement, the second broad theme of this chapter. During the 1910s and 1920s, at a time when some degree of self-expression was tolerated, strikes, riots, and other forms of social unrest were not uncommon. By the end of the period examined in this chapter, however, these freedoms would be completely suppressed through measures imposed by the government as a means of instilling a greater a sense of national unity, a sentiment that would be necessary to wage a full-scale war. Growing tensions accompanied by the rise of a labour movement brought about social change, the third theme of this chapter, which resulted in a massive transformation of consumption patterns, gender relationships, and business practices.

4.1 The rise of industrial capitalism in a shifting geopolitical environment (1895–1910s)

The full emergence of industrial capitalism coincided with two changes in the focus of economic activities: a shift from agriculture to industry and another from light to heavy industries. As a result, a growing number of labourers left their homes in the countryside and moved to cities in search of new factory work opportunities. The migration of labourers to large urban agglomerations had a marked effect on the populations of cities, namely Tokyo and Osaka. According to Andrew Gordon, between 1900 and the start of World War I, the size of the industrial workforce more than doubled from 400,000 to 853,000 persons, while in Tokyo alone the number of labourers tripled (Gordon, 1991, 20). Though factories continued to absorb the burgeoning number of workers, half of the entire labour force was still engaged in the agricultural sector as self-employed farmers, while one-fourth was employed in the tertiary sector of the economy in such professions as artisans and shopkeepers (Flath, 2000, 45). Of note is that a large portion of the urban workforce was male. However, thanks to the development of industry, females also began to enter the labour force in ever-greater numbers, often as factory workers. Women were essential to support Japan's industrial development in this period as well as the high-growth years (1951–1973) and beyond. In this period, they were particularly vital to its first major export industry, textiles, and later to others such as electronics (Partner, 2000). They also played a leading role in the social transformation that was taking place, which affected both family life and consumption patterns.

During this period the Japanese economy was marked by volatility and instability, in large part due to the nation's evolving geopolitical role in East Asia. As shown in Table 4.1, adjusted real GDP fluctuated between 8.9 per cent and minus 7.2 per cent between 1918 and 1936. The first major upswing in the economy came in the wake of the first Sino-Japanese War (1894–1895), due in part to the favourable terms of the Treaty of Shimonoseki at the conclusion of the war, which included a significant indemnity (Nagaoka, 1981, 1). In addition, the acquisition of new territorial possessions—one being Taiwan (Formosa)—sparked the growth of both Japan's economy and its imperialistic aspirations.

Accompanying these changes was a shift in the nation's investment priorities. From the late Meiji period into the 1930s, the government began channelling funds away from light industries such as textiles and instead

Table 4.1 Changes in adjusted real GDP, 1918–1936

Year	Adjusted real GDP
1918	8.7
1919	5.7
1920	−0.5
1921	6.9
1922	−3.8
1923	−7.2
1924	5.3
1925	6.2
1926	1.9
1927	4.0
1928	6.7
1929	0.6
1930	1.2
1931	−1.2
1932	6.1
1933	7.8
1934	8.9
1935	7.2
1936	2.6

Source: Utsunomiya (2008)

towards heavy industries, reflecting the underlying ideology of the slogan, 'rich nation, strong army' (*fukoku kyōhei*). Shipbuilding and iron and steel were two sectors that received government support. A related industry, shipping, also benefited from favourable legislation. According to the 1896 Shipping and Shipping Promotion Law, subsidies were granted to support its growth. After the Russo-Japanese War, heavy industry investments, particularly those relating to military build-up, would increase even further. In 1907, the first 20,000-ton cruiser was constructed at Yokosuka Shipyard, thus alleviating the need to import such large-sized vessels from abroad. In 1897, Yawata Ironworks was established, and in 1901 it began producing steel frames and plates as well as rails for a growing network of railways.

The second major conflict during this period, the Russo-Japanese War of 1904–1905, ended with a second victory for Japan; however, unlike the first Sino-Japanese War, it would contribute less to the development of business and the economy. This time Japan received no indemnities and was instead left with a large public debt, which by 1913 had reached 1.1 billion yen. The situation would reverse itself by 1920, however, when Japan would become a creditor nation with a surplus of over 2 billion yen (Nakamura, 1989 451).

The third major conflict was World War I (1914–1918), which, like the Sino-Japanese War, was highly favourable to Japan's development. The economy grew to levels that would not be witnessed again until the postwar high-growth period. The slowdown and in some cases cessation of exports from Europe to parts of Asia and Africa left Japanese businesses with an unprecedented opportunity to expand into markets that had, until then, been largely if not entirely untapped. Stock prices rose, and a factory construction boom got underway nationwide to respond to the new demand for Japanese goods in these new markets as well as at home. Import substitution got underway in earnest. As a result, goods such as steel, machinery, and chemicals for which Japan had once been import-dependent began to be produced domestically (Nakamura, 1989, 118).

Thanks to Japan's allegiance to the Allied side and geographical location, its involvement in the battles of World War I was limited, sparing it from major physical (infrastructure, homes, buildings, etc.) damage. Evidence of the positive effects of the war boom on the Japanese economy is evident from macroeconomic data. From 1914 to 1919, Japan's Gross Domestic Product (GDP) increased fivefold. A booming economy enabled it to reimburse all the foreign debts that had been incurred during the Russo-Japanese War and even allowed it to become a lender to overseas governments. According to the calculations of Angus Maddison, shown below in Table 4.2, growth of

Table 4.2 Growth ratios of real GDP in selected countries, 1913–1938

Country	Ratio (%)
Japan	**4.0**
Norway	2.9
Netherlands	2.2
United States	2.0
Italy	1.7
Germany	1.6
United Kingdom	1.1
France	0.9
Belgium	0.8
Canada	1.5
Average	**1.8**

Source: Maddison (2020), https://www.rug.nl/ggdc/historicaldevelopment/maddison/releases/maddison-database-2010

real GDP from 1913 to 1938 was impressively high, even in comparison to more economically developed nations (Maddison, 1983, 35).

A boom for Japanese business occurred thanks to strong overseas demand coupled by a depreciation of the yen. Exports of metals, machinery, and raw silk in particular, saw an increase. The availability of cheap Japanese products abroad sparked significant industrial development and demand, which was fuelled by severe shortages of goods in Europe and elsewhere. New territorial acquisitions also contributed to the growth of the domestic economy and stimulated further imperialistic expansion. To bolster the nation's self-sufficiency in armaments, investments in capital goods production such as steel, electrical equipment, and machinery rose. The combination of the changing geopolitical context and the growth in demand for Japanese exports propelled Japan from a marginal to a major player in the world economy.

In addition to the changing geopolitical circumstances, other factors contributed to the growth of business. Domestic firms were able to improve operational efficiencies. As the use of electric power became more widespread, cost reductions in some manufacturing industries were achieved, including fertilizers, thus providing a boost to productivity. Shipping and shipbuilding experienced a boom due to growing trade within Asia as well as other parts of the world.

The cessation of exports of some high-tech products from Western Europe aided in the development of important new industries, which benefited from policies designed to encourage key sectors of the economy. Until the outbreak of World War I, Japan had been dependent on imports of German chemicals and pharmaceuticals. Given the strategic importance of these sectors, however, in 1915 the Japanese government opted to provide direct subsidies to support self-sufficiency and import substitution. In 1917, policymakers introduced the Wartime Industrial Property Law (*Kogyō shoyūken senjihō*). According to this law the patents and other forms of intellectual property of the countries with which Japan was at war were no longer recognized. The introduction of this measure gave an unprecedented boost to the nascent chemical and pharmaceutical industries while also encouraging the establishment of in-house research (Yang, 2021, 19–37).

A final element that contributed to the development of business was the expansion of new markets for Japanese goods in its territorial possessions. While products made in and shipped from the Japanese mainland to these markets were not subject to duties, tariffs on Western goods were kept high. Given this propitious situation, domestic firms faced a less competitive environment, which provided them with an ever-wider range of new business opportunities. In response to the changes in geopolitics, some industries relocated their factories as well as their supplier networks. Japan's light industry activities were moved to the colonial possessions in Taiwan, Liaotung, the southern part of Sakhalin, Korea, and Southern Manchuria. Textile manufacturers such as Mitsui Bussan, Tōyō Menka, and Nihon Menka imported cotton and sold textiles in the markets of Korea, Taiwan, and China. Sugar production got underway in Taiwan, while pulp and paper products were manufactured in Sakhalin.

4.2 The rise of *zaibatsu* and the banking crisis (1920s–1930s)

A notable outcome of the developments described above was that it galvanized the position of the highly diversified, family-owned *zaibatsu* in the Japanese economy, a situation that would persist until their dismantling in 1945. As large-scale conglomerates, they would continue to expand and consolidate their operations thanks to their domination of certain industries. On the eve of World War I, Japan's major *zaibatsu* had secured large investments in all the key sectors of the economy including mining (Furukawa, Kuhara, Fujita), manufacturing (Asano, Kawasaki, or Matsukata), distribution (Okura, Suzuki, Iwai), and finance (Yasuda, Nomura, Murai) (Udagawa and Shōjima, 2011, 120). The largest and most highly diversified 'big three' *zaibatsu*, Mitsui, Mitsubishi, and Sumitomo, held assets in these sectors.

By the early 1900s, the operations of conglomerates spanned across Japan with trade networks and business interests in all the major overseas markets. While they were involved in every key industrial sector of the economy, two sectors in particular, mining and banking, had become the main sources of the capital they used to finance new businesses and, as shown below, to protect them during crises.

As shown in Table 4.3, the World War I boom would not endure. A long recession ensued from 1920 to 1929, which was punctuated by a shock known as the Shōwa Financial Crisis (*Shōwa kin'yu kyōfu*) of 1927. In the early aftermath of World War I, the country faced other economic ills, namely a trade deficit. The reason was the weakening competitiveness of Japanese goods in the home market, caused by changes in the exchange rate, which had made the price of Japanese products higher relative to imports from abroad and therefore less attractive.

Another significant occurrence, one that would have important ramifications on the Japanese economy and business, was a major natural disaster: the

Table 4.3 Summary of changes in the Japanese economy, 1914 to 1940

Trend	Event	Date(s)	Effects on the economy and business
Boom	World War I	1914–1919	High growth rates; inflation; increased economic output resulting in a bubble; trade surplus vis-à-vis directly involved in the war
Recession	Shōwa Recession	1920–1929	Mildly deflationary period; The Great (Global) Depression of 1929
Shock	Shōwa Financial Crisis	1927	Incomplete restructuring of business sector after World War I boom; outstanding bad loans of financial institutions; trade deficit
Depression	Shōwa Depression	1930–1931	Japan's return to the Gold Standard as the cause of severe deflation and general economic decline
Boom	Takahashi Economic Policy	1932–1936	High growth; modest inflation
Command economy	Wartime economy	1937–1940	High growth; rampant inflation

Source: Shizume (2009), 1–9

Great Kantō Earthquake of 1923. This earthquake would severely damage the physical infrastructure—homes and businesses—of Tokyo and its environs. One reason why the tremor was particularly devastating was the fires that ensued. In those days, highly flammable materials—wood and paper—were used in the construction of homes. Another reason was the timing of the earthquake. It occurred in the early morning when households were preparing breakfast, using flammable materials, such as wood and gas. The death toll was thus high not only because of the initial collapse of housing structures, but also because of the fires that quickly engulfed the city.

To understand the context and trace the causes of the post-earthquake banking crisis, it is necessary to provide some general information on the behaviour of businesses during the boom years of World War I. Thanks to the rapid rise in demand for Japanese goods, many business operators increased their productive capacities and invested in infrastructure such as new buildings and factories. To finance this expansion, firms took out loans from the large number of banks that were in operation at that time (Shizume, 2016). After the earthquake, many of these new structures for which the loans had been taken out were reduced to rubble, leaving the firms that had constructed them with significant debts. The earthquake directly impacted the liquidity of the banks, which issued business loans in its aftermath, a central cause of the Shōwa Recession (Shizume, 2009).

It is noteworthy that not all enterprises were affected in the same way by this situation. Some businesses were better positioned to shoulder their losses than others. Among those that successfully weathered the crisis were the 'big three' *zaibatsu*, also known as forerunner *zaibatsu* (*senkō zaibatsu*): Mitsui, Mitsubishi, and Sumitomo. The structure of their business operations and the types of investments they had chosen allowed them to shoulder huge losses during the crisis and beyond. In particular, the ownership of their own banks, known as *kikan ginkō*, allowed them to continue to borrow when necessary and to avoid bankruptcy. Moreover, a higher degree of diversification in a variety of industrial sectors, a key feature of the major *zaibatsu*, further bolstered their ability to cover their losses by absorbing them within the group. Among their holdings, the highly lucrative mining operations served as the strongest buffer against the shocks that occurred during this turbulent period. Paradoxically, by the end of the Shōwa Crisis and ensuing recession, the major *zaibatsu* were able to strengthen their operations, in some cases by purchasing the failed firms of other conglomerates, such as those of Suzuki Shōten.

Though numerous firms faced financial ruin in the aftermath of the 1923 Great Kantō Earthquake, none would experience failure on a scale that would match that of *Suzuki Shōten* (Suzuki & Company). Its bankruptcy caused repercussions that would reverberate throughout the economy of the Japanese mainland to its colonies. Its failure caused a banking crisis that was followed by reforms designed to restructure the banking sector. The Banking Act of 1927 placed stricter minimum capital requirements which in turn triggered a wave of mergers. Consequently, the number of banks, which stood at over two thousand in 1919, decreased to 650 by 1932 (Shizume, 2016, 13).

4.3 The rise and fall of Suzuki Shōten (Suzuki & Company)

Suzuki Shōten got its start in the late 1800s as a sugar-trading enterprise, founded in Kobe by Suzuki Iwajirō. Suzuki died in 1894, and was succeeded by his wife, Yono, who left the management of the firm to Kaneko Naokichi and Yanagida Fujimatsu. After Japan's victory in the first Sino-Japanese War, Kaneko decided that the firm would enter the camphor business in Taiwan, a move that first led to its connection to the Bank of Taiwan. The company's strategy of investing in raw materials such as camphor was facilitated by a powerful political connection, the Japanese government representative in Taiwan, Gotō Shinpei. Gotō was key to ensuring the firm's early success as he saw to it that Suzuki Shōten received the exclusive right to market Taiwanese camphor. Under Kaneko's direction, Suzuki Shōten also purchased a steelworks. In the early 1900s, its diversification spread even further afield into areas such as foods, chemicals, fish oil, tobacco, salt, cellulose, and so on.

Thanks to Kaneko's aggressive investments, Suzuki Shōten recorded rapid growth in the early decades of its operations; however, its expansion would take on a whole new dimension during World War I when Kaneko began to pursue investments in world markets. Suzuki Shōten achieved impressive financial results which allowed it to become a general trading company or *sōgō shōsha*, a type of firm that continues to serve an important function in Japanese business today. Yoshino (1975, 43) defines *sōgō shōsha* as one with '(1) domestic trade and trade between home and foreign countries; (2) third country trade; (3) diversification of merchandise; (4) strong investment activities; (5) industrial organizing; (6) trade subsidiary functions; (7) international information enterprise functions; (8) the organizing of international merchandise circulation'.

Through a series of speculative, but highly lucrative investments during World War I, the company's assets grew exponentially, placing it on a par in financial terms with the three largest *zaibatsu*. Thanks to its successes, Suzuki Shōten became known as one of the great business combines of the Taishō era (1912–1926) with an annual turnover in 1917 that even surpassed its rival, Mitsui Bussan (Katsura, 1975, 35 and 41).

Its success would, however, be short-lived. Diversification was a general strategy among all the *zaibatsu* during the Meiji and Taishō periods, one that was encouraged by the government as a means for achieving self-sufficiency in selected industrial sectors. Suzuki Shōten, however, had clearly over-diversified its investments with a disproportionately high number tied up in its subsidiaries. Another factor for its downfall was its business model, which was ill adapted to weathering severe crises. For their part, the business models of Mitsui and Mitsubishi were based on self-financing, which could be achieved by channelling funds from their internal banking system to their businesses when they were running low on capital. These *zaibatsu* also possessed extensive mining interests, purchased cheaply from the Meiji government (*haraisage*) as shown in Chapter 2, which remained lucrative, providing a 'safety net' during such times of crisis.

A final factor that contributed to Suzuki Shōten's downfall was the lack of necessary managerial capabilities to deal with the changing circumstances of the times. As mentioned in the previous chapter, most of the *zaibatsu* had undergone a major overhaul of their operations in the 1910s. As a result, highly competent professional managers with business-school degrees—as opposed to family members and other persons with limited or no business training—were placed in charge of their operations. These managers introduced drastic restructuring measures, the most prominent being the creation of holding companies (*gōmei*) to oversee the major sections of the group's operations (Yonekura, 1985). As a result, the governance structure of the major *zaibatsu* empires had become more decentralized, and their businesses were able to benefit from the introduction of modern business practices. The management style of Suzuki Shōten, on the other hand, would continue to be highly centralized and dictatorial in nature, as illustrated by Kaneko's strong reluctance to convert the operation to a joint-stock company and introduce the necessary rationalization measures to modernize its business and accounting practices (Katsura, 1975, 52–53).

Suzuki Shōten's total debt vis-à-vis its main bank, the Bank of Taiwan, reached approximately 379 million yen by 1927. In addition to these loans, the bank also lent to other companies, many of which were devastated by the Great Kantō Earthquake of 1923. Its outstanding loans totalled approximately 470 million yen, or the equivalent to nearly ten times the bank's capitalization. To remain solvent, the Bank of Taiwan had to resort to borrowing from city banks, the loans for which caused its debt to swell to 240 million yen by 1927 (Katsura, 1975).

For its part, the government introduced a one-month moratorium on debt to aid in the post-earthquake recovery. The Bank of Japan (BOJ) also issued earthquake bills as a means of further supporting the recovery efforts of the firms in the affected areas. By 1926, Suzuki Shōten and the Bank of Taiwan possessed nearly half of all these BOJ-issued earthquake bills. To improve the liquidity of the banks so that they could provide loans to the businesses in need, the BOJ was obliged to purchase the banks' commercial (earthquake) bills (Hunter, 2014).

Though many of Suzuki Shōten's debts were earthquake related, the company was heavily indebted even before the disaster. Reimbursing all the loans was highly problematic due to losses incurred through speculative investments made during the wartime boom years and over-diversification. The turning point for Suzuki Shōten, however, came in 1926 during deliberations in the Diet when the question of issuing additional earthquake bills was being discussed. The minister of finance, Kataoka Naoharu, inadvertently mentioned the total value of all the non-performing loans, a sum that far exceeded the amount that anyone present could have ever fathomed.

After Suzuki Shōten's dire financial situation came to light during the Diet deliberations, lawmakers voted down the bill to issue more earthquake bills. Kataoka's misstatement, which would soon appear in the press, triggered a new crisis causing a run on some of the banks. The situation further worsened when the Bank of Taiwan refused to extend any new loans to Suzuki Shōten, a development that resulted in yet another run on an even larger number of banks, one of which was the Bank of Taiwan.

A chain reaction of bank failures swept across the nation when the Bank of Japan decided not to offer new loans to the Bank of Taiwan or smaller banks. The long-term repercussion of the banking crisis was the merging or liquidation of banks whose operations were not strong enough to withstand it. The total number of banks dropped from 1,626 in 1924 to 779 in 1930, and 466 in 1935. Consolidation ensued, giving rise to 'the big five' banks of Mitsui, Mitsubishi, Sumitomo, Yasuda, and Daiichi, which held 18.5 per cent of all deposits in Japanese banks in 1920, and 42.5 per cent in 1935 (Miwa and Hara, 2007, 113). This would be the first major banking crisis, but not the last, as shown in other chapters on the bubble and post-bubble periods.

4.4 The formation of a labour movement in the context of industrial capitalism

In this chapter, the term 'factory' can be broadly defined as manufacturing facility employing five or more workers (Taira, 1970, 85). Over this period, the number and size of factories grew as did the labour force. Three major types of enterprise emerged at the end of Meiji period: *zaibatsu*, large joint-stock companies, and small firms, which continued to pursue their own course of development in the 1930s. In the context of a shift from light to heavy industries and growing competition in the domestic market, a duality could be witnessed, which was characterized by large-scale enterprises equipped with modern factories and a myriad of small-scale workshops.

While the factories of some of *zaibatsu* as well as those of the large joint-stock companies employed—at least by the standards of those times—large numbers of workers, most of the establishments had a workforce of fewer than a hundred employees. One salient difference between the small- and medium-sized firms and the *zaibatsu*/large joint-stock companies is that workers employed by the former were generally less efficient and received lower wages. One paradoxical feature of this period was an abundant labour force but a limited supply of factory workers (Taira, 1970, 85). The formation of a labour movement began in these large factories, as opposed to small workshops, where poor working conditions also existed. This movement was reflective of this period and had a marked effect on the relationship between society and business.

This period—one of great volatility for the Japanese economy—generated tumultuous changes in society and its relationship vis-à-vis business. Various forms of worker self-expression were suppressed through laws and police enforcement during most of the Meiji period. However, after 1900 the number of riots began to rise. Two of the largest ones were the 1905 Hibiya Anti-Treaty Riot and the Rice Riots of 1918, which came in response to a doubling in the price of the nation's staple food and mounting inflation. Harsh economic conditions were in large part to blame for the frequency, size, and in some cases, long duration of the protests.

It should be noted that the question of labour—while vital to one's understanding of the development of Japanese business—is not often a central theme in business-history literature. It does, however, merit coverage in this volume devoted to the development of capitalism and entrepreneurship for three reasons. First, the seeds of labour movement in Japan can be directly traced to the features of capitalism, especially *industrial capitalism*. Workers as participants in this movement perceived the notion of capitalistic development as running counter to their system of values based on agrarian, community-centred lifestyles, and strongly resisted capitalism's 'winner take all' underpinnings (Yui and Hirschmeier, 1975). Second, the rise of a labour movement sheds light on some of the origins of economic and social inequalities as well as the precarity of employment, which is often associated with capitalism not only in Japan but elsewhere (Piketty, 2014; Ozawa and Kingston 2022). According to Gordon (2003, 121), the rise of capitalism 'increased dramatically the numbers of urban poor and wage laborers; more importantly, it heightened the uncertain, dependent quality of their existence'. Finally, the focus on a labour movement in this section should serve to further clarify and contextualize the first theme covered in this chapter: the emergence of dualities found in business and in the workplace.

One distinctive feature of the early labour movement in Japan is that the demands of workers were rather broad. In other words, they did not focus simply on achieving improvements in their working conditions and the right to organize and strike. As Garon (1987, 17 and 43) points out, workers also sought to be treated with greater dignity by receiving greater recognition for their toil: 'Japanese workers, between 1890 and 1918 rarely phrased demands in terms of natural rights. Rather, they sought first and foremost to raise their lowly position within society and the workplace.' A second feature is that workers were not well organized until World War I. Though the first major strikes occurred around 1900, change occurred slowly and was met with great resistance on the part of employers. One reason for the reluctance of employers to raise wages and improve working conditions was their fundamental failure to recognize the connection between higher wages and higher profits (Taira, 1970, 86). Consequently, workers continued to toil in exploitative conditions for menial wages.

While the labour movement faced harsh criticism from industrialists, it found sympathizers in other fields. A small contingent of bureaucrats in various ministries, many of whom had received overseas training and exposure to labour issues, sympathized with the workers' plight and strove to encourage industrialists to improve labour practices and working conditions. There were other motivations for improving the conditions of the labour force. As expressed in the slogan, 'rich country, strong army' (*fukoku kyōhei*), some government officials supported the idea of improving factory conditions as the means to achieving imperialistic ends, an aspiration that could not be attained without a strong and healthy military force (Taira, 1970, 87). Thus, concessions to workers often came in a context of the growing need to keep them properly nourished and physically fit for battle. In this way, public health, worker productivity, and labour relations were all intertwined (Shimizu, 2021).

Resistance to change on the part of industrialists would grow to become an increasingly organized endeavour. By 1880, Japan's *zaibatsu* along with some large, non-*zaibatsu* firms formed the nation's strongest employers' association, the Japan Industrial Club (*Nihon Kōgyō Kurabu*), which served as a strong lobby against labour reform. They built a united front in opposition to introducing any laws that would interfere with their labour practices and refused to recognize unions. Industrialists also managed to thwart attempts to enact reforms by entering politics. Some heads of enterprise successfully ran for political office, while others made donations to political parties as seen in the example of Takuma Dan, the director-general of the Mitsui *zaibatsu*, who made regular donations to the *Seiyūkai* Party. Industrialists were thus on the defensive. When confronted with criticism—from both inside and outside Japan—for not upholding their moral obligation to protect workers, they would often respond with the counter-argument that such reforms were unnecessary in Japan due to their companies' long tradition of what Yui and Hirschmeier refer to as 'familism' (*daikazokushugi*) or what Taira calls the 'Japanese mystique' (Yui and Hirschmeier, 1975; Garon, 1987; Taira, 1970, 30).

Business, especially big business, was successful in staving off the introduction of any major legislation until the landmark decision in 1911 to enact the first Factory Law. This law provided minimum standards for protecting workers' health and safety. Some of the clauses of the new law included employer liability for injuries occurring at the workplace, limitations on the minimum age of recruitment to those over 12 years of age, and a ban on night work and workdays in excess of 12 hours for women and youths under 15 years of age. Despite these concessions, however, labour disputes persisted with growing intensity. From 1917 to 1919, strikes grew larger, longer, and more violent. Moreover, the number of unions quadrupled from 108 to 432 between 1918 and 1923 (Garon, 1987, 42).

With little control over the fluctuations in the economy during the boom-and-bust periods, business leaders grew increasingly powerless in their efforts to circumvent the widespread strikes, increasing rates of worker turnover, and labour shortages. Turnover was especially prevalent around 1900 in the heavy industries among skilled (shipyard) workers. It was not, however, limited to heavy industries; labour shortages could also be seen among low-skilled workers, particular in the textile sector. To remedy the problem, from the late 1880s through the early 1900s companies sent out recruiters to farm villages to search of a new pool of potential workers, the majority of whom were female (Garon, 1987, 14).

Measures to prevent turnover and labour shortages were put in place by what some might consider to be some of Japan's first social entrepreneurs. One well-known example is Kanebō (Kanegafuchi). In 1900, its president, Mutō Sanji (1867–1934) strove to improve the working conditions at the company's Hyōgo factory by introducing a mutual aid association, a factory nursery to care for children, a pension system, and so on. Despite these rare endeavours, however, Mutō was unable to improve the high turnover rate among his female workers in any significant way in the long term.

It is not surprising that the turnover rate was highest in industries with the harshest as well as most hazardous and unsanitary working conditions. In the mining sector, when renegotiating their contracts was unfeasible, workers—many of whom were women—would simply run away during the night (Garon, 1987, 13 and 15). Women, often the most vulnerable and most frequently subject to exploitation, were, however, an essential source of factory labour. From 1909 to 1930 over half of the workers in the textile sector were female. As members of the labour force, their contribution was vital to the development of the nation's first major export sector, textiles.

4.5 Characteristics of the early Japanese labour movement

As mentioned in the Introduction to this volume, during Japan's high-growth period (1951–1973), scholarly and popular works alike that connected Japanese-style management—particularly its harmonious employer–employee relationship—to business success began to appear in large numbers. These publications attracted an attentive audience of managers and students of business from around the world. What few may realize, however, is that the buds of Japan's management practices can be traced to this rather disharmonious period of frequent conflicts between industrialists and the labour force.

Examples of some of the first practices introduced were bonuses based on seniority and payments for good conduct by workers employed at shipyards and in steel manufacturing during World War I. This reward system was designed to discourage workers, particularly skilled, white-collar workers, from leaving their jobs, while also incentivizing them to engage in a more peaceful rapport with authority. Protection for blue-collar workers would not be put in place until the postwar period (Sugayama, 1992). Social welfare programmes similar to the ones introduced at Kanebō could also be found at some other companies during the 1917–1921 period (Garon, 1987, 44).

Two influences on the features of Japan's labour movement merit mention in this section. The first is the influence of international relations on its initial emergence. At the close of World War I, a delegation from Japan—the only non-Western nation to be represented—attended the Paris Peace Conference. What is significant about Japan's participation is that by signing the Treaty of Versailles in June of 1919, the Japanese government had also committed itself to allowing the organization of labour unions. Moreover, by recognizing workers' right to strike, industrialists could no longer consider their labour force as simply a commodity or 'unit of production', an important distinction that Japanese workers had long hoped to achieve. The treaty's signatories also pledged to create the International Labour Organization (ILO), whose first meeting took place in Washington DC in October of 1919. Japanese labour leaders were hopeful that Japan's participation in the first meeting of the ILO would bring noticeable improvements to labour relations. However, their hopes were dashed as the representatives of business present at the gathering, one being Kanegafuchi's Mutō, mentioned above, rejected demands to introduce reforms, asserting that Western-style standards were unnecessary and unsuitable for Japan's labour practices given the long tradition of familism, which according to the Japanese delegation, adequately ensured workers' welfare and protection (Yui and Hirschmeier, 1975).

The second feature of Japan's labour movement is the prominence of Christians—then and today a minority religion comprising approximately 1 per cent of the population—in its leadership, particularly at the time of its inception. One of the most prominent Christians to take part in the labour movement was Suzuki Bunji, the founder of *Yūaikai* or the Friendly Society. The *Yūaikai* was founded in 1912 and became the predecessor organization of the labour union, *Sōdōmei* (Nihon Rōdō Sōdōmei). The *Yūaikai* under Suzuki strove to find harmonious and cooperative solutions to resolve conflicts between workers and industrialists (Garon, 1987, 33). As Suzuki's approach was moderate, he was well respected among business leaders. According to George Large (1970), he was able 'to bridge the two worlds of business and labour' through mediation. This approach also allowed him to gain the trust of such imminent industrialists as Shibusawa Eiichi, who became his personal friend. Suzuki's measured stance would, however, draw criticism from more radical factions within his organization. He also began to question his own approach after making a visit to the United States, where he met with members of the AF of L (American Federation of Labor) in California (Large, 1970, 566).

Christians could also be found in important positions in the central bureaucracy and even among prominent politicians including Hara Takashi. These Christians, some of whom had decided to convert during their studies at Western institutions, took up the workers' cause and introduced legislation to protect their safety in the workplace and ensure such fundamental labour rights as being allowed to form unions and organize peaceful protests. The development of an international labour movement and the influence of these bureaucrats would also help to shape the course of business development in Japan as well as the early foundations of 'Japanese-style management', which is part of the Japanese Business System.

4.6 Social change: the rise of women in the workforce

The role of women in the workforce and in society as consumers would evolve over this period. It was not uncommon for women from the countryside to be recruited as factory workers before entering marriage. Though essential to Japan's industrial and economic development, they were however under-represented in unions, and made up less than 10 per cent of the unionized workforce even in the 1930s when it reached its pre-war peak. Women were frequently obliged to work under harsh and hazardous conditions for wages that were in most cases inferior to their male counterparts (Garon, 1987 16–7). Despite women's undervaluation as members of the workforce, their contribution to the growth of Japanese business is, however, indisputable: during World War I, they accounted for approximately half of the total labour force. As shown in Table 4.4, in some sectors women made up the majority of the workforce: the ratio of women working in the textile industry (silk-reeling, cotton-spinning, and weaving) in 1909 was 86.2 per cent and in the mining sector (ore and coal) it was 21.6 per cent (Sakamoto, 1977, 102).

Table 4.4 Comparison of the number of male and female workers (%) in the textile and mining industries in 1909

Industry	Males	Males (%)	Females	Females (%)	Total
Silk-reeling	9,611	5.2	174,786	94.8	184,397
Cotton-spinning	21,347	20.5	81,639	79.3	102,986
Weaving	17,648	13.8	109,793	86.2	127,441
Ore mining	61,657	83.2	12,448	16.8	74,105
Coal mining	184,766	78.4	51,943	25.3	62,515

Source: Sakamoto (1977), 32

During this period, little progress was made for women to improve the conditions of the environment in which they worked. Moreover, until the passage of the Factory Law, little attention was paid to the public health of the female labour force. The treatment of female and child workers was addressed in the Factory Act of 1911 followed by an amendment in 1923, which was put into force in 1928. These measures sought to protect women and children through the introduction of working hours, rest periods, minimum working age limits, etc. Such changes came against the backdrop of gatherings of the ILO where participants from around the world were also demanding better working conditions, including those for their female workforce.

Nonetheless, the working conditions in Japan's textile mills remained extremely poor, leading to the spread of contagious diseases, the most common being tuberculosis, and the high ratio of female workers in this sector left them especially vulnerable. Those workers with the longest shifts and most irregular hours were also the most susceptible to contracting infectious diseases. During the peak season, women workers had long hours, in some cases, 18-hour shifts (Hunter, 1993, 85–89). Like their male counterparts, women were also vulnerable to economic fluctuations: in the mines of Kyushu, the size of the workforce for both women and children grew rapidly during the boom years from 1909 to 1919, but dropped precipitously during the recession that followed World War I (Malony, 1991, 104).

As shown in Box 4.1, women not only occupied a significant place on factory floors and in mines. As new members of the consumer society of the period, they would also become the targets of novel forms of marketing. Some examples of their purchases were fashion items and cosmetics, which were sold in shops and department stores located in the urban centres of Tokyo followed by Osaka and other large cities. The young women who were the most interested in the latest Western fashions, media, and lifestyles—the so-called *moga* or 'modern girls' became Japanese urban society's new trendsetters, particularly during the interwar boom years described in this chapter.

Box 4.1 Shiseido: The early development of marketing and the rise of the female consumer

Though one generally associates Shiseidō exclusively with beauty products, it was co-founded by pharmacist-entrepreneur, Fukuhara Arinobu (1848–1924) as Japan's first Western-style pharmacy. Shiseidō opened in 1872 in Ginza, an area of Tokyo that remains one of the Japan's premier centres for shopping, art, and entertainment. After the launch of Shiseidō's first cosmetic, *Eudermine*, came other beauty products such as tinted facial powders in 1906 and a hair oil product called *Hanatsubaki* in 1907. It was not until 1907, however, when Shiseidō became a joint-stock company with the founder's third son Shinzō (1883–1948) as its president that the firm would shift from pharmaceuticals as the main product line to cosmetics, a pivot that was fully realized by 1915. During his tenure Shinzō endeavoured to find novel and artistic ways to cultivate Shiseido's image as a beauty company while educating customers about its products through advertising and marketing campaigns targeting female customers.

From medicines to beauty products

Like his father, Shinzō received training in Western pharmacy, becoming a certified pharmacist in 1907. In 1908, he left Japan to study pharmacy at Columbia University in New York. In 1910, after completing his degree, Shinzō decided to gain some practical experience by working for two years in the factory of a pharmaceutical company located in a New York suburb. In appreciation for his hard work, the owner allowed Shinzō to use some of his cosmetic formulas in Japan. Before returning home, however, Shinzō spent nearly two years visiting the major capitals of Western Europe. He was taken by the impressionist paintings he viewed in Paris, particularly the works of Monet and Renoir as well as by those of the Japanese painters residing in Paris at the time.

The company's shift from pharmaceuticals to cosmetics was accompanied by the decision to physically separate the cosmetics from the pharmacy/pharmaceuticals section of the business. To reflect this product and organizational modification, a second, modern-style building was erected in 1916 in the Ginza district to house the cosmetics section. It was in a laboratory located in this new building where beauty product development got underway. In 1924, a factory located in the same area began manufacturing a large array of novel products including cold cream, perfumes, and face powders.

Expanding Shiseido's appeal through advertising

In 1917, Shinzō established a new section, the Advertising Creation Department (*ishōbu*), which employed more than twenty artists. By doing so, the company's mission would be to create new cosmetics for its customers as well as foster a 'beauty culture' (Shiseidō Public Relations Department, 23; Guerra, 2016). One way this was accomplished was to invite fashionable Westerners to Japan to instruct Japanese women on skin and hair care. One example is the visit of the American hairdresser, Helen Grossman, who advised the company on its decision to establish hair salons equipped with the latest American hair-styling devices. In the 1920s, writers were

(continued)

Box 4.1 Continued

hired to pen articles for Shiseidō's new publications, which included a magazine and pamphlets. *Shiseidō Geppō* (Shiseidō Monthly), founded in 1924, contained articles on lifestyle and culture with a variety of themes ranging from recent fashions to how to brew coffee. Other pamphlets appeared with practical information on Shiseidō products. Examples include instructions on how to apply powder and facial cream as well as use other beauty care products including soap (Guerra, 2016, 22–28).

Shiseidō's publications were distributed to customers through its nationwide chain stores, whose owners sold Shiseidō products exclusively. In addition to this network of small-scale stores were large-scale department stores, where trained female staff provided beauty advice and sold products directly to shoppers for the first time in much the same way as in today's department stores. New forms of print advertisements promoted Shiseidō's domestic as well as its regional expansion into Asian markets, which got underway from an early date in 1938.

Japan's 'roaring twenties' and the emergence of the moga

Shiseido targeted a broad customer base by means of marketing to the 'New Japanese Woman', an image that blended traditional and Western looks (Guerra, 2016, 28). Within this broad category of the female population was a new trendy voice in Japanese society, known as the 'modern girl', often abbreviated in Japanese simply as *moga*. According to *Shiseidō Geppō*, the 'modern girl' could be defined as 'a young woman with a modern air who dresses in a Western manner rather than a Japanese manner, and is characterized by intelligence, marked individuality, and freedom from old stereotypes … [She] generally likes new things and is strongly affected by the U.S and motion pictures' (Shiseidō Public Relations Department, 2003).

The *moga* became symbols of a brief period of Japanese history during which the freedom of self-expression was tolerated, one that some have referred to as the *Taishō democracy*. After the 1923 earthquake, literary self-expression flourished with new works, some of which were penned by women. The changes in the fashions and lifestyles of women, encouraged through the development of marketing, were key factors in the expansion of the beauty business in Japan and the gradual transformation the role of women as an integral part of a new and thriving consumer society of this period and beyond.

4.7 Conclusions

The period extending from the 1890s to the 1930s was punctuated by fluctuations in the economy caused by internal and external shocks. It was also one that was characterized not only by the rise of industrial capitalism but also by the development of some distinctive features of Japanese business, namely the buds of Japanese-style management among workers, mainly at large firms. The emergence of a labour movement and worker shortages ushered in a fundamental shift in the old feudal-style relationship which had tied labourers to their employer. Dualities became increasingly manifest and could be clearly witnessed through the types of enterprise in operation during this period, ranging from the large-scale factories of the *zaibatsu* conglomerates to the traditional craft-producing workshops. As industrial capitalism advanced, a consumer culture also flourished, particularly in urban areas, bringing about a massive transformation in the Japanese lifestyle. Women as producers as well as consumers of all types of commodities, especially Western ones, stood at the forefront, bringing changes to the home, the factory shopfloor, and even the shelves of department stores.

5
The Role of Foreign Companies (1895–1930)

The advent of industrial capitalism explored in the previous chapter was, however, not a purely domestically inspired phenomenon. Foreign companies started to invest in Japan and played a major role in its economic and social transformation. The first foreign companies to establish operations in Japan's open ports of Yokohama and Kobe at the end of *shogunate* in the late 1850s and 1860s were mostly individual merchants and representatives of large companies specializing in trade between Europe and Asia or in regional trade within Asia. The largest one was the British multinational Jardine, Matheson & Co., founded in 1832. It came to Japan as early as 1859. Foreign companies did not carry out any manufacturing activity in Japan in early Meiji period, but some of them had a few investments in mining. The largest foreign direct investment (FDI) was the company co-founded in 1868 by the Scottish merchant Thomas Glover (1838–1911) and Saga Domain to exploit Takashima's coal mines. It was however taken over by the Meiji government in the early 1870s, and sold to Mitsubishi in 1881 (McMaster, 1963).

While evidence of international business activities could be found, Japan was relatively closed to foreign investors. To preserve the nation's sovereignty, maintaining control over industrialization and economic development was a high priority among Japanese bureaucrats. Thus, inward FDI was officially forbidden in 1881. As shown in previous chapters, the birth of industries based on import substitution was largely the outcome of the transfer of foreign technology, but this process relied on the actions of the government and private local entrepreneurs. Reliance on this model of development, however, started to yield bottlenecks in the 1890s, within the context of the second industrial revolution. While the first industrial revolution was linked to simple technologies (coal mining, steam machines, textile machinery) that were easy to copy by reverse engineering, the second relied on a new generation of technologies (oil, chemicals, electrical appliances, electric power, automobiles), which were much more complex and controlled internationally by multinational enterprises (MNEs). The pursuit of economic

Japanese Capitalism and Entrepreneurship. Pierre-Yves Donzé and Julia S. Yongue, Oxford University Press.
© Pierre-Yves Donzé and Julia S. Yongue (2024). DOI: 10.1093/oso/9780192887474.003.0006

development required the introduction of such technologies but in order to obtain them, Japan had to accept the presence of foreign companies on its territory.

The adoption of certain global institutions was necessary to attract foreign MNEs, and to provide them with a stable business environment. The yen was linked to the gold standard in 1897, and a new commercial law liberalizing the activities of companies with foreign capital was put into force in 1899. Finally, in 1900, Japan joined the Paris Convention for the Protection of Industrial Property, which allowed foreigners to apply for patents in Japan. At the same time, as Japan gradually recovered its customs autonomy after the first Sino-Japanese War (1895), the introduction of protectionist policies (the average import duty rose from 3.7 per cent in 1898 to 19.8 per cent in 1913 and 23.8 per cent in 1933) were important incentives for foreign companies to move production to Japan (Yamazawa and Yamamoto, 1979). However, some specific laws forbade the activities of foreigners in certain sectors including maritime transportation (1899), mining (1905), and gunpowder manufacturing (1910). There were also some restrictions placed on foreign entry into the insurance (1900), dyes manufacturing (1925) and banking (1927) industries (Mason, 1992, 25).

Table 5.1 provides details regarding the eighty-eight enterprises doing business in Japan in 1931 that had received foreign capital. Three main characteristics can be highlighted. First, about one-third of these companies did not engage in manufacturing. They were sales subsidiaries that invested in Japan to supervise the marketing and distribution of their goods. The overwhelming majority was engaged in machinery and electrical machinery, and the purpose for their entering the Japanese market was to increase the number of contracts and provide maintenance services for their equipment. Second, most of these companies came from three countries: the United States (40.9 per cent), the United Kingdom (23.9 per cent), and Germany

Table 5.1 Number of companies with foreign capital in Japan, 1931

Foreign capital (share)	Sales subsidiaries 100	Manufacturing and service companies 100	>50	≤50	Total
USA	15	6	6	9	36
UK	5	5	2	9	21
Germany	5	2	2	8	17
Others	4	–	–	10	14
Total	29	13	10	36	88

Source: Udagawa (1987)

(19.3 per cent). MNEs from these three countries dominated FDI throughout the world during the first global economy, and their strong presence in Japan was hence not an exception. Third, Japanese investors controlled about 40 per cent of these companies (including the management of a few companies with a 50/50 ratio of foreign to Japanese capital). The companies were mostly *zaibatsu* whose motivations were to found joint ventures with foreign partners to internalize specific knowledge and to develop their production capabilities in high-tech industries. During the first half of Meiji era, *zaibatsu* were more focused on international trade and finance than manufacturing (Fujita, 1990).

Sumitomo is a case in point. This *zaibatsu*, specializing in mining and finance during the Edo period invested first at the end of the nineteenth century in fields related to mining (refining, machinery, trade of lime), leading to the vertical integration of its businesses (Yamazaki, 2004, 63). Then, after 1900, the group moved to new industrial sectors and became a major actor in the second industrial revolution in Japan. To achieve this position, however, it needed to cooperate with foreign firms to obtain access to technology and know-how. Consequently, Sumitomo invested in several joint ventures; examples include the American glassmaker Libbey-Owens (1918), the French industrial gas producer Air Liquide (1930), and the Canadian firm Aluminum Ltd. (1931). Moreover, in the field of electrical appliances, Sumitomo purchased shares of Victor Talking Machine in 1929 and took a majority share in Nippon Denki (NEC) in 1932. All these investments in joint ventures contributed to making Sumitomo an industrial giant before World War II. The situation is similar for Mitsubishi and other *zaibatsu*.

According to the data of the Ministry of Finance, the stock value of inward FDI in Japan amounted to about 50 million dollars in 1913 and 122.5 million in 1929 (Mason, 1992, 46). In 1938, it had declined to about 100 million dollars. At that time, the stock of accumulated investment in Japan represented only 0.4 per cent of world FDI. Despite Japan's opening to foreign companies in the late 1890s, their presence was quantitively very low (Fitzgerald, 2015, 163). In 1941, before the outbreak of war between Japan and the Allied forces, the stock of FDI was estimated at 326 million yen (about 145 million dollars), of which more than half was held by the top ten largest companies (Udagawa, 1987, 17). These numbers are also relatively low from a domestic perspective. None of the foreign firms operating in Japan entered the ranking of the top 100 largest industrial firms in Japan in 1940 (Yamazaki, 2004, 410–411). Their importance is hence not related to their size, but rather to their contribution to the technological development of various industries, as the examples in the following sections show.

5.1 The electrical appliances industry

The electrical appliance industry is undoubtedly one of the most representative examples of the new businesses that emerged in the wake of the second industrial revolution. Electric power gave birth to a broad range of products, from electric lights and communication devices (telegraph and telephone) to electric engines. This new industry was soon dominated by a handful of large MNEs, essentially from the United States and Germany. Their characteristics were large capitalization, intensive research and development activities, and a patent strategy that enabled them to protect their innovations around the world (Chandler, 1990). Having access to such new technology and products was crucial for Japan's development, but to do so it needed to accept foreign direct investment.

The first joint venture founded in Japan was Nippon Electric Co. (NEC) (NEC, 2001). Its creation is related to the development of communications technology, which was necessary to connect the country with foreign countries. During the 1880s, Japanese engineers worked to acquire technology related to the telephone, through study trips to the United States and reverse engineering. The results were, however, insufficient for the founding of an industry, and the Japanese authorities decided to approach the American company Western Electric, which had produced and distributed the telephone developed by Alexander Graham Bell since 1881. They proposed to invest in a new company that would benefit from a monopoly in the telecommunication market in Japan. Hence, in 1899 NEC was founded with 54 per cent of Western Electric capital, while a minority stake was owned by two private entrepreneurs, among whom was Iwadare Kunihiko (1857–1941), a Japanese engineer who had lived in the United States and worked for Thomas Edison. The company experienced fast and impressive growth thanks to the extension of the domestic communication network (3,000 persons with a telephone connection in 1895 and 129,000 in 1910) and imperial expansion (Yanotsuneta Kinenkai, 2006, 490). It opened branches in Seoul (1908) and Lüshun (1909). Western Electric also transferred its Japanese knowledge and expertise regarding the development, manufacturing, and marketing of electrical appliances. This transfer was reinforced by sending Japanese engineers to its factories in the United States to learn about foreign technology. The development of NEC also required an increase of capital, and this led to the opportunity for the Sumitomo *zaibatsu* to become a minority shareholder in 1919. Specialized in the manufacturing of metal products, Sumitomo cooperated with NEC to develop cables. The collaboration between Sumitomo and Western Electric (renamed International Standard Electric in 1925) led to the creation of a second joint venture in 1932, Sumitomo Electric. During the 1930s, Sumitomo gradually increased its share of NEC capital and took full control in 1932 (see Chapter 7).

Following the example of Western Electric, all the major multinationals in the electrical appliance and electricity sectors invested in Japan after 1900. General Electric (GE) took a majority stake (55 per cent) in the electric light bulb producer Tokyo Electric (1905) and a minority stake (25 per cent) in the manufacturer of communications and heavy electrical equipment, Shibaura. Both companies were merged to form Toshiba in 1939. The German conglomerate Siemens, which had opened a branch in Tokyo in 1905, took a minority stake (10 per cent) in the medical equipment distribution company Goto Fuundo (1919) and 30 per cent in the joint venture Fuji Electric, co-founded with the *zaibatsu* Furukawa (1923). As for Westinghouse, the rival of GE in the United States, it had a 10 per cent share in the joint-venture Mitsubishi Electric organized with the shipbuilding company of Mitsubishi *zaibatsu* in 1923. Finally, the two companies that dominated the world market in the record and phonographic industry entered Japan in 1927. The American firm Victor Talking Machine opened a fully owned subsidiary, in which Toshiba and Mitsui invested two years later. Victor Company of Japan (JVC) was taken over after World War II by Matsushita Electric (today, Panasonic). As for the British firm Columbia, it took a majority share (59 per cent) in a local firm founded in 1910, which distributed music in Japan. It was renamed Nippon Columbia. All these ventures between Japanese and foreign multinationals started from a similar assessment: the Japanese were unable to produce electrical goods whose cost and quality could make them competitive against foreign goods. This was not only the case for the record and phonographic industry but also for light consumer goods (electric light bulbs) and for heavy equipment (turbines).

The impact of the investment of GE in the manufacturing of electric light bulbs is an excellent example of the impact foreign firms had on the development of the national industries (see Table 5.2). As shown in Chapter 2, domestic production, based on the imitation of foreign products, started at the end of the nineteenth century. It was dominated by a small company founded in 1890, which became Tokyo Electric. However, although this company developed, its gross sales were consistently lower than its import of foreign goods. In 1903 and 1904, foreign companies exported bulbs for a value that exceeded twice that of Tokyo Electric's production. The purchase of shares by GE changed the fate of this company. It started growing very fast and, in 1908, its sales of bulbs were almost three times larger than imports. This was of course the result of the decline of exports from the United States

Table 5.2 Market for electric light bulbs in Japan, values in yen, 1898–1908

Year	Tokyo Electric	Imports (total)	Imports (United States)	Imports (Germany)
1898	24,801	38,533	12,358	21,371
1899	38,466	67,712	19,789	24,002
1900	37,954	80,706	29,540	36,359
1901	31,205	95,584	25,081	56,231
1902	53,885	72,673	23,937	37,248
1903	40,996	122,649	40,841	68,580
1904	69,410	148,777	69,661	52,326
1905	87,038	146,888	93,027	34,455
1906	195,998	237,518	97,262	96,921
1907	268,533	126,790	34,303	49,522
1908	336,924	122,675	14,412	71,425

Source: Kikuchi (2007), p. 38

after 1906. However, as GE had begun producing in Japan, this was not the only reason. The American multinational introduced knowledge related to patent management to Japan, which included the practice of suing local companies that infringed GE patents (Nishimura, 2004). During the 1910s, Tokyo Electric took legal action against all the small domestic bulb producers, whose patents were cancelled by the Japanese courts, meaning that that they had no choice but to sign agreements with Tokyo Electric. This led to a concentration of bulb production in Japan under the control of Tokyo Electric. To dominate the market, this company also had to compete against its foreign rivals, especially those from Germany, whose exports to Japan continued to grow. After a long negotiation, Allgemeine Elektrizität Gesellschafft (AEG) signed an agreement with Tokyo Electric in 1914.

Technology transfer was the most important consequence of the presence of foreign companies. Working together with American, British, and German engineers and managers, the Japanese could learn about product development, manufacturing technology, protection of intellectual property, and marketing. Gradually, electrical appliance companies with foreign capital shifted from importing to producing electrical appliances in Japan, after which they adapted them to the local market and developed their own goods. Domestic production overtook imports for an increasing number of electrical goods, from fans (1914) and batteries (1915) to radios (1925) and turbines (1929) (Shimano, 1980). The increase in the number of patent applications also shows the localization of research in the early twentieth century. The total number for electric appliances went from twenty-three in 1900 (of which 82.6 per cent were applied for by foreigners) to 123 in 1910 (57.7 per cent). The composition of gross sales by the origin of products of Fuji Electric is another example of this gradual technology transfer. Figure 5.1 shows indeed that two years after the foundation of the joint venture, in 1925, it still relied mostly on imports of German products (6.4 per cent of sales). Domestic production developed smoothly and exceeded the 50 per cent mark during second half of 1929. It remained at over 90 per cent after 1933.

Finally, one should not forget that the Japanese electrical equipment industry was not created by foreign-owned companies alone (see Box 5.1). Companies like Hitachi (founded in 1908), Matsushita Electric (1918), and most railways, developed in this business without any foreign capital. They benefited however from an indirect and 'invisible' technology transfer (Uchida, 1991, 238). Human capital was a key resource for internalizing technological capabilities. Consequently, numerous Japanese engineers, employed by foreign-owned companies and trained in the United States, moved to so-called independent firms, and took charge of their development. In a similar way the Faculty of Engineering at Tokyo Imperial University employed Japanese engineers from foreign-owned firms like Shibaura. They taught new generations the knowledge they had acquired, and consequently played a major role in the process of indirectly transferring foreign technology. Licensing agreements and contracts for technological cooperation were also a means for transferring technology that did not rely on foreign capital. Hitachi for example signed contracts with AEG (1932) and the British company Yarrow (1935) (Uchida, 1991).

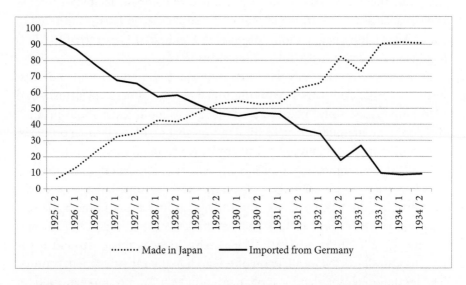

Figure 5.1 Percentages of gross sales by the origin of products at Fuji Electric, 1925–1934

Source: Udagawa (1987), p. 25

Box 5.1 Shimadzu, the Japanese company that challenged Siemens in the X-ray device market

The fact that foreign companies possessed a strong technological competitive advantage did not mean that local firms were unable to find ways to develop and eventually challenge the dominant position of multinationals in the Japanese market. The scientific instruments maker Shimadzu Co. is an excellent example of a domestic family firm which was able to take the lead in the market of X-ray devices during the 1920s (Donzé, 2018).

X-rays were discovered in 1895 by the German physicist Wilhelm Roentgen. The opportunities offered by this new technology to advance medical diagnostics attracted numerous companies around the world, which started manufacturing and improving X-ray devices. The world's largest producer was the German company Siemens. It had exported radiological equipment to Japan since the late 1890s and dominated the market. Yet, a major innovation allowed its competitor General Electric (GE) to enter this market. In 1913, GE developed the Coolidge tube, a technology that made the dosage of rays more precise and was consequently able to produce clearer X-ray images. GE focused on the mass production of tubes and supplied them to X-ray device assemblers. In Japan, tubes were produced by Tokyo Electric from 1915 and sold to various local assemblers. One of them was a company based in Kyoto, Shimadzu Co.

Founded in 1875 as a manufacturer of scientific instruments, Shimadzu was one of the first companies to take an X-ray image in 1896. It had a deep interest in this new technology and developed several machines; a major breakthrough was the launch of mass-produced simple X-ray device in 1915. Two years later, Shimadzu signed a contract with Tokyo Electric to secure its supply of tubes. Production of X-ray equipment rose to about 100 units in 1924 then skyrocketed to 2,500 units in 1934. This impressive development made Shimadzu the largest manufacturer of X-ray machines in Japan, overtaking Siemens.

How was it possible that a multinational like Siemens, being the world's largest manufacturer of X-ray devices, lost the Japanese market to a local company? The key reason is that the German company had been late to move production to Japan and to adapt its goods to the specificities of the Japanese hospital system, which was based on a high concentration of small private hospitals, meaning that their budget to acquire medical equipment was smaller than large hospitals in Europe and the United States. Siemens exported its goods without adapting to Japan, and although it co-founded a joint-venture with its Japanese importer in 1933 to manufacture

(continued)

> **Box 5.1 Continued**
>
> equipment in Japan under the name Goto Fuundo Manufacturing (GFM), this company basically assembled German machines without carrying out much innovation. In the mid-1930s, sales of medical devices by Siemens in Japan were about half the value of that of Shimadzu.
>
> As for Shimadzu, it implemented an aggressive strategy of cooperation with medical doctors to develop X-ray machines suitable for their needs (smaller, simpler, and cheaper). The firm carried out joint research activities with medical doctors. It was also very active in approaching academic societies in the medical field by showing its new devices during conference breaks and organizing its own conferences. Shimadzu also founded a training centre in Kyoto in 1927 for X-ray technicians, which had already instructed more than 350 students by the beginning of Pacific War. Marketing activities and the close relationship its forged with its customers (hospitals and doctors) were the main factors that enabled Shimadzu to challenge Siemens in one sector that is highly representative of the second industrial revolution.

5.2 The oil industry

Oil was one of the most important products of the second industrial revolution. It led to the foundation of several giant MNEs in the United States and Western Europe which have dominated the world market since the late nineteenth century. Industrial exploitation of oil started in the United States in the middle of the nineteenth century and gave birth to the Standard Oil Company, founded in 1870 by John D. Rockefeller, who built a monopoly in oil refining in America and largely dominated world markets at the beginning of the twentieth century. Standard Oil expanded internationally through the export of crude oil and the localization of its refineries. Its main competitor was the Royal Dutch Shell Company, founded through the merger of two large British and Dutch companies in 1907. The global demand for oil grew fast at the turn of the twentieth century, when its main use shifted from lighting oil to strategic products for military use, like fuels and explosives (Boon, 2020).

These two companies were the first to invest in the oil industry in Japan (Udagawa, 1987, 18-20). Despite the presence of crude oil in the country, especially in the areas in present-day Akita and Niigata prefectures, production was too small to respond to the needs of the domestic market. Moreover, local firms lacked refining capabilities. As early as 1893, Rockefeller established a new sales company, New York Standard Oil Japan in Yokohama. It oversaw two branch offices, Vacuum Oil (for the lubricating oil market, opened in 1892) and Socony (for the kerosene market, opened in 1893) (Kikkawa, 1991). It was followed in 1900 by Samuel Samuel & Co., a British firm owned by two brothers, who engaged in the formation of Shell, which had traded in Yokohama since the mid-1870s. They opened Rising Sun, a company specializing in selling oil products. These two foreign firms signed various agreements with the Japanese firms, Nippon Oil and Hoden Oil, the two largest distributors of oil in Japan at that time, to share the national market. In 1910, Standard Oil and Shell consequently controlled 65 per cent of the Japanese market (Kikkawa, 1991, 42).

For Japanese bureaucrats, the major issue was, however, not the trade in oil products (import and domestic distribution) but the acquisition of the necessary know-how to refine crude oil on Japanese soil. From a technological perspective this would be needed to support the development of this new industry but also the military, as oil had become the most important fuel for warships. In 1900, Socony (Standard Oil) founded a subsidiary specializing in refining called International Oil, which was sold in 1907 to Nippon Oil. The latter was a Japanese company founded in 1888 in Niigata and was already the largest producer of crude oil in the country. The takeover of International Oil made it possible to assimilate knowledge regarding refining. Socony concentrated on selling oil products in Japan by building a strong network of oil tanks throughout the country to strengthen its domination of this market. In 1929, Japan was its largest market for kerosene outside the United States, the fourth for gasoline, and the first for lubricants. As for Rising Sun (Shell), it also opened a refinery in the 1900s but stopped operations in 1915 to refocus on the distribution of oil products. This company was particularly competitive for gasoline. Together with Nippon Oil, it owned a large share of stations in Tokyo at the end of the 1920s (Kikkawa, 1991, 44–46).

Thanks to a change in customs policies, the transfer of production to Japan took a step forward in the early 1930s. The increase in tariffs for petroleum products (gasoline and kerosene) was higher than for crude oil. This was a clear incentive designed to attract foreign firms to invest in production in Japan. The revision of tariffs in 1926 led the American company Associated Oil, which became active in the Japanese market in the 1920s but was a small player in this business, to transfer technology and production to Japan. Its partner was Mitsubishi Corporation, the trading company of Mitsubishi *zaibatsu*. In 1923, both firms signed an agreement for the distribution in Japan of American Oil's products. In 1931, Mitsubishi and Associated Oil founded a joint venture with equal capitalization (50/50), Mitsubishi Oil. The American partner provided crude oil and technology, while Mitsubishi brought its expertise in distribution. It started production at the end of the year and was recognized as an important player in the domestic oil business. In 1932, oil companies present in Japan signed a cartel agreement to share the domestic market. Rising Sun (32.2 per cent) and Socony-Vacuum (21.2 per cent) still had half of the business, but domestic companies Nippon Oil (23.9 per cent), Ogura Oil, a small domestic firm based in Akita that merged with Nippon Oil in 1941 (12.5 per cent), Mitsubishi Oil (6.8 per cent) and others (3.4 per cent) were able to negotiate the other half (Kikkawa, 1995).

5.3 Ford and General Motors in Japan

The beginning of the motor-vehicle industry in Japan resulted from two major factors: the demand by the army (especially for trucks) and the development of motorization in Japanese society, particularly during the reconstruction of Tokyo and Yokohama after the Kantō Great Earthquake of 1923 (Mason, 1992, 60–72; Odagiri and Gotō, 1996, 179–190). Despite several attempts by Japanese entrepreneurs and the army, the production of cars in Japan before World War I was negligible. In 1918, considering the strategic importance of this industry, the state adopted the Military Vehicles Subsidy Law to provide financial support to Japanese private entrepreneurs engaged in this industry. It supported the manufacture of trucks by three companies (Tokyo Gas Electric, Kaishinsha, and Ishikawajima Shipyard), but the quality of production was very low and limited to military production. As for imports of full-sized cars, this developed after World War I; however, automobile production remained a niche market. Imports never exceeded the 2,000-car mark until 1923.

The Great Kantō Earthquake had a significant impact on the development of this industry, both in a short- and a long-term perspective. First, as the train system was disrupted in the Tokyo area, there was an urgent need for cars to deliver medical supplies and food. The city of Tokyo ordered a total of 1,000 Ford trucks to be used as buses (Mason, 1992, 66). As for Yanase Automobile Company, a firm founded in 1915 as the importer and distributor of GM automobiles, it ordered 1,000 Buick cars and Chevrolet trucks (Mason, 1992,

70). Second, the reconstruction of the Kantō urban area with larger avenues to replace the traditional dense network of narrow streets, facilitated the use of automobiles. Osaka soon followed with a policy to modernize the city's infrastructure (Hanes, 2002).

These new opportunities attracted the American companies that dominated the world market at that time. As import duties for car components were 25 per cent and 35 per cent for full-sized cars, these firms decided to establish assembly plants in Japan (Shinomiya, 1998, 22). Overseas production was not a new business for them. They had already acquired knowledge regarding foreign expansion through the localization of assembly. In 1923, Ford owned car assembly plants in Argentina, Belgium, Brazil, Canada, Denmark, England, France, Italy, Spain, and Uruguay (Wilkins and Hill, 2011, 434–435). Ford was already present in the Japanese market as an importer but needed to produce domestically due to rising import tariffs and to respond to increasing demand. Hence, Ford Japan was founded as a fully owned subsidiary in Yokohama in 1925. It started production the same year to strengthen the company's position in the domestic market. In 1926, the number of Ford cars assembled in Japan was nearly four times larger than imports (see Table 5.3). This success attracted competitors. In 1927, GM also opened a fully owned subsidiary in Osaka with the support of the local government. Both companies experienced fast growth during the early years of production, peaking at more than twenty-five thousand cars assembled in Japan in 1929. Imports of full-sized cars started to decline sharply from 1928. The contract signed that year between the Japanese company Kyoritsu and the American car marker Chrysler to assemble vehicles in Japan did not, however, challenge the duopoly of Ford and GM.

Business was severely hit by the Great Depression. In 1932–1933, the production of Ford and GM was only half that of the 1929 level. It recovered in 1934 but started to face a new challenge: the development of domestic car makers supported by the government. Nissan Motor was founded in 1933 as a spin-off of Tobata Casting, a manufacturing company integrated into the Nissan Group which began merging small passenger car manufacturers in 1931. As for Toyota, it started as an automotive division of the Toyoda Automatic Loom Company, before being separated as Toyota Motor in 1937 (Odagiri and Gotō, 1996, 185–190). These two domestic companies benefited from technology and knowledge transfer from Ford and GM after the state intervened to reorganize the national car industry (see Chapter 7).

Table 5.3 Japanese car market, 1916–1935

Year	Domestic production	Imports (full cars)	Import (KD)	Ford Japan (KD)	GM Japan (KD)	Kyoritsu (KD)
1916	–	218	–	–	–	–
1917	–	860	–	–	–	–
1918	–	1,653	–	–	–	–
1919	–	1,579	–	–	–	–
1920	–	1,745	–	–	–	–
1921	–	1,074	–	–	–	–
1922	–	752	–	–	–	–
1923	–	1,938	–	–	–	–
1924	–	4,603	–	–	–	–
1925	376	1,765	3,437	3,437	–	–
1926	245	2,381	8,677	8,877	–	–
1927	302	3,895	12,668	7,033	5,635	–
1928	247	7,883	24,341	8,850	15,491	–
1929	437	5,018	29,338	10,674	15,745	1,251
1930	458	2,591	19,678	10,620	8,049	1,015
1931	436	1,887	20,199	11,505	7,478	1,210
1932	880	997	14,087	7,448	5,893	760
1933	1,681	491	15,082	8,166	5,942	998
1934	2,247	896	33,458	17,244	12,322	2,574
1935	5,094	934	30,787	14,965	12,492	3,612

Note: KD means 'knocked-down', that is, disassembled cars assembled in Japan.
Source: Udagawa (1987), 82

The successful development of Ford and GM in Japan between the mid-1920s and the mid-1930s resulted largely from the new manufacturing technology they introduced, which included assembly lines, blueprints, and machine tools. Both companies also cooperated with numerous local manufacturing companies for the production of parts. For many entrepreneurs, this was a unique opportunity to learn about foreign technology. Moreover, the two American giants, Ford and GM, introduced new management regarding retail and sales. In 1924, when the head of the Ford export department visited Japan to evaluate the conditions of an investment, he explained in his report that 'dealers as we know them do not exist. [...] We must start from the very beginning to develop a real organization' (quoted by Wilkins and Hill, 2011, 150). Consequently, Ford and GM built a dense network of dealerships and introduced new management practices to improve the incentive to increase sales (e.g. larger commissions). These marketing techniques were also adopted later on at Toyota and Nissan.

5.4 Consumer goods

FDI in Japan during the first third of the twentieth century was, however, not limited to the sectors of the second industrial revolution. Several companies engaged in consumer goods established sales subsidiaries or even manufacturing facilities in Japan.

One of the first was American Tobacco Company (ATC), the world's largest cigarette manufacturer which expanded internationally through FDI in the 1890s (Bytheway, 2014, 153–161; Shibata, 2013, 28–33). It opened a branch in Yokohama in 1892 to organize the importation of cigarettes. The rise of custom duties on tobacco in Japan in 1899 led this American giant to look for a local partner. The following year, it founded an equally owned joint venture with a leading distributor of cigarettes in Japan under the name Murai Brothers & Co. ATC brought new technology (cigarette-rolling machines) and a broad range of brands. This cooperation strengthened the dominant position of Murai Brothers on the domestic market. However, the nationalization of the tobacco industry and the introduction of a state monopoly put an end to this business in 1904.

The movie industry was an important sector that contributed to the Westernization of Japanese society in a context of urban development. A total of nine American movie producers established subsidiaries in Japan, among which were Paramount Pictures, Universal, United Artists, and Warner Brothers (Rōdōkeizai kenkyūjo, 1948, 124–125). They distributed Hollywood movies throughout Japan and supported the development of movie theatres through cooperation with local entertainment entrepreneurs. For example, Paramount Pictures cooperated in the early 1930s with the music-hall and movie producer, Shōchiku (Shōchiku, 1985). These companies were still active during the 1930s, despite the development of nationalism, but were forced to withdraw after Pearl Harbor, in 1941.

Finally, two food companies were established in Japan during the interwar years, the American producer of dry fruits, Sun Maid and the Swiss dairy products company, Nestlé (Rōdōkeizai kenkyūjo, 1948, 125). The case of Nestlé provides an excellent example to demonstrate the conditions under which a food company moved production to Japan, for goods originally not related to Japanese material culture (Donzé and Kurosawa, 2013). During this period, dairy products were novelties that were gradually assimilated into the Japanese diet following a different sequence from Western countries. In 1913, condensed milk (national production value of 565,000 yen) was the most produced item in Japan, before butter (242,000 yen) and margarine (60,000 yen), while cheese (6,200 yen) and yogurt (5,400 yen) still had low volumes.

Nestlé is a Swiss company founded in 1905 through the merger of two companies founded in 1866-67, a manufacturer of powdered milk (Farine Lactée Henri Nestlé SA) and a producer of condensed milk (Anglo-Swiss Condensed Milk Co.). They diversified into chocolate in the early twentieth century. At the time of the merger, Nestlé already had a total of eighteen production centres, of which eleven were outside Switzerland. It exported its products throughout the world. In Japan, it started its business with the export of condensed milk through trading companies in the 1890s, before opening a branch office in Yokohama (1913), which moved to its current location in Kobe in 1922. The objective was to supervise the business of dairy goods directly in Japan, although distribution and retail were realized by Mitsui Trading. The sale of condensed and powdered milk was a profitable business in Japan. The value of imports grew from 178,000 yen in 1890 to 2.4 million in 1910 and peaked at 6 million in 1923. Other than Nestlé, a few companies from the United States (Borden Co. and Carnation Milk Products Co.) and Australia (Bacchus Marsh Co.) were active in this sector. However, this growth did attract new entrants from Japan, essentially the food companies Morinaga and Meiji that invested in condensed milk in the late 1910s through the takeover of small local producers. Thanks to their entry, the self-sufficiency ratio of condensed milk went from only 3.2 per cent in 1905 to 7.2 per cent in 1910 and 52.2 per cent in 1915. For Nestlé, the market became more and more competitive, which required an immediate response. First, the Swiss multinational fought off foreign competitors. It took over Bacchus Marsh in Australia (1921) and signed an agreement with Borden to distribute its goods in Japan (1926). Carnation was hence the only remaining foreign competitor by the mid-1920s. Second, an important rise in import duties in 1924 (followed by two other increases in 1926 and 1932) made it necessary to consider moving production to Japan. Between 1926 and 1931, Nestlé tried twice to form a joint venture in Hokkaido, first with small condensed milk companies, second with an association of dairy farmers. However, it had to give up both times due to the opposition from Morinaga and Meiji. This provides a clear example of a foreign company that had no specific technology to bring to Japan. Unlike the multinationals in the core sectors of the second industrial revolution, it had difficulties establishing operations in Japan, even during the Taishō democracy era, when Japan had a more liberal stance vis-à-vis foreign investment.

As it was impossible to find a partner in Japan, Nestlé decided to establish its own production facility. In 1934, it founded a separate company, Awaji Condensed Milk (abbreviated as ARKK in Japanese) that took over the factory of a small condensed-milk producer on the verge of bankruptcy.

However, due to the development of nationalistic policies against foreign companies and considering the long-lasting opposition of Morinaga and Meiji, Nestlé adopted a particular organization that enabled it to deal with the growing political risk (see Figure 5.2). ARKK was founded by seven Japanese nationals, and was hence legally a fully owned Japanese company with no foreign ownership. Yet in reality, Nestlé directly controlled this new company. The seven Japanese were employees or advisors of Nestlé Japan. They had received loans from the headquarters through intermediary companies to create ARKK. Moreover, technical assistance was provided via a contract with API, a subsidiary of Nestlé specializing in providing such services throughout the world. This arrangement served as the way to repatriate profits to Switzerland. The head of Nestlé Japan explained in a report dated in 1943 that 'economically speaking, ARKK was therefore a Swiss company' (quoted by Donzé and Kurosawa, 2013, 1327).

Such an organization was not limited to Japan. The cloaking of nationality was a strategy used widely by MNEs such as Nestlé around the world during the interwar years (Forbes et al., 2018). Nestlé started its production of condensed milk in Japan in 1934 and remained in the country throughout the war, resuming its operations in the early 1950s.

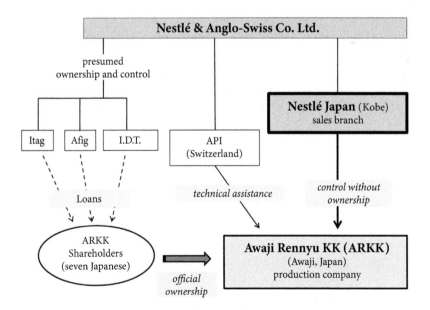

Figure 5.2 Ownership and control structure of Nestlé Japan and ARKK, 1934
Source: Adapted from Donzé and Kurosawa (2013)

5.5 Conclusions

The arrival and the development of foreign multinationals in Japan between the late 1890s and the early 1930s played a major role in the transfer of technology in sectors related to the second industrial revolution. They represented the foundations for the growth of such industries as automobiles and electrical appliances that would form the core of Japanese business during the high-growth period (1952–1973). Japan needed these firms, as they contributed to its technological and economic development.

However, despite the foundation of numerous joint ventures that led Japanese and Westerners to collaborate, in many cases foreign companies had to face a hostile environment. Local competitors, nationalism, and growing military power placed limits on the influence of foreign companies. Various pressures, such as bureaucratic red-tape, strikes, and mass demonstrations helped Japanese firms to gradually increase their capital ownership of joint ventures, allowing them to progressively takeover their control (Mason, 1992, 57–58). The outbreak of war with the United States put an end to the presence of most foreign companies, with some exceptions, namely Nestlé which was headquartered in a neutral country (see Chapter 7).

Hence, the first third of the twentieth century represents a particular period in the economic development of Japan. Opening the doors of the country to foreign capital was an opportunity for local entrepreneurs. However, only a handful of them were able to establish new businesses through international cooperation. One was an engineer, Iwadare Kunihiko, who co-founded NEC. Another was Murai Kichibei (1864–1926), the founder of Murai Brothers, who created a joint-venture with American Tobacco and another with the British textile company J. & O. Coats to produce silk in 1907. All these cases occurred during the 1890s and the 1900s, but they should be considered as exceptions. Foreign multinationals were looking for partners strong enough to make large investments in production and distribution. Consequently, *zaibatsu* were their most common choice of a partner for joint-venture investments. Mitsui, Japan's largest *zaibatsu* was an investor in Shibaura Works (later Toshiba, electric machinery), Toyo Babcock (machinery), Toyo Otis Elevator, and Nippon Construction Materials (Udagawa, 1987, 18–20). Joint ventures provided an opportunity to internalize new knowledge and to diversify into new sectors with a promising future. This strategy was not restricted to Mitsui but adopted in a similar way by other *zaibatsu*, notably Mitsubishi and Sumitomo. Consequently, FDI contributed not only to strengthening the competitive advantages of these conglomerates, but also to growing competition in the domestic market, as shown in this chapter through the case of electrical appliances. Opening the doors to foreign capital would only serve to further strengthen the position of the *zaibatsu* at the core of the Japanese economy.

6
Empire, War, and Business

The technological and industrial development of Japan between the end of *shogunate* and World War II is closely related to the rise of the military and imperialism, as expressed by the national slogan 'rich nation, strong army'. The development of most industries discussed in previous chapters, from condensed milk and apparel to oil and automobiles, was linked to the military. The need to protect the national sovereignty led not only to industrialization but also to the building of a military capable of defending and expanding the nation's sphere of influence in Asia. As Japan is a country largely lacking in natural resources, imperial expansion began in the 1890s as a mean to secure the supply of food and raw materials to fuel this industrial development (Sawai, 2016). This chapter explores the impact of imperialism and war on the development of enterprises in Japan.

6.1 Investments of Japanese firms in colonies

Imperialistic expansion is closely tied to the economic development of Japan. Soon after the Meiji Restoration, the Japanese government started an expansion policy in East Asia, marked by war and the formation of an empire. It took control of Hokkaido in 1869 by founding a Hokkaido Development Commission to supervise its administrative and economic modernization (see Chapter 2), followed by further expansion of control over the Kuril Islands in the north (1875) and the Ryūkyū Islands (Okinawa) in the south (1879). The First Sino-Japanese War led to the annexation of Taiwan (1895), while Korea was formally integrated into the Japanese Empire in 1910, after several decades of military and political interventions. Moreover, the victory in the Russo-Japanese War (1905) enabled Japan to extend its influence in Manchuria, a region rich in natural resources. The Japanese army invaded this region in 1931 and established the puppet state of Manchukuo the following year. It was colonized by Japanese, who continued to establish a military presence and enterprises until a second full-scale war with China broke out in 1937.

Among the various empires that dominated the world during the interwar years, the Japanese empire presents some specificities. Unlike the British or French empires, which spanned the world, Japan's empire had stronger cultural and religious commonalities, and was geographically concentrated. Control of its empire was hence not challenged by cultural and physical distance. Moreover, the economic dimension of the formation of the Japanese empire was much more significant than in the cases of Western empires. Colonies were important suppliers of food and raw materials for industrialization, as well as markets for manufactured goods. Japanese firms established manufacturing subsidiaries in the colonies. Hori (2008) qualified this process as 'a division of labour within the empire'. Table 6.1 clearly shows the large degree to which Taiwan and Korea were economically integrated into Japan's empire in 1937, with more than 80 per cent of their trade being with Japan. Manchuria was less strongly integrated, due to late colonization and the continuation of trade with neighbouring China. Nonetheless, half of its trade was with mainland Japan. Western empires were less economically integrated with their colonies, the sole exception being the Philippines, whose agricultural production relied on the American market. Indochina had the same level as Manchuria, while the Dutch and English colonies in Asia were loosely connected to their mainland. Even India relied on the United Kingdom for less than 40 per cent of its exports.

Colonies served a dual function in the Japanese economic system: suppliers of food and purchasers of manufactured goods. Japanese foreign trade statistics in 1935 clearly express these roles (Yamamoto, 2003, 248–249). First, colonies represented 31 per cent of all imports to mainland Japan that year. Agricultural products (60.6 per cent) exceeded industrial raw materials (25.9 per cent). Colonies were not suppliers of manufactured goods, which

Table 6.1 Dependency of the trade between the colonies and their mainland, 1937

Colony	Mainland	Imports (%)	Exports (%)
India	United Kingdom	39.0	33.2
Malaya	United Kingdom	15.1	8.8
East India	Netherlands	16.7	23.6
Indochina	France	53.4	55.2
Philippines	United States	60.8	80.4
Taiwan	Japan	83.3	92.5
Korea	Japan	85.0	87.4
Manchuria	Japan	52.8	47.7

Source: Hori (2008)

were imported from Western countries. Instead, they had a near monopoly as suppliers of food: 81.7 per cent of agricultural products imported to Japan came from the colonies. The share was far lower for industrial raw materials (14.6 per cent). This meant that the colonies had one dominant function: feeding Japan. Second, colonies absorbed 36.4 per cent of Japan's exports, essentially manufactured goods (82.4 per cent of all exports were to the colonies). However, Japanese high-quality manufactured goods with a high degree of international competitiveness, namely textiles, were exported to countries outside of the colonies (81 per cent). The colonies were an important market for heavy industrial goods (63 per cent) and various other manufactured goods (44 per cent) thus absorbing Japanese products that were not yet competitive on world markets.

The colonial trade and the economic integration of colonies were largely based on the investments by private companies supported by the colonial administration. This shows that the government trusted enterprises to implement national policies. This support by the state reduced the risks related to investing overseas (Peattie, 1989, 252). Some historians qualified these private companies as being the result of 'bureaucratic entrepreneurship' (Han-Yu and Myers, 1963), as private entrepreneurs were in charge of developing the colonies following the economic policies that were formulated in Tokyo. Direct investments in the colonies grew particularly fast during the interwar period climbing from 4.2 billion yen in 1926 to 8.0 billion in 1936 (see Table 6.2). The table also shows that Taiwan had the lowest share. Investments in Taiwan focused mainly on agriculture and light industries, while Korea, Manchuria, and China attracted investments in heavy industries. Many industrial *zaibatsu* were formed in these areas (see below, pp. 109–110).

After Taiwan was integrated into the Japanese empire, the colonial authorities oversaw its development by focusing on productivity improvements in

Table 6.2 Direct investments from Japan to its colonies, 1926–1936

| | 1926 | | 1930 | | 1936 | |
	Million ¥	%	Million ¥	%	Million ¥	%
Korea	1,127	26.7	1,507	27.9	2,409	30.0
Taiwan	519	12.3	685	12.7	707	8.8
Manchuria	1,402	33.3	1,757	32.6	2,919	36.4
China	1,166	27.7	1,446	26.8	1,994	24.8
Total	4,214	100.0	5,395	100.0	8,029	100.0

Source: Yamamoto (2003), 261

agriculture to increase crop yields in order to provide a higher volume of food to the mainland. They concentrated on the establishment of a sugar industry, a choice based on Taiwan's favourable climate and geographical conditions (Han-Yu and Myers, 1963). In order to attract investors from Japan, the governor general of Taiwan offered attractive incentives, such as a guarantee of a 6 per cent dividend for the first six years of operation, cheap land, and protection of factories by soldiers. Hence, a group of private entrepreneurs and politicians, supported by capital from Mitsui *zaibatsu*, founded Taiwan Sugar Manufacturing Co. in 1900. It started operations in 1901 and became the major exporter of sugar to Japan. In 1905, Mitsui had a share of 50 per cent of all sugar imported to Japan (Uemura, 1999, 11). This successful development, based on the application of modern production technology, attracted new investors. In 1906, Dai-Nippon Sugar Co. was founded in Japan through the merger of two firms (one founded by Suzuki Tosaburō, an investor in Taiwan Sugar Manufacturing, and another founded by Shibusawa Eiichi), which opened a subsidiary in Taiwan. The same year, Meiji Seika was formed. It produced sugar in Taiwan and engaged in the manufacturing of confectioneries in Japan, becoming one of the roots of Meiji Holdings, established in 2009. Under the Japanese colonial regime, Taiwan also experienced industrial development beyond the sector of sugar. The unification of the market on the island was an opportunity for hundreds of small local merchants to develop businesses: the number of workshops in Taiwan grew from 2,227 (of which 21.2 per cent had fewer than five employees) to 8,844 in 1940 (53.4 per cent) (Horiuchi, 2008, 141). These small firms, mostly controlled by local capital, were not only engaged in food processing but also in textiles, metalworking, and machinery. According to Horiuchi (2008), this transformation of the business structure provided the foundations of the postwar industrial development of Taiwan.

Like in Taiwan, the economic development of Korea by the Japanese colonial authorities started with agriculture, with a focus on rice. The rice riots of 1918 which contributed to labour unrest in Taishō-era Japan (see Chapter 4) had an important impact on rice production, and led to intensive efforts to modernize Korean agriculture in order to improve its productivity. However, this increase in production did not benefit the local population as it was mostly exported to the mainland. After World War I, ample natural resources and cheap labour attracted investment from Japanese companies in heavy industries. Factories to produce cotton yarn, metals, dyes, paper pulp, and other semi-finished industrial goods were opened in Korea. They exported their production to mainland Japan where they were transformed into finished goods. However, unlike Taiwan, the over-reliance on Japanese investment hindered the emergence of a dense network of local private companies (Fukuoka, 2008).

Manchuria was the most important location for Japanese investment in the empire, which started even before 1931 and accelerated after the formation of the Manchukuo state (see Table 6.2). The South Manchuria Railway company, founded in 1906, played a major role in this process (see Box 6.1), but it was not the only Japanese firm active in this region. The existence of natural resources attracted many private entrepreneurs in various fields of heavy industry, such as steelmaking, mining, and chemicals. Industrialization was financed largely by Japanese private banks in the early 1930s, then by the Industrial Bank of Japan, an institution founded in 1902 by the government to provide long-term loans to promote industrialization. In 1940, its loans accounted for more than 40 per cent of all the loans made to Manchurian manufacturing and mining companies (Rassmussen Kinney, 1982, 73). The *zaibatsu* also played a major role in the industrial development of Manchuria. Until 1941, private investments made by zaibatsu: Okura (21 per cent), Mitsui (17 per cent), Mitsubishi (8 per cent), and Sumitomo (5 per cent) collectively represented more than half of the total.

Box 6.1 History of the South Manchuria Railway Company

The expansion of Japanese imperialism in Korea and Manchuria intensified after the end of the war with Russia (1905) (Nakamura, 1989). The Japanese government founded a company in 1906 to operate the railway constructed by Russians in the late 1890s. The South Manchuria Railway Company (abbreviated Mantetsu) developed through the building and takeover of railway lines in northeastern China and occupied Korea. In 1939, it controlled a network in excess of 10,400 kilometres.

Moreover, this company diversified quickly into a broad range of sectors, from agriculture and power plants to coal mining and public utilities (houses, hospitals, schools, etc.). In 1911, Mantetsu was Japan's largest company. Its total assets amounted to 261 million yen, while the second largest, the maritime company Nippon Yusen, had only 59 million (Yamazaki, 2004, 400–411). It kept its incontestable lead until the end of the war. This firm developed thanks to the financial market, and about half of its capital was held by more than seventy-five thousand individuals.

After the foundation of the puppet state of Manchukuo in 1932, Mantetsu staff oversaw the industrial development of this region with the support of the government in Tokyo and the Kwantung army occupying the region. Characterized by an anti-capitalist ideology, the heads of Mantetsu and the Kwantung army introduced

> economic planning to promote the development of a heavy industry in Manchuria that would respond to the needs of manufacturing firms in mainland Japan. During the 1930s, the principle of this policy was to found a single company for each specific industry, in which Manchukuo government and Mantetsu would each take 30 per cent of capital, the remaining 40 per cent being sold to the public. This allowed Mantetsu to have the de facto control over the entire industry. Consequently, Mantetsu became both a railway company and a holding company controlling Manchukuo's industrial policy. In 1938, Manchukuo Heavy Industrial Development Co., founded one year previously, absorbed the heavy industry divisions of Mantetsu. The latter refocused on railway management and was dissolved in 1945 after the arrival of the Soviet Army.

Finally, some Japanese firms invested heavily in neighbouring independent China, considered by some historians as a part of the Japanese informal empire (Duus, 1989). This was particularly the case for the cotton industry. China had become an important market for the export of Japanese cotton yarn since the 1890s, and the emergence of local spinning companies led Japanese firms to invest and move their production bases to China, especially Shanghai. Trading companies were the first to invest, through the takeover of local firms. For example, Mitsui Trading purchased one in 1902, and founded Shanghai Spinning Co. Cotton companies such as Naigaimen, a private firm founded by Osaka investors, soon followed Mitsui's lead with the opening of a factory in Shanghai. In 1930, there was a total of eighty spinning companies in China. The top ten largest represented 48 per cent of the total production capacity. They included five Japanese companies, among which the largest was Naigaimen, followed by one British and four Chinese firms (Kuwahara, 2010). Japanese firms in China, however, faced difficulties from the 1930s, due to political tensions and the outbreak of war.

6.2 Military and technological development

Technological development is another issue that is closely related to military development. The concept of the National Innovation System (NIS) developed by economists in the 1990s is a useful tool for understanding how research and development (R&D) are organized in a country (Nelson, 1993). They argue that the interactions between the various organizations engaged in R&D (universities, private companies, and government bodies) rely on national specificities such as industrial structure, level of economic development, foreign affairs, the education system, and public policies.

In Japan, the research of Sawai Minoru sheds light on the formation and evolution of a NIS whose objective was to build Japan's industrial and military capabilities during the first half of the twentieth century (Sawai, 2012). He demonstrated that the technological development in Japan between 1900 and World War II relied on an intense cooperation between military research centres belonging to the army and navy, government organizations, universities, and private companies. The development of new weapons and the implementation of mass production methods indeed required the mobilization of science to support industrial development. A broad range of R&D centres were opened throughout the country. For example, by 1934, eighteen private companies had established research laboratories employing more than a hundred people, the largest being Nihon Optical Industry (Nikon, 2,200 researchers) and NEC (760 researchers) (Sawai, 2012, 47). The same year, there were more than thirty state-owned research organizations, among which were the Electrical Laboratory of the Ministry of Communication (1,090 researchers) and the Aviation Research Centre of Tokyo Imperial University (240 researchers) (Sawai, 2012, 51). Moreover, the army and the navy founded their own research centres, respectively in 1919 and 1923. The Research Centre of the Navy was one of the major and most prestigious research organizations in Japan before the war. In 1936, it employed 943 persons among whom were numerous engineers who had graduated from the best universities in the country (Sawai, 2012, 94). They cooperated intensively with private companies and universities to develop new weaponry and military equipment. Collaboration frequently took place on specific projects to develop a specific technology. Engineers from different organizations gathered and set up joint research programmes.

In addition to the military's initiatives, the government opened and developed faculties of engineering throughout Japan to fulfil the growing needs of research centres, armouries, and private companies. The total number of university graduate engineers working in Japan went from 1,921 in 1910 to 5,025 in 1920 to more than 41,000 in 1934 (Sawai, 2012, 473). A specific institution, the Department for Arms Production (DAP, *zohei gakka*) of Tokyo Imperial University, was founded in 1887 to carry out research and train engineers specialized in the development of weapons (Donzé, 2011). Between 1900 and 1940, DAP formed a total of 390 engineers. Their place of employment clearly shows the complementarity between the armouries and private companies, which were also engaged in arms production. A directory published in 1942 gives the place of work of 235 of them. The largest employers were the army and the navy, with about one-third of all DAP graduates (33.5 per cent in 1942). Many worked in aeronautics R&D centres but also in the development of sea mines and torpedoes, considered one of the most complex precision machineries at that time. The experience gained in this sector during the war was applied by several precision machine makers after 1945. One example is Suzukawa Hiroshi, who entered the second section of the Headquarters for Naval Vessels after graduating from DAP (1940) and joining Canon after the war, where he became head of the industrial design division in 1955 (Donzé, 2011).

More than half the graduates (50.3 per cent) worked in private companies (cf. Table 6.3). This means that some DAP-trained engineers entered private companies without having worked for the army or navy. Moreover, only a very small number of them were hired by private firms specializing in arms production: four engineers at Chuo Industry, one at Dai Nippon Arms, and one at Hitachi Arms. As all industries were engaged to some extent in war production at the time, the distinction between the military and the civilian industries in 1942 was blurred. The largest private employer was Mitsubishi Heavy Industries. It obviously hired these engineers to produce war materials: among them, one was employed by Nagasaki Munitions Works and seven by Tokyo Machine Works, a plant specializing in tank production (Mitsubishi jūkōgyō, 1956, 299–304). The other engineers were dispersed between the Nagoya Aircraft Works (two), the shipyards of Nagasaki (one), Kobe (one) and Yokohama (one), and the headquarters (one). The case of Japan Steel Works is remarkably similar. This steelmaker involved in weapons production was founded in 1907 as a joint-venture company between Hokkaido Colliery & Steamship Co. and two British arms manufacturers, Vickers, Sons & Co. and Armstrong and Whitworth & Co. (Nihon seikōjo, 2008). The actual work carried out by the five DAP engineers is unknown, but they may have been engaged in the production of weapons. Three of them are no longer mentioned in the 1955 *Gakushikai* directory, perhaps due to their death in the 1945 bombing of the main plant which killed some two hundred employees. Also, Japan Optical Industry (Nikon since 1988), the second largest private employer of DAP graduates in 1942, was a firm founded in 1917 to carry out R&D and produce optical instruments for the navy (Nihon Kogaku kōgyō 1960). As for the army, it sourced optical instruments from the company Tokyo Optical Industry (Topcon), founded in 1932 by the watchmaker Hattori (Tokyo kōgaku, 1982). It employed three DAP-trained engineers in 1942. Finally, one should mention the presence of Tokyo

Table 6.3 Private companies employing more than two DAP graduates, 1942

Name	Industry	Number of DAP graduates
Mitsubishi Heavy Industries	Machine	14
Japan Optical Industry (Nikon)	Optical instruments	9
Japan Steel Works	Steel	5
Toyo Precision	Testing instrument	5
Japan Special Steel	Steel	4
Tokyo Aircraft Instruments	Measuring instruments	4
Chuo Industry	Weapons	4
Sumitomo Metal Industries	Metal	4
Riken Industry	General	3
Kawasaki Heavy Industry	Machines	3
Hitachi Works	Electrical appliances	3
Tokyo Optical Industry (Topcon)	Optical instruments	3
Toshiba	Electrical appliances	3

Source: *Kaiin shimei roku* (1942)

Aircraft Instruments as one of the main employers. This firm began by producing measuring instruments for aircrafts and then participated directly in the war effort.

Finally, in 1942 there were also twenty-eight DAP graduates working outside the military and industry. Thirteen worked at universities and schools, especially at Tokyo Imperial University (five, including four at DAP) and Tokyo Institute of Technology (two), while the others primarily served at engineering faculties (one at Osaka University, one at Keijō University, Seoul) or at industry high schools (one at Yamanashi Industry High School and one at Ube Industry High School). Accordingly, their role was to train the new generation of engineers, to support the war effort, and subsequently the technological development of the industry after 1945 (Sawai, 2008). The administration was a source of employment for ten DAP graduates in 1942, five in some agencies of the Ministry of Commerce and Industry (MCI) (Patent Office and Machine Experiment Station) and one in the Scientific Division of the Cabinet Planning Agency (*Kikakuin*). Finally, six DAP graduates were employed by research centres, namely at the Aircraft Research Centre, the Riken Research Centre, and the Railway Research Centre.

After 1945, DAP was reorganized, redirected towards precision machines, and renamed the Department of Precision Engineering (*Seimitsu kōgakka*, DPE). It consisted of only three chairs, occupied until the beginning of the 1960s by professors in charge of DAP before and during the war. It trained students for employment in precision-machine firms and played an important role in supporting the technological development of the Japanese manufacturing industry in the context of the postwar military–civil conversion (*gunmin tenkan*, see Chapter 7).

6.3 The formation of new industrial *zaibatsu*

The big three *zaibatsu* Mitsui, Mitsubishi, and Sumitomo played a key role in the development of a heavy industry necessary to build a strong army (machinery, shipbuilding, aircraft), and exploited the resources in the colonies. However, a new type of *zaibatsu* emerged during the interwar period and took charge of similar activities. These organizations are commonly called 'new industrial *zaibatsu*' (*shinkō zaibatsu*) (Samuels, 1994; Udagawa, 2015). They worked closely with the army and experienced fast growth, based on their cooperation with military, financial support from the Industrial Bank of Japan, investment in Manchuria and Korea, and the organizational skills of a new generation of entrepreneurs (takeovers through M&A and the integration of numerous industrial companies). The most important ones were Nitchitsu (founded in 1908; specializing in chemicals and electric power), Nisso (1920, chemicals, steel and metals, mining, etc.), Riken (1927, industrialization of innovations developed by Riken Institute, established in 1917), and Nippon Sangyō (1928, machinery and mining).

Nippon Sangyō (Nissan) is a case in point for highlighting the specificities of these new industrial *zaibatsu*. The roots of this group go back to Kuhara Mining Co., the second largest producer of copper in Japan, founded in 1905 under the name Hitachi Mine. This company faced financial difficulties during the 1920s due to its over-diversification into a broad range of activities—one of them being the production of electric machinery that was spun out in 1910 as Hitachi. In order to rescue Kuhara Mining, one entrepreneur, Aikawa Yoshisuke (1880–1967), the brother-in-law of Kuhara Mining's owner, was appointed president in 1928. Aikawa earned a degree in engineering from the best school in the country, Tokyo Imperial University (today's University of Tokyo) and worked in Shibaura Works before travelling to the United States and returning to establish a foundry in Kyushu. He transformed the loosely integrated group by founding a holding company, Nihon Sangyō (abbreviated Nissan), to supervise the various industrial activities and investments of the group. At the time of its foundation, Nissan had eighteen subsidiaries and more than fifty affiliated companies engaged in seven different industries (Samuels, 1994, 102). One of them was Nissan Motors (see below, pp. 119–120). Then, in the 1930s Aikawa adopted an aggressive strategy to takeover firms in order to diversify risk (Miyajima et al., 2008). Once he had taken them over, he reorganized and re-listed them on the Tokyo Stock Exchange, making substantive financial profits that were re-invested to develop the conglomerate. Aikawa purchased stakes in 132 companies, giving birth to a large and diversified new industrial *zaibatsu*. The gross sales of the group increased from 1.2 million yen in 1931 to 30.8 million in 1934.

However, investing in Manchuria was the step that led to the real development of the group. The major *zaibatsu* were present in colonies but reluctant to invest heavily and cooperate directly with the army. Aikawa was then invited by his relative, Kishi Nobusuke (1896–1987), a bureaucrat at the MCI who was involved in the development of Manchuria, to invest in this region. Aikawa agreed to collaborate with the Kwantung army, which had de facto control over Manchukuo. In 1937, Nissan cofounded with the Manchukuo government an equally owned joint venture, Manchukuo Heavy Industrial Development Co. This firm was entrusted with the general development of resources and heavy industry (mining, steelmaking, metal smelting, machinery, shipbuilding, trucks, weapons, etc.), in cooperation with the military and local government. Aikawa received financial assistance from the Industrial Bank of Japan and the BOJ. In 1938, the headquarters of Nissan were moved to Manchuria. The Manchukuo Heavy Industrial Development Co. was merged with Nissan and the heavy industry division of the South Manchurian Railway Company (see Box 6.1) (Samuels, 1994, 103).

However, although he cooperated with the Japanese army in Manchuria, Aikawa did not share all the views of the military. In particular, he was against forming a pact with Germany and Italy. In 1942, under pressure from the Kwantung army, he resigned from his position as president of Manchukuo Heavy Industrial Development Co. and returned to the mainland, where he was elected to the Diet the following year. After the end of the war, Manchukuo Heavy Industrial Development Co. stopped its activities and was dismantled. At that time, the group included a total of 172 companies; most of them would go on to develop as independent firms (Udagawa, 2015, 88). Aikawa would be incarcerated until 1947 for his involvement in the war but would eventually return to politics and business. He was close to Kishi (who was also imprisoned until 1948 and appointed prime minister in 1957) and engaged in supporting SMEs in the 1960s (Udagawa, 2002a, 158–171).

The example of Nissan makes it possible to highlight some major characteristics of the impact of the military on business. First, the demand from the army and the navy was an important driver of the industrial transformation of the Japanese economy, from light to heavy industries. Between 1914 and 1942, the shares of textiles and food in industrial production dropped respectively from 45.2 per cent to 11.1 per cent and 16 per cent to 7.6 per cent, while it increased for metals (3.5 per cent to 20.1 per cent), machinery (8.1 per cent to 28.7 per cent), and chemicals (12.8 per cent to 17.2 per cent) (Miwa and Hara, 2007, 116). The new industrial *zaibatsu* played a key role in this transformation. Second, private companies like Nissan developed in an increasingly less competitive environment, particularly in the colonies. In the 1930s, the objective of building large conglomerates was not so much to achieve economies of scale and reduce production costs as to increase production in order to respond to growing military demand. Military procurement orders and financial means provided by the state supported fast development but with little consideration for the competitiveness of firms. Third, the central bureaucracy, embodied by Kishi in the case of Nissan, intervened to coordinate and plan industrial development. The MCI, established in 1925, intervened actively in the reorganization of domestic industry after 1931. It promoted industrial concentration by directly supporting the growth of the new industrial *zaibatsu*.

6.4 The control over foreign enterprises

Although the government had been welcoming to foreign companies since the late 1890s, the policy started to change in the early 1930s in a context of the fast development of heavy industries, expansion in China, and the rise of both militarism and nationalism (e.g. 'Buy Japan' campaigns). Taking control of foreign-owned companies or joint ventures with foreign capital became a major issue, particularly in the high-tech industries. Moreover, Japanese industrialists participated in this movement. The technological development of their firms made them less dependent on foreign technology, and to protect their interests, they pressured the government to restrict foreign investment. This was the case for Tokyo Electric, a firm that had been receiving capital from General Electric (GE) since 1905. Because it had organized its own research facilities, its management wanted GE to withdraw in the early 1930s. At the same time, local industrial gas manufacturers gathered in the Association of Japanese Oxygen Producers and tried to limit the activities of Air Liquide SA, the French multinational company that dominated this market (Mason, 1992, 52).

In this context, the finance minister, Takahashi Korekiyo informed the director of an American company in Japan in 1932 that Japan would continue to accept foreign firms 'provided that the industries in which the capital is invested are under the joint control of Japanese and foreigners' (quoted by Mason, 1992, 53). The legal framework for foreign direct investment also started to change. The Industrial Control Law, adopted in 1931, gave power to the state to intervene in specific industries in order to reorganize them. The main objective was to achieve a rationalization that would enable technological development and an increase in production to prepare for war (see below, p. 121). However, at the same time, through rationalization Japanese authorities could control the activities of companies with foreign capital through specifically applied laws. For example, the Petroleum Industry Law (1934) and the Automobile Manufacturing Industry Law (1936) introduced systems of licensing to produce in Japan that restricted the operations of foreign firms. Similar restrictions were introduced in the aircraft, machine tool, and shipbuilding industries. This situation led some foreign companies to divest from Japan. The American car companies of Ford and General Motors (GM) are a case in point (see below) but are not exceptions. For example, National Cash Register Company founded a joint venture in 1935 and opened a plant in Japan. However, it had to stop production and divest five years later, due to restrictions imposed by the government (Wilkins, 1974, 250).

This new legal framework in addition to pressure, harassment, and nationalistic campaigns led Western investors to accept a partial withdrawal from their joint ventures and to award majority ownership to their Japanese partners. Between 1930 and 1941, the proportion of foreign equity dropped from 50 per cent to 46 per cent for Carrier Co. (air-conditioned systems), 57 per cent to 9 per cent for Goodrich (rubber), 59 per cent to 20 per cent for International Telephone and Telegraph (ITT; communication), and 50 per cent to 25 per cent for Tidewater (oil) (Wilkins, 1974, 251). As for RCA Victor (phonographs and radios), due to various pressures ('Buy Japan' campaigns, tightening of foreign-exchange allowance, etc.), it had to sell the majority of its shares in the fully owned Japanese subsidiary to Nissan group in 1937 (Mason, 1992, 94–95). Government procurement was also a way to apply pressure to foreign multinationals. Although NEC, a company with Western Electric capital (taken over by ITT in 1925), had been a first mover in the development of telephone technology in Japan and had cooperated closely with the government to implement this infrastructure in the late 1920s, public authorities started to shift their orders to local telephone manufacturers such as Oki Electric and Toa Electric. In 1930, the Ministry of Communications decided to place its orders on a priority basis with Japanese-controlled firms (Mason, 1992, 95). This led ITT to withdraw from NEC and from 1932, progressively sell its share to Sumitomo (Udagawa, 1987, 18).

What were the effects of these controls and takeovers on Japanese companies? The car industry is an excellent example to use to elucidate this issue. It had experienced fast growth since the mid-1920s, following the investments of Ford and GM, which opened assembly plants in Japan (see Chapter 5). The growing needs of the military for trucks and vehicles resulted in direct government involvement to nurture a domestic industry in several ways (Mason, 1992, 72–93). First, as American companies were focused on automobiles, the authorities gave subsidies to three local manufacturers to develop midsized vehicles. This cooperation gave birth to Tokyo Automobile Industries Co., the predecessor of truck manufacturer Isuzu. Second, the government exerted various forms of pressure (e.g. restriction of trade to Manchuria and a requirement to combine Japanese subsidiaries with local capital) but the real turning point was the adoption of the Automobile Manufacturing Industry Law (1936). The production of cars became subject to a government licensing process, which could only be granted to Japanese companies. Ford and GM were allocated production quotas. Restrictions on imports also challenged the activities of these American companies. Both firms discussed the possibility of an arrangement with the two domestic companies that dominated the national car-making industry, Nissan and Toyota, but without success. Their production declined quickly, and they were soon overtaken by Nissan (1938) and Toyota (1939) (Mason, 1992, 90). Ford Japan and GM Japan were expropriated two weeks after Pearl Harbor.

While Ford and GM gained little from their business dealings in Japan, Nissan and Toyota benefited greatly from the knowledge provided by the American multinationals. Japanese producers started their operations in the automobile industry during the interwar years and adopted two different strategies regarding technology transfer (direct for Nissan and indirect for Toyota) (Odagiri and Goto, 1996, 185–190). When the new industrial *zaibatsu* Nissan was founded by Aikawa in 1928, some of the firms that merged to create it had already developed small-scale production of vehicles with the assistance of an American engineer, William R. Gorham (1888–1949). After 1928, he continued working for Nissan and developed a new model of a passenger vehicle under the brand Datsun in 1931. Gorham also organized a new industrial site in Yokohama, with equipment imported from the United States, where he aimed to implement a mass-production system inspired by Ford. As for Toyota, its roots go back to the textile machine manufacturing company, Toyoda Automatic Loom Works Co., where Toyoda Kiichirō (1894–1952), an engineer who graduated from Tokyo Imperial University and the son of the founder of the company, opened an automobile division in 1933. He sent one of his engineers to the United States for a seven-month study tour of car-manufacturing companies, among which was Ford. In 1935, Toyoda developed its first passenger vehicle modelled after a Chrysler vehicle through the process of reverse engineering and a truck similar to American ones. In 1937, Toyota Motors Co. was established as a separate company.

The two major sources of knowledge transfer in Japan were through the Japanese employees at Ford and GM and the network of independent parts suppliers built by the two American firms. As Table 6.4 shows, the first means of knowledge transfer was through Japanese managers who found employment in a domestic car company. This demonstrates that manufacturing technology was not the only knowledge that local producers sought. General management, marketing, and sales were also key factors to building competitive firms in the domestic market. Setting up a dealership network was vital. This knowledge was acquired through former Japanese employees of Ford and GM. The second means was via networks. Ford and GM nurtured a dense network of suppliers to manufacture the parts they needed to assemble cars in Japan. In 1935, tyres, batteries, electrical parts, chassis components, and body materials were provided by a broad range of Japanese companies (Mason, 1992, 82–84). The knowledge they acquired to manufacture high-quality parts also supported the development of Nissan and Toyota.

The outbreak of war with the United States and the other Allied powers in 1941 led to the policy of controlling foreign firms a step further. American and English assets were expropriated and transferred to Japanese firms. As

Table 6.4 Japanese employees that moved from Ford and GM to Nissan and Toyota

Name	Initial employer	Japanese employer and position
Tanaka Josaburō	GM Japan	Nissan, director
Maeda Isamu	GM Japan	Nissan, managing director
Hattori Seki	GM Japan	Toyota, managing director
Kamiya Shōtarō	GM Japan	Toyota Auto Sales, president
Hanasaki Shikanosuke	GM Japan	Toyota Auto Sales, managing director
Kato Masayuki	GM Japan	Toyota Auto Sales, president
Ashida Sadajirō	GM Japan	Nissan Auto Sales, managing director
Nakai Arano	GM Japan	Toyota Fukuoka, president
Konishi Yoshikazu	GM Japan	Nissan
Maehara Masanori	Ford Japan	Nissan, managing director
Tanaka Isamu	Ford Japan	Nissan, manager
Kawazoe Soichi	GM Japan, Ford Japan	Nissan America, vice-president
Takashima Tameō	GM Japan, Ford Japan	Nissan Auto Sales, head of Tokyo Office

Source: Udagawa (1987), 29 and Mason (1992), 87

for firms from Germany and neutral countries, most of them divested as it was impossible for them to continue to carry out business profitably, Nestlé being one of the very few exceptions (see Chapter 5).

6.5 The war economy

The growing intervention of the state in the economy occurred in the context of a recession and a growing will to support the shift of the manufacturing sector from light to heavy industries. Industrial policy was implemented by the MCI, established in 1925. In 1930, a Temporary Industry Rationality Bureau (*rinji sangyō gōri kyoku*) was founded by the government and attached to the MCI. Inspired by economic planning and scientific management, this body made plans to control enterprises, improve rationalization, and increase production (Johnson, 1982, 104). It worked in cooperation with representatives from *zaibatsu* and academia. The Industrial Control Law, adopted in 1931 is an outcome of this policy. This new legal instrument allowed the control of industrial organization and production. The law also enabled the government to intervene to oversee the reorganization of industries. When two-thirds of the firms in an industry had become affiliated with a specific control association, the law made joining compulsory for the other companies. At the end of 1937, there were a total of 1,172 control associations throughout Japan (Cohen, 1949, 11). They functioned like cartels and controlled notably the allocation of resources, and so on. The Industrial Control Law was followed by the adoption of several sectorial laws that introduced a system of official licensure for manufacturers. A mandatory licensing system for all producers was a way to eliminate foreign-owned companies (see above) and to support the concentration of production by a small number of firms in industries characterized by decentralization and a high concentration of SMEs. This law gave the government direct control over a broad range of firms' operations, like the expansion of equipment and production planning, in order to respond to military demands. Companies could also be granted special exemptions from taxes and land expropriation.

The implementation of these economic policies at the beginning of the Sino-Japanese War in 1937 was not a major departure from previous policies but rather the strengthening of the economic controls introduced in the early 1930s. The need to allocate capital, labour, and material resources to respond to military demand led to the adoption of a series of laws (Temporary Capital Adjustment Law, 1937; Temporary Export and Import Commodities Law, 1937; National General Mobilization Law, 1938) that strengthened the power of the government. This was followed by the introduction of price and wage controls in 1939. Representatives of the army and navy were then dispatched to private companies to supervise the production of munitions. The manufacturing production index shows a high level of growth between 1937 (100) and 1944 (124), but was almost exclusively based on armaments and plummeted during the final year of the conflict (53 in 1945) (Nakamura, 1989, 489).

6.6 Conclusions

The years 1931–1945, characterized by growing militarization and war, can be considered a period of both change and continuity for Japanese business. Pressure by Japanese authorities to force foreign firms to withdraw is the first major change. These enterprises contributed much to the technological development of Japan and played a key role in the shift from light to heavy industries. Most of them did leave Japan, and it would be difficult for them to make a successful comeback after 1945 (see Chapter 10). Second, the intervention of the state put an end to economic liberalism and free enterprise, a point that is significant in this volume on Japanese capitalism. Private companies did not disappear during this period but their development was highly impacted by Japan's imperialistic expansion and the preparation for war. The move of the Japanese towards a form of *wartime capitalism* with the *zaibatsu* at the core shaped their activities, from R&D and product development to production and to marketing. The government also set up important institutions, like the MCI, which had a broad influence on industrial organization and joint research projects. These organizations and their programmes continued in a different form after World War II, although their efficiency was limited (see following chapter). However, at the same time, the division of production implemented within the empire and the industrialization of colonies had long-lasting effects which were both positive and negative. The positive consequences of Japanese investment in those countries that were colonized remains a highly debated and sensitive issue in East Asian politics today. One must acknowledge that the infrastructure and human networks built by Japanese entrepreneurs and bureaucrats in the colonies greatly contributed to the first phase of their industrialization after 1945, particularly for some industries such as textiles. Economic historian Hori Kazuo has demonstrated for example that the four Japanese companies dominating the cotton industry in Korea during the 1930s, which were headed by Korean entrepreneurs after 1945, formed the core of the textile industry until the 1960s (Hori, 2008, 192). A similar trend can be observed in Taiwan and, to some extent, in mainland China. However, at the same time, colonization had disastrous effects on the lives of local populations, especially in Korea, and on the ability of local entrepreneurs there to contribute to economic development or even fulfil the nation's own needs.

Finally, considering entrepreneurship during this troubled period, it must be stressed that the growing presence of the military and government challenged and reduced the scope of action of private Japanese entrepreneurs. Capitalism shifted from an economic system based on the action of private firms in a competitive environment to a more bureaucratic system in which the government and the army had a growing weight. It was, however, not the end of entrepreneurship. Individuals, like Suzuki Tosaburō in Taiwan or Aikawa Yoshisuke in Manchuria, took the opportunities offered by Japanese imperialism to create firms focusing on the development of resources in the colonies. As for the pressure and struggle against foreign firms, this offered opportunities for the *zaibatsu* to consolidate their knowledge in the major high-tech industries like electrical goods, chemicals, metalworking, and automobiles. Lastly, the training of hundreds of engineers in universities throughout the country was aimed at providing the manufacturing industry with human capital in order to meet military demand. As shown in the following chapters, after 1945, a new generation of entrepreneurs would emerge specifically from this talented and well-trained corps of engineers and contribute to making Japan the world's second industrial economy by the late 1960s (see Chapter 8).

7
Business during the Occupation Period
Continuity and change

In addition to the high death toll of nearly three million people, World War II had profoundly devastating effects on Japan's urban infrastructure, businesses, and the economy. The most extensive destruction to its cities occurred in the final phases of war, resulting not only from the atomic bombs dropped on Hiroshima and Nagasaki, but also from the massive American airstrikes that ravaged Tokyo and Osaka. According to government estimates, at the end of the War approximately a quarter of Japan's national wealth was completely wiped out (Yonekura, 1994, 189). Given these circumstances, it is unlikely that any of those who observed firsthand the burned fields (*yakenohara*) of Japan's war-torn cities in the early days after the surrender could have ever predicted that the country would become the world's second largest economy by 1968. From the ruins, however, came an unprecedented opportunity to reconstruct the nation's physical assets and rekindle capitalism and entrepreneurship after a long period of strife.

The significance of the occupation period on Japan's long-term development is a subject that continues to spark lively discussions among historians even today. Though the path that the nation embarked upon in the early Shōwa years was indeed dark and destructive, one prominent historian, John Dower, boldly and persuasively contends that World War II—despite its final outcome—was 'useful' for Japan in terms of the institutional legacies that it left. Many key elements remained intact, namely the technological and scientific skills of its human capital, which would be necessary—once adapted to peaceful circumstances—to lead Japan towards recovery and its subsequent rise as an economic superpower. Interestingly, Dower also maintains—to the contrary of many postwar observers—that the end of the War was not a bright new beginning but the continuation of a gradual transformation that had already begun in the 1930s, if not before (Dower, 1990, 49–70).

This chapter argues that the postwar period was one of continuity but also one of great change. Continuity can be seen in the adaption of many of the institutions that had served Japan so well during its mobilization for war, though for different circumstances: a period of high economic growth (1954–1972). They would form the necessary bedrock for the phenomenal postwar business development that would occur in a context of political stability. Once reinstated and adapted, the old institutions of the war period would play a significant role in a new economic war which is epitomized by the popular slogan of the times: 'catch up with and overtake' (*oitsuki oiokose*) the West (Gotoh, 2020).

Along with these institutions was a corps of scientists and engineers, mentioned in the previous chapter, many of whom had been able to avoid being drafted for combat thanks to their specialized skills and knowledge. During the war, some had worked for private firms, which received commissioned work from the military to develop aircraft, weaponry, and other implements of war, but were left unemployed and idle after the surrender. Once the occupation ended, they would join forces with government and private enterprise to strengthen Japan's economy and its industries through innovation (Sawai, 2016; Dower, 1990; Gordon, 2003). They were aided by a propitious environment for technology transfer, particularly from the United States as well as private sector applications of military technologies for peaceful uses (*gunmin tenkan*) (Sawai, 2016). As described in Box 7.1, some of these scientists and engineers would begin working in research laboratories, while others, described in the following chapter through the case of Sony, would become entrepreneurs. Their expertise and skills were harnessed for use in numerous peacetime endeavours ranging from designing prototypes for new forms of transportation to overseeing massive infrastructure projects. This knowledge would serve as the foundations for the development and expansion of many new high-tech industries for which Japan would become famous around the world. At the same time, the void left by the collapse of state structures, the disorganization of businesses, and the departure of former company directors offered tremendous opportunities for young entrepreneurs, free to create and innovate. The postwar years were one of the richest periods for entrepreneurship (Kikkawa, 2023). Hence, the endeavours of entrepreneurs would help to re-define Japanese capitalism and entrepreneurship in the postwar period.

In this study of Japanese business development, the occupation period can be seen as a transition or 'bridge' between the dark path to economic ruin taken during the War and the new road to economic prosperity that would follow during the take-off. The purpose of this chapter is to examine the changes in capitalism and entrepreneurship during the occupation years to provide a better understanding of how this period prepared the nation for rapid growth. The structure of this chapter is as follows: (1) The general economic situation; (2) An overview of SCAP reforms; (3) The decline and

Box 7.1 The Shinkansen or Bullet Train

Japanese postwar business history is replete with examples of the transfer of technology, knowledge, and skills from the military to the civil industry (*gunmin tenkan*). Two well-known examples, are cameras and watches, whose high-tech features can be traced to wartime weaponry (Nelson, 1998). These products enabled Japanese manufacturers to refashion their image in overseas export markets from purveyors of 'cheap and shoddy' (*yasukarō warukarō*) goods to producers of high-tech, high-quality merchandise. Thus, they strengthened Japan's image as a peaceful nation, while also directly contributing to postwar economic recovery and prosperity. The *Shinkansen* or Bullet Train provides a particularly vivid example of the use of military technologies for peaceful purposes.

Shortly after Japan's unconditional surrender in the summer of 1945, the occupation authorities prohibited any involvement in the field of aeronautics, including the production of aircraft, an industry that would not resume until the 1970s. Revered as academic elites during the War, Japan's engineers were held in great disdain in its aftermath for their role in the nation's defeat and ensuing economic misery (Nishiyama, 2003 and 2007). Because SCAP authorities believed these men had directly contributed to the War and its destructive outcome, some 100,000 engineers, many of whom were aeronautical engineers, were purged and left jobless by the spring of 1946.

In a meeting on 15 August 1945, Horiki Kenzō (director of the Railway Board and the Minister of Health and Welfare in the 1950s) announced that it was the duty of the railroad industry to provide jobs to these unemployed engineers. The JNR (Japan National Railroad) absorbed hundreds of them, at least half from the military sector. Between 1945 and 1950, 267 new employees joined JNR some of whom would work at the Railway Technical Research Institute (RTRI), a branch of JNR and the place where the *Shinkansen* was conceived (Nishiyama, 2003).

Many individuals helped to design the *Shinkansen*. Thanks to their wide coverage in the media as heroes of the high-growth period, the stories of two former wartime aeronautical engineers, Miki Tadao and Matsudaira Tadashi have been particularly well documented. During the War, Miki was placed in charge of aircraft design, and it was he who designed the famous aircraft, the *Ōka*, deployed on the so-called *kamikaze* (*tokkōtai*) missions. This aircraft had a conical-shaped nose and lightweight body but no landing apparatus. Designs for the *Ōka* would inspire those used for the *Shinkansen*, and have been credited for its attainment of record high speeds. Achieving high speeds would make it feasible for postwar business travellers to use the *Shinkansen*, even for daily trips between Tokyo in Osaka. The

> *Shinkansen* would not only become a mode of transportation; it would also be a means to facilitate communication, a key to the development of business in postwar Japan.
>
> During the War, planes sent on missions would sometimes never reach their destinations due to accidents caused by vibrations known as 'flutter' resulting in the ignition and disintegration of the aircraft in midair. Matsudaira Tadashi found a solution to this problem and incorporated his findings into the development of 'the Zero' aircraft. Applying what he had learned from designing the Zero, Matsudaira remedied a similar problem for trains known as the 'hunting motion' which caused derailments and other serious accidents.
>
> Before the *Shinkansen*, travel by train was a dangerous undertaking. Of the 46,578 train accidents reported in 1946, some 488 were considered major accidents in which there was a collision or derailment (Nishiyama, 2007). Matsudaira's hypothesis challenged conventional wisdom, as many believed that the vibrations were not related to the engine but rather to the train tracks. Combining both theories and mathematical models, Matsudaira went about designing a new suspension system, the idea for which had come from a paper he read on the air suspension system used by the Greyhound Bus Company in the United States, which was made available by SCAP. His solution directly contributed to the comfortable ride that passengers aboard the *Shinkansen* enjoy today.
>
> The trial of the first *Shinkansen* represented in many ways the incarnation of Japan's postwar technological achievements and was broadcast live nationwide. The test run occurred shortly before the opening of the first Tokyo Olympic Games in 1964, another postwar symbol (see Chapter 12). The 1954 Games were to be a venue for Japan to showcase its scientific progress and return to the world stage as a peace-loving, democratic nation. In its trial run, the *Shinkansen* achieved a record speed of 256 kilometres per hour, surpassing the fastest train in operation at that time, the French TGV Mistral. The *Shinkansen* remains one of the fastest, most punctual, and safest trains in operation in the world today.

dissolution of the *zaibatsu* empires; (4) Entrepreneurship in the occupation period: the case of the steel industry; (5) Continuity and change: the reemergence of big business; and (6) Conclusions.

7.1 The general economic situation

Immediately after the War ended, some 13.1 million soldiers who had been stationed in parts of the Asian continent, were repatriated. This initially caused a sharp spike in unemployment; however, according to Nakamura (1989), a larger crisis was averted thanks to the dire circumstances of the times and the immediate need to rebuild the nation. Most quickly found work, in many cases in agriculture, which by 1947 had become the largest employment sector. As was the case during the War, providing food to the nation was a pressing issue. The loss of Japan's colonial possessions, the major suppliers of food, only aggravated the problem. The government rationing system (*haikyū seido*), which had been introduced during the war period as a mechanism for distributing food and other supplies to households, is one example of an institution that remained in place as a means for dealing with the dire circumstances in the immediate aftermath of the War. However, due to the inefficiencies of the system coupled by the insufficient supplies of food and other necessities, many Japanese resorted to making purchases on the black market (*yami'ichi*) or the so-called 'blue-sky markets' (*aozora ichiba*). At such markets, which sprang up across the country, one could find a variety of goods that could be bought and bartered. In this way, the truly desperate circumstances the Japanese faced at that time fostered a thriving grey economy. Low entry barriers provided ample opportunities for entrepreneurship in the largest sense of the term. Thus, it was from this context of resource scarcity—particularly financial capital—combined with ample human ingenuity that many early postwar period start-ups would emerge.

In addition to the scarcity of funds, food, and other basics, Japan lacked energy resources, namely coal that could be used to provide heat to households and power to factories, which were sorely needed to restart the economy. With the loss of its colonial territories, Japan could no longer rely on them as suppliers of coal or as a source of labour in its mines. A further challenge to the recovery effort was the failure of the rice crop in 1945–1946, which pushed the population even further towards the brink of starvation. In response to this dire shortage of food, US authorities provided little relief until 1947.

Economic recovery was also hindered by rampant inflation, a chronic problem since 1944. Inflation would not be curbed until the introduction of a drastic policy implemented in 1948 under Joseph Dodge, a former US banker, known as the Dodge Line. Dodge had gained experience in economic reconstruction planning and financial reform by working in West Germany before his arrival in Japan. The Dodge Line was designed to reduce the burden of the US aid used to foster Japan's economic recovery, a policy that had come under attack in the United States (Yonekura, 1994). The main aims of the Dodge Line were to balance the budget, get rid of government subsidies, put an end to the provision of loans from the Reconstruction

Finance Bank (*Fukkō kin'yū kōko*), and establish a single exchange rate of $1 = 360 yen. This fixed exchange rate was maintained until the 1970s and served as an indirect subsidy for Japanese exports. It would have important implications for Japan's recovery as well as the development of capitalism across East Asia. The demand for cheap Japanese exports provided new opportunities for entrepreneurship in one of Japan's principal markets, the United States as well as capital needed to restart FDI in Asian markets, one of the first being the former colony of Taiwan.

Though the occupation period is relatively short in comparison to the others examined in this volume—just six years eight-and-half months—it had a significant impact on Japanese society, its economy, and business development. The War and the lessons it provided deeply marked the national psyche and the fundamental values of all those who had experienced it, including the nation's entrepreneurs. As mentioned below, the Allied Occupation was almost exclusively overseen by the United States and was strongly influenced by American values. The US occupation of Japan would spark great changes in the workings of Japanese society, its aspirations, and lifestyle. Though this period would quickly draw to a close, the American military presence, especially in Okinawa, would continue to evoke a wide array of emotions among Japanese ranging from fear to admiration.

It is noteworthy that similarities have been drawn between the occupation and the Meiji period, a time when the nation also faced a foreign threat (Yui and Hirschmeier, 1975). The drive to rebuild the nation after a long war and regain political and economic sovereignty germinated a spirit of economic nationalism similar to that witnessed in the Meiji period, especially the latter half when many new enterprises were founded. Another similarity was a re-emergence of capitalism coupled by a flourishing of entrepreneurship in various forms.

7.2 An overview of SCAP reforms

Ideological underpinnings

From the time of the Japanese emperor's acceptance of the Potsdam Declaration on 15 August 1945 to Yoshida Shigeru's signing of the San Francisco Treaty in September 1951 followed by the full restoration of national sovereignty on 28 April 1952, Japan was subordinate to the occupation authorities, or SCAP (the Supreme Commander for the Allied Forces) under US General Douglas MacArthur. The two main pillars of the SCAP reforms were demilitarization and democratization. The impact of these reforms on Japanese society and business would be consequential on many levels with examples ranging from the measures to create a more equitable distribution of wealth to a new constitution which awarded Japanese women the right to vote.

Historians identify two distinct phases of the occupation period. During the first phase in 1945–1946, US authorities sought to punish Japan, a position that had particularly negative effects on Japan's economy and business recovery. The aim of the reforms introduced during this phase was to dismantle rather than to reconstruct the economy. The long-term objective of implementing such drastic economic measures was to prevent Japan from ever acquiring the means to re-arm or engage in future wars. The centrepiece of the economic reforms was the breaking up of the business empires or *zaibatsu* and other large corporate entities, which from SCAP's perspective were especially culpable for their wartime role.

Students of this period should keep in mind the historical context in which these business-directed reforms occurred. The designers of the reforms had experienced the New Deal in the United States and were influenced by the ideology upon which it was founded. The occupation followed a period in US history of 'trust busting' occurring in the early 1900s during the Roosevelt administration when efforts to break up big business empires such as those of the Rockefellers and Carnegies were undertaken. Large business entities with monopolistic control of certain sectors of the economy were perceived as detrimental not only to business development and entrepreneurship but also to society as a whole. The notion of a need to break up the *zaibatsu* empires was seen by SCAP as a prerequisite to ensuring free and fair competition—a defining element of capitalism.

The second phase from 1947 to 1948 was marked by the decision to reverse course. Like the first phase, this stance would also have direct effects on business development. Authorities' decision to 'reverse course' and to encourage rather than prevent the rebuilding of Japan's economy and businesses had notable ideological underpinnings whose roots can be traced to the escalation of the East–West tensions that were occurring during the Cold War. At that time, Western nations had become keenly concerned about the spread of communism in Europe and other parts of the world. Symbolic of this period was Winston Churchill's speech delivered in 1946 where he mentioned the Iron Curtain descending across Europe (National Archives, 1946). Changes in the international relations of the Asian region played a decisive role in this major policy shift. There was a fear on the part of American policymakers that a 'domino effect' was taking place in Asia and other parts of the world, and if left unchecked, would result in the formation of a communist stronghold (Kennan, 1947). When the Korean War (1950–1953) broke out, the United States under General MacArthur decided that Japan would make a better ally than an enemy. Faced with the rise of communism in Asia, the United States thus allied politically and cooperated economically with Japan by making it a major supplier for the Korean War.

There were also long-term economic aspirations embedded in this new relationship with implications for the development of Japanese capitalism in the long term. By making Japan a US ally, it had also created a new market for American goods. From both a political and business perspective, US-Japan relations would improve, giving rise to the formal military alliance that endures to this day. According to Article Nine of Japan's postwar constitution, drawn up by SCAP advisors during the occupation period, Japan could not engage in war. Unencumbered by having to maintain an offensive military force, Japan could rely on the US military stationed on bases, built mainly in Okinawa, a territory that would remain a possession of the United States until its reversion in 1971.

The result of the alliance was greater political stability for Japan, which would in turn have a favourable effect on the development of Japanese business in the long term. According to Japan's peacetime constitution, it could have a self-defence force whose budget would not exceed 1 per cent of GDP, a policy that remained intact until December 2022. Due to subsequent re-interpretations of its constitution, Japan has participated in overseas peace-keeping missions in warzones since 1996. Investments in defence-related sectors such as aeronautics and nuclear energy generation have continued to rise.

Indirect contributions to business development: agricultural, educational, and labour reforms

The purpose of this section is to highlight the agricultural, educational, and labour reforms that occurred during the occupation and to consider some of their effects on business development in the postwar era. Reforms specifically relating to business are addressed in the next section. As mentioned in the introduction, many of the reforms that SCAP introduced were not new. Indeed, some—namely those relating to agriculture and land redistribution—were underway before their arrival. One change that can be considered new, however, is the degree to which the land reforms changed the physical features of the Japanese countryside and affected agricultural policies in the long term.

The redistribution of land is often cited as being one of SCAP's most successful measures in terms of its effectiveness not only for equitably redistributing land to those who had for many years farmed it, but also for the new wealth it created. According to this reform, lands cultivated by tenants were expropriated from their absentee landowners thus allowing the former to own property. The result was a transformation of the Japanese countryside from one of large parcels of single-family properties to one of small, former tenant-owned plots. In terms of wealth generation, it is noted in the literature on this period that new technologies to improve rice yields were also introduced, thus contributing to an overall increase in agricultural productivity. While this viewpoint is generally accepted, some have challenged it (Flath, 2000). Though the degree to which new technologies boosted agricultural yields may be debatable, it is certain that the increase in food crop output improved the physical health of the average Japanese after the War, and that this contribution, though indirect, helped to raise the productivity of the nation's workforce.

A second area—a key element of SCAP reforms—was education. To the US authorities, Japan's wartime schools were places that were designed not to educate but to indoctrinate young Japanese with militaristic ideology. In response to their role in leading the nation on a destructive path towards war, schools were required to introduce sweeping changes to fundamentally reform the curricula and instil new ideas of democracy and peace. Other reforms were targeted at higher education with an aim of encouraging equality. In the pre-occupation period, university education was highly elitist. According to the occupation-period reforms, however, all Japanese—regardless of their socio-economic background—who possessed the knowledge to pass the state entrance examination could in principle be admitted to one of the prestigious national universities. This new reform applied not only to Japan's male but also to its female population, who had been barred from study at private and national universities until the arrival of SCAP. Based on the American ideals of democracy and freedom of expression, Japanese higher education became egalitarian and accessible to all those with the necessary qualifications. One important consequence of this reform is the growth of Japan's population of white-collar workers. Having a well-educated pool of human capital, who were both capable and well prepared to rebuild the country in the early postwar period, would help Japan to compete internationally during the high-growth period that followed.

A third reform target related to labour. As shown in Chapter 5, while Japan had an active prewar labour movement, legislative measures were enacted to stifle protest activities. In the early 1900s, under Article 17 of the 1900

Police Regulations, strikes and union organization were prohibited. Protests occurred, despite these measures; however, as the war approached, stronger countermeasures were introduced to quell any form of dissent. In 1940, the Japanese government implemented laws completely banning both labour unions and political parties.

Labour reform under SCAP was designed to encourage freedom of expression; thus, the US authorities initially encouraged protests and unionization. The Labour Union Law of December 1945 recognized unions and their right to strike, while the Labour Relations Adjustment Law of September 1946 contained stipulations regarding conciliation, mediation, and arbitration of labour disputes. The effects of these laws could be clearly seen in the ratio of unionized workers, which rose from 0 per cent in 1945 to 60 per cent of workers from 1948 to 1949. As of 1949, the largest number of unionized workers could be found in the local and national government sector with some 2,500,000 members. The government Railway Workers' Union had some 850,000 members. Other areas with a high degree of unionization were the electric power, coal mining, and textiles sectors. Membership in manufacturing, iron and steel, shipping, and others was also growing, though more gradually due to harsh economic conditions (Moran, 1949, 243). Of note is that the ratio was impressively high by global standards, given that the international average of unionized workers was 30 per cent (Gordon, 2003; Moran, 1949).

However, as membership in the Japan Communist Party (JCP) grew, SCAP's position evolved within the broader context of the Cold War. General MacArthur prohibited strikes on 31 January 1947, and directly intervened in 1948 and 1949 to prevent them (Moran, 1949, 245). The new stance taken by SCAP was reflected in legislation enacted during this period. Unlike the previous reforms that promoted self-expression, the Labour Relations Adjustment Law of July 1948 took the opposite position. Under this law, it became illegal for civil servants or employees of government enterprises, including the national railroads, to strike.

It is noteworthy that the move to restrict self-expression shocked labour representatives in the United States as well as the Russian and British representatives of the Allied forces (Moran, 1949, 247). The Red Purge that occurred in 1950 removed those with any affiliation to the JCP from their posts. Consequently, some thirty thousand employees who were said to be JCP members lost their jobs (Gordon, 2003). By 1955, the ratio of unionized workers dropped to only one third, and since the 1970s, the ratio has continued to decrease. The labour movement would reach a peak in the early postwar period. There are many examples of large-scale strikes in

Japan's early postwar labour history; however, perhaps those of Kawasaki Steel and Tōhō, a film, theatre, and film distribution company, are the most well known for their scale and intensity. Nishikawa Yatarō, the entrepreneur mentioned below is noted for his adeptness at negotiating with steel workers to bring an end to Japan's most disruptive strikes (Udagawa and Shōjima, 2011).

By around 2000 only around a quarter of all workers were members of unions (Flath, 2000, 83). Since then, fewer workers have become members of the large labour federations; however, there is a tendency for some to join 'enterprise unions', one of the three main features of 'Japanese-style management' (*nihon-teki keiei*) along with lifetime employment and seniority-based pay (Benson, 2008). Enterprise unions emerged in a context of the great political, economic, and social turmoil that resulted from the dire economic situation following Japan's defeat. According to Nimura Kazuo, one can make a clear distinction between the prewar labour movement and that of the early postwar labour movement in that the latter included both blue- and white-collar workers. Unlike labour movements in the West, which are industry- or occupation-based, Japan's unions are mainly employee- or enterprise-based (Nimura, 1998). Though the annual spring wage negotiations (*shuntō*) still occur, they are generally both cooperative and peaceful.

The trend towards harmonious relations between labour and management, a characteristic of the high-growth period, is to some extent tied to the existence of enterprise unionism. At the same time, however, there are economic aspects to consider. As the incomes of average Japanese workers increased and their jobs became more secure, many no longer felt a need to engage in disruptive and sometimes violent protests to gain concessions from employers. During the high-growth period under Prime Minister Ikeda Hayato, Japanese workers witnessed a doubling of their incomes, which allowed the average Japanese to join the middle class. Thanks to higher disposable incomes, both blue- and white-collar workers became consumers whose increase in purchasing power supported the nation's impressive double-digit GDP growth rates.

7.3 The decline and dissolution of the *zaibatsu* empires

Two phases of *zaibatsu* decline

As mentioned in Chapter 4, the *zaibatsu* began to undergo major organizational changes during the late Taishō and early Shōwa periods that would have a marked impact on their governance structures. The administration of the leading *zaibatsu* had shifted from family members to salaried or professional managers, thus weakening the direct and personal control that the former had once exercised over their operations. In addition to the decline of family-member-based management over the day-to-day operations as well as long-term planning, one can also identify two distinct phases of a more general decline of the *zaibatsu*, which was initially triggered by the economic circumstances of the Shōwa Depression of 1930.

The first phase got underway around 1937 with the start of the war with China, a development that intensified their need to raise capital in order to fulfil military orders. To acquire capital, the *zaibatsu* had to rely increasingly on outside sources as opposed to those within their empires. Over time, their financial stability would continue to weaken; moreover, the measures their organizations were forced to implement in response further eroded their ability to remain exclusively family owned. By the late 1930s, the leading *zaibatsu*'s self-financing capacities reached breaking point, which gave them little choice but to convert some of their operations to joint-stock companies through public stock offerings, a factor that largely contributed to the reduction in the ratio of family ownership (Morikawa, 1992, 233–237).

A second factor for their mounting financial and organizational fragility was reputational. Reports in the popular press stirred up public distrust in the *zaibatsu* empires and capitalism more generally. According to Morikawa, 'the formation of anti-*zaibatsu* opinion among the Japanese public in the early 1930s depended heavily on demagoguery, specifically the spreading of false rumors concerning dollar buying by the *zaibatsu*' (Morikawa, 1992, 224). These reports persuaded many that the sole pursuit of big business, particularly the leading *zaibatsu* was profit-making. As the War approached, the backlash against them intensified, becoming more menacing, a trend that the *zaibatsu* leaders attempted to assuage by founding charitable and community-focused associations and/or by making donations. In the case of the Mitsui *zaibatsu*, family members resigned from their posts and sold shares in some of their subsidiaries as a means of deflecting criticism, a move that further weakened family control.

The third factor for their decline can be traced to the rise of the so-called new *zaibatsu*, which became highly competitive during the War thanks to strong support from the military and bureaucracy. However, the *coup de grâce* for '*zaibatsu* capitalism' in Japan—whether leading or new—came during the occupation, when they were dismantled. In response, individuals, such as Mitsui's Edo Hideo, began trying to reorganize and regroup their former subsidiaries (Udagawa and Shōjima, 2011). Doing so, however, took time, and was hampered by legal obstacles as well as the general lack of coordination among the former *zaibatsu* affiliates.

The end of *zaibatsu* capitalism and the restructuring of big business

The US occupation authorities perceived the *zaibatsu* empires as bearing a significant responsibility for the war and as posing a threat to free and fair competition. To ensure that capitalism would flourish in a democratic postwar Japan, SCAP reformers decided to break up all forms of big business. In 1946, 40 per cent of their total stock was sold—some 167 million shares, valued at 8.1 billion yen. In December 1947, the Law for the Elimination of Excessive Concentration of Economic Power was introduced, followed by the Anti-Monopoly Law (*dokusen kinshihō*) in April of the same year. According to the former, some 325 companies were designated (*shitei kigyō*) for partition, representing some 65.9 per cent of all corporate capital in Japan. In 1947, Mitsui Bussan and Mitsubishi Shōji, Japan's two largest business entities were broken up, the former into 170 companies and the latter into 120 companies (Nakamura, 1984 24–25).

It is useful to consider the significance of the US authorities' decision in the wider context of Asian business development, since this can provide the reader with some insights into the role of 'big business' in latecomer economies more generally. In many emerging markets, large, diversified, and in most cases, family-owned conglomerates play a key role in economic development. Not only do these firms support growth; they often become early leaders of globalization in the countries where they were established (Colpan et al., 2010).

The Japanese views regarding SCAP's dissolution policy differed vastly from their American counterparts. The Japanese saw this US policy as highly detrimental to the nation's economic recovery and overly idealistic if not naïve. Though the average Japanese took a highly disdainful view of '*zaibatsu* capitalism' and their excessive control over the economy during the War, many were not unfavourable to the notion of having the state exercise a significant role in the economy—which it would do during the high-growth period—and were opposed to the notion of completely relying on market forces. Thus, proponents of a state-led approach to economic development could be found across a broad spectrum of the population from right-wing conservatives to left-wing labour leaders.

The founder of one of the large firms designated for dissolution was Matsushita Kōnosuke (1894–1989), one of Japan's most endeared entrepreneurs, who has even been referred to in the popular press as the 'god of management' (*keiei no kami*) (Udagawa and Shōjima, 2011; Kotter, 1997). His enterprise, Matsushita Denki (Matsushita Electric), later National and today, Panasonic, was designated a military contractor for its wartime activities, but also attracted attention for its distinctive M-shaped organization. This was the same modern business structure that was in use at many large US firms, including GE, but resembled—at least to US authorities—the holding company structure found at the *zaibatsu*. Holding companies were declared illegal in 1947, a legal constraint that would persist until 1997. The absence of such a structure serves as one of the reasons for the formation of firm networks or *keiretsu* in the 1960s (see Chapter 8). During the occupation, Matsushita, like other heads of large enterprises, was removed from his position as president of his own company.

In response to what he believed to be a highly detrimental decision both for the nation's economy and for the livelihoods of his employees, Matsushita visited SCAP headquarter regularly to try to convince the US authorities to allow him to resume his operations. He insisted that only by re-opening Japan's factories could the nation begin to achieve a full economic recovery. In a famous example in Japanese business history of worker loyalty, Matsushita's large workforce signed a petition which was submitted to the SCAP authorities requesting that the company be allowed to resume operations with Matsushita Kōnosuke as their president.

Though initially inflexible, SCAP's staunch 'punish Japan' stance in the first phase of the occupation would gradually mollify. SCAP had at the outset designated 325 subsidiaries for dissolution; however, by the time of the second, 'reverse course' phase of the occupation, only eighteen were dismantled. In fact, only the largest *zaibatsu* subsidiaries were broken up, namely Nippon Steel, Mitsui Mining, Mitsubishi Mining, Seika (Sumitomo) Mining, Toshiba, Hitachi Limited, Mitsubishi Heavy Industries, Oji Paper, and Dainippon Beer. Measures were introduced in 1949 and 1953 to relax the newly introduced anti-monopoly laws. While eighty-three factories had initially been designated, only seven were subject to seizure (Nakamura, 1981). Banks were excluded from the reorganization. As shown by the retraction of policies and reversal of decisions during this second or 'reverse course' phase of the occupation, measures to break up Japan's firms were significantly scaled back, and in practice, only leniently applied to business. This feature would have important implications for the speed of Japan's recovery and the re-emergence of the big business entities that would lead the economy in the postwar period.

As touched upon in the previous chapter, the structure of Japanese business had evolved during the war, thanks to the forced mergers introduced to rationalize (*tōseika*) the economy and enable industries that were important to the war effort to operate more efficiently. This transformation of business, which had started under the wartime regime, accelerated during the occupation thanks to the SCAP reforms. Through further break ups and subsequent mergers, the concentration ratios dropped in some cases to levels that were even lower than in the prewar period, a consequence that greatly benefited business development.

The resulting structure is what has been referred to in work on the steel industry as the 'competitive oligopoly system' (*kyōsōteki kasen seido*) whereby a specific sector is comprised of three to six competing firms, none of which possesses a controlling share of the market (Udagawa and Shōjima, 2011). This particular industrial structure fostered a healthy form of competition and encouraged innovation. Through this system, which took shape largely as a result of SCAP's reforms, postwar Japanese capitalism and entrepreneurship were unleashed. As shown in the following chapter, this new market structure would contribute to innovations that would support Japan's economic expansion during the high-growth period.

7.4 Entrepreneurship in the occupation period: the case of the steel industry

The effects of the purge on the steel industry

The steel industry provides a vivid illustration not only of the effects of SCAP policies on business during the occupation period but also of the nature of entrepreneurship. The first phase of the purge beginning in 1946 targeted militarists, ultranationalists, and others whom SCAP perceived as having been directly responsible for the war. The second purge in 1947 focused more on the economy and included the removal of the business leaders in large enterprises from their posts. More than two hundred thousand people were subject to the economic purge, including 2,210 executives of some 632 companies. Such individuals were prohibited from engaging in public service for a period of ten years, though some of those purged from the upper echelons of corporate management would return after the occupation ended in 1952. In most cases, however, the younger generation of leaders remained in their posts even after the US forces had departed.

These younger executives were initially the objects of scorn in the popular press, and were sometimes referred to as 'third-rate executives' (*santō jyūyaku*) due to their lack of experience. The removal of the wartime corporate top brass provided an extraordinary window for entrepreneurial opportunity as it allowed a younger generation of business executives to engage in more radical forms of innovation and risk-taking than their predecessors. One of the most famous examples of this new brand of entrepreneurship is that of the steel industry executive, Nishiyama Yatarō (1893–1966).

Nishiyama's idea, first put forward in the early days of the occupation, was to build new state-of-the-art integrated steel mills like those then found in the United States. He proposed this when the notion of even having a steel industry seemed unrealistic to many and preposterous to some, given Japan's lack of even basic resources such as food and energy. The founding of Japan's first integrated steel mill, a private-sector initiative, is a case that sharply contrasts with those one so commonly reads about in the same period, which give much of the credit for Japan's postwar economic success to adept government policymakers and bureaucrats. Nishiyama, whose large statue still stands in front of JFE Steel Corporation in Chiba prefecture, was a true maverick and prescient for recognizing the importance of Japan's steel industry to its economic development. He was a central figure in putting steel production on track to becoming a competitive, world-class industry in the postwar period (Yonekura, 1994, 189–211).

The state of the steel industry in the early postwar period

At the end of the war, steel, like so many other industries, was on the verge of collapse. Two of the fundamental causes for its particularly dire situation were the nation's heavy dependence on the imported raw materials necessary to produce steel and the lack of fuel (coal) to power its plants. Consequently, representatives of the government and steel industry alike felt that Japan should simply abandon steel production and focus instead on the development of light industries, due to their potential as a steady source of capital. Indeed, few saw as Tessa Morris Suzuki points out, the connection between a vibrant steel industry and the future development of key industries. Indeed, the production of steel would be used to support a wide range of sectors, including two that would be especially vital to Japan's international competitiveness: shipbuilding and automobile production (Morris Suzuki, 1994, 189–190).

Despite its critics, the rebuilding of the steel industry did gradually get underway as early as 1946, with the adoption of a new policy called the 'priority production system' (*keisha seisan hōshiki*). According to this system, the steel industry was able to benefit from the Economic Stabilization Board's subsidies for selected industries. In 1947, the Reconstruction Finance Bank began providing loans not only to steel producers but also to other industries such as coal mining, electric power, and fertilizers. This favourable situation, however, would abruptly end due to the introduction of the Dodge Line in 1948 which abolished the use of subsidies for industry, including steel. Though drastic, the Dodge Line had favourable long-term consequences by triggering what Yonekura Seiichiro called 'a paradigm shift for change', which enabled the steel industry to modernize and become one of the nation's most innovative industrial sectors (Yonekura, 1994, 194–197).

Kawasaki Steel's Nishiyama Yatarō and his innovations

Thanks to SCAP's decision to purge those serving in the executive echelons of major corporations, Nishiyama found himself at the helm of the newly created Kawasaki Steel. Nishiyama's interest in metal which would later lead him to devote himself to the task of promoting the growth of Japan's steel industry started from a young age, as his family owned a blacksmith shop. While a student at Tokyo Imperial University, he studied ferrous metallurgy, and after graduation he joined Kawasaki Shipyards. In 1933 he won the prestigious Hattori Prize for his work on the open-hearth steel-making method, and was sent to the United States and Europe to observe steel production, a trip that influenced his views on steel-making while also contributing to his prescience regarding the need for Japan to invest in the most sophisticated, yet costly, integrated steel factories as opposed to simply refurbishing existing ones.

As the head of Kawasaki Steel, Nishiyama would eventually succeed in realizing his vision of building an integrated steel works, whose layout would serve as the model for postwar steel mills not only for Japanese manufacturers but also for those in other parts of the world. The location of the factory along the coastline was one of Nishiyama's key innovations, one that went against conventional wisdom. Unlike the steel mills of England, the birthplace of the Industrial Revolution, which were built near the mines from which the raw materials used in the steel manufacturing process were extracted, the location of the Chiba works was situated along the coastline of Tokyo Bay. By doing so, Kawasaki Steel was closer to its markets in Tokyo and other large cities. In later years, the mill's coastal location would also facilitate the transport of steel to Japan's global markets as well as its imports of raw materials. Steel provides but one example of a 'seaside industry' (*rinkai sangyō*) and a business model that would spread in postwar Japan in tandem with the growth of Japanese export industries. The papermaking and chemical industries are two other important embodiments of this organizational model. Although Japanese bureaucrats and SCAP representatives strongly opposed Nishiyama's idea to invest in the steel industry due to its phenomenal costs, he nonetheless persevered. Kawasaki Steel became the first Japanese company to take out a large loan from the World Bank, though others would follow his example.

7.5 Conclusions

As shown in the case of the steel industry, even during the occupation, when business activities were limited due to controls and a lack of resources, evidence can be found of entrepreneurship. This trend was not exclusive to large corporations. Examples can also be seen in the form of new start-ups such as Sony, founded in 1946, Pioneer (incorporated in 1947), Amada (1948), Honda (1948), Wacoal (1949), and Sanyo Electric (1950). Though initially small and often struggling operations with few employees, these firms embodied a new brand of Japanese entrepreneurship that would define the high-growth period, covered in the following chapter.

These start-ups were aided rather than hindered by the severity of SCAP reforms for several reasons. First, because their activities were small in scale, they were unaffected by the labour unrest that was rife at such large companies as Kawasaki Steel or Tōhō. Second, they were not burdened financially by the need to transition their existing factories from military to civilian production at the end of the war. Third, one could argue that the sheer lack of material resources may have worked to their advantage by kindling the 'hungry spirits' needed for capitalistic development and entrepreneurship. The novel means by which the founders responded to the severe shortages of basic resources necessary to start and operate a business, ranging from capital and equipment to raw materials, tested their ingenuity and determination to find solutions such as cost-saving substitutes. Many of the early postwar start-ups were founded by engineers, whose innovations targeted niche markets, a strategy used to avoid direct competition with larger, more established firms. Moreover, some of firms such as Sony (Ibuka Masaru and Morita Akio) and Honda (Honda Sōichirō and Fujisawa Takeo) were partnerships, producing a favourable balance of technological expertise and clever marketing. These factors and others discussed in the next chapter helped start-ups to overcome their weaknesses and provided them with advantages as high-growth enterprises and early globalizers. The occupation period, even its 'punish Japan' phase, proved to be an especially propitious one for entrepreneurship and new enterprise formation.

Compared to other periods covered in this volume, the occupation was a short but nonetheless important period of Japanese business history. The reforms, many of which were already underway during the prewar period, advanced more quickly thanks to the SCAP reforms, thus preparing Japan to 'catch up and overtake' the West in some key sectors. Thanks to the redeployment and streamlining of the wartime institutions for a peaceful postwar context, Japanese business was ready to embark on a new era of capitalistic development. Though much coordination on the part of bureaucrats would be necessary to put in place the optimal environment for business, one can find examples as seen in the case of the steel industry where private entrepreneurship played—not an ancillary—but an essential role in Japan's impressive postwar ascent.

8
The 'Japanese Miracle'

In 1979, Ezra F. Vogel, a sociologist and professor at Harvard University, who was considered at that time to be one of the foremost specialists of East Asia, published a book entitled *Japan as Number One: Lessons for America* (Vogel, 1979). While the United States was facing economic decline in the 1970s, characterized by a trade deficit, high inflation, and de-industrialization, Japan was a booming economic power. It had not only become the world's second largest economy in 1968; it was also a major exporter (2.4 per cent of world exports in 1955 and 7.1 per cent in 1980) (Miwa and Hara, 2007, 40) and one of the largest holders of foreign-exchange reserves at the end of Bretton Woods in 1971. Such success attracted the attention of other American scholars. In his book Vogel examined how Japan was different from the West, with its group culture, modern corporations, efficient bureaucracy, and self-disciplined workers. His book became a best-seller both in the United States and Japan. It was followed by quite a few others in the early 1980s that emphasized similar, culture-focused explanations, namely how Japanese firms were becoming more competitive because they were different from Western ones (Johnson, 1982; Abegglen and Stalk, 1973).

The 'Japanese Miracle' did not result from Japan's cultural differences but essentially from the initiatives of entrepreneurs and firms that were able to catch-up technologically with the United States in the 1950s and the 1960s and to innovate in terms of product development and production technology. The formation and growth of competitive companies in world markets were, however, not merely the outcome of entrepreneurship. The government also played a key role through the implementation of a broad range of legislative measures and institutions that supported companies in their efforts to develop their organizational capabilities, improve their technological level, and strengthen their international competitiveness. The importance of the state, particularly the Ministry of International Trade and Industry (MITI), was strongly emphasized by Chalmers Johnson (1982). Other scholars, however, have demonstrated that the impact of industrial policy was limited to the catch-up phase and depended largely on the determination of large private companies to respond the guidance of the bureaucracy and to changes in the market (Okimoto, 1989; Callon, 1995).

Japanese Capitalism and Entrepreneurship. Pierre-Yves Donzé and Julia S. Yongue, Oxford University Press.
© Pierre-Yves Donzé and Julia S. Yongue (2024). DOI: 10.1093/oso/9780192887474.003.0009

In terms of its timing, most scholars agree that the high-growth period or 'Japanese Miracle' began in the early aftermath of World War II and ended with the first oil shock in 1973. Some economic historians, however, have demonstrated that although GDP grew again after the oil shocks, the rate was lower than in the 1950s–1960s but higher than in most Western countries. Given this relative decline, some mainly Japanese specialists refer to a stable growth period, ending around 1990. As this book is a general synthesis addressed to a global audience, the high and stable growth years are discussed from two perspectives: the formation of competitive firms and the role of industrial policy (Chapter 8) and the changes in society and business that were caused by the rise of a consuming middle class (Chapter 9).

Hence, this chapter tackles the role played by these actors and discusses in particular the different forms of business activity that emerged during this period. Section 8.1 introduces the horizontal diversified *keiretsu* (*kigyō shūdan*) that dominated the Japanese economy during the high-growth era. Section 8.2 presents the evolution of industrial policy, and section 8.3 evaluates the impact of the liberalization of trade and capital on business. It also shows how vertical manufacturing networks, or vertical *keiretsu*, were formed, by taking Toyota as an example. Finally, section 8.4 looks at the development of outward FDI.

8.1 *Keiretsu* and the birth of the Japanese Business System

The Japanese economy experienced impressive development between the end of Korean War (1953) and 1985, characterized by high-growth rates until the first oil shock (1973). Of all the sectors of the economy, the manufacturing industry experienced the most dramatic expansion. The index of the total production of this sector went from 7 in 1955 to 100 in 1985 (Miwa and Hara, 2007, 13). This development was based first on the domestic market. Urbanization and population growth led to new needs fulfilled by private enterprises (see Chapter 9). Second, foreign markets also supported industrial growth. Exports were booming from the mid-1960s, and the balance of trade became slightly positive in 1965 and 1966, a rather impressive feature since the opening of the country had occurred only one century earlier. It was positive in 1969–1972, then negative due to the oil shock, but largely positive again after 1976 (Foreign trade statistics, 2020). This demonstrates the growing competitiveness of Japanese companies in world markets.

The industrial structure also experienced a major change during the high-growth period. The developing sectors of the manufacturing industry in terms of number of employees were the machinery industry, including cars and electric appliances (20.9 per cent of workforce in manufacturing in 1950 and 34.3 per cent in 1980) and metalworking (11.7 per cent and 13.2 per cent). Textiles declined (23.5 per cent and 11.6 per cent), while other sectors like chemicals, oil, and food remained stable (Miwa and Hara, 2007, 12). The automobile industry, whose production increased tenfold between 1960 and 1980, became one of the major sectors of the economy. It directly employed 8.6 per cent of the total workforce in manufacturing in 1980 and had indirect effects on a broad range of sectors through its suppliers (mechanical components, glass, steel, tyres, etc.) and related services (insurance, leasing, trading, etc.). The development of most Japanese firms during the high and stable growth periods occurred within a specific organizational framework: *keiretsu* or business groups (*kigyo shudan*). *Keiretsu* are business groups without any strong centralized control, although the informal meetings of the presidents of the main member firms were a way to coordinate the activities at the level of the group. They formed in response to SCAP's dissolution of *zaibatsu*, the banning of holding companies, and the strict limitations on shareholding by companies, which made it difficult to build large, highly concentrated groups after the war. However, to sustain the high economic growth witnessed during this period required companies to organize themselves in order to stabilize their resources (especially labour and capital). In this sense, Japan became a typical example of a coordinated-market economy, like Germany, as opposed to a form of liberal-market economy that characterizes the United States and the United Kingdom, for example (Hall and Soskice, 2001). Six major business groups formed in the early 1950s: three came from former *zaibatsu* Mitsubishi, Mitsui, and Sumitomo, and three others were organized around Fuji Bank, Sanwa Bank, and Dai-Ichi Bank. They share three main features (Okumura, 1993).

First, firms within a *keiretsu* were linked to each other through a dense network of cross-shareholding. The anti-monopoly law limited the possession of shares in any one company by banks to 10 per cent until 1977, so that direct control of a firm was not possible. Hence companies in a *keiretsu* purchased each other's minority stakes. The shares owned by other members of the *keiretsu* is called 'stable shareholding' (*antei kabunushi*). This developed during the 1960s and 1970s, making *keiretsu* very stable organizations, and enabling the firms within to avoid hostile takeovers—particularly by foreign companies after the liberalization of FDI in the 1970s (see below, pp. 148–156).

(See the section on the changes in corporate governance during the Abe administration which brought about the system's weakening in Chapter 12).

The second characteristic was the function fulfilled by the main bank of the *keiretsu*. It was not only a minority shareholder in nearly all the companies in the group, but also a major supplier of capital through long-term loans. Banks did not take control of the firms they financed. They usually did not send bankers to join the board of directors. The objective was instead to ensure long-term growth through credit. This enabled the funding of ambitious or risky industrial projects which took time to generate profits. Sony, for example, was supported by Mitsui Bank, while Honda was backed by Mitsubishi Bank. However, in cases where a manufacturer ran into managerial or financial difficulties, the main bank intervened. It dispatched managers to reorganize the company, solve problems, and upon completion of their duties, return to the bank.

A famous example is the case of the automobile manufacturer Toyo Industries (*Tōyō kōgyō*, today Mazda). In the early 1970s, it had low productivity and produced engines with high fuel consumption. It was severely hit by the recession after the oil shock, as customers became more sensitive to petrol prices. The management of the firm was unable to take effective actions to overcome the crisis. Consequently, in 1976, five managers of Sumitomo Bank, the main bank of Toyo Industries, were dispatched to save the firm. They took charge of the general management, finance, marketing, and organization of workshops. The following year, the engineer who took charge of the rationalization of the production system, Yamazaki Yoshiki (1914–2014), was promoted to company president, the first appointment outside the founding Matsuda family. He launched new cars, negotiated with the labour unions and dealerships, and was able to return the company to profitability. As for the bankers, they returned to their positions at the main branch of the bank. This case, which is far from unique, clearly illustrates a major function the main banks fulfilled within the *keiretsu* (Miyamoto et al., 2014, 204–208).

Third, *keiretsu* are present in a broad range of industries and services. They are comprised of banks, securities companies, insurance companies, general trading companies (which take charge of imports and exports for the group's manufacturing firms), and several industrial and service corporations in all the major industries, including construction, chemicals, steel-making, and transportation. The companies that dominated the Japanese economy fiercely competed against each other. For example, Toshiba (Mitsui), Mitsubishi Electric (Mitsubishi), NEC (Sumitomo), Oki Electric (Fuyo), Sharp (Sanwa), and Fujitsu (Daiichi Kangin) were rivals in the electronics industry, as were Kirin (Mitsubishi), Sapporo (Fuyo), and Suntory (Daiwa) in the beer industry (Okumura, 1993, 202–203).

Beside this general form of business group, also called horizontal or financial *keiretsu*, two other types of inter-firm networks formed in the postwar years: vertical manufacturing (such as Toyota and its suppliers) and distribution (retail networks such as Matsushita and Shiseido) (Lincoln and Shimotani, 2009, 3, Shimotani, 1995 and 2012). The integration of suppliers or retailers offered notable advantages, one being cost reduction. Companies in the same group were able to share scarce resources to facilitate cost savings. The sharing of information along with various forms of risk were also advantages of this form of organization. The latter was important in the early postwar period since smaller subsidiaries were especially vulnerable to takeover by non-related companies. Group formation also helped to improve stability and facilitate long-term corporate planning, a feature often associated with Japan's success in the high-growth period. Business groups provided one engine for economic growth and offered an example of cooperation reinforced through inter-firm ties, combined with a distinctive form of coordinated competition, what is referred to as '*communitarian capitalism*' in later chapters.

Moreover, the stability of the Japanese business system was strengthened by a highly regulated labour market whose objective was to provide a stable workforce to enterprises. The three characteristics of the employment system during this period were lifetime employment, seniority-based pay, and enterprise unions. Companies recruited employees upon their competition of high school or university, offered them in-house or on-the-job training, and kept them until their retirement. The middle-class white-collar 'salaryman' became an iconic figure of Japanese corporate culture and society (Dasgupta, 2017). During the high-growth years, most Japanese considered themselves as belonging to this class (Sudo, 2019). One must, however, avoid idealizing the stability of the Japanese employment system or perceiving it as the general norm. Lifetime employment positions represented only a minority of all jobs and excluded workers in agriculture and SMEs as well as workers engaged by large companies under specified contracts. Temporary workers represented more than 40 per cent of Toyota Motor Company's workforce during the 1960s (Johnson, 1982, 12).

The *keiretsu* offered private companies a stable environment and hence contributed to their development until the end of the bubble economy period. Economic growth was the outcome of this business system. However, *keiretsu* were not closed organizations. Cross-shareholding went beyond the boundaries of the *keiretsu*, and most companies also received long-term loans from financial institutions which were not part of their *keiretsu*. *Keiretsu* were such flexible and informal organizations that some economists have even argued that they never existed and were the pure invention of Marxist scholars (Miwa and Ramseyer, 2006). This is, however, an extreme view, considering management practices like internal long-term transactions or rescues made by main banks in cases of financial difficulties.

Moreover, all firms were not strictly included in *keiretsu*. Some of them developed independently by obtaining capital from financial markets and building their own network of suppliers and distributors. This was particularly the case for what economist Nakamura Hideichirō called the leading medium-sized enterprises, whose specificities were product specialization, mass production, and large investments in equipment. This enabled them to strengthen their core competitiveness and expand internationally while remaining independent. Examples include the producer of components for bicycles Shimano; ophthalmic equipment company Nidek; confectionery maker Ezaki Glico; and automotive parts producer Imasen. All experienced fast development during the high-growth years (Ferguson, 2008). Finally, SMEs were not directly part of any business group but were in some cases affiliated. During the years 1955–1985, they were essentially in a relationship of dependency vis-à-vis large companies, which outsourced some activities in periods of growing demand. Japanese economists talk about a dual structure of the economy, whereby large companies can compete on world markets because they are well endowed with capital, skilled labour, and technology, while SMEs cannot because they are globally uncompetitive, focused on the domestic market, and lacking in essential resources like capital and technology (Tsuchiya and Mori, 1989).

8.2 Industrial policy and the acquisition of foreign technology

The development of competitive companies in Japan after World War II was not the mere result of the formation of a distinctive business system that enabled long-term growth in a stable environment. Japan lagged behind the United States and Western Europe in terms of industrial technology. The acquisition of foreign knowledge in sectors like chemicals, machinery, and electronics was a necessity. However, as during the first three decades of Meiji period, the postwar Japanese government wanted to avoid inward FDI and domination of the domestic economy by Western multinationals (see Chapter 3). Foreign technology without foreign capital was the objective of the state until the 1970s.

The government introduced two major laws that made it possible to control the activities of foreign firms in Japan (Sawai and Tanimoto, 2016, 316–317). The first was the Foreign Exchange and Foreign Trade Control Law, passed in 1949. It regulated the use of foreign currencies in Japan and was hence a major instrument to control the activities of foreign multinationals in the country. They were required to obtain approval from the Ministry of Finance to procure yen to invest in Japan or to receive foreign exchange in order to repatriate their profits to their home country. One example is the Swiss company Nestlé, which remained in Japan during the war, made profits by selling condensed milk during the 1950s, but was not allowed to exchange its yen against Swiss francs to send these profits back to the headquarters (Donzé, 2020). Similarly, Japanese companies that wanted to invest in the United States also had to obtain approval from the Ministry of Finance in order to be allocated the US dollars necessary to launch their businesses overseas. Foreign exchange was a scarce resource after the war, and the government wanted to use it to import the technologies and raw materials required for industrial development.

The second was the Foreign Investment Law, adopted in 1950. It controlled the investments by foreign enterprises in Japan, and decided whether to validate technical cooperation agreements. Each investment proposed by a foreign company was investigated by the Ministry of International Trade and Industry (MITI), set up in 1949 as the successor of the MCI. To be approved, the proposed investments had to be considered beneficial to the development of the Japanese economy. However, representatives of private companies intervened through MITI working committees and by lobbying to stop investments by companies that would challenge their position in the domestic market (Mason, 1992). For example, Coca-Cola Company, which arrived with the first GIs stationed in Japan in 1945, had to wait until 1960 to establish its business operation in the country. It had to negotiate with the government to be allocated US dollars to import beverages, then ingredients to produce them domestically. Moreover, it had to face opposition from the beer companies Asahi, Kirin, and Sapporo, which wanted to develop their own soft drinks but feared competition from Coca-Cola. In 1959, the American multinational decided to cooperate with Mitsubishi Heavy Industries to manufacture bottling machines, and Kirin—a member of Mitsubishi *keiretsu*—to distribute Coke in the Kansai area. This collaboration with one of the most powerful groups in Japanese economy has allowed Coca-Cola to carry out full operations freely since 1960 (Mason, 1992, 161–173).

Hence, during the 1950s and 1960s, signing a technical cooperation agreement was the most common way for Japanese firms to acquire foreign technology. These contracts included various clauses, mostly regarding the use of patents, together with technical training, against fixed fees or royalties for a determined time. The total number of contracts grew quickly, from seventy-six in 1950, to 588 in 1960, and 1,768 in 1970. At the same time, the share of long-term contracts (more than one year) also increased, rising from 45.5 per cent in 1950 to 75.2 per cent in 1970 (Nakamura, 1979). While Japanese firms were initially looking for specific knowledge, their development in the 1960s made it possible for them to enter into more long-term relationships with foreign partners.

The chemical and machinery industries were the main sectors of this technology transfer because they were precisely the ones in which the gap between Japan and the United States was the greatest. For all of the 1950–1975 period, the largest providers of long-term contracts were the United States (54.4 per cent), Germany (12.1 per cent), the United Kingdom (8.1 per cent), France (6.5 per cent), and Switzerland (5.8 per cent) (Nakamura, 1979). In terms of value, the technology balance of payments clearly illustrates the growing importance of these contracts over time. Imports of technology grew slowly until the mid-1960s (from 2.6 million US dollars in 1950 to 166 million in 1965), then accelerated, reaching 433 million in 1975, and exceeded 1 billion in 1978. Industrial development did not put an end to the importance of technology and instead only strengthened it. At the same time, the technological development of Japanese firms made it possible for them to export their own technology. Exports amounted to only 59 million in 1970 but accelerated during the 1970s reaching 342 million in 1979.

Despite the strong control of the government, foreign firms were not excluded from Japan. Their number was, however, very limited. In 1975, the share of companies with foreign capital in gross national sales was only 1.9 per cent for all the manufacturing industries. It was particularly low in traditional industries like food (0.5 per cent) but showed a larger presence than the average in electric machinery (3.2 per cent), chemicals (6 per cent), rubber (24.8 per cent) and oil (41.7 per cent) (Nakamura, 1979, 136). Foreign firms thus had a limited role, but were important for technological catch-up in some specific industries.

The chemical industry is a case in point. Japan lagged behind the United States and needed American technology to develop, in particular for the production of nylon, other synthetic fibres (e.g. polyester), and plastic materials like polypropylene. Other products and activities also included oil refining, fertilizers, and pharmaceuticals. The Japanese textile industry had developed the production of rayon and artificial fibres during the interwar years, but it was necessary to shift to a new generation of materials after the war, especially to respond to the demand for cheaper and more resistant fibres for the manufacturing of fishing nets and school uniforms, which was booming in the early 1950s (Nakaoka et al., 2001, 313). American companies invested massively in the Japanese chemical industry after 1950. Their presence was much welcomed by the Japanese government and entrepreneurs because they supported the growth of a new industry and had a positive and deep impact on many other sectors. Table 8.1 shows that a total of 124 Japanese companies in the chemical industry had American capital in 1977. FDI started slowly, with ten companies in the 1950s, most of them with at least 50 per cent of Japanese capital, and expanded rapidly in the following decades.

FDI in these 124 companies was carried out by a total of sixty-nine American companies, including all the dominant firms of this industry. The five giants Dow Chemicals, DuPont, Union Carbide, Monsanto, and Procter & Gamble represented 54 per cent of the total American capital invested in the Japanese chemical industry.

The example of DuPont illustrates well the broad range of businesses transferred to Japan. It started its investment in Japan in 1960, with the foundation of two joint ventures in which it held half of the capital: a company to manufacture plastics and rubber, co-founded with Showa Denko (a member of Fuji Bank *keiretsu*), and another to produce polyethylene, co-founded with Mitsui Sekiyu Kagaku under the name Mitsui Polychemicals. Three years later, in 1963, it set up two new joint ventures, again with 50 per cent of capital: one to produce fibreglass with Mitsui Sekiyu Kagaku, and a second to make polyurethane with Toray, a manufacturer of synthetic fibre and an affiliate of Mitsui *keiretsu*. DuPont pursued its expansion with the Mitsui group and took stakes in the three subsidiaries of Mitsui Polychemicals between 1970 and 1972. Finally, in 1972, it opened a fully owned subsidiary, DuPont Japan, to import and sell its goods in the Japanese market.

Table 8.1 Japanese chemical companies with American capital, 1950–1977

	1950–1959	1960–1969	1970–1977	Total
Joint-ventures, <50% capital US	5	21	14	40
Joint-ventures, 50% capital US	3	26	28	57
Joint-ventures, >50% capital US	1	5	6	12
Subsidiaries, 100% capital US	1	5	9	15
Total	10	57	57	124

Source: Nakamura (1979), 152–156

Despite the impressive presence of firms with American capital in the chemical industry, they were largely controlled by Japanese, although a change can be observed after 1970. For the entire 1950–1977 period, the overwhelming majority of companies were joint ventures with a minority foreign stake (32.5 per cent) or equally owned (46 per cent). There were only fifteen fully owned subsidiaries, essentially focused on import and distribution, rather than production, like Cyanamide Japan (1950), Monsanto Japan (1969), DuPont Japan (1973), Union Carbide Japan (1974), and Penwalt Japan (1974).

The Japanese partners of these joint ventures were generally the large chemical firms that wanted to improve their technological level and diversify into new products. Most of them were members of a *keiretsu*. For example, Mitsubishi co-founded companies with Monsanto (1951 and 1971), Sun Chemicals (1962), Union Carbide (1963), Polymer (1966), Cardorundeem (1972), Upjohn Co (1972), and Kalver Co (1974). The Mitsui group was affiliated with DuPont, as mentioned above, but also with Continental Carbon (1960), Catalysts Chemicals (1966), Texaco (1967), Continental Oil (1968), Liquid Carbonic (1971), and Crown Zellesbach International (1971). As for Sumitomo, it created joint ventures with Upjohn Co (1959), Upjohn States Rubber (1963), Hooker Chemicals (1965), Travenol Laboratories (1969), Atlantic Richfield (1972), Carborundum (1972), and Allied Chemicals (1975). The *keiretsu* were major partners of American chemical firms for various reasons. First, they had chemical firms which needed technological upgrading in their own group and had a real interest in cooperation. Second, they were able to invest capital in these new businesses, through their banks, insurance companies, and other companies. Third, they could introduce firms from their network to assist the new ventures with various issues such as trading and distribution.

Electronics is another major industrial sector that developed in the 1950s and 1960s through technology agreements and foreign capital. After World War II, the United States had the uncontested lead in this emerging industry. Western Electric (WE) and Texas Instruments (TI) developed transistors in the early 1950s, and the latter realized an integrated circuit (IC) in 1958. This new technology, which caught the attention of Japanese firms, again sheds light on the major role played by the government in making this knowledge available. In the early 1950s, Tokyo Tsūshin Kōgyō (renamed Sony in 1958), wanted to buy WE's patent to manufacture transistors in Japan but had to face the opposition from MITI whose approval was necessary to get the US dollars necessary to purchase the technology. MITI bureaucrats did not believe in the transistor's potential as a major technology, and Sony was only a small company at that time (see Box 8.1). After a long negotiation, Sony finally received approval in 1953, and was hence able to market its first hit in 1955: a portable radio (Morita, 1986). Matsushita Electric (renamed Panasonic in 2008) also acquired this technology through licencing agreements with the Dutch multinational Philips, and NEC did the same with the American company Fairchild (Mason, 1992, 180).

> **Box 8.1 A disruptive innovator: Sony**
>
> In 1979, Sony released the world's first portable cassette player equipped with stereo headphones: the Walkman. About fifteen years after the invention of the cassette tape by the Dutch multinational Philips, it became possible not only for the listener to bring music outside the home, but to enjoy it privately without disturbing others. This new product soon became a mega-hit around the world. Sony sold more than one hundred million Walkman in the 1980s and 1990s, an iconic good of those decades that could also be associated with the health craze, particularly the growing popularity of jogging. Sony updated this product with the launch of the world's first portable CD player (1984) and mini-disc recorder (1992), followed by various digital versions after 2000.
>
> The Walkman is a typical example of the disruptive innovation as conceptualized by Harvard Business School professor Clayton M. Christensen; that is, an innovation which creates a new market based on a new application of an existing technology. The cassette tape existed well before the launch of the Walkman but it was used on home devices or on portable players but without noise privacy. However, the Walkman changed the way consumers used cassette tapes and listened to music. It fuelled a high demand for cassettes tapes around the world, and contributed to their overtaking the sales of vinyl discs.
>
> The Walkman was, however, not Sony's first disruptive innovation. This company had been founded under the name Tokyo Tsūshin Kōgyō in 1946 by two engineers, Ibuka Masaru (1908–1997) and Morita Akio (1921–1999). It was a small company that focused first on the development of tape recorders. They were large pieces of equipment sold essentially to the government and schools. In 1952, while he was in the United States to investigate the possibilities of selling its tape recorders, Ibuka heard about transistors developed by Bell Laboratories. After returning to Japan, he was able, after hard negotiations with the MITI, to acquire the patent for the transistor from Western Electric (co-owner of Bell Laboratories). The objective was to develop a first disruptive product: a portable transistor radio. At that time, the dominant players in the Japanese electrical appliance industry, Matsushita, Sharp,
>
> *(continued)*

> **Box 8.1 Continued**
>
> and Toshiba, had already been producing radios for several decades. These radios were large devices, targeted at home use, and largely considered mature products. Hence, when these firms looked for transistor technology, it was not to change the nature of the radio, but to develop a new range of high-tech products such as televisions. Tokyo Tsūshin Kōgyō launched its first transistor radio (1955) and pocket-size radio (1957) based on a new concept: one radio per person, instead of one radio per home as its competitors did. This became the company's first iconic product, which was renamed in 1958 after the brand-name used for its radios: Sony. The pocket-size radio achieved a success beyond the domestic market and provided the opportunity to expand internationally. Sony Corporation of America was opened in 1960.
>
> Innovation in consumer electronics continued in the following decades, with a portable transistor TV (1960), color TV (1968), video-cassette recorder, Betamax (1975), the world's first CD player (1982), a video-camera (1984), the video-game PlayStation (1994), the personal computer, VAIO (1996), and a personal robot, Aibo (1999). It became one of the world's leading companies in this industry. According to Fortune's Global 500 ranking, Sony was thirtieth in the ranking of the largest firms in the world in 2000. Sony also diversified into music production in cooperation with the American company CBS (1970), finance with the co-foundation of Sony Prudential Life Insurance (1980), movie production with the takeover of Columbia Pictures (1989), banking (2001), and telecommunication (2001). The move from consumer electronics to services became important at the beginning of the twenty-first century, and is symbolic of the loss in competitiveness of the Japanese electronics industry (see Chapter 12) (Kikkawa, 2019, 162–182; Sony, 2020).

TI was against licensing out its technology. Hence, it tried to invest in Japan to manufacture and sell its semiconductors and electronic components (Mason, 1992, 174–197). The company opened subsidiaries in Europe in 1957–1960 and wanted to extend its network of factories in Asia. Fairchild founded one in Singapore in 1960, and was quite interested in entering the Japanese market, considering the development of several electrical appliances companies that offered an opportunity to expand its business. A first negotiation with Tokyo Tsūshin Kōgyō in 1959 did not yield any results, and, in 1963, TI applied for permission to open a fully owned subsidiary in Japan. MITI and several private companies which were developing their own transistors and IC chips at the time, notably Hitachi, NEC, Mitsubishi Electric, and Toshiba, firmly opposed TI's plan. However, MITI had to change its perspective from opposing to promoting the export of electronics to the United States: many Japanese companies used IC produced with TI technology, which was unpatented in Japan to manufacture goods that were sold in America, for example Sony pocket radios (1966) and Sharp calculators (1967). An agreement was hence necessary with TI. In 1966, MITI proposed the foundation of an equally owned joint venture with a Japanese manufacturer. After long negotiations, TI agreed to co-found a joint venture with Sony in 1968, which would be fully acquired after three years of operation. In the meanwhile, the American company also agreed to license its patents related to IC technology to all major Japanese companies.

Finally, IBM followed a path similar to TI. The company had been present in Japan during the interwar years through a subsidiary founded in 1937 under the name Watson Tabulating Machines (Mason, 1992, 118–130). It was expropriated after the start of Pacific War, and a subsidiary of Toshiba took over IBM's patents. The American parent company recovered its ownership after the war and founded IBM Japan in 1949. However, its activities were restricted by the legal framework established in 1949–1950. For example, in 1956, MITI refused to allow IBM Japan to import technology from the United States to manufacture computers. The American multinational would need to open a joint venture with a local partner, but it refused to do so. A compromise was found in 1960: IBM was allowed to import technology and develop its Japanese subsidiary, but in return it had to provide licenses for using its patents to the main Japanese electronics companies, Fujitsu, Hitachi, NEC, and Toshiba. This example illustrates an important feature of capitalism during the high-growth period, which relied on government coordination to build winning industries, as opposed to one or two leading firms. Thanks to these measures, rival firms were awarded equal access to the same leading technologies, a factor leading to synergies that benefited the development of this new sector.

From a Japanese perspective, IBM was, however, not the only provider of computer technology. The technical agreements with General Electric and Radio Corporation of America (RCA) enabled Hitachi to manufacture its first computer in 1957 and establish itself as a leading company in this industry in the 1960s. Hitachi became the largest maker in the Japanese market and directly challenged IBM by launching a copy of the IBM computer—but sold more cheaply—in 1974.

Although industrial policy and technology transfer supported the foundations of important industries such as chemicals and electronics, all the major sectors of the Japanese manufacturing industries did not develop on this basis. In some cases, like in automobiles, innovation related to production technology and intense competition nurtured the growth of domestic firms. While the automobile industry benefited from the protection of the domestic market until the 1960s, companies did not follow the plans of the government regarding the merger of manufacturers and product development. Toyota and Nissan kept their dominant position after the war but several new companies entered this industry, particularly as a strategy to expand beyond the production of motorbikes and scooters to automobiles. Suzuki (1955), Subaru (1958), Mazda (1960), and Honda (1962) joined the automobile industry and remained car producers. The development of automobiles relied on R&D and on the implementation of a mass-production system that enabled these firms to offer good quality cars at an affordable price. Toyota implemented the so-called 'just-in-time' production system characterized by the drastic reduction of stocks and the outsourcing of components from independent suppliers. The production of automobiles, including trucks and buses, went from 481,600 in 1960 to 5.3 million in 1970, and 11 million in 1980. The share of exports also grew steadily from 8.1 per cent in 1960 to 20.5 per cent in 1970, and 54 per cent in 1980. Japan overtook the United States as the world's largest car producer in the 1970s (Miwa and Hara, 2007, 162–163).

8.3 A gradual liberalization of trade and capital

The protectionist policy adopted in 1949–1950 did not aim to close the country in the long term, but to offer protection to Japanese companies during their phase of technological and organizational catch-up. The objective was to nurture competitive firms in order to allow them to expand into foreign markets. Becoming a strong exporter was the strategic goal of Japanese bureaucrats, designed to compensate for the country's reliance on imports of raw materials, energy, and food supplies. In 1955, Japan's share of world exports dropped to 2.4 per cent compared to 5.3 per cent in 1938 (Komiya and Itoh, 1988, 174). Protectionism was hence considered necessary in the 1950s.

In 1955, Japan became a member of GATT, yet several major economies, namely France, the United Kingdom, and India, refused to grant it most favoured nation status in their bilateral trade relations. These countries were followed in the early 1960s by several former British and French colonies. The most important market to Japanese companies was also the one with the easiest access and the largest in the world: the United States. By becoming a member of GATT, however, Japan had to give up import quotas, but replaced them with high tariffs. European restrictions were gradually relaxed after the

Japanese government announced its plan in January 1961 to liberalize trade. The number of items with import restrictions decreased from 1,443 in 1960 to 161 in 1970 and seventy-eight in 1980 (Komiya and Itoh, 1988, 192). At the same time, Japanese exports experienced fast development and the balance of payments became positive.

The gradual liberalization of trade in the 1960s also included technology transfer contracts, with a flexible application of the Foreign Exchange and Foreign Trade Control Law. Until 1960, a contract was accepted only if it had a positive impact on the Japanese economy, but afterwards it was accepted if it had no negative impact. This enabled Japanese firms to import foreign technology more easily. Moreover, in 1968, an automatic approval was decided for contracts with annual royalties below 50,000 US dollars, except in a few sensitive sectors (e.g. aeronautics, nuclear power, defence) (Ozawa, 1974, 22).

Pressures from international organizations (GATT, IMF, OECD), foreign governments, and domestic corporations to liberalize inward FDI grew in the mid-1960s. The Japanese authorities responded by liberalizing this activity slowly. In 1967, the government drew up a list of industries in which foreign investments would be automatically approved. They were, however, very specific sectors in which foreign firms were fundamentally weak or absent, such as soy sauce or geta sandals (Mason, 1992, 202). This partial-opening policy was pursued through various administrative measures but the real liberalization started in the 1970s. In 1971, the Japanese government declared it would approve all inward FDI with up to 50 per cent of foreign ownership, except in seven sensitive industries. Two years later, the limit for automatic approval was extended to 100 per cent foreign ownership except in twenty-two industries, then to five industries including mining, oil, and agriculture in 1976. The government completely abolished the Foreign Investment Law in 1980. However, this opening was accompanied by countermeasures adopted to protect Japanese firms from foreign hostile takeovers. In 1966, the revision of the Commercial Code made it possible for Japanese companies to issue new shares to third parties of their choice (Mason, 1992, 205). This institutional instrument was used by firms within the *keiretsu* to increase cross-shareholding and to strengthen links between them, so that it became difficult for foreign firms to acquire a controlling interest. Between 1965 and 1981, the percentage of capital in a *keiretsu* owned by other firms in the *keiretsu* (i.e. level of cross-shareholding) went from 23.7 per cent to 36.9 per cent for Mitsubishi, 14.3 per cent to 23.1 per cent for Mitsui, and 28 per cent to 36.6 per cent for Sumitomo (Okumura, 1993, 141). Some large manufacturing companies like Matsushita Electric, Toshiba, and Toyota also organized their operations to protect them from capital liberalization. They exchanged

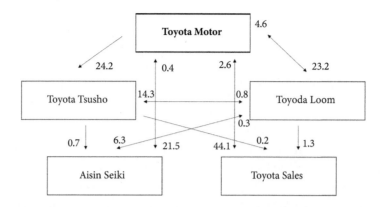

Figure 8.1 Toyota *keiretsu*, simplified organization and cross-shareholding structure, 1981
Source: Drafted by the authors based on Kitahara (1983), p. 94

shares with their suppliers and related companies, giving way to a specific kind of business organization, called vertical *keiretsu*.

For example, Toyota Motor not only strengthened its integration within Mitsui *keiretsu*, but built its own group. Between 1956 and 1981, the proportion of capital owned by the top ten shareholders grew from 21.4 per cent to 36.5 percent. In 1981, the top twenty largest shareholders had more than 50 per cent of Toyota Motor's capital. They included Mitsui Bank and related companies, but also firms affiliated to the car manufacturer, like its sales company (Toyota Sales) and former parent company (Toyoda Loom). Moreover, the core of the vertical *keiretsu* built around Toyota also included a component supplier company (Aisin Seiki) and a trading company (Toyota Tsūshō). It thus became virtually impossible for a foreign competitor to carry out any hostile takeover of any company related to Toyota (see Figure 8.1) (Kitahara, 1983).

8.4 Investing abroad

The period between the end of Korean War and the bubble economy was also one during which Japanese companies started to invest in foreign countries and to open subsidiaries abroad. Export was not the only way to expand internationally. The outward stock of Japanese FDI amounted to 1.5 billion US dollars in 1967. This was only 0.9 per cent of Japanese GDP that year. It then grew to 19.6 billion in 1980 (1.9 per cent) (Dunning and Lundan, 2008, 24). Scholars of international business distinguish between 'market-seeking' and 'resource-seeking' strategies (Dunning, 1980). What was the main driver of Japanese outward FDI?

First, until the early 1970s, most of Japanese FDI was market-seeking. Japanese manufacturing companies had built competitive production capabilities and exported their goods massively. As North America was the largest trading partner (35.1 per cent of Japanese exports in the 1960s and 31.2 per cent in the 1970s), many companies opened subsidiaries there (Miwa and Hara, 2007, 25). For all the period 1950–1975, 60 per cent of all Japanese FDI was realized in the United States, and most of the rest in European countries, particularly in the United Kingdom (11.3 per cent) and Switzerland (6.1 per cent). A handful of trading companies set up businesses in the United States in the early 1950s before merging into Mitsubishi International Corporation in New York in 1954 (Wilkins, 1990, 601–602). Mitsui and Sumitomo did the same over the same period, followed by several banks. Other companies invested directly to control their own operations, examples being Toyota (1957) and Sony (1960). Opening sales subsidiaries was important to supervise marketing activities, which included advertising and retail network management. It also helped Japanese companies to adapt their products to the specific needs of American customers.

Honda Motor Co. is a case in point (Demizu, 2005). This company was created in 1948 by Honda Sōichirō (1906–1991), a mechanic who founded a small company to produce pistons for vehicles in 1937 and launched the production of motorcycles after the war. In order to build the Honda brand internationally, the company started to participate in motorcycle races around the world in 1954, winning a first victory at the Isle of Man in 1961. To market this fame, Honda decided to expand its sales network in the United States by targeting the market for small capacity motorcycles (below 305cc at the time of the arrival), dominated at that time by European companies. After long negotiations with MITI to be granted the necessary US dollars to start a business overseas, Honda opened a subsidiary in Los Angeles in 1959. As Americans were used to driving large motorcycles able to run at a high speed, Honda had to position its products differently: an economical means of transportation which could be used by all. Thanks to its launch of a moped, it experienced a great success and fast growth—moving later into larger motorcycle models.

The end of the Bretton Woods system was a turning point for Japanese outward FDI. The yen started to appreciate (from 360 yen to 1 USD in 1949–1971 to 227 yen in 1980) and harm exports from Japan. Moving production facilities to countries with cheaper wages became a widespread phenomenon in the Japanese manufacturing industry. Resource-seeking also became the new driver of Japanese outward FDI in the 1970s. Some companies opened assembly plants in the United States. Table 8.2 gives an overview of the thirteen Japanese companies with the largest foreign operations in 1977. Matsushita Electric (today, Panasonic) was uncontestedly the largest Japanese multinational, with 884 million US dollars-worth of production output in its fifty-six subsidiaries. It was followed by electric appliances and electronics companies (NEC, Hitachi, Sanyo Electric, Toshiba) and automobile producers (Nissan, Toyota), but also chemical (Teijin, Toray, Toyobo), metalworking (Nihon Tokushu), and other manufacturing companies (Ishikawa, Yoshida). All of them were among the most competitive exporters in the 1960s

Table 8.2 Japanese companies with overseas production worth more than 150 million US dollars, 1977

Company	Production, USD million	Number of foreign subsidiaries	Main countries
Matsushita Electric	884	56	Philippines, Malaysia, Taiwan, United States, Brazil
Sanyo Electric	582	40	Korea, Hong Kong, Thailand, Brazil, Singapore
Toray	570	52	Korea, Taiwan, Hong Kong, Thailand, Indonesia
Teijin	423	33	Taiwan, Thailand, Singapore, Mexico, Brazil
Ishikawa	270	18	Singapore, Korea, Brazil, Spain
Yoshida (YKK)	266	38	Taiwan, Thailand, Canada, Costa Rica, Brazil
Nihon Tokushu	257	7	Thailand, Malaysia, Indonesia, United States, Brazil
Nissan	246	16	Singapore, Turkey, Mexico, Peru, United States
NEC	243	24	Korea, Taiwan, Malaysia, Brazil, Australia
Hitachi	200	30	Taiwan, Malaysia, Singapore, Mexico, Brazil
Toshiba	172	45	Korea, Taiwan, Thailand, Iran, Brazil
Toyota	160	15	Thailand, Indonesia, Peru, Brazil, Australia
Toyobo	159	22	Thailand, Malaysia, Indonesia, United States, Brazil

Source: Nakamura (1979), 208

and had to shift their production centres after 1971 in order to maintain their positions. The main countries where these firms invested clearly illustrate the importance of labour costs in overall production outlays. Most of them were located in South East Asian nations from which assembled goods could be re-exported throughout the world, principally to the United States and Western Europe. In the cases of Brazil and the United States, the new assembly plants targeted domestic customers.

The manufacturing subsidiaries opened abroad by Japanese companies contributed to the development of local industries through the transfer of knowledge, since they sent engineers from Japan to organize and supervise the work in their foreign plants. At the same time, thousands of local technicians were invited to Japan and trained in domestic factories. For example, by 1983, a total of 12,612 foreign technicians had been sent to Japan. Of them, 74.5 per cent came from Asian countries, especially Indonesia (15.3 per cent), China (12.1 per cent), and South Korea (12 per cent), while the United States (4 per cent) and Europe (5.3 per cent) had only small shares (Chin and Hayashi, 1995, 68). However, East Asian countries remained for the most part technologically dependent on Japanese and other foreign multinationals. Building a competitive domestic industry from spillover effects was particularly difficult in the car industry. For example, in Thailand the opening of manufacturing joint-ventures or subsidiaries by Toyota (1964), Mitsubishi (1966), Hino (1967), Isuzu (1974), Mazda (1975), Nissan (1977), and Honda (1984) did not lead to the emergence of a Thai car industry—although numerous domestic suppliers developed (Ueda, 2007).

Despite the opening of many overseas production facilities, Japanese companies continued to produce at home—and export. Process innovation, like the implementation of the lean production system by Toyota, and product innovation, particularly in electronics, strengthened the competitiveness of Japanese companies notwithstanding the high yen. The growing flow of exports to the United States and Europe led, however, to trade frictions in the 1970s and early 1980s. Electronics companies like Sony (1972), Matsushita Electric (1974), Sanyo Electric (1977), and Toshiba (1978) opened plants to assemble colour television sets in the United States, hence avoiding criticism and pressure by the American authorities. However, these companies soon diversified their activities into semiconductors by purchasing various American firms, which led to a negative reaction on the part of the US government. In 1987, Fujitsu had, for example, to abandon its plan to take over 80 per cent of the capital of Fairchild Semiconductor Co., a leading company in this industry and a supplier to the US Defense Department (Wilkins, 1990, 612–613). Yet, in the car industry the conflicts were more violent, with strong opposition by American labour unions towards Japanese imports. Japanese manufacturers voluntarily agreed to reduce their exports through VERs (Voluntary Export Restraint, 1981–1984) and to invest in the United States. Consequently, Honda (1982), Nissan (1983), Toyota (1984), Mazda (1987), and Mitsubishi (1988) opened production units on American soil (Hsu, 1994, 18).

In Europe, trade frictions led also to conflicts, particularly with France and Italy, which introduced a series of non-tariff barriers and quotas to restrict the import of Japanese electronics products. This led Japanese firms to invest in the United Kingdom, after an agreement was made in 1981 between Prime Minister Thatcher and the Japanese government (Abe, 2015). Toshiba (1981), NEC (1982), Sharp (1983), and Brother (1985) opened subsidiaries in the United Kingdom and exported to the entire European Economic Community. At the same time, it provided employment in industry at a time when British manufacturers were facing a deep crisis. In 1983, among the 173 Japanese companies established in Europe, 20 per cent were based in the United Kingdom. The high concentration of Japanese firms in the United Kingdom was advantageous to Japanese firms during this period but would become an important concern for Japan–UK trade relations post-BREXIT.

8.5 Conclusions

The successful development of Japanese companies between 1955 and the early 1980s is the outcome of an effective industrial policy focusing on nurturing competitive firms, a particular business system organized to allow high growth in a stable environment, and the expansion of domestic consumption (see next chapter). It has attracted the attention of numerous scholars from the United States and Europe who wanted to understand the sources of this impressive competitiveness. Most of them provided cultural explanations, arguing that, because the Japanese were different from Westerners, they had been able to create special organizations that allowed for stronger competitiveness: the culture of the group led to the formation of a specific business system characterized by cooperation, long-term relations, and self-sacrifice of employees. These factors are important but do not fully explain the success of Japan's capitalist model.

Many scholars, both in Japan and abroad refer to the features of capitalism during this period through the term, 'Japanese Business System' or as 'Japanese-style management'. However, such terms carry a strong culturalist connotation, as they are based on the premise that business in Japan was structured and operated differently from other countries for cultural reasons as opposed to a much broader range of possible factors. Though some Japanese business experts did challenge this culturalist interpretation by pointing out workplace commonalities, especially with the United States, they did not explore the historical context for the implementation of this system with the same depth seen in this volume (Koike, 1988 and 1993). The business-history approach provided in this book goes beyond this culturalist interpretation and demonstrates that the Japanese postwar business system was implemented in a specific context, under specific institutional circumstances, and had a clearly defined objective of catching up and competing with Western nations, particularly the United States. Achieving this required significant governmental coordination and guidance as well as cooperation between firms.

The Japanese Business System was hence the expression of a specific variety of capitalism, called *communitarian capitalism,* a concept proposed by Anchordoguy (2015). According to her work, this form of capitalism is characterized by cooperation and consensus-building behaviour between Japanese business, the state, and the workforce through various forms of paternalism (*onjyō shugi*). The protracted reliance on this development model to achieve success, even after the circumstances had evolved, was the cause of Japanese firms' slowness to adapt to the new competitive environment of the 1980s, a point that is re-explored in Chapter 12 (Anchordoguy, 2015, 5; Porter et al., 2000). It should be noted that catch-up industrialization, a term that was coined by Suehiro Akira, and communitarian capitalism both describe Japan's postwar development pattern, but with different focal points (Suehiro, 2008). What then accounted for the growing competitiveness of Japanese firms during the period described in this chapter? Western and Japanese management scholars alike have discussed the reasons at length. While international management studies were dominated by authors like Michael Porter who argued that a firm's competitiveness was a matter of strategy and positioning, Japanese scholars have emphasized that the resources of firms were their source of their strength. In 1995, Nonaka Ikujiro and Takeuchi Hirotaka published a book entitled *The Knowledge-Creating Company*, in which they demonstrate that Japanese companies established themselves as leaders in world markets because they were able to build a specific organization based on traditional Buddhist culture. Their ability to share tacit knowledge within a group and other cultural specificities were presented as the competitive advantages of Japanese companies (Nonaka and Takeuchi, 1995). Such views were largely shared during the first part of the 1990s, just before the Japanese economy started to witness a long decline.

One must also look beyond organizations and acknowledge the role played by individual entrepreneurs to explain Japan's success. The postwar business system tends to downplay the role of such individuals between 1955 and 1985, due to the domination of the *keiretsu* in the Japanese economy, the importance of middle management in decision-making in large corporations, and a career path whereby CEOs are mostly selected in-house. However, the economic and technological catch-up that characterized this period enabled a form of entrepreneurship based on taking advantage of new opportunities offered by social and economic changes. Exporting to the United States, importing new technology, and launching new products involved risk-taking by entrepreneurs. As Kikkawa Takeo has recently argued, if the founders of Honda Motor and Sony were financially supported respectively by Mitsubishi Bank and Mitsui Bank, it was because the latter trusted these companies and their founders and believed in their ability to establish themselves as dominant firms in world markets (Kikkawa, 2019, 178–182).

9
Business and Consumerism in the High and Stable Growth Periods

In 1971, McDonald's opened its first restaurant in Japan at Mitsukoshi Department Store in Nihonbashi, Tokyo. Founded in California in 1937 by two brothers as a drive-through store, McDonald's became a burger shop after World War II that rapidly developed in the US market in the 1960s. It then started its international expansion into Canada in 1967, and shortly after into Europe (1970) and Japan (1971). In Japan, working together with Fujita Den (1926–2004), McDonald's experienced rapid growth and soon established itself as the country's largest restaurant chain (Jones, 2005, 143).

The success of American fast-food in Japan was not however merely the result of an attractive and innovative food business model. It was supported by strong urban middle-class demand, which was fuelled by growing purchasing power, a desire to consume Western products, and an increasingly Westernized lifestyle. This chapter discusses the rise of consumerism and its subsequent effects on retailing. From these developments came a mutation in the places where Japanese consumers made their purchases and the ways that goods reached retailers.

While examining the shift from high to stable economic growth rates during this period, this chapter also explores of the limitations of growth, particularly its negative consequences or the dark side of capitalism. By providing a brief overview of the environmental damage caused by rapid industrialization and burgeoning consumerism, Box 9.1 gives the reader another perspective on Japanese business through the lens of a technological innovation introduced by what was then just a small-scale Japanese automobile manufacturer, Honda Motor Company. Such innovations were vital throughout the high and stable growth periods for their contributions to new businesses and to the many changes they generated in Japanese society.

Japanese Capitalism and Entrepreneurship. Pierre-Yves Donzé and Julia S. Yongue, Oxford University Press.
© Pierre-Yves Donzé and Julia S. Yongue (2024). DOI: 10.1093/oso/9780192887474.003.0010

Box 9.1 'The dark side of capitalism' as an opportunity for reinvention and innovation

Japan's catch-up occurred over a much shorter period than in the countries where the Industrial Revolution first originated. Industrialization indisputably brought numerous positive spillovers in terms of higher living standards. However, rapid economic growth also had detrimental effects on the environment and public health due in no small part to air and water pollution. Contributing to this problem was a perception that formed during the high-growth period of 'consumption as a virtue'. However, as Eiko Maruko Siniawer notes in her history of waste in Japan this notion would soon be challenged: by the 1970s, garbage disposal resulting from the mass-production and mass-consumption society that had emerged would become a social and environmental bane, especially for the residents of Tokyo (Siniawer, 2018).

As shown in Table 9.1, environmental damage caused by business development is not limited to the high and stable growth periods. Japan's first major industry-induced environmental disaster occurred in the 1880s and was caused by pollution from the Ashio Copper Mine in Tochigi prefecture. Like all forms of industrial pollution, this problem would have short- and long-term consequences on public health and the environment. It would also influence labour relations: the pollution from the Ashio Mine incited riots and gave birth to an early environmental movement.

Table 9.1 Japan's 'worst four' environmental disasters caused by pollution (*yondai kōgai*)

Year	Source	Cause	Prefecture	Disease
1912	Mitsui Mining and Smelting	Cadmium poisoning	Toyama	Itai-itai
1956	Chisso (nitrogen) Corporation	Methylmercury	Kumamoto	Minamata
1961	Showa Denko	Methylmercury	Niigata	Niigata Minamata
1960–1972	Petrochemical producers in Yokkaichi	Sulphur dioxide (caused by the burning of petroleum/crude oil)	Mie	Yokkaichi asthma

Walker (2010)

Governments around the world have generally been slow to take action against environmental damage caused by industrial pollution. However, one book called *Silent Spring*, which was written in 1962 by an American biologist, Rachel Carson, and translated just two years later into Japanese, would have a considerable impact on public policymaking relating to environmental protection worldwide (Carson, 1962). In the United States, the first significant measure to prevent environmental degradation was the creation of the Environmental Protection Agency in 1970. A similar organization, Japan's Environmental Agency, was founded in 1971. According to the 1963 Clean Air Act (revised in 1970, 1977, 1990), the US government would begin to monitor and regulate air pollution. While this legislation was enacted in the United States, it would have an especially significant impact on Japan's automobile manufacturing industry, which at that time had just begun building the foundations for global expansion in the United States.

In 1975, US congressman Edmund Muskie put forth a bill to amend the 1963 Clean Air Act, often referred to as the 'Muskie Act'. This amendment was designed to make a reduction of car emissions mandatory. The Big Three automobile manufacturers, Chrysler, Ford, and General Motors, strongly resisted the change. For Honda, however, this situation offered a unique opportunity to enter the US market:

> In 1974, about three years after entering the U.S. car market, Honda stunned the American auto industry by introducing a four-door Civic that met stringent Clean Air emission standards, which called for a 90 per cent decrease in carbon monoxide, hydrocarbon, and nitrogen oxide levels by 1975 compared with 1970 vehicles. This was the first car in the world to qualify under the new rules and it hit the streets just as the large U.S. automakers and Toyota were lobbying Washington to soften requirements, claiming that it was impossible to economically produce an engine that accomplished the act's goals. (Rothfeder, 2015).

Honda's low emission CVCC engine would become the new standard for the automobile industry. While environmental degradation caused by industry continues even today, this early example of Honda and its efforts to develop a low emissions engine provides evidence that through innovation and determination, companies can increase profits while also contributing to society.

9.1 The birth of a consuming middle class

At the conclusion of World War II, three major shifts occurred that would have a profound effect on the development of Japanese business. The first change was demographic—one that significantly impacted the size of the domestic market. The sudden rise in the population was triggered by two baby booms: the first in 1947–1949, followed by the second in 1971–1974. The children born during the first boom would come of age in the 1960s, causing fierce competition not only to enter schools and universities but also to join the labour force. This hardworking, increasingly educated demographic would become the impetus for Japan's economic development during the high-growth period. Some of the 'baby boomers' would enter companies as white-collar salaried employees or *salaryman*, while others would join the blue-collar, factory labour force. Thanks to a postwar situation characterized by robust economic growth and full employment, the baby boomers would be able to enjoy a significantly higher level of disposable income than previous generations. While the popular press has referred to high-growth period as the 'economic miracle', Japan's postwar ascent is more likely the fruit of these baby boomers' long working hours, unwavering drive to 'catch up with and overtake' (*oitsuki oikose*) their Western counterparts, and rising demand for new material goods.

The increase in employment opportunities during the high-growth period encouraged migration to urban areas. In the 1950s and 1960s, some one million people left the countryside and settled in cities. In the 1950s, just 38 per cent of the population resided in urban areas; however, by 1975, the figure had risen to 75 per cent. The structure of the Japanese family also changed. By 1975, some two-thirds of families were nuclear as opposed to the previous pattern of a large extended family living under the same roof (Gordon, 2003). The labours and desires of these migrants were embodied in a wide range of new purchases. Modern household electrical appliances as well as entertainment items such as television sets to improve both the convenience and comfort of daily lives would soon fill the homes not only of Japanese nuclear families, but also those of households around the world.

The generation of postwar baby boomers constituted the new middle class, and the fulfilment of their needs gave rise to what is referred to in Japanese business literature as the consumption revolution *(shōhi kakumei)* (Yoshino, 1971, 35–90). During the high and stable growth periods, the most sought-after consumer goods were 'the three treasures' (*sanshu no jinki*): a refrigerator, washing machine, and black-and-white television set, followed by 'the three Cs' (*san C*): a colour television, air conditioning, and car. High rates of postwar economic growth were fuelled in large part by increasing purchases of these popular items.

Despite their initially high price tags, appliance purchases rose precipitously as the following example illustrates. In 1957, just 20.2 per cent of households owned a washing machine. However, by 1962, the figure grew to 58.1 per cent and in 1967, it reached 96.1 per cent. By 2004, virtually all households—some 99.0 per cent—would own their own washing machine (Cabinet Office-Naikakufu, 1967, 1962, 1967, 2004). Related to the rapid growth of consumerism was another major change, the so-called distribution revolution (*ryūtsū kakumei*). The modernization of the distribution or marketing system, which gradually led to greater operational efficiency, evolved out of the synergies generated by the growth of mass production and mass consumption. As shown below, Japan's consumption and distribution revolutions heralded significant changes in the types of business where daily household items were sold, how these items reached retail establishments, and who purchased them.

9.2 Science, technology, and innovation

Symbols of progress in the high-growth period

The second major change—one that would indirectly support the expansion of consumerism—was a new orientation for the uses of science and technology. As mentioned in Chapter 7 on the occupation period, new institutions helped to redirect science and technology towards peaceful purposes. This change in focus would in turn contribute to rebuilding the economy and the development of business. Even before these new institutions were put in place, a call to hard work and the achievement of progress was made in the *Imperial Rescript of the Termination of the War*, delivered by the Shōwa Emperor on 14 August 1945, thus setting the tone for the decades to follow:

> Unite your total strength to be devoted to the construction of the future. Cultivate the ways of rectitude, foster nobility of spirit, and work with resolution—so that you may enhance the glory of the imperial state and keep pace with the progress of the world.

In the high-growth period, some of the first fruits of the new uses of science and technology could be witnessed in the daily lives of the Japanese. One concrete example is Tokyo Tower, which would become a highly visual landmark and symbol of progress as well as a vector for marketing to consumers. Tokyo Tower was erected in 1958, to which radio and television transmission antennae were added in 1961. These additions made it possible for public and private broadcasters not only to diffuse news programmes but also to promote the mass consumption of novel goods through advertisements featuring a wide array of novel and convenient 'made-in-Japan' products.

The circumstances of the Cold War helped to fuel the flow of advanced science and technology from the United States. Legislation such as the Foreign Exchange Control Law of 1949 was introduced by MITI, the overseer of the types of technology that Japan would import and how it would be used to develop the nation's industries (see Chapter 8). It is indisputable that the Japanese state played a vital role in directing the development of the postwar economy and promoting a new high-tech Japan through such legislation. The government would also provide direct financial incentives to companies to encourage the modernization of factories and purchases of new equipment in order to improve product quality and boost productivity.

Yet, as was also shown from a different perspective in the previous chapter, the role of the state, though important, should not be overestimated. Moreover, imports of foreign technology and legislation alone did not make Japan an industrial powerhouse; domestic innovations on the part of firms and entrepreneurs were also key components for Japan's emergence as a high-tech, scientifically advanced nation. Private-sector enterprises took an active role in fostering innovation by constructing new laboratories for conducting research and development. Between 1959 and 1975 the number of researchers at private companies more than tripled (Morris Suzuki, 1994, 169). Innovations occurred not only at large corporations but also at small start-up firms, particular those relating to the development of consumer goods. Examples can be found in a variety of forms ranging from a new time-saving kitchen appliance, Toshiba's rice cooker, launched in 1955, to a pocket transistor radio, marketed by Sony in 1958 (Macnaughtan, 2015, 79–104).

Innovations were not only material; they could also be found in the form of new management approaches, employing both theories and statistical analyses, designed to boost worker productivity and product quality. One vector for spreading Japanese management was the Japan Productivity Centre (JPC, *Nihon Seisansei Honbu*) founded in 1958. Though it is often assumed that GHQ bought scientific management to Japan, a movement to improve the quality of Japanese goods through a variety of statistical methods was already underway in Japan before the end of the War (Tsutsui, 1996). Management training courses organized by JPC contributed to more efficient management and higher product quality, which in the long term also helped to foster more harmonious labour–management relations.

The stable growth period and innovation

As shown in previous chapters, small-scale start-ups led the way to new markets by creating demand and need for products that had not previously existed. Some of Japan's earliest and most famous postwar start-ups such as Sony and Honda, would also be among its first global enterprises. Their founders were trailblazers and in some cases visionaries with a strong inclination for risk-taking. Moreover, rather than simply relying on the sales and distribution channels of existing companies, these firms established their own marketing networks and brands. As newcomers to well-established markets, they did not attempt to compete with the dominant brands. They searched instead for niches within an existing sector where there would be few or no competitors and thus a greater likelihood for success through innovation. As mentioned in the previous chapter, Sony's innovation in radios changed the way people enjoyed music, soon making previous products obsolete (Christensen, 2016). Innovations such as this one not only gave birth to new uses and customer needs; they sometimes changed society and its established norms, or what Schumpeter referred to as 'creative destruction' (Schumpeter, 1994). Such innovators could be found not only in manufacturing but also in Japan's service sector.

Kiyonari Tadao was perhaps the first scholar in Japan to provide a definition for 'start-up' (*benchā kigyō*), which he described it as a leading, newly founded company, established by an entrepreneur, which is modern, knowledge-intensive, and innovative (Kiyonari et. al., 1971; Yamazaki, 2004. Udagawa and Shōjima identify three venture capital booms: the first from 1970 to 1973; the second from 1982–1986; and the third from 1994 (Udagawa and Shōjima, 2011, 277–279). The first wave of domestic entrepreneurship came in the wake of the early trends in Silicon Valley in California in the 1960s. Though this wave would be interrupted by the first oil shock in 1973, some of the firms remained in operation in the long term. Some examples of the second and third waves of start-ups can be found in Table 9.2.

Table 9.2 Early start-ups of the 1970s and 1980s

Company	Founding	Main activity	Founding location
Roland	1972	Musical instruments	Osaka
NIDEC	1973	Small motors	Kyoto
Konami	1973	Digital entertainment	Osaka
Keyence	1974	Sensors	Osaka
HIS	1980	Travel	Tokyo
SoftBank	1981	Telecom	Tokyo
Tsutaya	1982	Book and videos/DVDs	Osaka
Square Enix	1983	Video games, etc.	Tokyo

Source: Compiled from the websites of the firms listed above

Innovations conceived by start-ups led to the development of new business sectors and were off-shoots of the changes that were also occurring in Japanese lifestyles. This was particularly evident in the growing demand for new forms of entertainment—both inside and outside the home—ranging from products for enjoying music and video games to travel, a trend that reflected the gradual increase in leisure time and the lifting of overseas travel restrictions in the stable growth period. Other new businesses were able to tap into the high precision instruments sector which included small motors and sensors, areas where Japan was able to capture a high, if not a dominant, global market share.

9.3 Social change and its consequences

The third major change could be seen in consumption patterns. This trend emerged in part in response to an evolution in the role of women in both the home and workplace. During the 1960–1970 period, the ratio of women who worked outside the home increased from 42 to 53 per cent. Opportunities to work outside the home grew thanks to the proliferation of convenient appliances, which allowed women to devote less of their time than in previous generations to meal preparation (Macnaughtan, 2012). Although the number of working women steadily rose, the division of labour in the workplace changed little. Women engaged mainly in traditionally female-held jobs such as secretarial and factory work (Gordon, 2003) The 1985 Equal Employment Opportunity Law, which prohibited discrimination against women in recruitment, job assignment, and promotion, was seen as an advancement for women. It was passed in the Diet but lacked the legal teeth to force employers to comply. The introduction of the spousal tax exemption system, which came under discussion only recently in the context of Abe's womenomics, served as a fiscal disincentive for Japanese women to work full-time since doing so would cause them to forgo their tax-exempt status (Yokoyama and Koyama, 2018). Thus, many married women chose to stay at home to raise their children as full-time housewives. This may explain why Japanese women have continued even today to shoulder a greater burden than their spouses in childrearing, housework (cleaning and meal preparation), and taking care of elderly family members.[1] Such institutional barriers

---

[1] https://www.mof.go.jp/english/pri/publication/pp_review/fy2017/ppr14_02_03.pdf

are to blame for the enduring problem of gender inequalities in the Japanese workplace. (See Chapter 12.)

Changes in the Japanese lifestyle impacted consumption patterns, not only for working women. With the increase in the time that all Japanese were devoting to activities outside the home—whether for work, education, leisure, or others—the demand for quick and convenient foods rose proportionally. This shift in turn sparked innovations in the food and beverage industries, as seen in the proliferation of processed foods. In 1958, the founder of Nissin, Andō Momofuku, launched the company's first instant noodle product, *Chicken Ramen*, the preparation of which took just three minutes and only required hot water. Nissin's instant ramen became an unprecedented success that was copied and adapted to different tastes around the world. Like Sony and Honda, Nissin would also become one of Japan's truly global brands (Kawabe, 2017). Nissin's cup ramen product would even accompany astronauts into outer space.

In 1960, Morinaga became the first company in Japan to launch an instant coffee product. Its pleasing taste and convenience made it highly successful, though the top-selling brand was the foreign firm, Nestlé (Donzé, 2020). In addition to the growing demand for caffeinated beverages, one key to Morinaga's high sales was the development of new Japanese drying technologies which contributed to more efficient mass production, not only for instant coffee but also for coffee creamer. Industries ranging from processed foods to medicines benefited from the applications of such technologies, providing a boon to many of Japan's manufacturing industries (Morinaga Nyūgyō, 2018, 52; Arai et al., 2022). In 1963, Otsuka Foods (today part of Otsuka Group) launched its first major hit, Bon Curry. This product's main marketing demographic was not housewives but single men, and was sold in easy-to-serve individual portions. The 'retort pouch', another Japanese innovation, launched in 1971, made it possible to prepare Bon Curry simply by boiling the unopened pouch in water for three minutes. Pouches of *Bon Curry* could be heated then served on top of rice, prepared in another convenient innovation of the high-growth period, the automatic rice cooker. During the same period, preparation would be further simplified thanks to microwave ovens, launched in Japan in the late 1960s. They would gradually become a common appliance in Japanese homes and a must for convenience stores, discussed below.

Frozen foods sales also grew in popularity for their convenience. Thanks to the spread of two-door refrigerators (one for frozen foods), half of all frozen foods consumed were ready-made. Demand for such quick and easy processed foods along with soft drinks (carbonated and fruit beverages) rose precipitously. With the spread of vending machines from 1975, new beverages, including canned coffee, sports drinks, and oolong tea, also increased in popularity.[2]

During this period the Japanese diet evolved and became increasingly Westernized (see Table 9.3). Moreover, through the transformation in the Japanese diet and food culture came a change in the Japanese identity (Hopson, 2020). Over time, the Japanese would consume less of the staple food, rice, and more flour-based products, the most popular being bread and noodles. This was the result not only of Westernization but also of trade policies that encouraged imports of American wheat products (Moen, 1999). Caloric intake rose as did the calorie sources. This was due to a rise in the sheer volume of food consumed combined with better nutrition compared to the previous periods as well as increased use of ingredients commonly found in Western foods, namely sugar and oil.

Growth in the economy translated into a corresponding rise in the living standards and personal consumption expenditures. Domestic policy measures were a major impetus for the growth of the economy and the ensuing changes in consumption patterns: in 1960, Prime Minister Ikeda Hayato introduced an income-doubling plan. As a result, Japan's Engel coefficient (the ratio of one's income spent on food) would gradually decrease leaving consumers with more disposable income to make purchases of an ever-wider variety of mass-produced, mass-marketed goods.

Table 9.3 Westernization of the Japanese diet: daily caloric intake per capita (%)

	1934–38	1951–55	1956–60	1961–65	1970
Caloric intake	2,128kcal	2.045kcal	2,264kcal	2,385kcal	2,529kcal
Rice	56.7	48.1	48.5	46.8	36.7
Flour	4.6	12.0	10.8	11.1	12.3
Livestock products	1.4	1.9	3.3	5.5	9.0
Sugar	6.8	5.5	6.4	7.5	11.2
Oil	2.0	2.4	3.8	6.1	9.0

Source: Kikkawa and Takaoka (1997)

---

[2] Statistics Bureau of Japan, https://www.stat.go.jp/data/kakei/longtime/index3.html; Ministry of Agriculture, Fisheries, and Forestry, https://www.maff.go.jp/j/wpaper/w_maff/h22/pdf/z_appendix_03.pdf

9.4 Distribution patterns during the high and stable growth periods

The changes in Japan's distribution system, which began in earnest in the 1960s, became a major interest not only for those directly involved in marketing but also for the general Japanese public. Perhaps the most vivid example of this heightened interest is Hayashi Shūji's 1959 bestseller entitled, *The Distribution Revolution (Ryūtsū Kakumei)* (Hayashi, 1962). As shown in the case study of Daiei below, the modernization of Japan's distribution system significantly affected how goods reached consumers as well as the relationships between retailers, manufacturers, and wholesalers. However, an overhaul of Japan's distribution system was much needed by the 1960s due to its inefficiencies and low productivity. Conversely, in the United States during the 'second industrial revolution' that took place in the mid-nineteenth century, new mass-production techniques were applied to revolutionize the retail sector giving rise to the massive development of chain stores as early as the 1920s (Bernstein, 1997, 493–494).

From department stores and shops to large-scale supermarkets

Against the backdrop of distribution-system reform, important changes were also occurring in terms of the places where consumers purchased daily food items. Three significant influences on this evolution in Japanese shopping patterns were: (1) fluctuations in the economy, (2) the emergence of large-scale supermarkets, and (3) new needs. In Chapter 3, the rise of iconic department stores, namely Mitsukoshi and Takashimaya, which were built in cities, some in the late 1800s, was briefly described. Thanks to the growth of railroads, new large-scale department stores such as Seibu, Tōkyū, and Hankyū were constructed in the buildings attached to major train terminals. However, such forms of shopping were mainly for affluent consumers. The average Japanese housewife made most of her daily purchases at small, family-owned shops located in shopping arcades and/or neighbourhood markets.

During the stable growth period in particular, this trend would completely reverse, as shopping in large-scale supermarkets would become an activity of the masses. In the 1960s, the first supermarkets would begin to appear in towns and suburbs, thus allowing shoppers to make use of their cars, another popular consumer purchase.

Table 9.4 Ranking by sales of retailers by year (1962–1972)

	1962	1964	1967	1970	1972
1	Daimaru	Daimaru	Daimaru	Mitsukoshi	Daiei
2	Mitsukoshi	Mitsukoshi	Mitsukoshi	Daimaru	Mitsukoshi
3	Takashimaya	Takashimaya	Takashimaya	Takashimaya	Daimaru
4	Matsuzakaya	Matsuzakaya	Matsuzakaya	Daiei	Takashimaya
5	Tōyoku	Hankyū	Daiei	Seiyū Store	Seiyū Store
6	Hankyū	Isetan	Seibu	Matsuzakaya	Seibu
7	Isetan	Seibu	Isetan	Seibu	Jusco
8	Seibu	Tōyoko	Hankyū	Jusco	Matsuzakaya
9	Sogō	Daiei	Tōkyū	Uny	Nichie
10	Matsuya	Matsuya	Seiyū Store	Isetan	Uny

Notes: Supermarkets are highlighted in grey. Seiyū Store is part of Saison Seibu Group, a railroad company that diversified into a large department-store chain after 1964. Originating from a silk-trading business which was established in 1758, JUSCO became part of AEON Group in 1989. Uny opened Nagoya in 1912. Across two generations, it became the amalgamation of a number of stores, mainly specializing in the sale of kimonos. Nichie first opened for business as a small sports-apparel retailer in Hiroshima prefecture before its incorporation in 1962.
Source: Maeda (1991)

Table 9.4 below illustrates this new trend. By the eve of the first oil shock in 1972, supermarkets, highlighted in grey had succeeded in overtaking department stores as the most popular shopping venues. Though Daiei was the clear winner, other supermarkets, namely Seiyū Store, Jusco, Nichie, and Uny also joined the ranking. In 1980, Itō-Yōkado, mentioned in the next section, would rank second, with Daiei in first place. Faced with competition from supermarkets, which offered similar products at lower prices, the popularity of department stores waned.

Nakauchi Isao and the rise of the supermarket chain, Daiei

One entrepreneur, Nakauchi Isao (1922–2005), served as a major impetus behind the shift in shopping preferences and the modernization of the distribution system. One of his most significant contributions to Japanese business during the stable growth period was to make the American-style supermarket chain a common feature of Japan's nationwide shopping landscape. He did this by bringing the concept of the hypermarket or superstore to Japan and filling them with a variety of low-priced products, available in large volumes.

The introduction of Japan's first major supermarket chain, Daiei, provides a useful tool for understanding how Japanese capitalism evolved during the high and stable growth periods. The introduction of the supermarket chain was revolutionary not only in terms of how it changed the way Japanese shopped. It also altered the way goods were distributed from manufacturers, wholesalers, and suppliers to their retailers.

Supermarket chains can be distinguished by several features. First, they are 'self-service' operations, allowing for the reduction of personnel costs by alleviating the need for employees to accompany customers while they shop. As the prices of products are fixed, customers do not need to negotiate them with sellers. Second, as supermarkets are larger than shops, they have more opportunities for economies of scale. Their low-cost advantage is reflective of their superior bargaining power vis-à-vis suppliers and wholesalers. Third, they offer a larger selection of goods than small shops. This distinction helps supermarkets to ensure stable earnings and greater profitability since they can rely on the revenues from popular items when demand for others declines (Udagawa and Shōjima, 2011, 261–262).

Though Nakauchi was a pioneer in introducing the American-style supermarket model to Japan, he was not the first to establish a store with one or some of the features mentioned above. In 1953, Kinokuniya opened a store in Aoyama with a self-service produce section. In 1956, Maruwa Food Center followed suit by opening two stores with self-service shopping and a wide range of products targeting housewives. Though there were these early efforts, the sheer scale of Nakauchi's Daiei chain store model placed it in a class of its own.

In 1957, Nakauchi opened his first business in Osaka, a drugstore called Store for housewives, *Daiei Drugstore*. However, he soon discovered that he could not compete with more established drugstores without offering a wider range of discounted products. To attract the shoppers of his rivals, he began selling snacks and cosmetics. In 1958 and in 1961, he opened larger stores with an even wider array of items, including clothing. Thanks to the appeal of a broader range of goods sold at low prices, Nakauchi was able to rapidly expand his business. The first major turning point in his career, however, came in 1962 when he attended a large supermarket convention in the United States as Japan's representative. He returned to Japan with a plan to bring the American-style large-scale supermarket chain-store model he had witnessed firsthand. Based on this model, he opened a chain of hypermarkets or SSDDS (self-service discount department store, known in Japan as GMS or General Merchandise Store). His five-storey complexes, stocked with a full range of products, were situated in suburbs and smaller cities across the country. As tenants could rent and sell goods in the spaces offered in these large complexes, they became venues to which customers could drive their cars and make purchases of food, clothing, and many other items. Shoppers could also take advantage of services such as banking and various forms of entertainment for all age groups.

While Nakauchi's business model naturally pleased many housewives, the methods he employed to achieve his ends generated great ire among his suppliers, which he constantly pressured to cut costs. His fiercest critics, however, were his competitors, namely Seiyū Store, numerous manufacturers, including Nissin, Morinaga, Toyobo, Kao, and Matsushita, and even one of his siblings. Problems arose with his main rival, Seiyū Store when Nakauchi decided to build a new supermarket in the large suburban city of Akabane. In proximity to the station, there was already a Seiyū Store, which Nakauchi proceeded to try to force out of business. This dispute is humorously referred to in business literature and the popular press as the 'Akabane War' (*Akabane sensō*).

His most intense and longest battles were fought against two large-scale manufacturing firms, Kao Corporation and Matsushita Electric. The so-called '30-years' war' waged between Nakauchi and the founder of Matsushita Electric, Matsushita Kōnosuke, one of Japan's most respected and beloved entrepreneurs, is interesting as it reveals some of the particularities of their approaches to capitalistic competition. Nakauchi used his superior bargaining power as a large-scale retailer to force sellers to reduce their prices by cutting their profit margins, while Matsushita as a large-scale manufacturer strove to achieve 'coexistence and co-prosperity' (*kyōzon kyōei*) with all of his affiliated sellers in large part by organizing them into a distribution network or *keiretsu*, discussed at length in the previous chapter. Matsushita's aim was to prevent a common occurrence during this period of expanding mass production combined with high growth, known as 'excessive competition' (*katō kyōsō*). Such cutthroat competition often occurred when large numbers of sellers began often drastically to reduce their prices in unison in order to secure market share. Matsushita insisted that this form of competitive behaviour should at all costs be avoided, and instead he encouraged his 'fair pricing movement' (*seika hanbai undō*). Matsushita's stance—the embodiment of 'communitarian capitalism'—was the polar-opposite of Nakauchi, who believed that the market alone should determine prices.

Of note is that the features of Japan's distribution system would become a thorny issue not only among the domestic players. As the Japanese market grew to become the second largest in the world, its distribution system, specifically the structural characteristics of the *keiretsu* and the barriers they created for newcomers would become a point of great tension between

Japan and its US and European trading partners in major trade negotiations in the following decades, known as the MOSS Talks (Market-Oriented, Sector-Specific) in 1985 and SSI (Structural Impediments Initiative) in 1993. For the foreign companies hoping to penetrate Japan's markets, the *keiretsu* system was perceived as a non-tariff barrier, while for foreign governments, it was seen as the source of an exploding trade imbalance (Japan's Keiretsu System Hearing, 1991).

Nakauchi's disagreement with his brother would cause the latter to leave the business. This quarrel stemmed from Nakauchi's belief that even if some of his stores were unprofitable their losses could be recouped if the combined sales of the chain remained profitable. One should note that prioritizing growth and market share over the profitability of individual stores was an inherent flaw in Nakauchi's business model, which would become increasingly difficult to sustain, particularly in the aftermath of the economic bubble.

The fall of Nakauchi and the rise of new shopping patterns

With sales of one trillion yen in 1980, Daiei became Japan's largest retail store, a position Nakauchi would not retain for long. Udagawa and Shōjima identify three main factors for his downfall. The first was the stagnation in consumer spending at the end of the high-growth period. The second relates to government policy. In order to protect small retailers, MITI introduced the Large-scale Retail Store Law in 1974, which by 1978 greatly restricted the building of large-scale supermarkets, but, as shown below, would benefit convenience stores. The third, and perhaps the most important one was the change in consumer preferences. Unlike the high-growth period, wage levels during the stable growth period would stagnate. At the same time, because consumers' *basic* needs had been met, they would begin to lose interest in purchasing large quantities of discounted, mass-manufactured products. The Japanese shopper of the 1980s and 1990s would instead value convenience, a trend that would give convenience stores a decisive competitive edge over large-scale supermarkets (Udagawa and Shōjima, 2011, 270–280).

During the high-growth period, Nakauchi, once known in the popular press as the 'King of Distribution' *(Ryūtsū no Ō)*, was considered one of Japan's most successful self-made men and a hero for housewives. The decline of his supermarket empire and eventual bankruptcy were symbolic of the coming of a new era in Japanese business. Perhaps the greatest factor for his decline was his inability to anticipate and adapt to this change. The take-off for Nakauchi's supermarket chain occurred when Japanese aspired to fill their homes with basic amenities—a refrigerator, television, and washing machine—and to enjoy the abundance of Western foods, including meat, one of his top-selling items and an especially scarce commodity during the war. As Japanese incomes began to rise in the early postwar period, the availability of an abundance of products at low prices was important to sustaining competitive advantage. However, once those needs had been fulfilled and economic growth began to decelerate, consumer desires again changed.

The fatal flaw in Nakauchi's business model was that he believed land prices would continue to rise indefinitely, what the Japanese business literature refers to as 'the land myth' (*tochi no shinwa*). Even when he was most heavily in debt, Nakauchi continued to purchase land to construct new supermarkets by taking out loans from banks with his existing properties as collateral in the belief that its value would rise. After a decade of aggressive expansion starting in the early 1980s, his stores began to operate at a loss. As sales stagnated, Daiei implemented drastic reforms, which led to the closing of 2,000 stores. Despite these efforts, sales did not significantly improve. The scale of the damage following the bursting of the land bubble in the early 1990s and the 1995 Hanshin Awaji Earthquake, whose epicentre was Kobe, the site of his first stores, left Daiei with even more debt. Nakauchi officially resigned as president in 2001. Daiei partnered with AEON in 2006, but was still unable to recover. In 2014, AEON took the majority share.

9.5 Seven-Eleven: harbinger of the third industrial revolution

Japan's convenience stores began as 'voluntary chains' set up by groups of small retailers and wholesalers, one early example being My Shop, which opened in 1969. It is important to note that the large-scale supermarket chains described above also joined the trend. In 1973, Seiyū Store (Saison Group) became the first supermarket to open a convenience store called Family Mart in Sayama in Saitama Prefecture. In 1975, Daiei followed suit with the opening of Lawson in Sakurazuka, Osaka. However, the true pioneers of the modern business model for the convenience store in Japan were Suzuki Toshifumi and the owner of Itō-Yōkado, Itō Masatoshi. As shown below, Seven-Eleven Japan blended the two shopping models. Suzuki also helped to modernize all the aspects of his convenience-store operations—from the manufacturer and wholesaler to the retailer—by introducing information technology.

Itō-Yōkado and the founding of Seven-Eleven Japan

Suzuki joined Itō-Yōkado's supermarket chain store in 1963 at mid-career after having worked from 1956 for a publication distribution firm called TOHAN or Tokyo Shuppan Hanbai. Like Nakauchi, Itō was also exposed to American-style merchandising on a visit to the United States as a delegate to the Third Modern Merchandising Method Seminar. While there, he was especially impressed by the response of Sears, Roebuck, and Company, then the world's largest retailer, to the decline of the department store model. Upon his return to Japan, Itō-Yōkado embarked on the founding of a chain of supermarkets, the first of which was built in 1961 in Kita Urawa in Saitama prefecture (Kawabe, 2015, 255).

As the high-growth period was drawing to a close and sales were in decline, the management of Itō-Yōkado, like many other Japanese companies, felt the need to search for fresh new business ideas in the United States and Europe. In the early 1970s, while setting up an agreement in the United States to open Denny's family restaurants in Japan, Suzuki came upon the idea of establishing a convenience store chain. This idea would materialize in the form of an agreement with Southland Corporate in 1973. At the time of the agreement, Southland, founded in 1927 as what may have been the world's first convenience-store chain, was a highly successful company. In the early 1970s, it had already become a franchise with nearly ten thousand stores in operation across the United States and parts of Canada, and was listed on the New York Stock Exchange (Bernstein, 1997, 494–495).

While Suzuki did have the support of Itō, he faced opposition from within the corporate organisation, as the convenience-store model went against the conventional wisdom of the times. As shown above in the example of Daiei, the competitive advantage for large-scale supermarkets was their ability to offer the same products as convenience stores at lower prices, thanks to economies of scale and scope. Despite the initial lukewarm reception of Suzuki's idea, the first store opened in 1974 in Toyosu in Tokyo's Kota Ward, followed by a second store, located in Fukushima prefecture.

At the time of Seven-Eleven's entry, Japan's retail model was already experiencing great change due to the opening of large-scale supermarkets, such as Daiei. Supermarkets and convenience stores alike were met with strong opposition from small family-owned shops, which were unable to compete against superstores in terms of price and variety. To avoid tension with these small operations, Itō chose a conservative approach to market entry. Moreover, unlike Nakauchi, he did not purchase land to build new stores. Instead, he strove to convince small shop-owners, particularly liquor shops with a license to sell alcohol, to convert their operations to his convenience store model.

This strategy which was less disruptive to the existing status quo worked, and Itō-Yōkado's franchise system soon grew. In 1975 there were fifteen Seven-Elevens; in 1980, the figure rose to 801 shops; in 1986 to 2,651 and in 1995 to 5,952. Since its founding, Seven-Eleven Japan has been able to retain its position as the largest convenience-store operator in the country in terms of sales (Bernstein, 1997, 504–506) By the 1990s, convenience stores would overtake supermarkets, a position that would remain unchallenged until the Covid-19 pandemic, which brought a radical, though only temporary, change in Japanese lifestyles. The Covid-19 crisis was marked by a preference on the part of consumers to spend more time at home and to make their purchases in supermarkets or online rather than convenience stores (Nikkei Asia, 2021.

Seven-Eleven: factors for growth and resilience

The convenience store model continues to endure as an integral part of Japanese retailing for a number of reasons. First, it seized upon the shift in customer preferences, specifically the transition from a seller's market to a buyer's market by introducing measures to streamline the supply chain. The distinction between the two types of markets is important, as it encapsulates the transition from the high-growth period of the 1950s and 1960s when demand exceeded supply (i.e. a seller's market), to the opposite (i.e. a buyer's market) during the stable growth period, when buyers could dictate the product line-up in stores. By the 1970s, retailers increasingly had to entice their customers into their stores by offering new products and greater convenience to match changing lifestyles (i.e. a buyer's market). The situation evolved in the early 1990s when changes resulting from the burst of the bubble economy caused customers to demand even greater variety and cheaper goods. This need would provide an opportunity for new forms of retailing, a niche filled by '100-yen shops', led by the global chain store, Daisō.

Second, convenience stores were able to adapt to a changing regulatory environment, one in which policymakers sought to curtail the rapid expansion of large-scale superstores, in part to protect mainly family-owned shops from closure. The first major legislative change in this direction was the 1974 Large Store Law (LSL), which gave regional shopkeepers the decision-making authority to determine whether a new large-scale supermarket would be able to open in their area. At the same time, LSL restricted the operating hours of large stores, but not those of convenience stores. In 1978, the legislation expanded in scope to cover medium-sized stores of 500 square metres in size. Though LSL did slow the growth of large-scale supermarket chains, Daiei and similar chains responded by opening their own convenience stores. The entry of these convenience stores thus stymied the government's aim of protecting small shops from bankruptcy.

Regulators perceived that the introduction of LSL would yield advantages for Japanese business, as they believed that encouraging small shops to modernize their distribution system would enhance their productivity (Bernstein, 1997, 506–508). Efforts designed to shield small family-owned businesses from competition would however fail. Today, in some of Japan's suburban and rural areas, one can find entire shopping arcades filled with shuttered storefronts. Other forms of modernization introduced by convenience stores further increased the divide between the winners and losers. Under the direction of Suzuki, an increasingly more sophisticated information technology system was put in place to streamline the movement of goods and information at Seven-Eleven stores, further galvanizing their position within the Japanese shopping landscape.

Third was the choice of locations. Because convenience stores were situated in populous urban areas, they did not have to compete directly with large-scale supermarkets. Moreover, since Lawson (Daiei) was dominant in the Kansai area, Seven-Eleven instead targeted the Kantō region. Another locational strategy of Seven-Eleven was to gain market dominance in a relatively small geographical area by clustering shops in close proximity. Two benefits of this tactic were that it blocked competing convenience stores from setting up a business in the same area while also promoting cost-effectiveness. The latter was realized thanks to the rationalization of the distribution system via vendor consolidation; that is, deciding on a single wholesaler for the distribution of small quantities to the stores situated in a specific area. These measures and others helped to reduce inventories and increase profit margins (Bernstein, 1997, 512–513).

Fourth was the offering of new services, thus raising the notion of 'convenience' to a new level. As mentioned above, before the emergence of the convenience-store model, Japan had many family-owned shops, which catered to the needs of small neighbourhood communities by offering a wide variety of useful products. Convenience stores competed with these shops by providing novel services not offered by them such as utility bill payment and facsimile services as well as photocopying. As mentioned above,

Itō-Yōkado's strategy was to approach existing shops about becoming a convenience store franchisee to minimize tensions with local neighbourhood businesses, which, in some cases, were already under pressure due to competition from large-scale supermarket chains. (Bernstein, 1997, 508–510). The small shop owners who agreed to convert their operations to the Seven-Eleven model would in return enjoy the advantage of being able to rely on the parent company for managerial assistance. Seven-Eleven also devised manuals to help them manage their franchise operations and provided employee training.

Fifth was the introduction of new systems. Suzuki was a true pioneer in making use of information technologies in retailing. This change sparked Japan's transition from the second industrial revolution, relying on buying and selling in bulk, to the third industrial revolution, the hallmark of which was the introduction of advanced information technologies. This process got underway in 1978 when Seven-Eleven began replacing its telephone-based order system with one using computer-processed order slips. In 1982, Seven-Eleven became the first business in Japan to make extensive use of POS (point of sales) data. In the 1990s, it continued to upgrade its information technologies by implementing an Integrated Services Digital Network of POS data to analyse and diffuse data. This sophisticated system linked the stores and headquarters to manufacturers and distribution centres (McCraw, 1997, 491).

The upgrading of its information technologies was the harbinger for the introduction of one of Seven-Eleven's most novel innovations, 'tampin kanri', a system used to collect and diffuse purchasing information on an item-by-item basis. One of the distinguishing features of this system is that it empowered employees in individual stores by allowing them to participate in purchasing strategies by analysing the buying patterns of the customers who visit their stores. By using this system, they were able to implement strategies to fine-tune their purchasing forecasts and improve the management of their inventories. As part of Seven & i Group, Seven-Eleven has continued to augment the services it offers into new areas such as banking. It has also become a truly international company, which by 2013 had over fifteen thousand stores operating nationwide and over fifty thousand globally.

9.6 Conclusions

For Daiei and Seven-Eleven, the American chain store served as a business model and a new opportunity to promote the growth of consumerism in Japan. One can now find America-inspired supermarkets and convenient stores across the nation from Hokkaido to Okinawa. Though initially adopted wholesale, the American model was soon adapted to Japanese circumstances. In the long term, it has contributed to a change in the Japanese shopping culture and consumer identity.

Suzuki modernized the American convenience-store model by introducing information technologies to such an extent that a new Japanese model would surpass even its American originator. This was evident in the 1980s when the situation for Southland would resemble that of Japan at the end of the high-growth period. Southland faced mounting competition, causing a sharp decline in sales. Its *coup de grâce* would occur in October 1987 with the crash of the US stock market, which led to a massive selling-off of its assets. Seven-Eleven Japan would purchase fifty-eight of its stores in Hawaii, thus acquiring a controlling share in the company (McCraw, 1997, 521–524).

To keep pace with changes in consumer preferences, Japanese retailing would continue to evolve over time. In the 1970s and 1980s, competitive advantages were derived from the convenience of longer business hours, additional services, and new products. However, after the bursting of the bubble in the 1990s, low prices would once again become a priority for consumers. At the same time, new competition in the form of even larger, foreign supermarket chains such as Walmart and Carrefour entered the Japanese market with varying degrees of success (Toussaint, 2011). It remains to be seen how shopping in Japan—whether by department stores, supermarkets, convenience stores, or e-commerce—will change. Innovative forms of retail, especially those employing digital technologies, are likely to emerge.

10
The Bubble Economy and its Aftermath

In March 1987, Yasuda Fire and Marine Insurance Company acquired one of Van Gogh's *Sunflowers* for the sum of 39.9 million dollars at a Christie's auction in London. It was at that time the largest amount ever paid for a painting. Japan used to have another one of the seven *Sunflowers* done by the Dutch painter, in a private collection, but it was destroyed during an air raid in 1945. The insurance company, the world's fifteenth largest at that time, was founded in 1888, when Van Gogh started to paint his series of *Sunflowers*, and its centenary anniversary was seen as an opportunity to bring back one of these paintings to Japan. It was displayed—and still is today—in the firm's private museum at its headquarters in Tokyo.[1]

During the second half of the 1980s, newspapers were full of similar stories about Japanese individuals and companies purchasing assets around the world, from Bordeaux wineries to Australian Gold Coast real estate. In 1989 when Sony took over Columbia Pictures the business magazine *Newsweek* had a cover entitled, 'Japan Invades Hollywood'.[2] All of these episodes embody the financial power that Japan had gained. While it had often been short of capital and resources from the end of shogunate, it became one of the world's wealthiest countries and a creditor nation in the 1980s. The net inflow of capital into the country led to the formation of a financial bubble. It lasted for less than a decade but its impact on Japanese business, the economy, and society was deep. It represents the end of the 'Japanese miracle' and a turning point in modern Japanese business history. This chapter discusses the conditions for the formation of the financial bubble (section 10.1) and two related developments: the growth of outward FDI (section 10.2) and the increase in luxury product consumption (section 10.3). Finally, section 10.4 focuses on the collapse of the bubble and its consequences.

---

[1] *The New York Times*, 9 April 1987.
[2] *Newsweek*, 9 October 1989.

10.1 The formation of the financial bubble

The growth of the Nikkei index of the Tokyo Stock Exchange and land prices witnessed a brief period of stagnation following the 1973 oil shock, but started increasing steadily at the end of the 1970s (see Figure 10.1). The rise was however moderate. In 1985, the Nikkei index entered a new period of dramatic growth, going from 12,000 points in February that year to a historical peak at 38,915 points in December 1989. On paper, the value of Japanese firms tripled in just a few years. In 1989, the ranking of the world's top fifty largest companies based on market capitalization included thirty-two Japanese firms, among which the top five largest Nippon Telegraph and Telephone (NTT), a communications company privatized four years earlier, was the world's largest company, with a market value of more than 163 billion US dollars. It was followed by four Japanese banks, each with a value over 60 billion.[3]

Two years after the start of the rise of stock-market prices, land prices also began to escalate in Tokyo, with an average increase of 50.5 per cent in 1987 and 67 per cent in 1988. Osaka followed in 1988 and Kyoto in 1989 (see Table 10.1). According to an urban legend that became famous through the

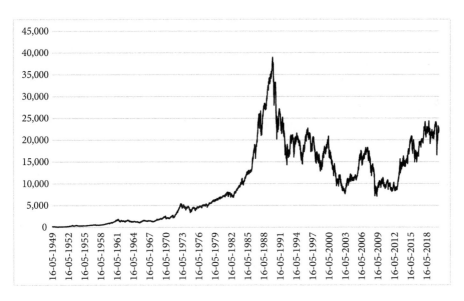

Figure 10.1 Nikkei Index, 1949–2019
Source: Bank of Japan Time-series Data Search

---

[3] Diamond Online, https://diamond.jp/articles/-/177641?page=2 (accessed 18 August 2020).

Table 10.1 Evolution of housing prices in major Japanese cities, as a percentage, 1985–1992

	1985	1986	1987	1988	1989	1990	1991	1992
Tokyo City	2.9	6.4	50.5	67.0	−6.3	−0.3	0.1	−10.3
Osaka Prefecture	n/a	3.3	4.3	20.6	35.5	58.6	2.1	−24.5
Kyoto Prefecture	n/a	3.2	3.4	8.9	31.8	67.1	14.9	−27.5

Source: Kinugawa (2002), 67–68

global media, at the peak of the land price bubble the dollar value of the Imperial Palace in Tokyo surpassed that of the entire state of California.[4] This is of course unverifiable as the palace has never been for sale on the market, but such an assertion expresses the strong impact that the rising land price bubble had on the world media.

Why did such a huge and unprecedented financial bubble occur in Japan during the second half of the 1980s? Many scholars have carried out research in macroeconomics and monetary policy to answer this question (Ito, 2003; Saxonhouse and Stern, 2004). Business historian Kikkawa Takeo has convincingly argued that, from a historical perspective, the enormous inflow of money into the Japanese financial market was something new in a country characterized by a lack of capital (Kikkawa, 2006). The sudden and growing availability of capital flowing into stock and land markets led to a bubble. There are three major causes for the fast increase in the inflow of capital.

First, the balance of trade became increasingly positive from the early 1980s, though it had been always slightly negative in the 1950s and 1960s. The trade surplus started to rise in the 1970s but the two oil shocks put an end to this growth—importing energy was costly and made the balance of trade negative. However, it became positive again in 1981. It grew very fast and remained positive until 2011, when the closure of nuclear plants throughout the country following the accident of Fukushima Daiichi led to the increase of imports of oil and gas, as shown in Chapter 12. During the 1980s, the total surplus amounted to on average 2.2 per cent of GDP (Fukao et al., 2018, 304). This surplus was the direct consequence of presence of competitive industries in world markets, notably automobiles and electronics.

A second major cause of the availability of capital was the international currency policy of the Bank of Japan (BOJ) (Garside, 2012, 68–69). In order to limit the appreciation of the yen after the Plaza Agreement, the BOJ cut

---

[4] See for example *The Guardian*, 27 March 2000 or *The Economist*, 11 October 2007.

the interest rate five times between 1986 and 1987, from five per cent in January 1986 to 2.5 per cent in February 1987. The liberalization of capital flows strengthened the presence of foreign investors in Japan. Goldman Sachs (1983), Credit Suisse (1986), and UBS (1986) opened subsidiaries in Japan. Hence, the BOJ's objective was to make accounts in yen less attractive to foreign investors and to support Japanese exporting industries. The outcome was also to make cheap yen available in the domestic market.

Third, one must stress the impact of a major change in corporate financing. The deregulation of the Japanese financial system enabled companies in the manufacturing industry to make greater use of the domestic financial market to finance their investments in the 1980s, rather than the long-term loans by their main banks. For example, the issuing of unsecured bonds was authorized in 1979. Toyota and Matsushita Electric were the first two companies to use this financial instrument that year. The number amounted to 175 firms in July 1985 and to about 500 in November 1988 (Hoshi and Kashyap, 2001, 229–230). Moreover, increasing revenues from exports also supported self-financing. Consequently, the main banks had to find new customers and offer loans to businesses with a higher level of risk. Between 1975 and 1990, there was a clear structural shift among corporate borrowers. For all Japanese banks, the loans to large enterprises declined from 40 per cent to about 20 per cent between those two years, while small firms saw their share climb from 35 per cent to 65 per cent (Garside, 2012). Consequently, the sudden and large inflow of available capital into the Japanese economy led private companies and banks to purchase assets such as stocks and land. This led to speculation and to the formation of a price asset bubble.

10.2 The development of outward FDI

The increasing availability of capital, low interest rates, and the growing value of the yen became strong incentives for Japanese to invest abroad in the 1980s. Moreover, Japanese companies and investors had more money, and foreign assets were cheaper to purchase. Figure 10.2 clearly shows that the 1980s, and particularly the mid-1980s, were a turning point in the internationalization of Japanese companies. It also emphasizes the impact of yen's appreciation, as the yearly average value of the US dollar dropped from 204 yen in 1980 and 201 in 1985 to 135 in 1990. It continued then to decrease and stayed at a low level throughout the 1990s, with an average of 116 yen. At the same time, the flow of outward foreign investment expanded more and more rapidly. While it had always been under 5 billion US dollars in the 1970s, it hit this mark for

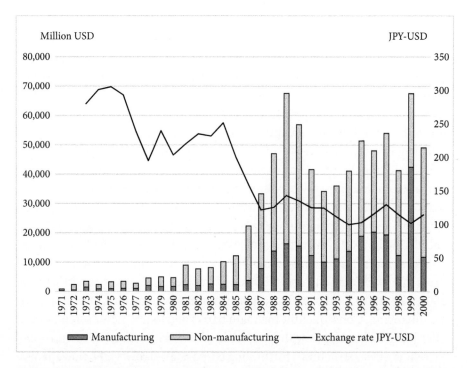

Figure 10.2 Japanese outward FDI, flows in million USD, and exchange rate with the US dollar, 1971–2000
Source: JETRO and BOJNote: data for fiscal years concerning FDI.

the first time in 1980 before climbing to 12.2 billion in 1985 and peaking at 67.5 billion in 1990. These investments contributed to increasing the global presence of Japanese business overseas. Until 1980, the value of the outward stock of Japanese FDI amounted to less than 1 per cent of GDP, which is very low by international comparison (8.1 per cent of GDP for the United States and 6.2 per cent for the European Union in 1980). It grew to 6.6 per cent of GDP in 1990, making the ratio of Japan closer to that of the United States (7.5 per cent of GDP). Measured as a proportion of world outward stock of FDI, the share of Japan went from 3.7 per cent in 1980 to 11.2 per cent in 2000 (Dunning and Lundan, 2008, 24).

Producing in and exporting from Southeast Asia in particular, had already begun during the 1970s (see Chapter 8), a move that had become much more profitable for Japanese firms, which pursued a strategy to invest abroad to strengthen their foreign presence. Hence, in 1990, the global ranking of the top 100 largest non-financial transnational corporations included a total of twelve Japanese multinationals. They were especially active in the production of electronics (Matsushita, Sony, Toshiba), cars (Honda, Nissan, Toyota), and rubber (Bridgestone). However, the manufacturing industry was not the main target of investment in the second half of the 1980s, and its relative share even decreased at that time. This sector amounted to 35.2 per cent of outward foreign direct investment in the 1970s and only 24.9 per cent in the 1980s.

Finance and real estate were the driving forces of the sharp increase in foreign investments. When the flow peaked, in 1989, the largest sectors were banks and insurance (15.4 billion US dollars), real estate (14.3 billion), and services (10.6 billion). In comparison, the entire manufacturing industry represented only 16.3 billion, and within it the largest sectors were electric machinery and electronics (4.5 billion), chemicals (2.1 billion), and vehicles (2 billion). For example, Sumitomo Bank experienced expansion throughout the world. During the high-growth years, it had founded branches in Germany, Hong Kong, Singapore, the United Kingdom, and the United States to support the activities of the firms in its *keiretsu*, particularly its trading company. However, in the 1980s, it started engaging in new banking activities around the world with no relationship to its *keiretsu*. In 1984, it took over a bank in Switzerland (Banca del Gottardo) and engaged in private banking in Europe. It then opened subsidiaries in Frankfurt (1988), Paris (1988), and in Ireland (1989). At the same time, Sumitomo Bank engaged in a securities business in the United States, taking an equity stake in Goldman Sachs & Co. (1986) and various financial companies in New York (1990). Finally, in Asia, Sumitomo opened branches and founded banks in China (1992), Thailand (1993), and Indonesia (1993) (Slager, 2004, 395–397). Similar trends can be observed for all the major banks and securities companies. Moreover, banks and investors did not invest abroad solely through direct investment. The level of portfolio investment (purchase of stocks and bonds without managing interest) and short-term positions became much higher. Between 1984 and 1989, the total amount of Japanese assets abroad grew from 341 to 1,771 billion dollars, with a stable share of direct investment (about 11 per cent).

Resort hotels in Australia and Hawaii were in particular the targets of Japanese investments in real estate. EIE International is a case in point (Nikkei, 2000, 100–158). In 1986, this medium-sized company, founded in 1972 to import and distribute magnetic tapes made by the American company 3M, had the opportunity to acquire the Hyatt Hotel in Saipan, with financial support from the Long-Term Credit Bank of Japan (LTCB). In the years to follow, it made similar investments on the Gold Coast (Australia) as well as in Hong Kong, London, New York, Los Angeles, and Tokyo. In 1991, the total assets of EIE International amounted to 293 billion yen (about 2.3 billion US dollars).

As for services, this sector included general trading companies which purchased various assets abroad to secure their supply of raw materials and increase their profits. Their business model shifted hence from pure trading activities to portfolio investment in a broad range of activities, from energy to machinery, food, and metals. Itoh, Marubeni, Mitsubishi, Mitsui, and Nissho Iwai were all present in the 1990 global ranking of the top 100 largest non-financial transnational corporations (UNCTAD, 1993, 26–27).

10.3 Luxury consumption in Japan

The rapid increase in disposal income and the high yen had a profound impact on domestic consumption. Japanese had more disposable income and used it to increase their purchases of personal goods. This led to the growth in consumption of Western luxury goods, making Japan the top market for this industry during the second half of the 1980s (Donzé, 2020). The attraction of Japanese customers to French fashion and American jewellery started earlier, and department stores had been introducing luxury goods in Tokyo and Osaka since the 1960s. However, the scope of consumption changed drastically as Japan became the base for the expansion of European luxury companies in the global market (Donzé and Fujioka, 2015). For example, Japan had already overtaken the United States in 1976 as the first market for the export of French leather goods, but the overall level was still low (82.8 million euro). It started its high growth in the following decade, and rose from 154.4 million euro in 1980 to 761.1 million in 1989. During the entire period, Japan had a growing share of exports: 8.7 per cent in 1976, 18.1 per cent in 1980, and 26.6 per cent in 1989 (Donzé, 2020). The trend was similar for other luxury goods.

Despite the growing interest of Japanese consumers in Western luxury goods, only a handful of companies had established sales subsidiaries in Japan when the bubble economy began. It started with the cosmetic makers, L'Oréal (1963) and Estée Lauder (1967), followed by a few watchmakers and jewellers such as Tiffany (1972), Boucheron (1973), and Longines (1974), as well as French leather goods and fashion brands like Louis Vuitton (1978), Chanel (1980), and Hermès (1983) (Bytheway, 2014). These companies focused on the import and distribution of their goods through existing retail channels, mostly department stores. They were, however, exceptions.

Department stores had established a unique position in the domestic luxury market since the beginning of the twentieth century. They offered consumers a broad range of goods, from traditional Japanese products such as *kimono* and ceramics, to imported goods like fashion, jewellery, and watches. After World War II, when French haute couture renewed its conquest of world markets, department stores were the key partners for their expansion in Japan. They had built business relationships with domestic apparel companies that produced Western-style clothing and were hence able to produce French fashion under license. Licensing was the first market-entry strategy for European luxury companies. Daimaru was a pioneer and in 1953 it had already signed an agreement with Christian Dior, the uncontested leader of postwar French fashion. Numerous department stores followed this trend by establishing similar partnerships with French designers: Takashimaya with Pierre Cardin (1959), Matsuzakaya with Nina Ricci (1961), Mitsukoshi with Guy Laroche (1963), and Isetan with Pierre Cardin (1963). Moreover, a few apparel firms signed licensing agreements directly with foreign fashion companies, like Sanyo Shōkai with Burberry (1969) and Kawabe with Yves Saint Laurent (1970) (Donzé, 2020).

In Western countries, luxury was, until the 1990s, a small business targeting a wealthy elite clientele. Japanese department stores, however, adopted a different approach that led to the democratization of luxury. Licensing allowed them to manufacture not only high-priced fashion, but also a broad range of branded accessories, from handkerchiefs and underwear to keyholders and necklaces. As these products were much cheaper than ready-to-wear clothing, they attracted a new and younger clientele, thus helping companies to expand the sales and profitability of their business. The shift to accessible luxury was later adopted by the European headquarters and applied to their worldwide operations. Japanese department stores were hence not simply retailers of foreign luxury goods. They adapted them to the specificities of the domestic market to support their expansion. Consequently, the gross sales of Japanese department stores—including items other than foreign luxury products such as food and domestic fashion—expanded steadily from the 1970s and experienced rapid growth during the bubble economy period. Their overall gross sales amounted to 1,824 billion yen in 1970 and 5,722 billion yen in 1980. It reached a historical peak in 1991, with 9,714 billion yen.[5]

Although foreign companies had a dominant position in expanding the domestic luxury market, Japanese companies were not completely absent. Some enterprises adapted their strategy to this growing market for accessible luxury. For example, Mikimoto made its cultured pearl necklaces a

---

[5] Japan Department Stores Association, sales statistics, https://www.depart.or.jp/store_sale/ (accessed 15 August 2020).

must-have item for wedding ceremonies, and focused on this business in the 1980s. It also attempted to diversify into accessories with the launch of cosmetics and perfume in 1979, then watches and writing instruments in the 1980s. It also engaged in in-flight sales in 1989 with the cooperation of Korean Airlines. Targeting the mass-market supported the fast development of sales, which doubled between 1980 and 1990. As for the watchmaker Seiko, which gained fame by marketing the world's first quartz watch in 1969, it did not want to allow the Swiss manufacturers to dominate the domestic luxury watch market. It consequently relaunched its sub-brand, Grand Seiko for high-quality mechanical watches in 1988, with the obvious objective of competing with Rolex and Omega (Donzé, 2020). However, in fashion, Japanese designers were unable to develop strong brands in cooperation with local apparel companies and department stores. Kenzō Takada, Issey Miyake, and Hanae Mori moved to Paris in the 1970s and 1980s to boost their careers, but it was difficult for them to become large international businesses in the same way as the Western luxury firms. Kenzo was acquired by LVMH in 1993, and the designers who went back to Tokyo pursued their careers as relatively small businesses (Donzé and Fujioka, 2021).

The collapse of the price asset bubble in 1991–1992 had a strong but not a dramatic impact on luxury consumption in Japan. The decline in sales at department stores (8,820 billion yen in 2000 and 6,292 billion in 2010) mirrors a similar deep crisis of the luxury business in Japan. The loss in competitiveness for the department stores was, however, not merely the result of the end of bubble economy. They suffered from the new brand strategy adopted then by European luxury companies, for whom they had been key partners since the 1960s. In order to manage global brands efficiently, European headquarters stopped licensing manufacturing and distribution to Japanese department stores. They took control of their distribution in the 1990s. Most of the largest luxury brands opened subsidiaries in Japan: Coach (1991), Miu Miu (1991), Bulgari (1991), Giorgio Armani (1995), Vivienne Westwood (1996), Tag Heuer (1997), Burberry (2000), Paul Smith (2002), Berlutti (2002), Prada (2003), Cartier (2003), and so on. They opened monobrand stores in the major shopping districts of central Tokyo and weakened their ties with department stores. The transformation of luxury retailing supported consumption during the 1990s. Japan kept, for example, its importance as the world's largest market for French leather goods, with a high share of 30 per cent in 1994–2003. However, it plummeted in later years (12.4 per cent in 2010; 4 per cent in 2019).

10.4 The collapse of the bubble economy and its consequences

The price asset bubble peaked at the end of 1989. On 29 December of that year, the Nikkei index reached its highest historical record, at nearly 39,000 points (see Figure 10.1). Real estate prices in Tokyo also had attained their highest level and started to decline slightly at the end of the year, but the land bubble shifted to Osaka and Kyoto where prices continued to climb until 1991 (see Table 10.1). The prices of these assets were not related to their real value, and the authorities felt a need to put an end to speculation. In 1986, the government had already organized a special group of cabinet members to deal with rising land prices. The following year, it introduced a tax on short-term capital gains for corporations. At the same time, BOJ intervened and tightened the money supply. It again raised the discount rate, which went from 2.5 per cent in May 1989 to 6 per cent in August 1990, in order to tighten the money supply (make money more expensive to borrow by raising interest rates) to reduce the amount of capital in the economy.[6] In the meantime, in April 1990, the government asked banks not to increase their lending to the real estate sector (Ito, 2003, 295). In 1991, the tax on capital gains on real estate rose from 32.5 per cent to 39 per cent. The government also introduced a new land tax (1992) followed by a special tax on unused land in metropolitan areas (1993).

All of these measures had a direct effect on the bubble economy. The value of stocks declined quickly. The Nikkei index dropped to nearly 20,000 points in October 1990 and hit a new low at under 15,000 points in August 1992 (see Figure 10.1). Real estate prices followed in 1992 with a dramatic decline throughout the country. In 1991 and 1992, the loss of value can be estimated at 178 trillion yen for stocks and 318 trillion for land (Iyoda, 2010, 81). The bursting of the bubble was dramatic for many enterprises as well as for individuals who had invested in assets that lost their value. Many real estate companies and financial firms became insolvent, meaning that they were no longer able to reimburse the loans they had made to purchase land. For example, EIE International was riddled with bad debts and lost the support of the LTCB in 1993. After a long decline, it went bankrupt in 2000. This case is far from isolated. In June 1995, 75.9 per cent of the total assets of the seven

---

[6] Bank of Japan, https://www.boj.or.jp/en/statistics/boj/other/discount/discount.htm/ (accessed 25 August 2020).

largest real estate companies were considered 'bad debts' or 'non-performing loans' (*furyō saiken*) (Kinugawa, 2002, 162).

Such bad debt became a national issue that threatened the stability of the financial system. In 1997, Sanyo Securities, a medium-sized company, and Yamaichi Securities, formed in 1897 as one of the oldest and largest companies in Japan in this sector, both went bankrupt. The same year, two banks closed due to insolvency: Hokkaido Takushoku Bank, one of the largest regional banks in the country, and Tokuyo Bank, a small bank in the Tohoku region. According to the Ministry of Finance, the total amount of bad debt was estimated at 77 trillion yen in March 1998 (about 600 billion US dollars that year) (Garside, 2012, 122). In response the government adopted several plans in 1998 to rescue banks and save the nation's financial system. Large amounts of public capital were injected to settle the bad debt in 1998 and 1999 but to no avail. At the end of 1998, the state nationalized the two important financial institutions, the LTCB and Nippon Credit Bank (NCB). Draconian measures were adopted to improve the balance sheets of these two banks and ensure their survival. In 2000, LTCB was sold to a group of American investors, and NCB to domestic investors, including Softbank. They were renamed respectively Shinsei Bank and Aozora Bank. The restoration of their profitability was pursued through strict measures against borrowers. Many borrowers' loans were terminated leaving them insolvent, a policy that led to the bankruptcy of thirty-two listed companies between 1997 and 2003, among them, Sogo Department Store and Dai-Ichi Hotel (Fukuda and Koibuchi, 2006, 239).

The difficulties faced by banks during the 1990s also resulted from an institutional change that occurred during the previous decade: the end of the so-called convoy system. During the high-growth period, the Ministry of Finance had introduced administrative guidance according to which a bank having financial difficulties had to be helped or merged by other banks. This policy, which reveals a feature of communitarian capitalism, contributed to the stability of the Japanese financial system, but was gradually abandoned in the late 1980s in favour of a more liberalized environment (Hoshi, 2002).

Numerous companies from the manufacturing industry and non-financial services were also severely hit by the bursting of the bubble, even though they were not directly linked to the bankrupt banks and securities companies. The new financial strategies adopted by many companies in the early 1980s, following the liberalization of corporate bond issuing in 1977–1981, had caused them to loosen their ties with their main banks. Yet, many companies did not have sufficient knowledge of finance, and they made risky investments outside their main activities of manufacturing or services. There was a strong belief in the 1980s that the new high-tech financial techniques—called *zaiteku*—had made investments safer. However, this was not always the case, and many companies incurred losses. This problem started before the burst of the bubble but worsened during the bubble period and its aftermath. For example, in 1987, Tateho Chemicals, a mid-sized company specializing in the production of ceramics and other materials, lost 28 billion yen (about 191 million US dollars at that time) in futures trading in the Japanese government bond market.[7] Such losses became more common in the 1990s, as seen in the examples of Sanrio (1991), Hanwa Industry (1992), Sumitomo Trading (1996), and Yakult (1998).[8] It also led to the bankruptcy of some companies like Tokyo Food Trading (1997) (Kikkawa, 2006). The common problem faced by all these firms was the lack of a monitoring system for investment activities. The regulations for trading were weak, and this gave way to risky investments that sometimes largely exceeded the scope of the company's total assets. However, the lack of financial know-how by manufacturing companies was not a general trend. Some firms, like Toyota Motor, acquired skills in equity finance, and were able to make efficient use of the financial system (e.g. maintaining cross-shareholding within its *keiretsu* and listing on the New York Stock Exchange in 1999) (Kikkawa, 2006, 117–118).

The collapse of the financial system put an end to forty years of fast economic development. Capital investment by companies, which had traditionally been the pillar of growth since the 1950s, as well as private consumption declined after 1991. The average rate of annual GDP growth dropped to 1.8 per cent in 1991–1996 and to 0.5 per cent in 1997–2002 (Hashimoto et al., 2019, 306). Economic stagnation also had a dramatic impact on the employment system. The rate of unemployment rose from 2.1 per cent in 1990 to 4.7 per cent in 2000 (Hashimoto et al., 2019, 314). The changes also affected the employment situation: the share of non-permanent jobs in the national workforce increased from 16.4 per cent in 1985 to 26 per cent in 2000.[9] Finally, the economic slowdown had a negative effect on tax revenues. The government again started to issue special deficit-financing bonds in 1994. The government's gross financial liabilities went from 63.9 per cent of nominal GDP in 1990 to 135.4 per cent in 2000.[10] The authorities intervened in an attempt to restart the economy and put an end to a deflationary cycle that had plagued it since 1992. BOJ gradually decreased the discount rate from 6

---

[7] *Financial Times*, 2 October 1987.
[8] *Financial Times*, 14 November 1991, 27 February 1992, 20 September 1996.
[9] Statistics Bureau of Japan, Labour Survey, https://www.stat.go.jp/english/data/roudou/index.html (accessed 25 August 2020).
[10] OECD Statistics, https://stats.oecd.org/ (accessed 25 August 2020).

per cent to 0.5 per cent between July 1991 and September 1995.[11] This move, however, had no effect, and the rates have not returned to the 1 per cent mark since then.

The liberalization of the financial system was at the core of the economic policy of the Japanese government during the post-bubble years (Toya and Amyx, 2006). Inefficient and bureaucratic, it was seen as an obstacle to the development of manufacturing companies and the recovery of the economy. This was, however, not a Japanese specificity; the deregulation of finance was also a major political trend in the United States and Western Europe during the 1990s. In Japan, the financial 'big bang' policy was implemented by Prime Minister Hashimoto Ryūtarō (1937–2006). A member of the LDP (Liberal Democratic Party) that had ruled Japan since 1955, Hashimoto had already had a long career in successive cabinets when he was appointed prime minister in January 1996. Of note is that he had been minister of transport under Prime Minister Nakasone Yasuhirō in 1986–1987, and was placed in charge of the privatization of Japan Railways (see Box 10.1). He was a neoliberal, meaning that he supported a small government and minimal intervention in business and the economy. The most significant measures in his 'big bang' policy were the liberalization of the foreign exchange business (1997) and the authorization of holding companies (1997) which had been forbidden since 1947 due to the anti-monopoly law, introduced during the occupation period. The liberalization of finance has been pursued by his successors until 2001, with major steps like the adoption of a law to reform the financial system that deregulated the activities of banks and insurance companies (1998), the authorization of online securities firms (1998), the liberalization of fees on securities transactions (1999), and the authorization of real estate investment trusts (2000).

Box 10.1 Nakasone and the privatization of state-owned enterprises

Neoliberalism is a policy that is strongly associated with the American president Ronald Reagan (1981–1989) and the British prime minister Margaret Thatcher (1979–1990). Facing high inflation and the decline of the competitiveness of their manufacturing industries, they adopted various policies characterized by non-interventionism, deregulation, and the privatization of state-owned enterprises.

---

[11] Bank of Japan, https://www.boj.or.jp/en/statistics/boj/other/discount/discount.htm/ (accessed 25 August 2020).

However, this policy went far beyond the United States and the United Kingdom, becoming a global phenomenon, from Latin American to Europe and Asia.

In Japan, neoliberalism rose to prominence under Nakasone Yasuhirō (1918–2019), who was prime minister between 1982 and 1987. While the LDP had ruled the country since 1955, it was divided into several internal factions. Until 1980, 'career bureaucrats-turned-politicians' (Gordon, 2003, 301) controlled the party and directed the cabinet. Most of them were from the most powerful ministries, Finance and International Trade and Industry. They believed in the role of the state to support the development of large competitive corporations. Yet, in the mid-1970s, after the technological catch-up had been achieved, the liberal faction asked for a withdrawal of the state and the deregulation of economy. Members of this faction were in office for a short time in 1972–1974 under prime minister Tanaka Kakuei (1918–1993), a self-made man who made his fortune in the construction industry, and dominated Japanese politics in the 1980s and 1990s (Gordon, 2003, 301–302).

Nakasone became a deputy in the House of Representatives in 1947, and was a supporter of Tanaka. One of the main features of Nakasone's economic policy was the privatization of large state-owned companies, namely Japan Tobacco and Salt Public Corporation (1985), Nippon Telegraph and Telephone Public Corporation (1985), and Japan National Railways (1987). The first two were renamed Japan Tobacco (JT) and Nippon Telegraph and Telephone (NTT) and were listed respectively in 1994 and 1987. As for the third one, it was reorganized in 1987 as Japan Railways Group (JR) which includes six regional passenger transportation companies, one freight transportation company, and two service companies. The government initially retained the ownership of these companies, but they were gradually privatized in the 1990s. JR East was listed in 1993, JR West in 1996, and JR Central in 1997. Finally, Japan Airlines (JAL), which from 1953 was a semi-governmental public corporation, was fully privatized in 1987, when the government liberalized the airline business. The objective of privatization was to improve their profitability, by closing or decreasing money-losing operations and introducing the principles of private-sector management. It also provided the political opportunity to weaken the labour unions and the Japan Socialist Party, which were traditionally strongly supported by these public corporations and posed a threat to LDP dominance.

The banking crisis and the liberalization of finance led to a profound transformation of the banking industry from the second half of the 1990s. While regulation had kept the financial system stable since the 1960s, a succession of mega-mergers gave birth to three large banking groups (see Figure 10.3): Mizuho Holdings, formed in 2000 through the merger of Dai-Ichi Kangyō Bank, Fuji Bank, and Industrial Bank of Japan; Sumitomo Mitsui

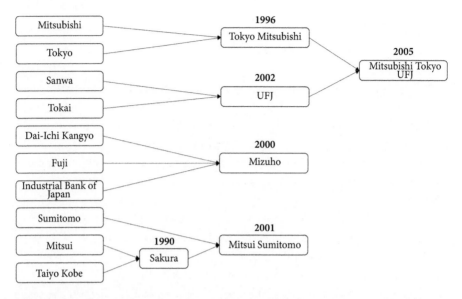

Figure 10.3 Waves of mergers and formation of mega banks in Japan, simplified chart
Source: Drafted by the authors

Bank, founded in 2001 with the merger of Sumitomo Bank and Mitsui Bank; MUFJ Bank, which resulted from the merger in 2005 of two groups, Tokyo-Mitsubishi Bank and UFJ Bank, formed through the merger in 2002 of Sanwa and Tokai Banks. Moreover, liberalization also contributed to the foundation of new banks by large corporations: Seven Bank (2001), Sony Bank (2001), Rakuten Bank (2005), and Aeon Bank (2006).

These mega-mergers brought together financial institutions that were once the main banks of *keiretsu*. This is the manifestation rather than the cause of the decline and the end of traditional *keiretsu*. Many companies had already moved to financial markets to obtain a supply of capital prior to the bubble, which led banks to focus on new businesses, as explained above. Hence, in the 1990s, the need for companies to get rid of their bad debts and increased competition in financial markets due to liberalization gave way to the formation of mega banks. In this context, the new driver of investment was profitability, and not ensuring the stability of the business system. Thus, cross-shareholding started to decline sharply after 1990. For all the companies listed on the Tokyo Stock Exchange, the proportion of 'insider shareholders' (shareholders that invest to keep capital stable), a feature of the Japanese Business System, declined from more than 60 per cent during the early 1990s to less than 45 per cent in 2000, and below the 35 per cent mark in 2005 (Hashimoto et al., 2019, 434). This enabled outsiders (investment funds, pension funds, individuals, and foreigners) to increase their weight and influence in Japanese companies. Thus, corporate governance started to change, which contributed to the decline of the traditional Japanese Business System (see Chapter 11) and the form of capitalism it embodied.

10.5 Conclusion

Beyond the price asset bubble itself, which left a lasting impression due to its excesses, the liberalization of finance was a turning point in the history of Japanese capitalism. It started before the bubble—which was one of the causes—and continued throughout the 1990s as a remedy for the crisis. Regulation of the economy and coordination of activities within the *keiretsu* had been the foundations of the postwar Japanese Business System. It was now fully threatened by the liberalization of finance which led to an environment characterized by increased competition. Entrepreneurs who were not risk averse seized the opportunities offered by this institutional change, like Takahashi Harunori (1945–2005), the CEO of EIE International who purchased real estate around the world. However, not all the real estate tycoons ended up bankrupt when the bubble collapsed. Mori Taikichirō (1904–1993), founder of Mori Building Company, became the world's richest person in 1991, according to the business magazine *Forbes*.[12] His descendants, active in real estate, are still ranked among the wealthiest Japanese today.

Yet, there is a need to look beyond the real estate magnates to understand entrepreneurship in the 1980s and 1990s. Deregulation, economic stagnation, and social change were also opportunities to launch new businesses, like Softbank (founded in 1981), Uniqlo (1984), and the telecom operator DDI (1984; today: KDDI). All three started as private companies, identified the potential growth of a new business (internet services, fast fashion, and mobile communication respectively), entered financial markets in the 1990s, and experienced fast growth after 2000 (see Chapter 12).

Outward FDI is another characteristic of the new business practices that emerged in the 1980s. The post-bubble crisis only had a limited impact on the internationalization of Japanese enterprises. Except in 1992 and 1993, the

---

[12] *Los Angeles Times*, 8 July 1991.

annual flow remained above 40 billion dollars until 2000 (see Figure 10.2). In 2000, the outward stock of FDI by Japanese amounted to 278.4 billion dollars, that is, 5.9 per cent of GDP. The weight of Japan in global outward stock of FDI declined (4.3 per cent in 2000) due to losses made by banks and real estate firms. A comeback in manufacturing investments (41.5 per cent of FDI in 1991–1995 against 22.6 per cent in 1985–1989) and an increased share in Asia (19.6 per cent of FDI in 1991–1995 against 12.2 per cent in 1985–1989) show that Japanese companies in the automobile and electronics industries pursued and developed internationally. The exchange rate (high yen or *endaka*) was a major push factor for the relocation of production overseas as the strong yen continued to make exports from Japan expensive.

11
Global Competition during the Lost Decades

In 2005, for the first time since World War II, the population of Japan, then 127.7 million people, showed a decrease from the previous year. The decline was still limited—about eight thousand people—and the population returned to a slight rise in the following years. However, after a peak at just over 128 million in 2007–2010, the population entered a period of continuous decline (124.8 million in August 2022). This demographic evolution results from a strong decline in births and particularly from a low level of immigration (2.3 per cent of total population in 2020). Although foreigners have supported population growth in Western Europe and North America since the late twentieth century, Japan did not follow this path.[1]

The aging and declining population caused a change in the paradigm for Japanese society and business. One must remember that Japan was the world's second largest economy from 1968 to 2010, when it was overtaken by China. Since the beginning of the Edo period at least, economic development and growth had relied on the domestic market, leading to a foreign policy and relationship with foreigners that was driven by the needs of local society and corporations. Yet, in the early twenty-first century, this was not possible any longer. Horioka (2006) has clearly demonstrated the impact of the stagnation of household consumption on the prolonged slowdown of Japanese economy. Consequently, Japanese companies had to cross their national borders to find new customers and increase their sales. The pursuit of economic growth abroad had become a necessity to cover increasing healthcare and social welfare expenses.

Thus, globalization became the major challenge for entrepreneurs and companies in nearly every sector of the economy. Moreover, this happened in a context characterized by the dramatic rise of global competition, with the advent of new competitors in South Korea, Taiwan, China, and other industrialized nations in Asia. The transformation of the world

---

[1] Statistics Bureau of Japan, https://www.stat.go.jp/ (accessed 25 August 2022).

Japanese Capitalism and Entrepreneurship. Pierre-Yves Donzé and Julia S. Yongue, Oxford University Press.
© Pierre-Yves Donzé and Julia S. Yongue (2024). DOI: 10.1093/oso/9780192887474.003.0012

economy negatively affected the competitiveness of the Japanese manufacturing industries precisely when they needed to strengthen their global expansion.

Although some scholars have described the 1990s and the 2000s collectively as the 'lost decades', Kikkawa Takeo has argued that each decade was distinctive. The 1990s were a period of crisis due to financial losses and bad debts after the bursting of the price asset bubble, but Japanese companies maintained their competitiveness in manufacturing, as expressed by a high trade surplus. However, during the first decade of the 2000s, these firms faced a severe crisis marked by the loss of competitiveness in their core activities. Except for the automobile industry, most Japanese manufacturing firms declined after 2000 (Kikkawa, 2006). Hence, the objective of this chapter is to discuss how the Japanese management and business environment changed in the context of globalization. After an overview of the transformation of corporate governance (section 11.1), the focus turns to the cases of the electronics (section 11.2) and automobile (section 11.3) industries. Next, this chapter tackles the development of foreign firms in Japan (section 11.4), start-ups and entrepreneurship (section 11.5), before concluding with an overview of the emergence of Cool Japan as an opportunity for growing business opportunities abroad (section 11.6).

11.1 A new corporate governance

The deregulation of the Japanese financial system during the 1990s had a deep impact on the organization of firms. The reorganization of the banking industry, characterized by mergers that led to the formation of three megabanks, put an end to the main bank system and weakened the *keiretsu*. Moreover, the government allowed the formation of holding companies in 1997—which had been forbidden by the anti-monopoly law put in place by the occupation forces after World War II. The change enabled enterprises to reorganize as groups. In October 2012, among a total of about 3,600 listed companies in Japan, 420 were holding companies (Hashimoto et al., 2019, 400). Mergers and acquisitions (M&A) became a common way to grow from the late 1990s. Whereas diversification relied traditionally on in-house innovation during the high-growth years, deregulation made it possible to enter new businesses. For example, Fuji Film Corporation repositioned itself as a medical device business, built on its expertise in X-ray films and medical imaging. To make this shift, it took over a total of seventeen companies specializing in healthcare in 2005–2010 (among which 11 were abroad), followed by sixteen others (10 abroad) in 2011–2020.[2]

In addition, the stable ownership by insider shareholders that had once characterized governance in Japanese Business System declined dramatically from the 1990s (see Chapter 10). New investors established themselves as dominant players in the Tokyo Stock Exchange, particularly foreigners (see Table 11.1). Moreover, within financial institutions, an important shift occurred between city and regional banks, whose share dropped from 15.7 per cent in 1990 to 2.9 per cent in 2019, to investment trusts, whose share grew over the same period from 9.8 per cent to 21.7 per cent. Together, foreigners and investment trusts owned a third of the capital of Japanese listed companies in 2000 and a half in 2019. Unlike insider shareholders that privileged the stability of ownership and *keiretsu*, these new investors gave priority to short-term profits. This put pressure on companies to adopt new management practices and new organization in order to improve their profitability.

The new corporate governance model could also be characterized by a smaller number of members on the board of directors. Traditionally, this body rewarded successful managers who were close to retirement by including them on their boards, and it had a weak influence on the management of the company. In the early 1990s, the boards of Toyota and Hitachi had for example more than fifty members (Hashimoto et al., 2019, 443). The crisis of the main banks, which used to monitor companies, made it necessary for companies to strengthen their internal mechanisms to control their activities. The number of members on the boards decreased, and directors

Table 11.1 Tokyo Stock Exchange, shareholding ratio by investor category, as a percentage, 1990–2019

	1990	2000	2010	2019
Number of companies	2,078	2,587	3,616	3,789
Financial institutions, %	43.0	39.1	29.7	29.5
Securities companies, %	1.7	0.7	1.8	2.0
Business corporations, %	30.1	21.8	21.2	22.3
Foreigner investors, %	4.7	18.8	26.7	29.6
Government (central and local), %	0.3	0.2	0.3	0.1
Individuals, %	20.4	19.4	20.3	16.5

Source: Tokyo Stock Exchange

---

[2] https://ir.fujifilm.com/ja/investors/performance-and-finance/m-and-a.html (accessed 20 September 2020).

from outside the company, including foreigners, began to be appointed. The new objectives of the boards were to decide a strategy for the firm and to oversee its execution, like in the United States. Some large companies also started appointing foreign CEOs, like Carlos Ghosn at Nissan (2000–2017) or Howard Stringer at Sony (2005–2012). They and others contributed to transforming management practices at large corporations. Known as the 'cost killer', Ghosn was able to return Nissan to profitability through the termination of relationships with its suppliers (Nissan sold *keiretsu* investments to reduce its own debt), the closure of five plants, the elimination of 21,000 jobs, and the introduction of a performance-based career system (as opposed to the traditional seniority-based promotion system) (Millikin and Fu, 2005).

The transformation of the employment system is another important change in the organization of Japanese firms since the 1990s. Deflation, increased competition, and pressure from shareholders led companies to adopt new employment practices to reduce the cost of the workforce. Although the profitability of companies increased over the latter half of the twenty-first century, the average monthly salary of employees peaked at a just over 420,000 yen in 1997 before decreasing constantly until 2009 (357,000 yen) and stagnating in the 2010s at 365,000 yen.[3] The absence of an unemployment insurance system like those in Western Europe and an underdeveloped market for changing jobs forced many employees to accept new contracts characterized by employment uncertainty. The share of non-regular employment, which amounted to 7.4 per cent of the workforce in 1985, rose to 22 per cent in 2015. For women, it grew from 32.1 per cent in 1985 to 57 per cent in 2015, contributing to greater gender inequality than in some other developed countries (see Chapter 12).[4]

11.2 The transformation of the Japanese electronics industry

After 2000, Japanese manufacturing companies had no choice but to focus on foreign markets to strengthen their global presence, due to economic stagnation at home. Macroeconomic indexes clearly illustrate this change. Exports took on a growing importance in the domestic economy, surpassing even the level of the early 1980s. While exports represented only 9.7 per cent of

---

[3] The Japan Institute for Labour Policy and Training, https://www.jil.go.jp/kokunai/statistics/timeseries/html/g0401.html (accessed 20 September 2020). This data is for companies with more than thirty employees.

[4] MHLW (https://www.mhlw.go.jp/file/06-Seisakujouhou-11650000-Shokugyouanteikyokuhakenyukiroudoutaisakubu/0000120286.pdf)

GDP on average in the 1990s, after a peak of 14.4 per cent in 1984, it grew steadily to more than 17 per cent in 2007 and 2008. Hence Japanese companies had become more and more oriented towards global markets, making the Japanese economy more dependent on the state of the global economy. This is one of the reasons why the country was particularly vulnerable to the global financial crisis. The share of exports to GDP returned to the 17 per cent mark only in 2014.[5]

Yet, Japanese firms were not the only ones to export more after 2000. Global trade entered a period of expansion in the 1990s, which was even faster than the development of Japanese exports. Consequently, the share of Japan's exports in world trade declined. In 1990, Japan was the second largest exporter after the United States, with a share of 8.2 per cent of world exports. It still amounted to 7.9 per cent in 2000 but dropped to 5.5 per cent in 2010, when Japan fell to the fourth largest exporter, behind China, the United States, and Germany. The decline continued in the following decade but at a lower level (4.3 per cent of world exports in 2018).[6]

However, exports are not the only way to access foreign markets. Foreign direct investments (FDI) are another, and numerous Japanese manufacturing companies adopted this means, notably through the acquisition of foreign firms, to expand abroad during the first phase of the twenty-first century. The total stock of Japanese outward FDI went from 278 billion US dollars in 2000 to 830 billion in 2010.[7] This represented 8.1 per cent of Japanese GDP in 2005 and 14.6 per cent in 2010.[8] Companies in all the sectors of economy, from food and electronics to banking and insurance, expanded their operations aggressively abroad during this period. They were losing their competitiveness as exporters but reorganized as multinational corporations. In order to discuss this change, the following section examines two major industries: electronics and cars.

The consumer electronics industry is one of the most representative sectors of the 'Japanese miracle' period. The development and mass production of audio and video devices, as well as personal computers and semiconductors, contributed to making Japan one of the world's largest exporters. This is also an industry in which companies relocated their low value-added activities to Sout East Asia and Latin America as early as the 1970s. However, the domination of Japanese companies over this industry was challenged by a

---

[5] World Bank, exports of goods and services https://data.worldbank.org/indicator/NE.EXP.GNFS.ZS (accessed 18 September 2020).
[6] World Bank, https://wits.worldbank.org/ (accessed 18 September 2020).
[7] JETRO, FDI statistics, https://www.jetro.go.jp/world/japan/stats/fdi.html (accessed 18 September 2020).
[8] OECD, https://data.oecd.org/fdi/fdi-stocks.htm (accessed 18 September 2020).

profound transformation after 2000. The economic and technological development of other Asian nations, particularly South Korea, Taiwan, and China, the change of product architecture from an integral to a modular model, and digitalization led to the formation of global value chains and the advent of new competitors. Japanese electronics companies gradually lost their competitive advantage in the manufacturing of finished goods. For example, in 2009, the largest producers of plasma TVs in the world were two Korean firms, Samsung (18 per cent of market share) and LG (10.6 per cent), followed by two Japanese companies, Sony (8.6 per cent) and Sharp (7.2 per cent), the Chinese group TCL (5.9 per cent) and the Taiwanese company TPV (5.3 per cent). Panasonic and Toshiba were lower, with shares below 5 per cent (Kasuya, 2012, 414). A similar picture could be drawn for nearly all consumer electronics goods.

Although they lost their competitive advantage in producing finished goods and equipment, Japanese electronics firms did not disappear. The ranking of the top ten largest global companies in electronics and electric appliances illustrates this evolution (see Table 11.2). While Japanese companies once dominated this industry, in 1995 they lost their position of first place to Samsung, which occupied it in 2010 and 2020. NEC vanished from the ranking in 2010, and Toshiba in 2020. At the same time, one can observe the emergence and growth of companies from South Korea, Taiwan, and China. Moreover, most Japanese firms that are still ranked experienced a deep mutation and largely moved out of the electronics sector altogether.

Table 11.2 Largest companies of the world, electronics and electrical appliances, revenues in million US dollars, 1995–2010

1995		2010		2020	
Name	Revenues	Name	Revenues	Name	Revenues
Hitachi (JP)	76,431	Samsung (K)	108,927	Samsung (K)	197,705
Matsushita (JP)	69,947	Siemens (D)	103,605	Hon Hai (T)	172,869
GE (US)	64,687	Hitachi (JP)	96,593	Hitachi (JP)	80,639
Siemens (D)	51,055	Panasonic (JP)	79,893	Sony (JP)	75,972
Toshiba (JP)	48,228	LG (K)	78,891	Panasonic (JP)	68,897
Sony (JP)	40,101	Sony (JP)	77,696	LG (K)	53,464
NEC (JP)	37,945	Toshiba (JP)	68,731	Pegatron (T)	44,207
Daewoo (K)	35,706	Hon Hai (T)	59,324	Mitsubishi E. (JP)	41,045
Philips (N)	33,516	Mitsubishi E. (JP)	36,116	Midea (CN)	40,440
Mitsubishi E. (JP)	32,726	Philips (N)	32,232	Honeywell (US)	36,709

Note: Japanese companies are in grey.
Source: Fortune Global 500, https://fortune.com/global500/ (accessed 20 September 2020)

Sony is a case in point. In 2000, the proportion of electronics in the company's gross sales rose to 69 per cent, other divisions (games, pictures, music, and insurance) having shares of only between 6 per cent and 9 per cent. However, 10 years later, the share of electronics had dropped to 53 per cent. In 2019, it was only 37 per cent. In the meanwhile, Sony diversified into new businesses namely banking (2001) and mobile communication through a joint venture with the Swedish company Ericsson in 2001 (fully taken over by Sony in 2012) and online games with the PlayStation Network (2006). As for electronics, one can observe a shift from traditional consumer goods to new areas of growth. Sony took over the digital single-lens reflex camera division from Konica-Minolta (2006) and founded a joint venture with Olympus related to medical solutions (2013). At the same time, it sold its divisions of personal computers and TVs (2014). Hence, after 2000, Sony changed from a consumer electronics company to a group focused on electronics solutions and services as well as finance.[9]

The second major feature of the Japanese electronics industry after 2000 is the successful growth of medium-sized companies specializing in the development of new materials for electronics components. These firms started developing parts for the Japanese manufacturers of consumer electronics and accumulated knowledge related to materials. After 2000, when companies like Sony moved out of consumer electronics, these specialized firms were able to shift their focus towards new consumers in East Asia, by developing components for Chinese, Korean, and Taiwanese companies (Hirano, 2017).

11.3 The transformation of the automobile industry

Unlike in electronics, Japanese automobile companies were able to maintain and strengthen their competitiveness after 2000 in the context of a fast-growing global market. The total volume of world production went from 58.4 million vehicles in 2000 to 77.6 million in 2010, and 91.8 million in 2019. Toyota, Nissan, and Honda maintained their presence among the top ten largest manufacturers over the years, Toyota being able to establish itself as the world's largest automobile producers in the early twenty-first century. While Toyota was ranked as the third largest car company in the late 1990s, it successively overtook Ford (2005) and General Motors (2006) to establish itself as number one. It has maintained this position even today, except for

---

[9] Sony Corporation, *Corporate Report 2020*, https://www.sony.net/SonyInfo/IR/library/corporatereport/CorporateReport2020_E.pdf (accessed 18 September 2020).

2011, when it dropped to third place behind GM and Volkswagen, due to the Great Kantō Earthquake which disrupted its domestic production network.[10]

Fujimoto Takahiro has argued that the competitiveness of Japanese car companies was related to the specificity of the automobile as a product. Unlike consumer electronics goods, a car is an extremely complex product which integrates technology from mechanics as well as electronics and requires the use of a huge number of components. Car manufacturers thus kept control over the design of a car and still dominate the supply chain organized to produce all the necessary parts. Japanese manufacturing companies were traditionally good at developing and producing their products completely in-house, and maintaining this model in the car industry has contributed to strengthening the competitiveness of Japanese automobile companies (Fujimoto, 2004). However, despite this shared characteristic, there are significant differences among the various car-makers in terms of the organization and management of their global operations.

Toyota Motor provides one of the most salient examples for showing how a company facing a decline in sales in a shrinking Japanese market successfully reorganized as a global company.[11] Domestic sales peaked at 2.5 million vehicles in 1990, then entered a long period of decline, decreasing from 1.8 million vehicles in 2000 to 1.6 million in 2010 and in 2019. In the meantime, foreign sales slightly exceeded domestic sales in 1992 and continued to grow, reaching 3.4 million vehicles in 2000, 6 million in 2010, and 8.1 million in 2019. Beyond numbers, one must emphasize the launch of innovative models that achieved success around the world, like the Toyota Prius, a hybrid electric automobile produced from 1997 and launched worldwide in 2000, or the premium brand Lexus, developed for the American market in 1989 and launched in other countries in 2005. Moreover, the dramatic development of Toyota on world markets relies on its global organization. First, exports from Japan continued to expand to support the development of this company at home. After the relocation of production centres to foreign countries, particularly to the United States in the context of the trade friction of the 1980s, Toyota's exports declined sharply until the late 1990s, before making a comeback after 2000. In the twenty-first century, more than half of Toyota's domestic production is exported. Second, at the same time, production abroad has constantly pursued its development since the mid-1980s. It surpassed the volume of exports from Japan in 2000 and the level of all domestic production in 2006. The globalization of production is characterized by the

---

[10] OICA, http://www.oica.net (accessed 19 September 2020).
[11] https://global.toyota/en/company/trajectory-of-toyota/history/ (accessed 18 September 2020).

opening of plants throughout the world, including emerging markets like those of China (foundation of three joint ventures in 2002–2006), Mexico (2006), and Russia (2007) (Shimizu, 2009). Yet, the global production network was reorganized after the Asian financial crisis (1997). While the role of foreign assembly plants had been mostly to produce for their national or regional markets, the crisis in Asia showed the danger of being too concentrated geographically. Toyota set up a new organization whereby foreign plants not only manufacture cars for the domestic market but also specific models for global markets (Kawabe, 2011).

Nissan, the second largest Japanese car-maker, has followed a different path of development, as its global expansion since 1999 occurred within the context of the strategic alliance made with the French automobile company Renault (Stevens and Fujimoto, 2009). Although it experienced fast development during the high-growth years, Nissan faced existential difficulties in the 1990s that led it into a financial crisis. This was due to its excessive emphasis on technology as opposed to customer demand, and its traditional lack of attention paid to profits. In 1999, Nissan was close to bankruptcy and formed an alliance with Renault to ensure its survival. The French company took a 36.8 per cent stake in the capital of Nissan against a payment of five billion euros and sent Carlos Ghosn to Japan to restructure the firm (see above, p. 206). At the same time, both companies founded an equally owned joint venture in the Netherlands, Renault-Nissan BV, commonly known as the Alliance, also managed by Ghosn. Its role was to coordinate the strategic management of the two partners, to manage common entities (logistics, sales, purchases, engines, etc.), and to benefit from synergies, for example regarding the development of new cars and the dealership network around the world. The relationship between both partners was strengthened in 2002, when Renault increased its stake in Nissan to 44.4 per cent (later decreased to 43 per cent) and Nissan received 15 per cent of Renault's capital. This cooperation was successful. Nissan became profitable again, and the Alliance established itself as the third-largest car manufacturer in the world behind Toyota and Volkswagen in 2011. The Alliance was enlarged in 2016 with the arrival of Mitsubishi, of which Nissan took over 34 per cent of the capital, and became closer to Toyota and Volkswagen. However, the interventions of the French government (which owns 15 per cent of Renault) and the concentration of power in the hands of Ghosn, whose objective was a merger between the members of the alliance, led to tensions at Nissan. The arrest of Ghosn, accused of financial mismanagement, by Japanese police in 2018 and his extraordinary escape to Lebanon in 2019 have challenged the future of the Alliance.

Finally, beyond the two different paths of global expansion taken by Toyota and Nissan, it is useful to briefly examine the strategy adopted by a smaller car manufacturer, Suzuki to find niches in world markets. Suzuki was the thirteenth largest vehicle producer in 2000 and is a company which has specialized in the production of light cars (*keijidōsha*) since the 1970s. These vehicles, characterized by their small size, light engine, and low price, were developed for the domestic market in the context of increasing oil prices and an urbanized lifestyle. It was however difficult to export them to Western markets where consumers wanted larger and more powerful automobiles. Suzuki was able to expand internationally by targeting markets where such a vehicle would find customers. India appeared as an excellent opportunity, considering the low incomes and congested metropoles.

Suzuki invested in India in 1982, taking a minority stake in Maruti Ltd., a company founded in 1971 by private entrepreneurs with the support of the Indian government. Suzuki increased its participation in Maruti to 50 per cent in 1992 and took the majority share in 2002. Suzuki's light cars produced in India were marketed first in 1983 with great success, leading the company to capture a market share of more than 60 per cent in the 1990s. It then decreased due to the emergence of numerous competitors, namely the Korean company Hyundai and the local conglomerate Tata, but was still number one in 2005–2009 with a share of about 40 per cent (Malhotra and Sinharay, 2013).

11.4 Foreign firms in Japan

The comeback made by Nissan in 1999 through its alliance with the French company Renault suggests that foreign companies are playing a growing role in the Japanese economy. However, their actual presence was still very limited at the beginning of the twenty-first century. The stock of inward FDI has developed dramatically, from 50.3 billion US dollars in 2000 to 214.7 billion in 2010 and 310.3 billion in 2019, but this expresses a general trend of growth in investment throughout the world.[12] Measured as a percentage of GDP, Japan has the world's lowest level of inward GDP (see Table 11.3). Although it doubled between 2005 and 2019, it is still below the 5 per cent mark, which is not only more than ten times lower than in the United States and European Union, but also far below China and India. Looking at this index, Japan is the country which is the least open to foreign companies.

---

[12] JETRO, Foreign trade statistics, https://www.jetro.go.jp/world/japan/stats/fdi.html (accessed 28 September 2020).

Table 11.3 FDI stocks, inward, as a percentage of GDP, 2005–2019

	2005	2019
Japan	2.1	4.3
India	6.2	14.5
China	20.6	20.4
Germany	22.8	27.6
United States	21.6	43.9
European Union (average)	30.3	59.7
Netherlands	70	188.9
Ireland	77.2	288.2

Source: OECD and World Bank

The weak presence of foreign firms in Japan is not the result of legal restrictions as it used to be in the decades following World War II (see Chapter 10). Inward FDI was liberalized in the 1980s, but important barriers, such as a complex bureaucracy and high corporate taxes have remained obstacles to investments by foreign firms in Japan. Moreover, differences in the language and culture make it difficult for Western companies to succeed in Japan.

Leeja Russel has demonstrated that more than half of foreign investments in Japan in 2014 were concentrated in three industries: finance and insurance (37.9 per cent), transportation equipment manufacturing (13.6 per cent, mostly Nissan), and electric machinery manufacturing (11.3 per cent). As for the home country of these foreign multinationals, it was essentially the United States (63.7 per cent) and China (10.1 per cent) (Russel, 2017). American firms strongly dominate the insurance sector (Aflac, Gibraltar, Met Life, Prudential), information technology (Amazon, Google, Yahoo), and various services (Costco, McDonald's, Starbucks). They are also present in the electric machinery industry through the takeover of several Japanese firms. For example, the investment fund KKR opened an office in Tokyo in 2007 and took over Panasonic Healthcare in 2013.[13] As for Chinese firms, their growing weight is especially impressive: their total stock of capital invested in Japan went from 84 million US dollars in 2000 to 399 million in 2010 and 4.9 billion in 2019.[14] Here again, Japan is not a specific case as the global expansion of Chinese firms has taken a step forward since 2015. Most of Chinese companies investing in Japan are looking for technology through the acquisition

---

[13] *Financial Times*, 27 September 2013.
[14] JETRO, Foreign trade statistics, https://www.jetro.go.jp/world/japan/stats/fdi.html (accessed 28 September 2020).

of firms or divisions of firms, like the solar system company MSK, taken over by Suntech Group in 2006 or the white goods division of Sanyo Electric purchased in 2011 by Haier.[15]

Beside the cases of American and Chinese firms, one must mention the presence of hundreds of small foreign firms specialized in the sales of their products in the Japanese market, similar to the European fashion and luxury companies that opened subsidiaries in the post-bubble years (see Chapter 11). Cultural barriers are a significant challenge in the consumer goods industry. For example, the food industry is dominated by Japanese companies, Coca-Cola and Nestlé being exceptional cases of foreign firms that encountered success in this business. The Swiss multinational Nestlé is an excellent example of how the localisation of management enabled a foreign firm to internalize marketing knowledge related to the Japanese market and consequently develop new goods adapted to local consumers (Donzé, 2020). In 1960, Nestlé founded a new subsidiary in Japan, specializing in the production and sales of Nescafé, which experienced impressive growth until the 1980s. However, the food market became extremely competitive in the post-bubble era, and the need to adapt global products to local tastes was a new challenge in the 1990s. Nestlé responded to these changes by localising its management. In 2001, a Japanese national, Fujii Shinichi, was appointed CEO of Nestlé Japan for the first time. Moreover, nearly all his managers and employees were Japanese so that the company was a de facto domestic firm, despite belonging to a multinational based in Switzerland. The most emblematic expression of this localisation was adapting the chocolate bar, KitKat to the Japanese market. Launched by the British firm Rowntree in the 1930s and taken over by Nestlé in 1988, KitKat was a brand used for a product sold without adaptation throughout the world—in Japan since 1973 by the food confectionery company Fujiya. Then in 1989, Nestlé Japan took over the management of KitKat from Fujiya, and after 2000 developed a broad range of new KitKats, using tastes other than milk chocolate, ranging from green tea and *sake* to banana and milk coffee. Moreover, in 2015, Nestlé Japan opened KitKat boutiques in department stores to distribute luxury versions of their famous chocolate. As for coffee, it also developed into new directions, with the opening of a café Nescafé in Kobe (1999), the launch of Barista coffee machines (2009), and the implementation of a system of coffee ambassadors for the Nescafé (2012). These new strategies were also implemented to cope with the growth of another foreign firm that was experiencing impressive success in Japan, Starbucks Coffee.

---

[15] *Reuters*, 28 July 2011 and Japan *Times*, 1 August 2012.

Founded in 1995, the Japanese joint venture opened a first coffee store in Ginza, Tokyo in 1996, before a surge in growth (117 stores in 1999 and 453 in 2002) (Umemoto, 2015). Hence Nestlé had to react to keep its competitive edge in the coffee market. Various activities carried out by Nestlé Japan after 2000 demonstrate that the localisation of management enabled a foreign firm to overcome the strong cultural barriers of the Japanese consumer goods market.

11.5 Start-ups and the problem of entrepreneurship

Although the end of the traditional Japanese business system, social change, and globalization offered a broad range of new opportunities, Japan is characterized by its very low level of entrepreneurship from an international perspective. According to the White Paper on Small Enterprises in Japan published in 2017, the proportion of people *not* interested in business start-ups in Japan amounted to 77.3 per cent in 2012, compared to 22.9 per cent for the United States, 30.6 per cent for Germany, and 39.2 per cent for France.[16] As a consequence, the enterprise creation ratio is low. In 2001–2015, new businesses represented a share of about 5 per cent of all companies, compared to 10–14 per cent for the United States, Germany, and France.[17] Moreover, Japanese firms are much more likely to survive than Western. For companies established between 2007 and 2013, the survival rate of five years after starting was 81.7 per cent in Japan compared to 48.9 per cent in the United States, 40.2 per cent in Germany, and 44.5 per cent in France.[18] Hence, Japanese entrepreneurs tend to found fewer firms but have a relatively high rate of survival. This lack of a risk-taking mentality towards the founding of start-ups has four major causes.

First, the development of digitalization and the formation of global value chains led to a new dominant paradigm in innovation, which did not develop in Japan. Instead, Japanese manufacturing companies based their technological development and growth during the second half of the twentieth century on incremental innovation, that is, on the gradual improvement of production technology and products. These firms used to exert strong and direct control over R&D, production, and sales. Yet, since 2000, companies in Asia

---

[16] *White Paper on Small Enterprises in Japan*, National Association of Trade Promotion for Small and Medium Enterprises, p. 110. https://www.chusho.meti.go.jp/pamflet/hakusyo/H29/PDF/2017shohaku_eng.pdf (accessed 22 September 2020).
[17] Ministry of Economy, Trade, and Industry, https://www.chusho.meti.go.jp/pamflet/hakusyo/H29/h29/html/b2_1_1_2.html (accessed 22 September 2020).
[18] *White Paper on Small Enterprises in Japan*, p. 115.

and the West have shifted their innovation practices to a new system based on inter-firm cooperation and a focus on the specific segments of the product development process, called 'open innovation' (Yonekura and Shimizu, 2015). In this context, numerous entrepreneurs in the United States and Asia took the opportunity to create firms to exploit opportunities for specific niche products, particularly in information technology and biotechnology, but not in Japan.

Second, venture capital is underdeveloped in Japan. Financial companies specializing in investments in start-ups developed in the United States in the 1970s and in Western Europe in the 1980s. Venture capital supported the foundation and development of numerous firms like Apple and Intel. However, in Japan, the formation of a capital market for such relatively high-risk investments occurred later and relied initially in large part on limited public funding. Fewer private companies or individuals invested in venture capital in the 1970s, though there are examples of successful spinoffs such as FANUC (1972), which began as a subsidiary of the large computer firm, Fujitsu in 1950s.

There are also fewer university start-ups compared with the United States. However, some firms have stepped in to facilitate their entry. The first private company specializing in financing university start-ups was Mirai Securities, established in 1998 by Japan Asia Investment Company. The number of its investments in start-ups went from eight in 2000 to 271 in 2008. Numerous other venture capital (VC) funds were created in the following years, and the JASDAQ Securities Exchange was opened in 2004 as a section of Tokyo Stock Exchange specializing in high-tech companies and start-ups; however, the total value of capital invested still lagged behind that of Western countries. In 2005, Japanese venture capital funds reached a total of 860 billion yen invested, while the amount was 31,320 billion yen in the United States and 27,210 billion in Western Europe (Hamada, 2009). Venture capital in the early 2000s was also used to create in-house start-ups at large corporations, such as Sony (Kneller, 2007). New VC funds emerged around 2008, the most important being World Innovation Lab, which had invested 1.9 billion US dollars in more than a hundred firms in the United States and in Japan in 2023, including the online consumer-to-consumer flea market Mercari (its IPO in Tokyo in 2018, raising about 550 million dollars, was the largest in Japanese history).[19] Moreover, megabanks have recently engaged in this business, Sumitomo Mitsui Financial Group (SMFG) having for example

---

[19] https://wilab.com/ (accessed 20 July 2023).

announced in 2023 the launch of a 210 million dollar VC fund.[20] Despite these developments, Japan still lags far behind Silicon Valley's standards.

Third, the persistence of the traditional employment system in most large corporations has been an obstacle to the creation of spin-offs by employees. Leaving one's employment to found one's own company is highly risky, as a failure could severely limit one's prospects of finding a new employer. Moreover, it might also mean foregoing all one's social welfare benefits, a feature associated with the permanent employment system at large corporations.

Fourth, one must also mention the existence of an education system whose objective is the training of a labour force with a high level of general knowledge and technical skills, but which has tended to place less importance on personal development, creativity, and communication skills in both Japanese and other languages. Japanese graduates are trained to fulfil a broad range of needs at large corporations, not to act independently or question conventional wisdom. The features of such an education system have had an impact on the ability and the desire of graduates to seize opportunities and to create new enterprises.

These obstacles to entrepreneurship largely explain why Japan after the 1990s was unable to sustain the industrial lead it had gained during the high-growth period. All the major businesses related to information and communications technology (ICT) were created outside Japan. When Steve Jobs came back to Apple in 1997, the American manufacturer of personal computers established itself as the new benchmark in consumer electronics with the launch of iconic products such as the iPod (2001) and iPhone (2007). Moreover, Amazon (founded in 1994), Google (1998), Alibaba (1999), Skype (2003), Facebook (2004), YouTube (2005), Twitter (2006), Instagram (2010), and Zoom (2011) were all companies created outside of Japan, mostly in the United States. In 2018, the number of 'unicorns' or privately owned start-ups valued at more than 1 billion dollars, amounted to only two in Japan, while there were 117 in the United States, seventy-three in China, and eighteen in the United Kingdom (Hoshi and Lipscy, 2021, 400).

Some Japanese entrepreneurs seized the opportunities offered by ICT to create new firms, but nearly all of them focused on the domestic market so that only a handful grew as truly global firms through mergers with foreign firms. This was the case of the internet service (e-commerce, finance, media, travel, etc.) company Rakuten, founded in 1997 by Mikitani Hiroshi (born in 1965), a former employee of the Industrial Bank of Japan. The company went

---

[20] Nikkei Asia, 10 June 2023 (https://asia.nikkei.com/Business/Finance/Japan-s-SMFG-to-start-210m-venture-fund-to-develop-unicorns, accessed 20 July 2023).

public on the JASDAQ Securities Exchange of the Tokyo Stock Exchange in 2000 and started its global expansion in 2005 with the acquisition of LinkShare Corporation, an American company specializing in marketing. It engaged in e-commerce abroad in 2006 when it launched Taiwan Rakuten Ichiba. Revenues of Rakuten Group went from 9.9 billion yen in fiscal year 2002 to 346.1 billion in 2010 and 1,263.9 billion in 2019. However, despite this impressive development, the firm has depended largely on the domestic market (81.8 per cent of revenues in 2010 and 77.8 per cent in 2019).[21]

11.6 The business of Cool Japan

The decline in the competitiveness of Japanese manufacturing companies, the relocation of production in the United States and in Europe, and the emergence of companies from other East Asian nations in electronics and machinery have changed the image of Japanese goods throughout the world since the 1990s. While Japanese products were once seen as the embodiment of a 'yellow peril' during the second half of the twentieth century, they have shifted to something more positive, namely the incarnation of Cool Japan—based on Japan's unique culture and the result of creative activities. This expression was coined by the American journalist Douglas McGray who wrote an article in *Foreign Policy* in 2002 where he argued that *anime*, video games, and manga had enabled Japan to strengthen its global cultural influence and that Japan's Gross National Cool had to be considered as a form of 'soft power' or 'a reminder that commercial trends and products, and a country's knack for spawning them, can serve political and economic trends' (McGray, 2002, 53).

The *anime* industry is a good example of the development of Japanese cultural industries abroad. The broadcasting of Japanese cartoons on American and European TV channels started in the 1960s and 1970s with narratives and characters inserted into a Western background (Lu, 2008). *Anime* studios adapted their techniques and know-how to foreign markets. However, in the following decades, successful *anime* were not adaptations but rather products developed for a Japanese audience, featuring superheroes and creatures for the domestic market, which were diffused abroad. Dragon Ball was a hit in Western markets in the 1990s and Pokémon after 2000. Foreign sales in the Japanese animation industry (including movies and TV) grew faster than domestic market sales in the early twenty-first century, going from 373 billion

---

[21] https://global.rakuten.com (accessed 22 September 2020).

yen in 2002 to 522 billion in 2005 thus offering hope for further global expansion. Yet, it declined sharply in the following years and stagnated at around 250 billion in 2009–2012, before entering a new phase of fast growth due to the expansion of sales in China and the spread of smartphones, peaking at 1,009 billion in 2018.[22] Yet, although *anime* is one of the major embodiments of Cool Japan, sociologist Mori Yoshitaka has demonstrated that this industry is strongly anchored in transnational networks in Asia (Mori, 2011). The production of *anime* is a labour-intensive business and, in order to improve profitability, large Japanese studios began to outsource part of their production to low-waged neighbouring countries. It started with Korea in the 1960s with Toei Animation, one of the largest producers, which signed contracts with Korean and Taiwanese subcontractors. The wage increases in South Korea then led to a new shift of its production to China in the 1980s. In the early twenty-first century, Shenzhen had become a major hub for producing Japanese *anime*. These Sino-Japanese relations led to cross-border cooperation to develop original *anime* for Chinese TV, like Condor Hero, a series co-created in 2001–2002 by Nippon Animation (scenario writing and character design) and the Hong Kong based company Jade Production (selection of original story, production, marketing, and sales). Mori concludes his analysis by arguing that the global success of Japanese *anime* is not different from electronics and other manufactured goods whose production base shifted from Japan to East Asia. *Anime* produced domestically for the local market are considered 'too sophisticated, positioned in a detailed way within the Japanese cultural context [so that] those who live outside Japan cannot enjoy or even understand them easily' (Mori, 2011, 40).

Food is another example of the global success of Cool Japan. The export of a broad range of products, from green tea, *sake*, and Kobe beef to instant noodles and soy sauce has expanded since 2000. It benefited from rising health concerns throughout the world and the favourable reputation of Japan's food culture. The case of *sake* shows how a traditional alcohol was able to find niches abroad after 2000 (Hamamatsu and Kishi, 2018). *Sake* brewing has been a declining industry since the 1970s, in the context of a shift in consumer preferences towards other alcoholic beverages (beer and wine) and a shrinking market. Exports were, however, an exception. They represented less than 1 per cent of national production in the 1990s. Yet, the situation started to change in the early twenty-first century. Exports went from three billion yen in 2000 to 8.5 billion in 2010 and 15.5 in 2016, while the share of

[22] Anime Industry Report 2019, https://aja.gr.jp/download/anime_ind_rpt2019_summary_en (accessed 30 September 2020).

foreign markets grew from 1 per cent of national production in 2000 to 4.1 per cent in 2015. Over the same period, the average price per litre doubled, from 400 yen in 2000 to 800 yen in 2016. This expansion was supported by the fast growth in consumption in the United States (largest outlet), Korea and, more recently, mainland China. This growing demand is linked to the rapid expansion of Japanese restaurants overseas for which the Ministry of Agriculture, Forestry, and Fisheries introduced a certification system in 2016, following the inclusion of Japanese traditional food (*washoku*) in UNESCO's Intangible Cultural Heritage list three years earlier. Thus, several *sake* brewers took the opportunity to focus on this expanding market, the largest being Takara Shūzō, a company founded in 1842 which established a sales subsidiary in the United States in 1983 and whose foreign operations grew to 13 per cent of gross sales in 2013 and to 33 per cent in 2017.[23]

The promotion of *anime*, *sake*, and other cultural industries overseas is supported by the government and various ministries. The Ministry of Foreign Affairs (MOFA) started a programme for cultural diplomacy in 2003, and five years later made the *anime* character Doreamon a cultural ambassador. As for the Ministry of Economy, Trade, and Industry (METI, formerly MITI), it opened a Cool Japan Bureau in 2010 to promote exports, and in 2013 created the Cool Japan Fund to co-invest with private companies in various projects to promote the expansion of the Japanese fashion, food, and content industries overseas.

11.7 Conclusions

The liberalization of finance following the post-bubble crisis and the decline of the domestic market due to the aging population gave Japanese companies a strong incentive to expand abroad to pursue their development (see Box 11.1). The two largest manufacturing companies in 2001, Toyota Motor and Panasonic, witnessed a rapid increase in their overseas sales. For the former, it went from 58 per cent in 2000 to 74 per cent in 2010, and 75 per cent in 2019, while it increased from 21 per cent in 2000 to 48 per cent in 2010 and 52 per cent in 2019 for the latter.[24] All indexes, from the share of exports to GDP to the level of outward FDI, show that Japanese firms have become much more outward looking than before 2000. This expresses the transformation of Japanese capitalism towards a model that is much more

---

[23] *The Japan Times*, 1 August 2018.
[24] Toyota Motor Co. and Panasonic Co., SEC filings. Data is for fiscal years.

similar to other countries, as it is shaped by global competition and pressure from financial markets. However, the stronger dependence of Japan on overseas markets presented various challenges and issues—which could be transformed into opportunities.

Box 11.1 A successful fast fashion brand: Uniqlo

Today, Fast Retailing Company, whose apparel brand is Uniqlo, is one of the top four fast fashion brands along with H&M, The Gap, and Zara in the world in terms of scale. The successful development of Uniqlo is an excellent illustration of the way a Japanese company was able to achieve growth in the global marketplace.

The roots of this firm go back to a unisex casual-wear store opened in Hiroshima in 1984 by Yanai Tadashi (born in 1949). Yanai was the son of the owner of a small company that sold menswear in Ube, a small city in neighbouring Yamaguchi Prefecture. His store, 'Unique Clothing Warehouse', gave birth to the brand name Uniqlo, which was renamed Fast Retailing in 1991. While most apparel brands in Japan had adopted an extreme segmentation of their market and developed hundreds of brands (e.g. the apparel company World launched 69 new brands in the 1980s),[27] Uniqlo decided to do something completely different: offering one brand of clothing for everyone.

Uniqlo was still a small retailer in the 1980s but adopted a new strategy for growth during the following decade, based on the SPA model (specialty store retailer or private label apparel). Yanai built an extensive network of stores throughout Japan where only Uniqlo garments were sold (Sugihara and Somehara, 2017, 19 and 35). The company focused on design and product development, while manufacturing was outsourced to independent companies, based essentially in China. The number of stores went from twenty-nine in 1991 to 433 in 2000, most of them in suburbs, along roads, and in shopping malls.[28] Its impressive expansion was supported by capital raised on the Hiroshima Stock Exchange where Fast Retailing was listed in 1994—then on the Tokyo Stock Exchange in 1999. Uniqlo became the largest apparel retailer in Japan in 2000. Its success expresses the deep transformation experienced by the Japanese apparel industry after the collapse of the bubble economy, characterized by the drop in clothing consumption (15,300 billion yen in 1991 and 10,500 billion in 2013), the relocation of production overseas (share of domestic production of the apparel market dropped from 50 per cent in 1990 to 3 per cent in 2014), and the shift in retailing (from department stores to single-brand stores). Moreover, the low-price strategy adopted by Uniqlo responded to the needs of the overwhelming majority of consumers, whose incomes started to either stagnate or decrease from the late 1990s.

(continued)

> **Box 11.1 Continued**
>
> The years 1999–2001 were a turning-point in the history of Uniqlo, as Yanai decided to strengthen product development by moving production to foreign markets. A subsidiary was opened in Shanghai in 1999 to better supervise production in China. The same year, a collaboration got underway with the Japanese chemical company Toray for the development of special fibres to manufacture new kinds of functional underclothing. In 2004, a design centre opened in New York. As for retail, Uniqlo opened its first store abroad in London in 2001. Others followed in Shanghai (2002), Seoul (2005), Hong Kong (2005), and New York (2006). The concept of the flagship store, that is, a large shopping space offering the entire range of goods launched by the company to embody the value of its brands, was developed in the shopping areas of global cities, and brought back to Japan in 2012, with the opening of similar centres in Ginza, Tokyo, and Shinsaibashi, Osaka.
>
> Its growth in global markets was very fast, with the total number of stores reaching 2,203 in 2010 and 3,589 in 2019.[29] Moreover, online sales started in 2000. These figures also include a second brand launched by Fast Retailing in 2006, under the name GU as well as a few American and French brands purchased after 2000 but whose weight is not significant. In 2019, the revenues of Fast Retailing came essentially from Uniqlo (83 per cent), while GU and global brands only had 10.4 per cent and 6.6 per cent respectively.[30]
>
> Fast Retailing has achieved impressive development in the global markets. Hardly noticeable in 2000, Uniqlo International represented only 8.9 per cent of revenues in 2010 before growing to 35.9 per cent in 2015, and 44.9 per cent in 2019. It overtook Uniqlo Japan in 2017. As for Yanai Tadashi, he became one of the richest entrepreneurs in Japan, ranking as the wealthiest person in Japan for the first time in 2009 according to the American business magazine *Forbes*, and has continued to retain his spot ever since.[31]

The first was the need for companies to hire more internationally minded employees. The language barrier had never been considered a real obstacle until 2000 when the domestic market had little to offer in terms of growth. Yet, the young Japanese population was not only declining as a demographic. Its interest in learning new languages and engaging in cross-cultural exchange

---

[27] *World 50th Anniversary Book*, Kobe: World, 2009, p. 329.
[28] Fast Retailing Co., Annual report, 2019.
[29] Fast Retailing Co., Annual report, 2019.
[30] Fast Retailing Co., Annual report, 2019.
[31] *The Guardian*, 13 January 2020 and https://www.forbes.com/billionaires/ (accessed 6 October 2020).

was also declining. For example, the number of Japanese studying in the United States dropped from 46,497 students in academic year 2000/01 to 21,290 in 2010/11 and 18,105 in 2018/19.[25] This decline represents an important challenge for companies in need of an increasing number of employees capable of working in an international environment.

Second, the growing orientation towards foreign markets meant that Japan had become much more sensitive to fluctuations in the global economy. Its businesses were severely affected by the world financial crisis following the Lehman Shock, and the economy experienced a deeper recession than in the United States or Western Europe. In 2009, Japan experienced a growth rate of minus 5.2 per cent, while it amounted to minus 4.1 per cent in the European Union and minus 2.4 per cent in the United States; growth was positive in China at 8.7 per cent.[26] The liberalization of the employment system enabled manufacturing companies to dismiss thousands of non-regular workers to adapt more flexibly to the economic downturn. However, this led to a severe social crisis as the welfare system was not adapted to deal with such a situation.

Hence, in the early 2010s, Japan found itself in a paradoxical situation, characterized by the stronger international orientation of its economy and companies, and its youth much more domestically focused than older generations. Cultural differences were a major barrier, as expressed by the low level of inward FDI. However, they also provided an opportunity, as demonstrated by the successful adaptation of KitKat products by Nestlé Japan in the domestic market and by the growing popularity of Cool Japan abroad, which celebrates them.

---

[25] Institute of International Education, Open Doors, https://opendoorsdata.org/data/international-students/leading-places-of-origin/ (accessed 30 September 2020).
[26] IMF, *World Economic Outlook*, 2010.

12
Rebooting Global Competitiveness in Post-3.11 Japan

The Rio Olympics closed on 21 August 2016 with one unexpected guest, the host of the 2020 summer games, Prime Minister Abe Shinzō (see Figure 12.1). His appearance in the ceremony was remarkable not least for its rarity since few serving prime ministers take part. However, what he will most likely be remembered for is not that he attended it, but how. Abe ascended to the stage dressed as the Nintendo character, Super Mario. Was this a symbol of the new Japan he wished to convey to the world?

The 2020 Tokyo Olympics was not the first event to make use of imagery. The Tokyo Games which took place in 1964 have since become an important symbol of Japan's high economic growth period. Hopes were high that the 2020 games would also herald in a new era of economic expansion. The tourism industry was seen as key to realizing the government's revitalization plans, particularly in areas facing depopulation. Fukushima, one of the games' main venues, was to symbolize the nation's resilience and rebirth following the 2011 earthquake and nuclear disaster, referred to in Japan simply as 3.11. Because of Covid-19 concerns, however, the 2020 games opened on 23 July 2021 to a largely empty stadium under tight public-health restrictions. Abe, who had been so instrumental in winning Tokyo's bid to host them, was no longer prime minister and did not attend. This chapter highlights the post-3.11 period leading up to the 2020 games and traces the changing competitive environment for Japanese business.

The bursting of Japan's asset bubble in the early 1990s marked the start of a long period of economic stagnation, initially referred to as 'the lost ten-years' (*ushinawareta jūnen*) and later as 'the lost twenty years' (*ushinawareta ni-jūnen*) or the Heisei Recession. Attempts to resolve the problems it caused were stymied by setbacks, the two most significant being the 2008 global financial crisis, often called the 'Lehman Shock' in Japan, followed by the *coup de grâce* on 11 March 2011, the Great Tōhoku Earthquake and Tsunami. These crises presented new obstacles in Japan's fragile path to economic recovery.

Japanese Capitalism and Entrepreneurship. Pierre-Yves Donzé and Julia S. Yongue, Oxford University Press.
© Pierre-Yves Donzé and Julia S. Yongue (2024). DOI: 10.1093/oso/9780192887474.003.0013

Figure 12.1 Abe dressed as Super Mario at Rio Olympics closing ceremony, 2016
Source: Wikimedia Commons Fernando Frazão/Agência Brasil, CC BY 3.0 BR, https://creativecommons.org/licenses/by/3.0/br/deed.en via Wikimedia Commons https://commons.wikimedia.org/wiki/File:Cerim%C3%B4nia_de_encerramento_dos_Jogos_Ol%C3%ADmpicos_Rio_2016_1039534-21082016-_mg_8618.jpg

The triple Fukushima disaster—an earthquake, tsunami, and nuclear-power-plant explosion—was a tragedy for the entire nation and its economy, but especially that of the Tōhoku region, home to many SMEs, some of which supplied parts to the nation's most globally present corporations. The threat of radioactivity to agricultural and marine products triggered a massive drop in exports as well as a reputational blow to 'the Japan brand', brought on by the association between nuclear contamination and Japanese products (*Nikkei newspaper* editorial, 4 April 2011). The same year, China overtook Japan to become the third largest economy in terms of GDP, a psychological blow for many Japanese.

In the immediate aftermath of the disaster, Prime Minster Kan Naoto, during his short term in office from June 2010 to September 2011 made the decision to shut down all of Japan's nuclear-power plants. Considering the serious safety concerns that Fukushima raised, he ordered new inspections at all the sites nationwide and began an appraisal of Japan's energy policies. The decision to halt operations shook the foundations of Japan's postwar economy, which had been powered in no small part by the nuclear-power industry. The abrupt shutdown prompted a fundamental shift in Japan's energy mix (see Figure 12.2).

In the immediate aftermath of 3.11, the effects of decreased energy capacity and rolling blackouts were felt in some parts of the country (Samuels, 2013). A debate on the future of Japan's energy policy got underway, involving a wide array of stakeholders ranging from pro-nuclear policymakers and representatives of the utility monopolies to concerned citizens' groups. Reducing Japan's dependence on nuclear power led to a reckoning among the different interests and the search for alternatives, including various forms of renewable energy (Scalise, 2012; DeWit and Son, 2011; Huenteler, Schmidt, and Kanie, 2012, 7; Fraser and Aldrich, 2020). One company, Softbank specifically addressed this issue through its business strategies (see Box 12.1).

Box 12.1 SoftBank's Son Masayoshi and a new age of environmental challenges for Japanese business

Son Masayoshi (1957–), founder of SoftBank and principal investor in Vision Fund, which at the time of writing this chapter was the world's largest tech fund, has gained a reputation as an outspoken and innovative entrepreneur both inside and outside Japan (Nicolas et al., 2019). SoftBank Vision Fund has made investments not only in China's digital economy. It has also provided funds to economies that have not traditionally attracted Japanese business, namely Saudi Arabia. Son's background sets him apart from the other Japanese entrepreneurs mentioned in this volume and provides a rare example of a highly successful 'minority entrepreneur' (Udagawa, 2002a). During Japan's colonization of the Korean Peninsula, Son's grandfather was sent to Japan where he was forced to work in the coalmines of Kyushu in southwestern Japan. His father owned pachinko parlours, a business often associated with Japan's ethnic Korean minorities, who remained in Japan after World War II, yet often did not opt to be naturalized as Japanese citizens. Due to a long history of discrimination that might have prevented him from enjoying the same employment opportunities as Japanese, Son decided at the age of 16 to leave Japan to pursue his studies in California. After finishing high school, he entered UC Berkeley, and in 1977, while still a student, he collaborated with a professor to create an automatic translation device which he sold to the electronics manufacturer, Sharp.

In 1980, Son started a software wholesaling business followed by publishing in 1981, initiatives that grew to become SoftBank Group. His entry into the telecommunications arena began in the mid-1980s thanks to the privatization of NTT, mentioned in the Box 10.1 in Chapter 10, and deregulation measures carried out by the

Nakasone government. Son would achieve recognition in Japan in this sector thanks to the patenting of his innovative routing device. However, it was two investments in e-commerce—one in Yahoo in the 1990s and another in Alibaba in the 2000s at a time when both firms were still in their infancy—that would place Son's SoftBank in a class of its own. It was such bold moves that helped to create the image of Son Masayoshi as a global visionary, and enabled him to make even larger investments, notably his most recent one, Vision Fund, founded in 2016.

Son was chosen for this box since his business achievements help to elucidate the changes in the context for doing business in Japan after the bubble period. His case also illustrates—in contrast to the examples mentioned above—some of the positive effects that deregulation had on the business environment, entrepreneurship, and development of Japanese capitalism. The purpose of this box, however, is not simply to provide an overview of Son's businesses but to delve into how 3.11 and the massive environmental damage it caused influenced the notion of sustainability at SoftBank and in Japanese business and society more generally.

The 3.11 disaster as a new growth arena for Son's SoftBank

In the aftermath of 3.11, Son decided to create the Japan Renewable Energy Foundation. The mission of this operation was to harness his experience in business to encourage Japan to shift away from nuclear power towards a greater reliance on renewable energy. One strategy he proposed to was to create a solar belt by expanding the use of solar power in Japan (DeWit and Son, 2011). He also founded the Renewable Energy Institute to study ways to promote the shift towards renewables; since 2016, through the Global Energy Interconnection Development and Cooperation Organization, efforts have been made to connect Japan and other Asian nations to the same renewable energy grid (Renewable Energy Institute). Most recently Son founded SB Energy to strive to become a platformer and service provider of renewable energy. This venture seeks to create linkages between his existing businesses and the energy sector (SB Energy).

Son's endeavours, connecting business with the environment, are impressive, and may constitute a form of 'social entrepreneurship', as defined by the creation of businesses with a clear social mission whose primary goal of generating social value and change takes precedence over profit-making (Dees, 1998). Japanese business history has many examples of entrepreneurs who have contributed to society through their business activities, ranging from Shibusawa Eiichi in the Meiji period to Honda Sōichirō in the high-growth period, who succeeded in becoming the first to develop a novel car engine with lower emission levels. Of note is that all the entrepreneurs dealt with in this volume have in some way strived to create value and enact social

(continued)

> **Box 12.1 Continued**
>
> changes through various means, whether it was by providing housewives with low-priced foods (Nakauchi Isao) or by giving people of all ages around the world new ways to have fun through the development of entertainment products (Ibuka Masaru and Morita Akio).
>
> ### Looking ahead: SDGs and the future of Japanese business
>
> Japanese society faces environmental challenges that require novel forms of social entrepreneurship. Through the Kyoto Protocol and other international treaties, Japan has become directly involved in finding solutions to climate change. At the United Nations Sustainable Development Summit in 2015, seventeen SDGs (Sustainable Development Goals) were adopted, and 169 targets were set to 'address key issues in economic, social, and environmental fields, such as sustainable economic growth, elimination of economic inequalities, and measures against climate change' (Takehara and Hasegawa, 2020, vi). Consequently, all Japanese companies are implementing new strategies to achieve their SDGs by 2030 (UN Global Compact Japan, 2021 Tōyō Keizai, 3 July 2021).
>
> SDGs are applicable in many areas and are relevant to the many yet unresolved issues discussed in this chapter ranging from gender equality (SDG 5) to decent work and economic growth (SDG 8). A company's environmental record can significantly impact its reputation and future investment prospects, as seen in the growing importance of ESGs (Environmental, Social, and Governance). Corporate Social Responsibility (CSR) is not a new theme in Japanese business, nor is industry-induced environmental degradation. However, both concepts have taken on a new meaning since 3.11, which is Japan's—and perhaps one of humanity's—worst ecological disaster to date. The search by Japanese companies for sustainable ways to limit climate change and prevent further environmental damage provide important new themes for business-history studies and will continue to directly affect the development of Japanese capitalism and entrepreneurship in the years to come.

The disaster would have a notable effect on Japanese attitudes towards nuclear power, as it called into question the long-held myth that a reliance on nuclear power posed no danger to society, the environment, and human health. Indeed, before the disaster, most Japanese were in favour of using nuclear power (Fraser and Aldrich, 2020, 3) as a clean and safe source of energy. The disaster caused untold damage to the lives and livelihoods of those in the affected areas but also to the national psyche, thus renewing

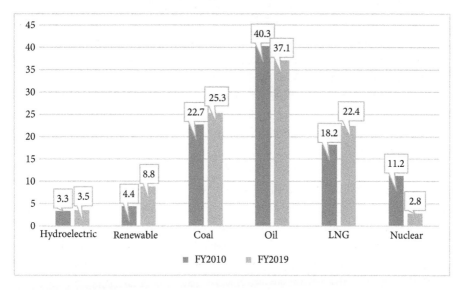

Figure 12.2 Ratio of Japan's energy mix, fiscal years 2010 and 2019 in %
Source: METIhttps://www.enecho.meti.go.jp/en/category/brochures/pdf/japan_energy_2021.pdf

the sense of Japan's inherent vulnerability vis-à-vis the forces of nature. A national debate got underway regarding the implications of 3.11 and the viability of a model of capitalism whose modus operandi hinged largely on achieving continuous growth and global competitiveness (Kato, 2010; Pilling, 2014; JSPS, 2015; Saito, 2020). Since the disaster and the subsequent reduction in the supply of nuclear power, Japan's reliance on imports of fossil fuel has increased significantly making it more difficult to reach its current climate-change-reduction commitments (see Figure 12.2). The situation in Ukraine, an important supplier of fuel, and changes in geopolitics have further destabilized the situation both in Japan and globally.

12.1 Abenomics and the emergence of a 'new Japan'

In 2007, after stepping down prematurely due to health reasons, Abe Shinzō (1954–2022) returned as prime minister in December 2012. He would remain in office until his successor, Suga Yoshihide officially took over as prime minister in September 2020, thus making Abe the longest continuously serving prime minister in Japanese history. Abe's two terms would strongly impact Japan's political economy and institutions (Harris, 2020). Abe was able to introduce sweeping changes thanks to his predecessors who had implemented legislation designed to centralize the decision-making process, allowing the Prime Minister's Office as opposed to the administration and the Diet to take the initiative (Lechevalier and Monfort, 2017). Thus, legislative measures and administrative reorganizations under Hashimoto and Koizumi in the 1990s and 2000s had strengthened the power of the prime minister. This can be illustrated by the number of civil servant appointees attached to the Cabinet Secretariat which rose from 822 in 2000 to 2,971 in 2018. This change gave the central government the power it needed to carry out reforms and propose new policies, even in the face of opposition from ministries (Hoshi and Lipscy, 2021).

From the start of his second term, Abe provided a strong response to the nation's most immediate problem, 3.11, by introducing a measure that would shock observers both inside and outside Japan for its counter-intuitiveness: he proposed the restarting all of Japan's nuclear reactors (Saoshiro and Maeda, 2012). To prevent a deeper recession and to arrest the many chronic problems facing the economy—deflation, low levels of consumption, and low productivity compared to other OECD nations—he introduced a reform package, known as Abenomics, consisting of three targets or arrows.

In his own words, the purpose of Abenomics was 'to break down any and all walls looming ahead of the Japanese economy and map out a new trajectory for growth' (The Government of Japan, 2021). Thus, Abe set out, as had his predecessors, to encourage investment by making Japan a more favourable place for doing business through various measures such as decreasing the corporate tax rate. Through policy he endeavoured to strengthen the competitiveness of domestic firms, a move that was particularly advantageous for large corporations.

Some have viewed Abe's economic reforms as a major departure from those of his predecessors, while others have argued that they were nothing more than the 'repackaging of old policies' (Shibata, 2017; Harris, 2020; Katz, 2014). This chapter argues that the reform package was both. Building on several decades of past reforms, Abe went a step further by implementing measures that are likely to be more enduring. The industrial sectors deemed to have a strong potential for economic growth were pegged for expansion, a central focus being tourism. The initial thrust to develop the tourism sector gained momentum thanks to Japan's successful bid in 2016 to host the 2020 summer Olympic Games in Tokyo, the fruit of a campaign in which Abe as prime minister had been personally invested. In addition to tourism, his policies prioritized innovation in areas relating to digitalization, AI (artificial intelligence), and applications for Big Data. By tapping into such fields, Abe believed he could promote entrepreneurship and help build the foundations for a 'new social model', one that could respond to Japan's major demographic challenges: an aging population and a shrinking workforce caused by a low birthrate.[1]

This chapter examines Japan's most recent period, one that is still in search of a name. Though the themes dealt with in this chapter are far from exhaustive, they should provide readers with a general overview of some of the major debates affecting the development of Japanese business and society since 3.11 and the context in which they occurred. This final chapter is comprised of the following sections: (12.2) Abenomics and the end of communitarian capitalism?; (12.3) The political economic context for Abenomics; (12.4) Abe Shinzō's three arrows of reform; (12.5) New areas of growth: tourism and the Tokyo Olympics; (12.6) Conclusions, and a box: SoftBank's Son Masayoshi and a new age of environmental challenges for Japanese business (see Box 12.1).

12.2 Abenomics and the end of communitarian capitalism?

Public sentiment plays a determining role in a nation's economic performance, and thus it is useful to note the shifts in opinion. During Abe's tenure, public confidence in his ability to bring an end to the 'lost decades' evolved over time from being generally negative to largely positive, particularly from the perspective of certain segments of the population. According to an opinion poll conducted by the Pew Research Center, at the beginning of Abe's second term, over half of the Japanese surveyed had a negative view of their own future economic prospects, despite first quarter economic growth in 2013 of 3.5 per cent (Stokes, 2013). One reason for their pessimism is that the rewards of Abe's reforms tended to be unequally distributed across the population. His policy to raise the consumption tax from 8 to 10 per cent, which was first proposed in 2014, then postponed before being implemented on 1 October 2019 provides an example. While the revenues gained from the tax were to benefit society, it was detrimental not only to individuals in the low-income bracket but also to the average household. At the same time, he reduced the corporate tax burden, providing a boon to large companies and their shareholders (Inoue, 2018). As shown in Table 12.1, while dividends increased dramatically, wages remained largely unchanged, evidence that the distribution of the rewards of Abenomics accrued mainly to large companies and their stockholders.

[1] https://www.japan.go.jp/iichics/index.html

Table 12.1 Effects of Abenomics on profits, labour costs, cash equivalents, and capital investments in FY2009 and FY2018 in trillion yen

FY	Recurring profits	Employees' salary/bonus	Capital investment	Dividends	Cash equivalent
2009	17.9	41.3	17.4	7.0	40.9
2018	48.2	43.9	24.7	18.9	66.6
Amount of increase	30.3	2.6	7.3	11.9	25.7
Ratio (%) of increase	170	6	42	170	63

Note: Includes all industries except finance and insurance and companies with capital stock exceeding 1 billion yen.
Source: METI https://www.meti.go.jp/shingikai/economy/sustainable_kigyo/pdf/001_05_00.pdf, accessed on March 2, 2022; Policy Research Institute, Ministry of Finance Japan (https://www.mof.go.jp/pri/reference/ssc/index.htm).

Changes in Japan's corporate governance model were underway before Abenomics was introduced (Aoki, Jackson, and Miyajima, 2007, 1–47). During his term, however, Abe took them a step further. Before the bursting of the bubble, Japan's model of corporate governance was based largely on long-term relationships between companies and their 'insider stakeholders' (board members, main bank, and loyal shareholders). These relationships had helped to shape Japan's particular way of doing business—its own brand of capitalism—which has been discussed at length in other chapters. As the economy continued to stagnate during the long recession, however, these relationships began to be challenged (Buchanan, Chai, and Deakin, 2012).

In view of bringing about further reforms, the Abe government issued a policy report called *Japan Revitalization Strategy 2014*.[2] According to the findings of the report, Japan's corporate governance model contained inherent flaws which needed to be addressed if the nation was to 'revitalize'. The problems discussed in the report were (1) low ROE (return on equity); (2) a slow response to changes in the business environment, necessitating more M&A (merger and acquisition) and restructuring; and (3) excessive cash deposit holdings combined with lower capital investments than in other developed nations. Japan's model of corporate governance, as described by Kinouchi Toshihisa, senior staff writer at the *Nikkei* newspaper, prevented Japan's poorly performing companies from reducing the size of their regular workforce, hindered changes in management, and limited returns to shareholders (Kinouchi, 2020, 19).

---

[2] https://www.kantei.go.jp/jp/singi/keizaisaisei/pdf/honbun2JP.pdf

The changes in Japan's corporate governance model had important implications not only for stakeholder relationships but also for management practices (Aoki, Jackson, and Miyajima, 2007, 8). The well-established 'social contract', one based on job security for full-time employees in exchange for lifetime service to the firm was called into question (Schaede, 2020). Accordingly, Japan's paternalistic system designed to protect and retain workers—one which had once been credited for producing the 'economic miracle'—was perceived as the cause of its stagnation (Ouchi, 1981; Vogel, 2006).

Thus, Abe's reforms provided firms with a strong legal framework to facilitate the shift from stakeholder to shareholder capitalism. By doing so, corporate Japan moved towards the 'shareholder value model of capitalism' which had become commonplace at Western, particularly American, companies since the 1980s (Jones, 2017, 12). The rise of a shareholder-value model of capitalism, however, would carry with it an unfortunate social cost of increased economic inequalities, particularly for Japan's precariat (Piketty, 2014; Moriguchi, 2017).

The context for reform

To better understand the underlying motivations for Abe's reform policies, which built on those of his predecessors, it is useful to provide an overview of the context for Japan's long recession and the influences on policy and business. Perhaps one of the best analyses of the major issues for Japan in the post-bubble period is that of Marie Anchordoguy. In her book focusing on the telecommunications industry, she blames the slow recovery on Japan's 'communitarian capitalism' model, which she asserts was ill suited to the post-bubble situation. Japan's system was a double-edged sword that 'helped to accelerate economic development under the conditions that existed up to 1980s but is also responsible for the economic paralysis that followed'. She defines 'communitarian capitalism' as one with an activist state that encourages market forces without allowing them to disrupt the social order. This type of postwar capitalism shunned big winners that could push weaker firms out of the market and big losers that could pose a threat to social stability (Anchordoguy, 2015, 3–11). While her work focused on the telecommunications industry, her findings were applicable to other once globally competitive industries which peaked in the high and stable period, as described in Chapters 8 and 9.

Ulrike Schaede's work, *Choose and Focus: Japanese Business Strategies for the 21st Century*, published on the eve of the 2008 global financial crisis, provides an optimistic view of the strategies implemented at some companies in the late 1990s and early 2000s to deal with this situation. According to Schaede (2008), a major transformation—'an inflection point'—was occurring at Japanese companies at that time, causing them to redirect investments from unrelated to core business areas, by shedding costly paternalistic employment practices and restructuring. Between 1998 and 2006 huge strides were being made at the large Japanese companies in her sample to adjust to the competitive global environment they faced. 'Choose and focus' (*sentaku to shūchū*), which became a buzzword during the recession, was the reversal of a dominant strategy among Japanese companies from the postwar period to diversify their business into a wide range of sectors, often into fields completely unrelated to the core activity. This practice was introduced both to reduce risk and to take advantage of growing consumer demand. Schaede (2008) emphasised that Japanese companies which were able to let go of their non-core operations and focus their attention on the core business performed better. To accomplish this task, however, restructuring and changes in the company's relationship with its employees were requisites. Such firms abandoned the long-held Japanese management practice of lifetime employment in favour of 'performance-based pay' (*nōryoku-shugi*).

In a third study of the private sector, Stephen Vogel provides an analysis of a selection of Japanese companies from different industries and their responses to the recession. In his survey, he found that the degree to which a company restructured was correlated to its sector of operations, level of foreign versus government influence, and overseas versus domestic market presence. Accordingly, the banking sector, which was heavily reliant on government bailouts, introduced the least radical reforms. On the other hand, companies with the highest degree of foreign ownership introduced the most robust restructuring strategies, as illustrated by the massive layoffs and factory closures at Nissan, mentioned in the previous chapter. Companies with a strong dependence on the domestic market, such as department stores and supermarkets, were initially slow to restructure, though this situation evolved over time. As seen in the case of Toyota, the more globally focused the company, the quicker the response to the introduction of adjustments designed to bolster international competitiveness (Vogel, 2006).

The politico-economic context for Abenomics

Changes in Japan's institutional environment for business began before Abenomics. In the 1990s, Prime Minister Hashimoto Ryūtarō (1996–1998) implemented measures designed to improve the nation's competitiveness through deregulation. His policies were known as the Japanese Big Bang, which got its name from similar initiatives taken by Margaret Thatcher and Ronald Reagan in the 1980s. The latter introduced Reaganomics, a set of neo-liberal (free-market) economic policies. Whether this was the inspiration for Abe's choice of the term, 'Aben*omics*' to describe his policies is unknown. Hashimoto's deregulatory measures, which his successors in the LDP (Liberal Democratic Party) built on, had a significant impact on the evolution of Japanese capitalism over time.

Another reformer, Koizumi Jun'ichirō (2001–2006), believed that economic recovery could only be achieved by fundamentally altering the relationship between business and politics, a message that was clearly articulated in one of his campaign slogans: 'Change the LDP, Change Japan'. Koizumi instigated important systemic reforms, which were met by great resistance from within his own party. Opposition stemmed in large part from his aim to break up two state monopolies, which had been the cash cows for the public works projects that had fuelled the LDP's political machine since the days of Tanaka Kakuei, particularly in rural areas (Tanaka, 1973). Opposition from within his own party, however, eventually led him to compromise (Takenaka, 2008). Because his reform attempts fell short of their initial expectations, he has been criticized for failing to live up to his commitment to achieve real change (Maclachlan, 2004).

While Koizumi's postal and highway system reforms were important, more noteworthy to the purposes of this study of capitalism were those relating to labour. In 2003, Koizumi's economic and finance minister, Takenaka Heizō amended the 1985 Dispatched Workers Law (*Haken Rōdōsha hō*) making it easier for companies to employ non-regular workers. What is most significant about this measure is that it further weakened Japan's system of lifetime employment, and caused an increase in the number of low-paid workers with unstable employment contracts (see Figure 12.3).

Many would blame these labour reforms on the subsequent widening of socio-economic disparities (*kakusa shakai*) and the erosion of the middle class. It is undeniable that inequalities plague all capitalist economies; however, those in Japan were once smaller than they are today (Piketty, 2014). The reforms would also have significant implications for gender equality, since women occupy a larger proportion of the non-regular posts than men. Consequently, it was women—more often than men—who were dismissed from their jobs when their employers found it necessary to reduce the size of the workforce. The fact that some of the women who fill non-regular positions are also single mothers meant a rise in gender inequality, child poverty, and other social ills (Abe, 2008).

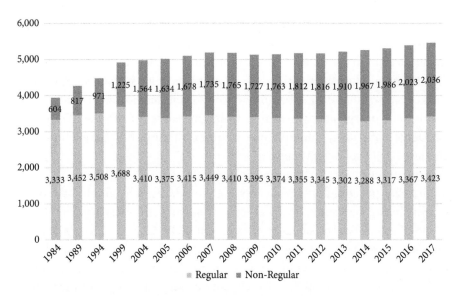

Figure 12.3 Regular and non-regular workers, 10,000 persons, 1984–2017
Source: Based on MHLW (https://www.mhlw.go.jp/file/06-Seisakujouhou-11650000-Shokugyouanteikyokuhakenyukiroudoutaisakubu/0000120286.pdf)

Because these measures made it easier for employers to dismiss non-regular workers, the latter would become especially vulnerable during the global recession of 2008–2009, when restructuring occurred on a large scale. Japan's welfare-state model, which lacks a strong 'safety net' in comparison to some other OECD nations, aggravated the situation for Japan's precariat, hampered recovery efforts, and contributed to a further widening of socio-economic disparities (Sekine, 2008). Non-regular employment issues would not be fully addressed until the introduction of the 'work-style reforms', described below.

Takenaka's reforms were designed to make Japanese firms more competitive, while also making Japan a more attractive place for foreign direct investment, but were highly controversial from the outset. By providing the necessary legal framework to do so, large companies that were struggling to recover from the recession were able to reduce the size of their workforce and 'play by the same rules' as their major trading partners. As noted by Gotoh (2020), however, the neo-liberal reforms implemented since Hashimoto were criticized by many Japanese politicians, business representatives, and society, who opposed the full transition from Japanese-style stakeholder capitalism, discussed in previous chapters, to a more liberal American (global) model. Thus, not all the economic reforms were aimed at destroying Japan's business system or at only prioritizing financial markets.

Over the lost decades period, prime ministers, including two who were not members of the LDP, tried to devise measures to stimulate the economy and end the long recession, with little success. During his short term as prime minister, Asō Tarō (2008–2009) introduced a 5 trillion yen (US$52 billion) economic stimulus package to boost consumer spending and stimulate economic growth through the issuing of shopping vouchers, followed by an eco-point system to encourage new household appliance purchases. While some of his policies did achieve their desired goal—a rise in consumption—the effects were only temporary. Thus, measures to restore consumer confidence to a level needed to attain a full, sustained recovery fell short of the mark (Sakajiri, 2008).

12.3 Abe Shinzō's three arrows of economic reform

Abe's centrepiece policy, Abenomics, was a reform package consisting of three arrows. The first was fiscal policy, which raised the level of government spending, the overarching aim of which was to promote GDP growth. This policy was to be realized in large part through Keynesian-style government spending on public works projects, financed by a rise in the consumption tax in October 2019 from 8 to 10 per cent. The aim of Abe's second arrow was a monetary stimulus designed to increase liquidity through quantitative easing. The overarching goal was to spark a rise in the inflation rate, whose target was set at 2 per cent. Both the first and second arrows are of great importance to historians of economic policy and finance; however, given this volume's focus on the development of business, they are only mentioned in this chapter.

Boosting global competitiveness by expanding trade opportunities was a major area of interest for the Abe government. One example of this was his decision to enter the Trans-Pacific Partnership (TPP), signed in 2018 by twelve nations for the purpose of creating a free-trade zone. The United States under Barack Obama decided to participate in the agreement. However, Obama's successor, Donald Trump, took a difference stance, preferring a bilateral as opposed to a multilateral approach to trade relationships. As of the writing of this chapter, the United States had not signed the TPP agreement.

Abe's third arrow specifically addressed the issue of enhancing global competitiveness through structural reform through the introduction of a reform package that would affect the way Japanese worked, known as 'work-style reform' (*hatarakikata kaikaku*). This reform package sought to respond to a variety of issues, including the declining birthrate, labour shortage, and low participation rate for women in the workforce, especially in executive management-level positions.

Structural change in the workplace

'Work-style reforms' contained a legal framework according to which all companies regardless of size were obliged to implement. On 6 July 2018, in the 196th Ordinary Session of the Diet, the Work-style Reform bill was passed into law and took force on 1 April 2019. The bill amended eight existing laws, including the Labour Standards Act (LSA) and the Industrial Safety and Health Act (ISHA). Collectively, these amendments represented the first major reform of the Labour Standards Law in seventy years (Labor Issues, 2018 5; Prime Minister of Japan and his Cabinet 2018). Some of the most important changes in the LSA are summarized below.

In addition to reforming workplace practices, there were other aims. First, they addressed Japan's low productivity (as measured by the ratio of GDP to hours worked)—the lowest among the G7 nations despite—or perhaps due to—its long working hours (Japan Productivity Centre; OECD iLibrary 2017). Legal limits on the number of working hours were introduced along with penalties for employers who did not comply. The government's rationale behind the efforts to change Japan's long working-hours culture was based on the notion that providing workers with a wider range of work-style choices could also help to solve another problem, the nation's low birthrate. Though not addressed in Table 12.2, work-style reform it was thought, might also help to tackle Japan's socio-economic disparities, which are correlated to the differences in the treatment of regular and non-regular (including both part-time and fixed contract/dispatched) workers.

Table 12.2 Amendments to the Labor Standards Law

Amendment	Enforcement date
Enhancement of flextime system	1 April 2019*
Introduction of legal limits on working hours	1 April 2019
Raise in extra wage rate for overtime working hours	1 April 2023
Ensuring use of a certain number of days of annual paid leave	1 April 2019
Establishing a 'highly professional' work system allowing certain professions such as physicians to continue to work long hours	1 April 2019

Note: * enforcement date for SMEs of April 2023.
Source: 'Key Aspects of the Work Style Reform Bill' in *Japan Labor Issues*, vol. 2, no. 10, November 2018, p. 6

Contextual factors for changing Japan's work culture

Changing a nation's work culture is not an easy task since one's work philosophy—as was also shown in the first chapter of this volume—is often deeply entrenched in underlying cultural values and norms (Hofstede, 1980; Meyer, 2014). Despite strong evidence of a correlation between long working hours and inefficiency, overwork is commonplace in industries and countries where competition is fierce (*Economist*, 2021). The tendency to overwork is not a uniquely Japanese feature. It can be seen in other Asian 'latecomer economies', such as China (IIwamoto and Nakamura, 2016).[3] Overwork has shown to cause physical illnesses, such as heart attacks and strokes as well as psychological ones, including depression and suicide, known in Japanese as *karō-jisatsu* (suicide by overwork) (Araki and Iwasaki, 2005).

The historical context also plays a role in shaping the work culture. The expectation for workers to put in long hours was widespread during the high-growth period when the Japanese population was united to achieve a common goal of 'catching-up and overtaking' Western nations. Japan's corporate work practices became a focal point of global interest in the 1980s when the term, *karōshi* or 'death by overwork' first appeared in the popular press. *Karōshi* emerged in the context of the bubble period when Western nations' political tensions with Japan were high due to growing trade deficits. Measures to legally define *karōshi* were introduced in Japan, and compensation was paid to the families of the victims.

Japan's unhealthy work culture was captured in the spotlight on Christmas Day 2015, when Takahashi Matsuri, a graduate of a top Japanese university and employee of prestigious advertising firm, Dentsū, took her own life by jumping from the company dormitory. At that time, although her contract with Dentsū limited overtime work to 70 hours per month, Takahashi was working over 100. The courts would later recognize the correlation between her death and the unhealthy working environment at Dentsū, and force the firm to provide her family with compensation (National Law Review, 2018; Ennahachi, 2019).

The Work-style Reform Act, introduced in June 2018 in the aftermath of this case, specifically addressed the problem of *karōshi* by requiring employers to implement measures to instil a healthier workplace culture as well

---

[3] MHLW 2021 https://www.mhlw.go.jp/stf/seisakunitsuite/bunya/hukushi_kaigo/seikatsuhogo/jisatsu/jisatsu_year.html

as legal safeguards to limit overtime hours. Compliance by all companies, regardless of size, is now mandatory. While the reform is seen as a landmark in worker protection legislation, there is still room for improvement. As shown in Table 12.2, loopholes for professions such as physicians and consultants mean that they can be asked to work excessively long hours (Japan Labor Issues, 2018 7). Ironically, the bureaucrats in Japan's ministries—some of whom were responsible for implementing measures to improve the situation for workers in the private sector—are not protected by the new legislation. One example is the bureaucrats at the Ministry of Health, Labour, and Welfare who put in especially long hours in the early phases of Covid-19, though such practices existed long before the pandemic (Timinsky, 2019). Despite these measures, overwork is still commonplace in many Japanese companies and indeed in most capitalist economies. Given the severity of Japan's chronic labour shortage, the problems described above are not likely to be solved without a serious debate on immigration policies and an acceptable definition of 'work–life balance' for all.

A new competitive advantage: harnessing the power of women

One of the work-style reforms' most highly publicized features was a policy that was not initially part of Abenomics; Womenomics was designed to increase the participation of women in the workforce. Abe's statement made on 26 September 2013 at the 68th session of the general assembly of the United Nations provides a brief overview of its central aims:

> There is a theory called 'womenomics', which asserts that the more the advance of women in society is promoted, the higher the growth rate becomes. Creating an environment in which women find it comfortable to work and enhancing opportunities for women to work and to be active in society is no longer a matter of choice for Japan. It is instead a matter of the greatest urgency. Declaring my intention to create 'a society in which women shine', I have been working to change Japan's domestic structures. (Prime Minister of Japan and his cabinet, 2013)

While implementing specific measures to empower the female population was a first for the Abe government, the term womenomics and the need for greater female workforce participation were not new concepts. Womenomics was initially put forth in 1999 by Kathy Matsui, an executive at Goldman Sachs, as a means for making it easier for more Japanese women to join the workforce at any stage of their lives and contribute to economic development (Matsui, Suzuki, and Ushio, 1999).

A discussion on how to make Japan a country 'in which women shine' was long overdue. As Helen Macnaughtan pointed out in her assessment of womenomics, the role of Japanese women in the workforce had not evolved significantly since the postwar period. During the high-growth period in the 1960s, women were seen as essential for achieving economic growth; at the same time, however, they were not given the same status as men. Women were thus regarded as temporary fixtures in the workplace, employed simply to fill a gap in which male domination was considered normative. Accordingly, women often joined companies as regular employees after completing their education; however, once they married, they were expected to quit their jobs to raise children. While some women did return to work after child-rearing, their status was lower than their male counterparts since the Japanese employment system awards higher pay and promotions to those with long service to the company through the seniority-based pay system. In most cases, the women who returned to work were only offered part-time (non-regular) as opposed to full-time (regular) positions. Thanks to the institutionalization of this employment pattern as the general norm, Japan's workforce has become highly gendered with, in the words of Macnaughtan, 'an employment system that allocates productive roles to men and reproductive roles to women' (Macnaughtan, 2015).

Though the number of Japanese women who participate actively in the workforce continued to rise, which Abe claimed was proof of his policy's effectiveness, it was mainly for non-regular positions. Since the introduction of womenomics, there have been improvements; however, Abe's numerical targets for women on corporate boards and other leadership positions have not been reached (Crawford, 2021). Today, fewer Japanese women occupy executive management positions than their Western counterparts (International Labor Statistics, 2020).

Japan's gender gap is also high in terms of wage differentials. According to 2014 OECD statistics, Japan has the third highest gender wage gap among member nations, surpassed only by Estonia (second) and South Korea (first). This reflects the fact that in the private sector, only 9 per cent of employees with managerial responsibilities were women. One reason why it is more difficult for women to advance to positions of leadership is the lack of childcare facilities and labour shortages, particularly in urban areas. Other contributing factors are low government spending on early childcare education and a taxation system that has encouraged women to take low paying, part-time jobs to avoid exceeding the tax deduction threshold of 1.03 million yen, as mentioned in Chapter 9 (OECD Data, 2021; OECD Entrepreneurship at a glance, 2017).

The gender gap can be illustrated by the so-called *M-curve* in women's employment patterns, a trend that emerged in the 1960s. In Japan, female graduates join the workforce after completing their education in roughly equal numbers as their male counterparts, causing the workforce participation curve to slant upwards for women in the same way as men. However, the curve starts to dip downwards as women leave the workforce to bear children, forming the first hump of the M in the M-curve. As women re-enter the workforce after their children enter school, the curve again rises, forming the second crest of M-curve. By contrast, for men who generally do not leave or rejoin the labour force to engage in child-rearing, similar dips and rises in the labour participation ratio do not occur until after retirement. As a result, the shape of the curve for male workforce participation forms an inverted U.

It is noteworthy that in other OECD nations, except South Korea, the labour participation curves for men and women do not differ significantly. Because Japan's work practices often make it more difficult to take a leave of absence for child-rearing, the women who quit and rejoin the workforce face greater obstacles than their female counterparts in other OECD nations. Indeed, Japanese women who leave the workforce for an extended period most often return as non-regular employees with lower pay, limited benefits, and more precarious employment contracts than their full-time (male) counterparts.

New ways of working: 'Englishnization' and teleworking

Evidence of initiatives designed to change the workplace culture in order to bolster global competitiveness can also be found in the private sector. Two of Japan's most celebrated entrepreneurs, Yanai Tadashi (UNIQLO) and Mikitani Hiroshi (Rakuten), mentioned in the previous chapter, implemented measures intended to modify their workplace culture through English. Mikitani Hiroshi, Rakuten's founder, made English part of his corporate strategies: On 1 March 2010, he announced the 'Englishnization' of his operations. Accordingly, English became the company's lingua franca regardless of the location of the operations. Thus, it is used for all communications, even between Japanese in Japan, not only for meetings but also for other forms of written and verbal communication. It is even used for the vending machines in the corporate cafeteria. Employees were given two years to reach the mandated level of proficiency or risk demotion (Neeley, 2013).

The intensification of competition in the domestic market is the result of a changing business environment discussed in this chapter and the previous one. In particular, deregulation—achieved by the removal of barriers to entry and the opening the domestic market to overseas competition—has for some companies done away with various legal protections and eroded their domestic market advantages. For others, however, it has provided new opportunities, one example being the telecommunications maverick, Son Masayoshi, mentioned in Box 12.1. The deregulation of the publishing sector combined with the increased use of digital technologies were factors that provided Rakuten's Mikitani with an opportunity to compete against global online retailers such as Amazon.

The global pandemic has given some Japanese businesses an opportunity to introduce changes in the workplace, which go beyond the work-style reforms. Teleworking is one example. Working remotely did not become widespread until the outbreak of Covid-19 and the government's issuing of the first state of emergency declaration in April 2019. Prior to the pandemic, the government had encouraged companies to adopt more flexible working practices to allow women to work from home after giving birth and to provide all employees, regardless of their gender, with the opportunity to care for their elderly parents. NTT (Nippon Telegraph and Telephone Corporation) was the first company to promote teleworking, a move that was facilitated by its early investments in a networking infrastructure. The government also encouraged firms in Tokyo and its surrounding areas to carry out simulations to allow firms to prepare for teleworking during the 2020 Tokyo Olympics when public transportation would be stretched to overcapacity due to the large influx of foreign spectators.

As seen in this example of the spread of remote work, Covid-19 has been the source of some highly 'disruptive' innovations at Japanese firms—both large and small, and it has also brought about modifications in the business culture and norms. Without the pandemic, the government's promotion of digitalization and discouragement of the use of personal seals (*hankō*) and face-to-face meetings might have seemed less urgent. However, given the initial resistance by some companies to respond to the new environment and the swift return to former practices as soon as the infection numbers began to subside, it is uncertain whether teleworking will ever become a permanent fixture in the Japanese workplace.

12.4 New areas of growth: tourism and the Tokyo Olympics

In 2016, the International Olympics and Paralympics Committee approved Japan's bid to host the 2020 Tokyo Summer Games. While the decision meant that spectators and athletes from around the world would be flocking in droves to Tokyo to watch them and participate, the tourism sector had already been pegged as a new and promising area for growth. The popularity of Japan as a tourism destination had steadily risen since the collection of statistics first began in the 1960s. Figure 12.4 shows a gradual increase in visitor arrivals with one major interruption following 3.11, and another caused by Covid-19. According to a McKinsey&Company report, from 2011 to 2015, the growth rate for the Japanese tourism sector was among the fastest in the world (Andonian et. al., 2016).

One feature of the tourism industry is that most inbound tourists are Asian. One reason for Japan's attractiveness is its proximity to other Asian nations; however, there are other factors to consider. First, in 2013, Japan ratified the 'open sky' agreement, which increased the number of arrivals to Japan's major airports. This, combined with airline deregulation, triggered a rise in the number of low-cost carriers (LCCs), whose activities have experienced varying rates of success. Some LCCs were launched by Japan's two main carriers, JAL (Japan Airlines) and ANA (All Nippon Airways), while others such as Jet-Star (Qantas, Australia) and AirAsia (Malaysia) were foreign-owned. Peach, once a Malaysian carrier, began its activities in Japan through a partnership with ANA but was, at the time of the writing of this section, fully owned by the latter. JAL (ZIPAIR) entered, then exited its LCC strategy, while ANA has continued to pursue it through partnerships and acquisitions. Skymark, the only independent Japanese LCC, once filed for bankruptcy but is

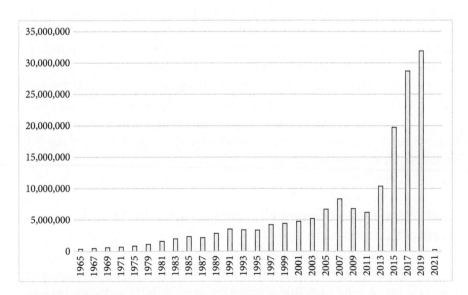

Figure 12.4 Inbound visitors to Japan by year, 1965–2021
Source: JNTO (https://statistics.jnto.go.jp/en/graph/#graph—inbound—travelers—transition)

back in operation. The situation is likely to evolve significantly as the global pandemic and fluctuating fuel costs continue to pose a threat to the survival of LCCs and the airline industry more generally. A second factor in the rise of tourism among Asians is the relaxation of immigration and visa regulations. This decision led to notable increases in the number of tourists from China, Malaysia, and Thailand.

Against a backdrop of the precipitous rise in inbound Asian tourism, the term *bakugai* sometimes translated as 'bomb-buying' entered the Japanese vocabulary. This term describes a consumer behaviour mainly attributed to Chinese tourists who make large purchases of high-quality 'made-in-Japan' products at drug and department stores, sometimes completely depleting their stocks. The growth in Chinese tourism was made possible not only thanks to the relaxation of Japan's visa restrictions but also to the rapid rise of the Chinese economy and the growth of the disposal income of its large population. These factors made China the top source of Japan's tourism revenues until the pandemic. The third factor for the general rise in tourism is the depreciation of the yen, one of the aims of Abenomics. Consequently, Japanese goods have become more competitive (i.e. cheaper), contributing to Japan's attractiveness as a destination not only for Asian consumers, but also for a growing number of European and American travellers, who had initially not chosen to visit Japan due to a perception of high prices.

Thanks to the combination of the above factors, incentives offered by the Japanese government, and Japan's genuine allure as a destination, the tourism industry was booming on the eve of the global pandemic, but not without significant consequences. The negative effects of the tourism boom could clearly be seen in the chronic shortage of hotel accommodations, especially in Tokyo, Kyoto, and other major cities. At that time, deregulation once again became a buzzword as measures were taken to officially allow *minpaku*, the Japanese term for the Airbnb business model, initially in limited parts of Tokyo, as well as the ride-sharing service, Uber. Another negative consequence of the boom was the overcrowding of pedestrian areas and public transportation systems, an increasingly urgent issue in tourist spots, such as Kyoto. A discussion of sustainable ways to deal with the growing number of inbound tourists was already underway before the outbreak of Covid-19, though solutions had yet to be found. Residents of popular tourist destinations complained of the disruptive effects of unrestricted tourism on their daily lives, while those in the regions generally welcomed their arrival and the positive spillovers that it was having on the revitalization of local businesses and the economy in general (*Nikkei* newspaper, 18 April 2019). It remains to be seen how the changing geopolitical situation, particularly in Asia, and the fluctuations in the global economy will affect this industry in the years to come.

12.5 Conclusions

Abe left his post as prime minister in September 2020 at the beginning of a new wave in the Covid-19 global pandemic. What will be his legacy for Japanese business? Abe missed his goal of a 2 per cent target for inflation (first arrow), while the debt-to-GDP ratio surpassed 250 per cent and continued to rise (second arrow) (Ito, 2020). On the other hand, on the eve of the pandemic, stock prices reached levels not witnessed since the bubble economy years. Pre-pandemic employment statistics for new university graduates were also favourable (*Kyodo News*, Sept 2021). While Abenomics did bring a surge in profits to firms and an increase in dividends to shareholders, the lives and livelihoods of the average worker changed little and their wages remained stagnant. Purchasing a home, especially in or near central Tokyo, has grown increasingly out of reach for the average Japanese. The impact of higher housing costs, however, has to some extent been offset by the rise of teleworking, an outcome of the pandemic. Though it is uncertain whether the trend will continue, working from home has allowed some Japanese to move to rural areas where housing is cheaper, a boon not only for workers but also for Japan's regional economies.

For the Japanese economy and business, the effects of Covid-19 pandemic have been uneven. Some sectors performed well, such as video games company, Nintendo or new home delivery services of foods and other necessities. In March 2022, Sony, which benefited from extraordinary growth of sales of online games and services during the pandemic, announced operating profits above one trillion yen for FY2021. Until then, only Toyota had been able to achieve such favourable results (*Kyodo News*, 10 May 2022). According to an article published in June 2021 in the *Nikkei* newspaper, one-third of Japan's listed companies intended to increase dividends in FY2022 (*Nikkei*, June 2021). Efforts to reboot the post-Covid economy, however, were exacerbated in part by one of the slowest vaccine rollouts in all the OECD nations, due in part to a lengthy approval process (OECD, 9 March 2021).

Against the advice of public health officials, the government decided to launch the first 'GoTo Travel Campaign' in 2020 to encourage through subsidies the domestic tourism industry, which predictably resulted in a surge in

Covid-19 cases (Anzai and Nishiura, 2021). The policy was soon reversed, but is representative of a dilemma that policymakers have faced over the last few decades: how to respond to societal needs while also promoting economic growth. This is a fundamental issue facing the future of capitalism, not only in Japan but in other developed economies. The Japanese government has remained more cautious than most governments regarding the re-opening of borders not only for tourists but also for business and student travellers. Nonetheless, in early 2022 Japanese authorities began to gradually re-open them. The havoc wreaked by the long pandemic has created an unprecedented opportunity to open a new debate on how to achieve not only a more sustainable form of tourism but also a new model of capitalism—one that can provide benefits to both the economy and to all those who support it. Whether this opportunity will be seized or not remains to be seen.

Conclusion

This volume explored a variety of forms of Japanese capitalism and entrepreneurship over a period of more than two centuries from both a domestic and an international business perspective. This conclusion offers a general discussion of the changes that took place over this period, the main factors for the evolution of Japanese capitalism and entrepreneurship, and some implications for business development in Japan and other major capitalist economies.

Some of the fundamental features of Japanese business have their roots in the Edo period, one example being the many old and often family-owned and operated firms whose longevity can be explained in large part by one of Japan's distinctive systems, adult adoption. Other early institutions played an important role in the development of Japanese business in the long term. The alternate residence system, a politically motivated decision, served as a major catalyst for the creation of a transportation infrastructure for both goods and people, which linked the nation's regions to the capital in Edo, and provided the basis for an early system of monetary exchange. Another was the rice-based taxation system. This promoted the regional economies by stimulating competition for new product development relying on indigenous technologies, another characteristic of Japanese business. A group of entrepreneurial actors, the 'rural capitalists', who produced and sold goods to sustain the Edo economy, would stand at the forefront of business development in the Meiji period.

The opening of the nation to global trade in the Meiji period created a new environment, one that was especially conducive to the emergence of new forms of capitalism and entrepreneurship. The growth of business was witnessed through two vectors: state enterprises and those run by private entrepreneurs. A third vector was foreigners. They were the major agents of technology transfer and a significant influence on the development of Japanese capitalism throughout the Meiji period and beyond. Two new institutions of business, the Stock Exchange and the Chamber of Commerce were imported from Western Europe through such individuals as Shibusawa Eiichi, the so-called father of Japanese capitalism. He directly contributed to the growth of business through the formation of numerous joint-stock companies. Others such Fukuzawa Yukichi propagated printed sources of practical business knowledge and provided training and employment opportunities to aspiring entrepreneurs at new business schools. From this period until the end of World War II, private investors (*zaibatsu*) built business empires and forged close relationships with the help of the political elite. This allowed them to accumulate vast amounts of capital for the building of modern industries in which they possessed a majority stake.

Economic expansion during the Taishō period, the result of the introduction of a mass-production system, heralded in a new era, referred to as *industrial capitalism*. Accompanying its emergence were changes in the relationship between business and society, witnessed through the birth of a labour movement, the growth of the female workforce, and the rise of consumerism. Japan's geopolitical ambitions contributed to the expansion of business overseas, especially in its newly acquired colonial markets in Asia, bringing an unprecedented economic boon. At the same time however, Japan's full integration into the global economy made its firms increasingly vulnerable to the shocks occurring in the 1920s and 1930s. With the approach of World War II, cooperation between military research centres, government, universities, and private enterprises was encouraged, leading to the birth of a national innovation system, an important advancement both for business and science with implications for a postwar pattern of growth which was highly technology-driven.

Under the control economy of World War II, capitalism and entrepreneurship were severely restricted as the government put in place measures to curtail the market mechanism and redirect all available resources into the war effort. With the entire nation mobilized for war, the structure of business evolved, becoming highly concentrated, especially in sectors relating to the production of weaponry. The war's protraction, however, brought severe shortages of food and supplies, and aggravated tensions between Japan's wartime government and its entrepreneurial elite: the executive managers of the *zaibatsu*. Perceived by the public and government as merely taking advantage of escalating wartime demand to increase their own personal wealth, these executives became symbols of the evils of capitalism and the targets of criticism, government sanctions, and even assassination attempts.

Japan's defeat and the US occupation from 1945 to 1952 did not prevent the emergence of a new form of capitalism, influenced by the entrepreneurship of a new generation of businessmen. The destruction of the nation's physical infrastructure and the lack of the necessities, namely food, clothing, and shelter, provided new opportunities for business development. As a defeated nation, the loss of political sovereignty combined with a strong desire to rebuild the war-torn economy created a climate that was similar to that of the Meiji period when economic nationalism was especially intense.

As in the Meiji period, the Japanese state also played a central role during the high-growth period. The government provided a favourable environment for private enterprise by encouraging business development in certain sectors and by offering preferential treatment to industries perceived as having the greatest potential to boost economic growth, often through exports. The institutional environment was propitious for capitalist activities, thanks to structural reforms which especially benefited business development. The SCAP's decision to dismantle the *zaibatsu* and other major industries, such as steel, encouraged a healthy form of competition as well as a flourishing of innovation. After the occupiers left, the former *zaibatsu* companies formed business groups, overseen by professional managers as opposed to family members. Large numbers of tiny start-ups also appeared, one being Sony. These firms not only contributed to economic reconstruction but also to a sea change in the quality and image of Japanese products abroad. During this period, Japan's image transformed from a manufacturer of 'cheap and shoddy' goods into a high-tech superpower. The success of private-sector businesses was rooted in their innovations, many of which relied on peacetime applications of wartime technologies, and in some cases guidance from the state. The exponential growth of the Japanese economy during the high-growth period was also supported by a growing population and the rise of a middle-class consumer society.

In 1968, Japan reached a new milestone when it became the second largest economy in the world in terms of GDP—a position it held until 2010. The nation's success in achieving this rapid ascent was referred to in the popular press as the 'Japanese miracle' and was emulated across East and South East Asia. The blue-collar management system, now almost synonymous with Toyota, made Japan's factories some of the most productive and widely imitated in the world. While Japan does merit praise for its achievements, its model of rapid industrialization revealed 'the dark side of capitalism' in the form of industrial pollution and environmental degradation. Public protests took place in response, but were not always met by swift and expedient government action. The problems that occurred in Minamata for example were debated in the courts for decades before a settlement was finally awarded to the victims in 2014.

The stable growth period marked a new phase in the evolution of Japanese capitalism and entrepreneurship. To cope with this climate, large manufacturers strengthened their relationships with firms in the same sector as well as their *keiretsu* affiliates. The explanations for lower growth rates are complex but largely tied to changes in consumer preferences and growing competition in Asia. Responding to these changes were entrepreneurs, such as Nakauchi Isao and Suzuki Toshifumi, who introduced American models of business which challenged existing business practices and created new patterns of consumer purchasing. Looking for new business ideas in the United States, as these two did, is a recurring theme throughout this volume. Working through diplomatic channels as well as their partner companies, foreign firms also effected major changes in Japan's institutional and business environment.

The characteristics of Japanese capitalism during the boom periods were influenced by firms' desire to gain greater control of their markets, while also ensuring a stable source of labour. The early formation of a distribution system in the prewar period helped manufacturers to deal with market imperfections caused by fluctuating demand. Japanese management practices of lifetime employment, enterprise unions, and seniority-based pay, which were institutionalized during the high-growth period, served as the foundations for the strong and stable bond that was built between the management at large firms and mostly male white-collar employees. The 'social contract', based on reciprocity: worker loyalty in exchange for long-term employment, and the formation of cooperative intra-firm networks were two features of the *communitarian capitalism*, described in this volume. Japanese firms received accolades in the 1970s and 1980s for achieving harmonious, cooperative workplaces and high productivity at a time when tensions in Western countries with their labour forces threatened their global competitiveness. The same relationships would be judged differently, however, during the post-bubble recession, when Japan's model of capitalism came under pressure to adjust to new circumstances, despite the absence of a strong social safety net.

The combination of the deregulation of the banking system, low interest rates, and a strong yen led to an asset bubble that burst in the early 1990s, marking another watershed for Japanese capitalism. During the bubble period, average Japanese began investing their savings in the equity market, which reached heights that have only recently been replicated. The frenzy to purchase shares produced a new climate for business and another form of capitalism, referred to in this volume as *financial capitalism*. Entrepreneurship in the form of speculative financial products and property development failed when the bubble burst. The luxury goods and overseas travel industries performed well during the bubble period thanks to the rise in disposable income for some and a stronger yen. At the time of the bubble's peak, to observers around the world, Japan seemed to have finally been able to catch up with and perhaps even overtaken the West.

The crash that ended the bubble economy provided an opportunity for serious collective reflection. Some Japanese blamed the economic collapse on governmental mismanagement and corporate greed, while others saw the culprits as speculative financial capitalism and the abandoning of a fundamental key to Japan's postwar success: manufacturing (*monozukuri* or 'making things'). The recession that followed endured for over two decades. With the bursting of the bubble came a decline in consumer confidence and low demand, which was reinforced by two increasingly troubling demographic trends: the decreasing birthrate and an aging population. The government employed countermeasures to stimulate the economy and increase global competitiveness, with perhaps one of the most controversial being the deregulation of the labour market. Over time, the latter increased precarity for workers and exacerbated social inequalities, which has since led to a serious questioning of the sustainability of a capitalist system founded on communitarian values. The decline in disposable income during this period did, however, bring new opportunities for entrepreneurship as seen in the expansion of the low-priced clothing retailer, Uniqlo and Daiso's 100-yen shops across Japan and in overseas markets.

The final chapter in this volume focused on the long-term repercussions of 3.11 and the introduction of Abenomics. Abenomics addressed a wide range of economic issues, stemming from Japan's demographic challenges and declining global competitiveness. Changes in the corporate governance model, which were already underway during previous administrations, pushed Japan one step further towards the shareholder-focused, financialised model of capitalism, seen especially in the United States. 'Work-style reform', including greater opportunities for the advancement of women in business were placed high on the policy priority agenda, as was the expansion of one relatively new industry, tourism. Abe was succeeded by Suga Yoshihide then Kishida Fumio, whose centrepiece campaign pledge was to introduce 'a new form of capitalism' (Prime Minister's Office of Japan, 2022). To date, Kishida's definition of capitalism has been vague. Moreover, his measures to encourage investment in start-ups and stimulate economic growth are not new (The Economist, 2022).[1]

At time of the publication of Ezra Vogel's 1979 best-selling classic, *Japan as Number One*, countries in both the developing and developed world

---

[1] Nikkei Asia, 21 June 2022, https://asia.nikkei.com/Spotlight/Asia-Insight/Japan-startups-see-Kishida-s-new-capitalism-as-road-without-map.

were looking to Japan as a model for success in business, education, and labour relations. Today factories around the world employ Japanese labour practices with favourable results, as evidenced in their high rates of productivity, worker satisfaction, and profitability. The twenty-first century has been called the Asian Century, whose foundations Japan has in no small part helped to build. Asian latecomer economies emulated the Japan's postwar catch-up industrialization model, based on a variety of factors including administrative guidance, private entrepreneurship, technology transfer, and others (Suehiro, 2008). This development pattern aided them to achieve, to varying degrees, their own 'miracles' of rapid, high economic growth. Today, as policymakers and business leaders around the world search for ways to deal with their sluggish economies and increasing social ills, they might once again turn to Japan whose experiences during the 'lost decades' in particular, might provide some cautionary lessons.

As latecomer economies have introduced and adapted the Japanese model to suit their own distinctive historical circumstances, natural endowments, and changing economic environment, there have naturally been some divergences. China's approach to capitalism has been more authoritarian, while another nation, Thailand, adopted a weak-state approach. Though one can find some similarities in the business models across Asia thanks in part to their common cultural features, convergence towards a single form of Asian capitalism seems unlikely, despite the assumptions of some scholars of the political economy that it would (e.g. Amable, 2003).

The influence of Western nations, especially the United States, has been an important undercurrent in the development of Japanese business history. Whether it was in the context of the arrival of the 'black ships' in Tokyo Bay or the threat of trade wars, Japanese have often viewed foreign contacts with trepidation. Since the end of World War II, thanks to a growing population, Japan was able to keep the forces of globalization at bay. Legal frameworks as well as cultural barriers served as buffers to protect the domestic market and by extension to defend the livelihoods of its workers. Over the last two decades, however, Japan's gradual embrace of an Anglo-Saxon, neoliberal form of capitalism has challenged these arrangements.

As economists in recent years have asserted, capitalism as an economic system is inherently flawed in no small part for its tendency to produce social inequalities. This is clear in the Japanese example: during the high-growth period, many Japanese thought of themselves as members of the middle class; the same is no longer true today. Economist Thomas Piketty, whose book, *Capital in the Twenty-First Century*, was a worldwide best-seller, made a visit to Tokyo in 2015. Both during his stay and in his book, he criticized

Japan's policies since the 1990s for their tendency to widen wage differentials, which according to his analysis, have resulted in greater social inequalities. While less conspicuous than the gaps seen in the United States, the situation has continued to worsen over time. As Moriguchi Chiaki has shown, Abenomics benefited the highest earners, while the wages of workers with lower incomes, especially the non-regular workforce, have stagnated (Moriguchi, 2017; Moriguchi and Saez, 2010).

While the objective of this volume is not to address the ideological dimensions of Japanese capitalism, the importance of Marxism as a dominant force in intellectual circles in Japan in the twentieth century is worth mentioning (Walker, 2016; Takeuchi, 1974). Since that time, Marxism has been an important undercurrent in Japan's most reputable economics departments, particularly during certain periods of its development. This academic tradition fostered critical debates on the long-term economic development of Japan, which went beyond the income inequalities that Piketty and others identified. The author of a third best-seller is Saitō Kōhei, a Marxist philosopher and historian of economic thought, who offers another critique of capitalism through his work on the connections between climate change and economic development. Only through policies designed to achieve degrowth, he argues, can a catastrophic global climate crisis be averted (Saito, 2020). In a series of articles in one of Japan's most widely circulated newspapers, the *Mainichi*, he discusses a broad spectrum of issues directly related to the development of Japanese capitalism, ranging from the pollution problems caused by Minamata to questions concerning diversity and inclusivity in Japanese society. His insights are gaining popularity among those who are most likely to be affected by climate change and shrinking economic prospects: Japan's youth.

What is the future of Japanese capitalism and entrepreneurship? At the end of World War II, Japan was a country that few outside Japan understood; today that is no longer the case. Japan must cope with many of the same challenges that those in other countries around the world also face. It is hoped that this general survey of Japanese capitalism and entrepreneurship over time provides students of Japanese business, economics, and society not only with ample information for discussion and debate, but also with some ideas for how to confront these common challenges.

References

Publications in English

Abe, T. (2015). The 'Japan problem': The trade conflict between the European countries and Japan in the last quarter of the 20th century. *Entreprises et histoire*, 3: 13–35.
Abegglen, J., and Stalk, G. (1973). *Kaisha: The Japanese Corporation*. New York: Basic Books.
Alexander, J. W. (2013). *Brewed in Japan: The Evolution of the Beer Industry*. Honolulu: University of Hawaii Press.
Amable, B. (2003). *The Diversity of Modern Capitalism*. Oxford: Oxford University Press.
Anchordoguy, M. (2015). *Reprogramming Japan: The High-Tech Crisis under Communitarian Capitalism*. New York: Cornell University Press.
Andonian, A., Kuwabara, T., Yamakawa, N., Ishida, R. (2016). The future of Japan's tourism: path for sustainable growth towards 2020, McKinsey Japan and Travel, Oct. 2016.
Anzai, A., and Nishiura, H. (2021). 'Go to Travel' campaign and travel-associated coronavirus disease 2019 cases: A descriptive analysis 2020, July–August 2020. *Journal of Clinical Medicine*, 10: 398.
Aoki, M., Jackson, G., and Miyajima, H. (2007). *Corporate Governance in Japan*, Oxford: Oxford University Press.
Arai, I., Yongue, J., and Tsutani, K. (2022). The development of the Kampo medicines industry: 'Good Practices' and health policy making in Japan, in *Asian Medical Industries: Contemporary Perspectives on Traditional Pharmaceuticals*, S. Kloos and C. Blaikie, eds. London: Routledge, 81–109.
Araki S., and Iwasaki, K. (2005). Death due to overwork (*Karoshi*): Causation, health service, and life expectancy in Japanese males. *Journal of the Japanese Medical Association*, 48(2): 92–98.
Arano, Y. (2005). Concept of the border: Nations, peoples, and frontiers in Asian history, the foundation of a Japanocentric world order. *International Journal of Asian Studies*, 2(2): 185–215.
Bartholomew, J. R. (1989). *The Formation of Science in Japan: Building a Research Tradition*. New Haven, CT: Yale University Press.
Beckert, S., and Desan, C. (2018). *American Capitalism: New Histories*. New York: Columbia University Press.
Bellah, R. N. (1985). *Tokugawa Religion: The Cultural Roots of Modern Japan*. London: The Free Press.
Benson, J. (2008). The development and structure of Japan's enterprise unions. *Asia Pacific Journal, Japan Focus*, 6(11): 1–9.
Bernstein, J. R. (1997). 7-Eleven in America and Japan in T. K. McCraw, Creating Modern Capitalism: How Entrepreneurs, Companies, and Countries Triumphed in Three Industrial Revolutions. Cambridge, MA: Harvard University Press.
Boon, M. (2020). The global oil industry in *The Routledge Companion to the Makers of Global Business*, T. Da Silva Lopes, C. Lubinski, and H. J. S. Tworek (eds). Oxon and New York: Routledge, 467–482.
Braudel, F. (1979). *Civilisation matérielle, économie et capitalisme, XVe et XVIIIe siècles*. Paris: Armand Colin.

Buchanan, J., Chai, H. D., and Deakin, S. (2012). *Hedge Fund Activism in Japan: The Limits of Shareholder Primacy*. New York: Cambridge University Press.

Bytheway, S. J. (2014). *Investing Japan: Foreign Capital, Monetary Standards, and Economic Development, 1859-2011*. Cambridge, MA: Harvard University Asia Centre.

Callon, S. (1995). *MITI and the Breakdown of Japanese High-Tech Industrial Policy, 1975-1993*. Stanford, CA: Stanford University Press.

Carson, R. (1962). *Silent Spring*. Houghton Miffin Company.

Chandler, A. D. (1990). *Scale and Scope: The Dynamics of Industrial Capitalism*. Cambridge, MA: Harvard University Press.

Christensen, C. M. (2016). *The Innovator's Dilemma: When New Technologies Cause Great Firms to Fail*. Cambridge, MA: Harvard Business Review Press.

Cohen, J. B. (1949). *Japan's Economy in War and Reconstruction*. Minneapolis, MI: University of Minnesota Press.

Colpan, A. M., Hikino, T., and Lincoln, J. R. (eds) (2010). *The Oxford Handbook of Business Groups*. Oxford: Oxford University Press.

Crawford, M. (2021). Abe's womenomics policy, 2013-2020: Tokenism, gradualism, or failed policy. *The Asia-Pacific Journal Japan Focus*, 19(4): 1-16.

Dasgupta, R. (2017). Articulations of salaryman masculinity in Shôwa and post-Shôwa Japan. *Asia Pacific Perspectives*, 15(1): 36-54.

Daykin, J. (2015). International ambitions at an exposition at the margin: Japan's 1903 Osaka exhibition in *Cultures of International Exhibitions 1840-1940: Great Exhibitions in the Margins*, M. Filipová, ed. Dorchester: Dorset Press, pp. 332-349.

Dees, J. G. (1998). Enterprising non-profits: What do you do when traditional sources of funding fall short? *Harvard Business Review*, 76: 55-67.

Demizu, T. (2005). The origins and development of Honda's globalization. Motorcycles: The establishment of the Honda brand, and the localization of sales and production. *Japanese Research in Business History*, 22: 83-108.

De Vries, J. (1994). The industrial revolution and the industrious revolution. *The Journal of Economic History*, 54(2): 249-270.

DeWit, A., and Son, M. (2011). Creating a solar belt in East Japan: The energy future. *The Asia-Pacific Journal Japan Focus*, 9(38): 1-8.

Dilworth, D. A., and Hurst, C. G. (2008). *Fukazawa Yukichi, An Outline of a Theory of Civilization*, Vol. 1 (revised translation). Tokyo: Keio University Press.

Donzé, P.-Y. (2010). Studies abroad by Japanese doctors: A prosopographic analysis of nameless practitioners. *Social History of Medicine*, 23(2): 244-260.

Donzé, P.-Y. (2011). The Department for Arms Production of the University of Tokyo and the beginnings of the Japanese precision machine industry (1930-1960). *Osaka Economic Papers*, 61(1): 37-59.

Donzé P.-Y. (2017). *Industrial Development, Technology Transfer, and Global Competition: The Japanese Watch Industry from 1850 to the Present Day*. New York: Routledge.

Donzé P.-Y. (2018). *Making Medicine a Business: X-ray Technology, Global Competition, and the Transformation of the Japanese Medical System, 1895-1945*, Basingstoke: Palgrave Macmillan.

Donzé, P.-Y. (2020). L'expansion des multinationales suisses en Extrême-Orient: Nestlé au Japon de 1945 à nos jours. *Taverse*, 1: 48-61.

Donzé, P.-Y. (2022). Luxury Business in Japan in *Oxford Handbook of Luxury Business*, P.-Y. Donzé, J. Roberts, and V. Pouillard (eds). Oxford and New York: Oxford University Press, pp. 445-460.

Donzé, P.-Y., and Fujioka, R. (2015). European luxury big business and emerging Asian markets, 1960-2010. *Business History*, 57(6): 822-840.

Donzé, P. Y., and Fujioka, R. (2021). The formation of a technology-based fashion system, 1945–1990: The sources of the lost competitiveness of Japanese apparel companies. *Enterprise & Society*, 22(2): 438–474.

Donzé, P.-Y., and Kurosawa, T. (2013). Nestlé coping with Japanese nationalism: Political risk and the strategy of a foreign multinational enterprise in Japan, 1913–1945. *Business History*, 55(8): 1318–1338.

Dore, R. (2000). *Stock Market Capitalism: Welfare Capitalism: Japan and Germany versus Anglo-Saxons*. Oxford: Oxford University Press.

Dower, J. W. (1990). The useful war, Daedalus Vol. 11, No. 3, Cambridge, MA: MIT Press, pp. 49–70.

Dunning, J. H. (1980). Toward an eclectic theory of international production: Some empirical tests. *Journal of International Business Studies*, 11(1): 9–31.

Dunning J. H., and Lundan S. M. (2008). *Multinational Enterprises and the Global Economy*. Cheltenham: Edward Elgar.

Duus P. (1989). Japanese Cotton Mills in China, 1895–1937 in *The Japanese Informal Empire in China, 1895–1937*, P. Duus, R. H. Myers, and M. R. Peattie, eds. Princeton, NJ: Princeton University Press, pp. 65–99.

Economist, The (2021). Bartleby: The dangers of decision fatigue, why breaks are actually good for productivity, 29 May.

Economist, The (2022). Kishida Fumio's 'new capitalism' is many things but it is not new, 12 February.

Ennahachi, Z. (2019). The death that shook Japan's earth: A case study of Matsuri Takahashi. Master's thesis, Ritsumeikan University.

Ericson, S. J. (1996). *The Sound of the Whistle: Railroads and the State in Meiji Japan*. Cambridge, MA: Harvard East Asian Monographs.

Ericson, S. J. (2014). The 'Matsukata Deflation' reconsidered: Financial destabilization and Japanese exports in a global depression, 1881–1885. *The Journal of Japanese Studies*, 40(1): pp. 1–28.

Ferguson, E. (2008). *The Rise of the Japanese Specialist Manufacturer: Leading Medium-Sized Enterprises*. Basingstoke: Palgrave Macmillan.

Fitzgerald, R. (2015). *The Rise of the Global Company: Multinationals and the Making of the Modern World*. Cambridge: Cambridge University Press.

Flath, D. (2000). *The Japanese Economy*. Oxford: Oxford University Press.

Forbes, N., Kurosawa, T., and Wubs, B. (2018). *Multinational Enterprise, Political Risk and Organisational Change: From Total War to Cold War*. Oxon and New York: Routledge.

Francks, P. (2015). *Japanese Economic Development: Theory and Practice*. Oxon and New York: Routledge.

Fraser, T. and Aldrich, D. P. (2020). *The Fukushima Effect at Home: The Changing Role of Domestic Actors in Japanese Energy Policy*. Wiley Interdisciplary Reviews: Climate Change, John Wiley&Sons Vol. 11(5) Sept. pp. 1–11.

Fridenson, P., and Kikkawa, T. eds. (2017). *Ethical Capitalism: Shibusawa iichi and Business Leadership in Global Perspective*. Toronto: University of Toronto Press.

Fruin, W. F. (1994). *The Japanese Enterprise System: Competitive Strategies and Competitive Structures*. Oxford: Clarendon Press.

Fujita, N. (1990). Ties between foreign makers and *zaibatsu* enterprises in prewar Japan: Case studies of Mitsubishi Oil Co. and Mitsubishi Electric Manufacturing Co. In T. Yuzawa and U. Masaru, eds. *Foreign Business in Japan before World War II: Proceedings of the Fuji Conference*. Tokyo: University of Tokyo Press, pp. 118–139.

Fukuda, S., and Koibuchi, S. (2006). The impacts of 'shock therapy' under a banking crisis: Experiences from three large bank failures in Japan. *The Japanese Economic Review*, 57(2): 232–256.

Fukasaku, Y. (1992). *Technology and Industrial Development in Pre-War Japan. Mitsubishi Nagasaki Shipyard, 1884–1934*. London/New York: Routledge.

Futaya, T., and Blaikie, C. (2021). Reshaping the Toyama medicines industry in Japan in *Asian Medical Industries: Contemporary Perspectives on Traditional Pharmaceuticals*, S. Kloos and C. Blaikie, eds. London: Routledge. pp. 110–136.

Garon, S. (1987). *The State and Labor in Modern Japan*, Berkeley and Los Angeles, CA: University of California Press.

Garside, W. R. (2012). *Japan's Great Stagnation: Forging Ahead, Falling Behind*. Cheltenham: Edward Elgar.

Gordon, A. (1991). *Labor and Imperial Democracy in Prewar Japan*. Berkeley, CA: University of California Press.

Gordon, A. (2003). *A Modern History of Japan: From Tokugawa Times to the Present*. Oxford: Oxford University Press.

Goto, T. (2006). Longevity of Japanese family firms in *Handbook of Research on Family Business*, Cheltanham: Edward Elgar Publishing, pp. 517–536.

Gotoh, F. (2020). *Japanese Resistance to American Financial Hegemony: Global versus Domestic Social Norms*. Oxon and New York: Routledge.

Guerra, J. (2016). Consumerism, commodification, and beauty: Shiseido and the rise of beauty culture. *Rice Historical Review*, Spring 2016: 28–36.

Hall P. A., and Soskice, D. (2001). *Varieties of Capitalism: The Institutional Foundations of Comparative Advantage*. Oxford: Oxford University Press.

Hamada, Y. (2009). Venture capital in Japan. *Economic Journal of Hokkaido University*, 38: 1–12.

Han-Yu, C., and Myers, R. H. (1963). Japanese colonial development policy in Taiwan, 1895–1906: A case of bureaucratic entrepreneurship. *The Journal of Asian Studies*, 22(4): 433–449.

Hanes, J. E. (2002). *The City as a Subject: Seki Hajime and the Reinvention of Osaka*. Berkeley and Los Angeles, CA: University of California Press.

Hanley, S. B. (1968). Population trends and economic development in Tokugawa Japan: The case of Bizen Province in Okayama. *Daedalus*, 97(2): 622–635.

Hanley, S. B. (1987). How well did the Japanese live in the Tokugawa period? A historian's reappraisal. *Economic Studies Quarterly*, 38(4): 319–320.

Hanley S. B., and Yamamura, K. (1971). A quiet transformation in Tokugawa economic history. *The Journal of Asian Studies*, 30(2): 373–384.

Hannah, L. (2015) A global corporate census: Publicly traded and close companies in 1910. *The Economic History Review*, 68(2): 548–573.

Harris, T. (2020). *The Iconoclast: Shinzo Abe and the New Japan*. London: C. Hurst & Co.

Hauser, W. B. (1983). Some misconceptions about the economic history of Tokugawa Japan. *The History Teacher*, 16(4): 589–583.

Hayami, A. (2015). *Japan's Industrious Revolution: Economic and Social Transformations in the Early Modern Period (Studies in Economic History)*. Tokyo: Springer.

Headrick, D. R. (1988). *The Tentacles of Progress: Technology Transfer in the Age of Imperialism, 1850–1940*. Oxford: Oxford University Press.

Hirano, S. (2017). Small, hidden and competitive: The Japanese chemical industry since 1980 in *Industries and Global Competition*, B. Boouwens, P.-Y. Donzé, and T. Kurosawa (eds). Oxon and New York: Routledge, pp. 153–172.

Hobsbawn, E. J. (1975). *The Age of Capital, 1848–1875*. London: Weidenfeld and Nicolson.

Hobsbawn, E. J. (1987). *The Age of Empire, 1875–1914*. London: Weidenfeld and Nicolson.

Hofstede, G. (1980). *Culture's Consequences: International Differences in Work-Related Values*. London: Sage.

Hopson, N. (2020). Ingrained habits: The 'kitchen cars' and the transformation of the Japanese diet and identity. *Food, Culture, and Society*, 20(5): 589–607.

Horioka, C. Y. (2006). The causes of Japan's 'lost decade': The role of household consumption. *Japan and the World Economy*, 18(4): 378–400.

Hoshi T., and Kashyap A. (2001). *Corporate Financing and Governance in Japan*. Cambridge, MA: MIT Press.

Hoshi, T., and Lipscy, P. Y. (eds) (2021). *The Political Economy of the Abe Government and Abenomics Reforms*. Cambridge: Cambridge University Press.

Hoshi, T. (2002). The convoy system for insolvent banks: How it originally worked and why it failed in the 1990s. *Japan and the World Economy*, 14(2): 155–180.

Howe, C. (1996). *The Origins of Japanese Trade Supremacy*. London: Hurst & Co.

Howell, D. L. (1992). Proto-industrial origins of Japanese capitalism. *The Journal of Asian Studies*, 51(2): 269–286.

Hsu, R. C. (1994). *The MIT Encyclopedia of the Japanese Economy*. Cambridge, MA: MIT Press.

Huenteler, J., Schmidt, T. S., and Kanie, N. (2012). Japan's post-Fukushima challenge—implications from the German experience on renewable energy policy. *Energy Policy*, 45: 6–11.

Hunter, J. E. (1976) A study of the life of Maejima Hisoka, 1835–1919. PhD dissertation, St. Anthony's College, Oxford University.

Hunter, J. (ed.) (1993). *Japanese Women Working*. London and New York: Routledge.

Hunter, J. (2003) *Women and the Labor Market in Japan's Industrializing Economy: The Textile Industry before the Pacific War*. London and New York: Routledge.

Hunter, J. E. (2005). Understanding the Economic History of Postal Services: Some Preliminary Observations from the Case of Meiji Japan. CIRJE-F-344, Retrieved 20 May 2021 from https://core.ac.uk/download/pdf/6341601.pdf.

Hunter, J. E. (2014) 'Extreme confusion and disorder'? The Japanese economy in the Great Kantō Earthquake of 1923. *Journal of Asian Studies*, 73(3): 753–773.

IMF (2010). *World Economic Outlook*. Washington, DC: IMF.

Inoue, S. (2018). Inequality and precarity in Japan: The sorry achievements of Abenomics. *The Asia-Pacific Journal Japan Focus*, 16(6): 1–12.

Ito, T. (2003). Retrospective on the bubble period and its relationship to developments in the 1990s. *World Economy*, 26(3): 283–300.

Ito, T. (2020). An assessment of Abenomics: Evolution and achievements. *Asian Economic Policy Review*, 16(2): 190–219.

Iwamoto K. and Nakamura Y. "The dark side of growth in Asia's race for prosperity and profit workers are paying the price." *Asia Nikkei*, Dec 16-25, 2016.

Iyoda, M. (2010). *Postwar Japanese Economy: Lessons of Economic Growth and the Bubble Economy*. Springer Science & Business Media.

Japan Department Stores Association, sales statistics, https://www.depart.or.jp/store_sale/ (accessed 15 August 2020).

Japan's keiretsu system, Hearing before the Committee on Finance United States Senate, 102nd Congress, 1st Session, 1–159, (Oct. 16, 1991).

Japan Labor Issues (2018). 'Work-style reform enacted: discussions underway at the Council on the Contents of Specific Procedures'. *Japan Labor Issues*, 2(10): 2–9.

Johnson, C. (1982). *MITI and the Japanese Miracle: The Growth of Industrial Policy, 1925–1975*. Stanford, CA: Stanford University Press.

Jones, G. (2005). *Multinationals and Global Capitalism: From the Nineteenth to the Twenty-First Century*. Oxford: Oxford University Press.

Jones, G. (2017). *Profitability and Sustainability: The History of Green Entrepreneurship*. New York: Oxford University Press.

Jones, H. J. (1985). The Griffis thesis and Meiji policy toward hired foreigners in *The Modernisers: Overseas Students, Foreign Employees and Meiji Japan*, A. W. Burks, ed. Boulder and London: Westview Press, pp. 219–253.

Kato, N. "Japan and the ancient art of shrugging." New York Times, 21 Aug. 2010.

Katz, R. (2014). Voodoo economics: Japan's failed comeback plan. *Foreign Affairs*, 93(4): 133–141.

Katz, R. (2016). Nurturing entrepreneurship in Japan is not easy. *The Oriental Economist*, 5 July 2016, retrieved from: https://toyokeizai.net/articles/-/125103

Katsura, Y. (1975). The role of one sogoshosha in Japanese industrialization: Suzuki & Co., 1877–1927 in *Proceedings of the Business History Conference*, second series, Vol. 3. Cambridge: Cambridge University Press, pp. 32–61.

Kawabe, N. (2015). The Seven and i Group in *Handbook of East Asian Entrepreneurship*, F.-L. T. Yu and H.-D. Yan, eds. London: Routledge, pp. 252–263.

Kennan, G. F. (1947). The sources of Soviet conduct. *Foreign Affairs*, 25: 566–582.

Kikkawa, T. (1991). Business activities of the Standard-Vacuum Oil Co. in Japan prior to World War II. *Japanese Yearbook on Business History*, 7: 31–59.

Kikkawa, T. (1995). International oil cartels and the Japanese market. *Japanese Yearbook on Business History*, 11: 33–51.

Kikkawa, T. (2006). Beyond the 'lost decade': Problems confronting Japanese companies, and solutions. *Japanese Research in Business History*, 23: 107–126.

Kikkawa, T. (2023). *History of Innovative Entrepreneurs in Japan*. Singapore: Springer.

Kneller, R. (2007). *Bridging Islands: Venture Companies and the Future of Japanese and American Industry*. Oxford: Oxford University Press.

Kocka, J. (2016). *Capitalism: A Short History*. Princeton, NJ: Princeton University Press.

Koike, K. (1988). *Understanding Industrial Relations in Modern Japan*. Basingstoke: Palgrave MacMillan.

Komiya, R., and Itoh, M. (1988). Japan's international trade and trade policy, 1955–1984 in *The Political Economy of Japan, Vol. 2*, T. Inoguchi and D. Okimoto, eds. Stanford, CA: Stanford University Press, pp. 173–224.

Kotter, J. P. (1997). *Matsushita Leadership: Lessons from the 20th Century's Most Remarkable Entrepreneur*. New York: Free Press.

Large, S. S. (1970). The Japanese labor movement, 1912–1919: Suzuki Bunji and the Yūaikai. *The Journal of Asian Studies*, (29)3: 559–579.

Lechevalier, S., and Monfort, B. (2017) Abenomics: Has it worked? Will it ultimately fail? *Japan Forum*, 30(2): 277–302.

Lu, A. S. (2008). The many faces of internationalization in Japanese anime. *Animation*, 3(2): 169–187.

McGray, D. (2002). Japan's gross national cool. *Foreign Policy*, 130(1): 44–54.

McKinsey & Company (Andonian, A., Kuwabara, T., Yamakawa, N., and Ishida, R.) (2016). The future of Japanese tourism: Path for sustainable growth 2020. Retrieved on 9 July 2021.

Maclachlan, P. L. (2004). Post office politics in modern Japan: The postmasters, iron triangles, and the limits of reform. *The Journal of Japanese Studies*, 30(2): 281–313.

Maclachlan, P. L. (2011). *The People's Post: The History and Politics of the Japanese Postal System (1871–2010)*. Cambridge, MA: Harvard University Asian Center.

McMaster, J. (1963). The Takashima mine: British capital and Japanese industrialization. *Business History Review*, 37(3): 217–239.

Macnaughtan, H. (2012). Building up steam as consumers: women, rice cookers, and the consumption of everyday household goods in Japan in *The Historical Consumer: Consumption and Everyday Life in Japan (1850–2000)*, P. Francks and J. Hunter, eds. London: Palgrave Macmillan.

Macnaughtan, H. (2015). Womenomics for Japan: Is the Abe policy for gender employment viable in an era of precarity. *Asia-Pacific Review*, Japan Focus, 13(1): 1–19.

McCraw, T. K. (1997). *Creating Modern Capitalism: How Entrepreneurs, Companies, and Countries Triumphed in Three Industrial Revolutions*. Cambridge, MA: Harvard University Press.

Maddison Project Database, version 2020. Bolt, Jutta and Jan Luiten Van Zanden (2020), "Maddison style estimate of the evolution of the world economy. A new 2020 update".

Malhotra, G., and Sinharay, A. (2013). Maruti Suzuki—Reigning Emperor of Indian Automobile Industry. *Journal of Case Research*, 4(1): 1–38.

Malony, B. (1991). *Activism among Women in the Taisho Cotton Textile Industry*. Santa Clara, CA: Santa Clara University Scholar Commons, College of Arts and Sciences.

Mason, S. (1992) *American Multinationals and Japan: The Political Economy of Japanese Capital Controls, 1899–1980*. Cambridge: Cambridge University Press.

Matsui, K., Suzuki, H., and Ushio, Y. (1999). *Womenonmics: Buy the Female Economy*. Goldman Sachs Japan: Portfolio Strategy, 13 August.

Mendels, F. F. (1972). The first phase of the industrialization process. *The Journal of Economic History*, 32(1): 241–261.

Metzler, M. (1994). Capitalist boom feudal bust: Long waves in economics and politics in pre-industrial Japan. *Review (Fernand Braudel Center)*, 17(1): 57–119.

Meyer, E. (2014). *The Culture Map: Breaking through the Invisible Boundaries of Global Business*. New York: Public Affairs.

Millikin, J. P., and Fu, D. (2005). The global leadership of Carlos Ghosn at Nissan. *Thunderbird International Business Review*, 47(1): 121–137.

Miwa, Y., and Ramseyer, J. M. (2006). *The Fable of the Keiretsu: Urban Legends of the Japanese Economy*. Chicago, IL: University of Chicago Press.

Miyajima, H., Imajo, T., and Kawamoto, A. (2008). Mergers and acquisitions in Japan from a historical perspective: Understanding M&A waves in the prewar era. Unpublished paper given at the Fujicon Conference, Waseda University, Tokyo, 26 January.

Miyamoto, M. (1989). The products and market strategies of the Osaka Cotton Spinning Company: 1883–1914. *Japanese Yearbook on Business History*, 5: 117–159.

Miyamoto, M. (1996). The management system of Edo period merchant houses in Japanese Yearbook on Business History *1996, Vol. 13*. Business History Society of Japan, pp. 97–142.

Moen, D. G. (1999). The postwar Japanese agricultural debacle. *Hitotsubashi Journal of Social Studies*, 3(1): 29–52.

Moran, W. T. (1949). Labor unions in postwar Japan. *Far Eastern Survey*, 18(21): pp. 241–248.

Mōri, Y. (2011). The pitfall facing the Cool Japan project: The transnational development of the anime industry under the condition of post-Fordism. *International Journal of Japanese Sociology*, 20(1): 30–42.

Moriguchi, C., and Saez, E. (2010). The evolution of income concentration in Japan (1886–2005) in *Top Incomes Global Perspective*, A. B. Atkinson and T. Piketty, Oxford: Oxford University Press, pp. 714–734.

Morikawa, H. (1992). *Zaibatsu: The Rise and Fall of Family Enterprise Groups in Japan*. Tokyo: University of Tokyo Press.

Morikawa, H. (2001). *A History of Top Management in Japan: Managerial Enterprises and Family Enterprises*. Oxford: Oxford University Press.

Morita, A. (1986). *Made in Japan: Akio Morita and Sony*. Boston: E. P. Dutton.

Morris Suzuki, T. (1994). *The Technological Transformation of Japan from the Seventeenth to the Twenty-first Century*. Cambridge: Cambridge University Press.

Nagaoka, S. (1981). Indemnity consideration in Japanese financial policy after Sino-Japanese War (1894–96). *Hokudai Economic Papers*, 11: 1–29.

Nakamura, S. (1979). *Sengo nihon no gijutsu kakushin* (Technological innovation in postwar Japan). Tokyo: Otsuki shoten.

Nakamura, T. (1989). Depression, recovery and war, 1920–1945 in *The Cambridge History of Japan, Vol. 6*, P. Duus, ed. Cambridge: Cambridge University Press, pp. 451–493.

Nakamura, T., and Kaminski J. (trans) (1984). *The Ppostwar Japanese Eeconomy,*. Tokyo: University of Tokyo Press.

National Archives (1946). Winston Churchill, 'Iron curtain speech', 5 March. Retrieved 27 May 2021 from https://www.nationalarchives.gov.uk/education/resources/cold-war-on-file/iron-curtain-speech/

Neeley, T. (2013). Language and globalization: 'Englishnization' at Rakuten. Harvard Business School Case 9-412-002.

Nelson, P. A. (1998). Rivalry and cooperation: How the Japanese photography industry went global. PhD dissertation, University of Warwick.

Nelson, R. R., ed. (1993). *National Innovation Systems: A Comparative Analysis*. Oxford: Oxford University Press.

Nicholas, T., Nanda, R., and Roth, B. (2019). Masayoshi Son and the Vision Fund. Harvard Business School Case 9-819-041, 13 February.

Nikkei Asia (2021), Japanese retailers focus on health products and delivery amid COVID, April 9, 2021.

Nimura, K. and Gordon, A. (ed.) (1998). *The Ashio Riot of 1907: A Social History of Mining in Japan*. Durham, NC: Duke University Press.

Nishimura, S. (2004). General Electric's International Patent Management before World War II, *Japanese Research in Business History*, 21, 101–125.

Nishimura, T. (2012). The activities of the Yokohama Specie Bank in the foreign trade financing operations for raw cotton before the First World War in *The Origins of International Banking in Asia: The Nineteenth and Twentieth Centuries*, S. Nishimura, T. Suzuki, and R. C. Michie, eds. Oxford: Oxford University Press, pp. 174–195.

Nishiyama, T. (2003). 'Cross-Disciplinary Technology Transfer in Trans-World War II Japan: The Japanese High-Speed Bullet Train as a Case-Study'. *Comparative Technology Transfer and Society*, 1(3): 305–325.

Nishiyama, T. (2007). War, peace, and nonweapons technology: The Japanese National Railways and the products of defeat, 1880s–1950s. *Technology and Culture*, 48(2): 286–302.

Nonaka I., and Takeuchi H. (1995). *The Knowledge-Creating Company: How Japanese Companies Create the Dynamics of Innovation*. New York and Oxford: Oxford University Press.

Odagiri, H., and Gotō, A. (1996). *Technology and Industrial Development in Japan: Building Capabilities by Learning, Innovation, and Public Policy*. Oxford: Oxford University Press.

OECD ilibrary (2017). Eurostat Entrepreneurship Indicators Programme, Entrepreneurship at a glance 2017, pp. 110–122. https://www.oecd-ilibrary.org/industry-and-services/entrepreneurship-at-a-glance_22266941. Accessed 8 September 2021.

OECD Data (2021). Gender wage gap. Accessed on 8 September 2021. https://data.oecd.org/earnwage/gender-wage-gap.htm

Ogilvie, S., and Cerman, M. (1996) *European Proto-industrialization: An Introductory Handbook*. Cambridge: Cambridge University Press.

Ohno, K. (2006). *The economic development of Japan: a path traveled by Japan as a developing country*. Tokyo: GRIPS Development Forum.

Ohno, K. (2017). *The history of Japanese economic development*. London: Routledge.

Okimoto, D. I. (1989). *Between MITI and the Market: Japanese Industrial Policy for High Technology*. Stanford, CA: Stanford University Press.

Olejniczak, T., Pikos, A., and Goto, T. (2019) In search of continuity: Theoretical and methodological insights from a case study of Polish centennial company. *Journal of Management History* 25(4): 565–584.

Oqubay, A., and Ohno, K. (2019) *How Nations Learn: Technological Learning, Industrial Policy, and Catch-Up*. Oxford: Oxford University Press Scholarship Online.

Ouchi, W. G. (1981). *Theory Z: How American Business Can Meet the Japanese Challenge*. Reading, MA: Addison-Wesley.

Ozawa, M., and Kingston, J. (2022). Precaritarization of work in Japan in *Japan in the Heisei Era (1989–2019): Multidisciplinary Perspectives*, N. Murai, J. Kingston, and T. Burrett, eds. London: Routledge, pp. 127–139.

Ozawa, T. (1974). *Japan's Technological Challenge to the West, 1960–1974: Motivation and Accomplishment*. Cambridge, MA: MIT Press.

Partner, S. (2000). *Assembled in Japan: Electrical Goods and the Making of the Japanese Consumer*. Berkeley, CA: University of California Press.

Peattie, M. R. (1989). Japanese Treaty Port Settlements in China, 1895–1937 in *The Japanese Informal Empire in China, 1895–1937*, P. Duus, R. H. Myers, and M. R. Peattie, eds. Princeton, NJ: Princeton University Press, pp. 166–209.

Pempel, T. J. (1987). The unbundling of 'Japan Inc.': The changing dynamics of Japanese policy formation. *The Journal of Japanese Studies*, 12(2) Special Issue: A Forum of the Trade Crisis: pp. 271–306.

Piketty, T. (2014). *Capital in the Twenty-First Century*. Cambridge, MA: Harvard University Press.

Pilling, D. (2014). *Bending Adversity: Japan and the Art of Survival*. New York: Penguin Press.

Porter, M., Takeuchi, H., and Sakakibara, M. (2000). *Can Japan Compete?* New York: Perseus Publishing.

Pratt, E. E. (1999). *Japan's Protoindustrial Elite: The Economic Foundations of the Gōnō*. Cambridge, MA: Harvard University Asia Center.

Prime Minister of Japan and his Cabinet (2013). Speeches and Statements made by Prime Minister Shinzo Abe, The Sixty-Eighth Session of The General Assembly of The United Nations, 26 September. Accessed on 2 September 2021, https://japan.kantei.go.jp/96_abe/statement/201309/26generaldebate_e.html

Prime Minister of Japan and his Cabinet (2018). Policy speech by Prime Minister Shinzo Abe to the 196th session of the Diet, 22 January. Accessed on 8 September 2021, https://japan.kantei.go.jp/98_abe/statement/201801/_00002.html

Rasmussen Kinney, A. (1982). *Japanese Investment in Manchurian Manufacturing, Mining, Transportation, and Communications, 1931–1945*. New York: Garland Publishing.

Ravina, M. (1999). *Land and Lordship in Early Modern Japan*. Stanford, CA: Stanford University Press.

Robinson, A. (ed.) (1979). *Appropriate Technologies for Third World Development: Proceedings of a Conference Held by the International Economic Association at Teheran, Iran*. London: Palgrave Macmillan.

Rothfeder, J. (2015). *Driving Honda: Inside the World's Most Innovative Car Company*. London: Penguin Books.

Sakajiri, N. (2008). Aso's 'cynical' stimulus, *Far Eastern Economic Review*. https://asiasociety.org/mr-asos-cynical-stimulus

Samuels, R. J. (1994). *'Rich Nation, Strong Army': National Security and the Technological Transformation of Japan*. New York: Cornell University Press.

Samuels, R. J. (2013). *3.11: Disaster and Change in Japan*. Ithaca, NY: Cornell University Press.

Saoshiro, S. and Maeda R. 'Japan's push to restart nuclear plants sparks anger'. Reuters, 19 January 2012.
Scalise, P. (2012). Hard choices: Japan's post-Fukushima energy policy in the 21st century in *Natural Disaster and Nuclear Crisis in Japan*, J. Kingston, ed. Nissan Institute/Routledge studies series, Hoboken, NJ: Taylor and Francis, pp. 140–155.
Sawai, M. (ed.) (2016). *Economic Activities under the Japanese Colonial Empire*. Singapore: Springer.
Saxonhouse, G. (1974). A tale of technological diffusion in the Meiji period. *Journal of Economic History*, 34(1): 149–165.
Saxonhouse, G., and Stern, R. (eds) (2004). *Japan's Lost Decade: Origins, Consequences and Prospects for Recovery*. Oxford: Wiley-Blackwell.
Schaede, U. (2008). *Choose and Focus: Japanese Business Strategies for the 21st Century*. New York: Cornell University Press.
Schaede, U. (2020). *The Business Reinvention of Japan: How to Make Sense of the New Japan and Why It Matters*. Stanford, CA: Stanford Business Books.
Schumpeter, J. A. (1994) [1942]. *Capitalism, Socialism, and Democracy*. London: Routledge.
Sekine, Y. (2008). The rise of poverty in Japan: The emergence of the working poor. *Japan Labor Review*, 5(4): 49–66.
Sheldon, C. D. (1958). *The Rise of the Merchant Class in Tokugawa Japan, 1600–1868: An Introductory Survey* Monograph (Association for Asian Studies). https://www.asianstudies.org/publications/asia-past-present/.
Shibata, S. (2017). Re-packaging old policies? 'Abenomics' and the lack of an alternative growth model for Japan's political economy, *Japan Forum*, 29(3): 399–422.
Shimada, M. (2017). *The Entrepreneur Who Built Modern Japan: Shibusawa Eiichi*. Tokyo: Japan Publishing Industry Foundation for Culture.
Shimizu, K. (2009). The uncertainty of Toyota as the new world number one carmaker in *The Second Automobile Revolution*, M. Freyssenet ed. London: Palgrave Macmillan, pp. 69–94.
Shimotani, M. (1995). The formation of the distribution Keiretsu: The case of Matsushita Electric. *Business History*, 37(2): 54–69.
Shimotani, M. (2012). Japanese holding companies: Past and present. *Japanese Research in Business History*, 29: 11–28.
Shiseido Public Relations Department (2003). *The Shiseido Story: A History of Shiseido, 1872–1972*. Tokyo: Shiseido.
Shizume, M. (2009). The Japanese economy during the interwar period: Instability in the financial system and the impact of the world depression. *Bank of Japan Review*, May 2009: 1–10.
Shizume, M. (2016). Financial crises and the central bank: Lessons from Japan during the 1920s. WINPEC Waseda Working Paper Series No. E1611, Tokyo: Waseda Institute of Political Economy, November.
Siniawer, E. M. (2018). *Waste: Consuming Postwar Japan*, New York and London: Cornell University Press.
Slager, A. (2004). Banking across borders. No. ERIM PhD Series, Erasmus University Rotterdam.
Sluyterman, K. (ed.) (2015). *Varieties of Capitalism and Business History: The Dutch Case*. Oxon and New York: Routledge.
Smith, T. C. (1989). *Native Sources of Japanese Industrialization 1750–1920*. Berkley, CA and London: University of California Press.
Stevens, M., and Fujimoto, T. (2009). Nissan: From the brink of bankruptcy in *The Second Automobile Revolution*, M. Freyssenet, ed. London: Routledge, pp. 95–111.

Stokes, B. (2013). Abenomics' challenge: The Japanese attitude. Pew Research Center, 27 May. https://www.pewresearch.org/global/2013/05/27/abenomics-challenge-the-japanese-attitude/.

Sudo, N. (2019). Why do the Japanese still see themselves as middle class? The impact of socio-structural changes on status identification. *Social Science Japan Journal*, 22(1): 25–44.

Suehiro, A. (2008). *Catch-up Industrialization: The Trajectory and Prospects of East Asian Economies*. Singapore: NUS Press.

Sugayama, S. (1992). Work rules, wage rules, and single status: The shaping of the 'Japanese employment system' in *The Origins of Japanese Industrial Power: Strategy, Institutions, and Organizational Capability*, E. Abe and R. Fitzgerald, eds. London: Routledge.

Taira, K. (1970). Factory legislation and management modernization during Japan's industrialization, 1896–1916. *The Business History Review*, 44: 84–109.

Takehara, M., and Hasegawa N. (2020). *Sustainable Management of Japanese Entrepreneurs in Pre-war Period from the Perspective of SDGs and ESG*. London: Palgrave Macmillan.

Takemura, E. (1997). *The perception of work in Tokugawa Japan: A study of Ishida Baigan and Ninomiya Sontoku*. New York and Oxford: University Press of America.

Takenaka, H. (2008). *The Structural Reforms of the Koizumi Cabinet, an Insider's Account of the Economic Revival of Japan*. Tokyo: Nihon Keizai Shinbun Shuppansha.

Takeuchi, Y. (1974). Marxism in Japan. *La philosophie japonaise contemporaine, Révue Internationale de Philosophie*, 8(107/108): 49–68.

Tanaka, K. (1973). *Building a New Japan: A Plan for Remodeling the Japanese Archipelago*. Portland: Simul International.

Tanimoto, M. (ed.) (2006). *The Role of Tradition in Japan's Industrialization*. Oxford: Oxford University Press.

Timinsky, S. J. (2019). The nation that never rests: Japan's debate over work–life balance and work that kills. *The Asia-Pacific Journal Japan Focus*, 17(10): 2.

Toussaint, A. (2011). You can't please all of the people all of the time: Walmart's adventures in Japan in *Case Studies in Japanese Management*, P. Haghirian and P. Gagnon, eds. Singapore: World Scientific: pp. 13–33.

Toya, T., and Amyx, J. A. (2006). *The Political Economy of the Japanese Financial Big Bang: Institutional Change in Finance and Public Policymaking*. Oxford: Oxford University Press.

Tsutsui, W. M. (1996). W. Edwards Deming and the origins of quality control in Japan. *The Journal of Japanese Studies*, 22(2): 295–325.

Uchida, H. (1991). The transfer of electrical technologies from the United States and Europe to Japan, 1869–1914 in *International Technology Transfer: Europe, Japan and the USA, 1700–1914*, D. Jeremy, ed. Aldershot: Edward Elgar.

United Nations Conference on Trade and Development (UNCTAD), *World Investment Report*, 1993.

Utsunomiya, K. (2008). Economic fluctuations in Japan during the interwar period: reestimation of the personal consumption expenditures. *Monetary Economic Studies*, December 2008: 331–158.

Vogel, E. F. (1979). *Japan as Number One*. Cambridge, MA: Harvard University Press.

Vogel, S. K. (2006). *Japan Remodeled: How Government and Industry Are Reforming Japanese Capitalism*. New York: Cornell University Press.

Wadhwani, D., and Lubinski, C. (2017). Reinventing entrepreneurial history. *Business History Review*, 91(4): 767–799.

Walker, B. L. (2010). *The Toxic Archipelago: A History of Industrial Disease*. Seattle: University of Washington Press.

Walker, G. (2016). *The Sublime Perversion of Capital: Marxist Theory and the Politics of History in Modern Japan*. Durham, NC: Duke University Press. https://www.historicalmaterialism.org/reading-guides/marxist-theory-japan-critical-overview

Westney, D. E. (1987). *Imitation and Innovation: The Transfer of Western Organizational Patterns to Meiji Japan*. Cambridge, MA: Harvard University Press.

Wilkins, M. (1974). *The Maturing of Multinational Enterprise: American Business Abroad from 1914 to 1970*. Cambridge, MA: Harvard University Press.

Wilkins, M. (1990). Japanese multinationals in the United States: Continuity and change, 1879–1990. *The Business History Review*, 64(4): 585–629

Wilkins, M., and Hill, F. E. (2011). *American Business Abroad: Ford on Six Continents*. Cambridge: Cambridge University Press (first edition 1964).

Williamson, O. E. (1981). The economics of organization: The transaction cost approach. *American Journal of Sociology*, 87(3): 548–577.

Wittner, D. (2000). Iron and silk: progress and ideology in the technological transformation of Japan. PhD dissertation, Ohio State University.

World (2009). *World 50th Anniversary Book*. Kobe: World.

Xia, Q., and Donzé, P.-Y. (2022). Surviving in a declining industry: A new entrepreneurial history of Nihonsakari since the 1970s. *Business History*, ahead of print (online preview).

Yamamoto, Y. (2003). Japanese Empire and Colonial Management, in *Economic History of Japan, 1914–1955: A Dual Structure*, T. Nakamura and K. Okada, eds. Oxford: Oxford University Press, pp. 223–146.

Yamamura, K. (1969). The role of the merchant class as entrepreneurs and capitalists in Meiji Japan, *Vierteljahrschrift für Sozial- und Wirtschaftsgeschichte*, 56: 105–120.

Yamamura, K., and Streeck, W. (2005). *The Origins of Nonliberal Capitalism: Germany and Japan in Comparison*. New York: Cornell University Press.

Yang, T. M. (2021). *A Medicated Empire: The Pharmaceutical Industry and Modern Japan*. New York: Cornell University Press.

Yokoyama, I., and Kodama, N. (2018). Women's labor supply and taxation—analysis of the current situation using data, Policy Research Institute, Ministry of Finance. *Public Policy Review*, 14(2). Retrieved 28 May 2021 from https://www.mof.go.jp/english/pri/publication/pp_review/fy2017/ppr14_02_03.pdf

Yonekura, S. (1985). The emergence of the prototype of enterprise group capitalism—the case of Mitsui. *Hitotsubashi Journal of Business and Management*, 20(1): 63–104.

Yonekura, S. (1994). *The Japanese Iron and Steel Industry, 1850–1990: Continuity and Discontinuity*. Basingstoke: Palgrave MacMillan.

Yongue, J. S. (2016). Academia–industry relations: Interpreting the role of Nagai Nagayoshi in the development of new businesses in the Meiji period and beyond in *Science, Technology, and Medicine, the Modern Japanese Empire*, D. G. Wittner and P. C. Brown, eds. London: Routledge.

Yoshino, M. Y. (1971). *The Japanese Marketing System: Adaptions and Innovations*. Cambridge, MA: MIT Press.

Yui, T., and Hirschmeier, J. (1975). *The Development of Japanese Business (1600–1980)*. London: Routledge.

Publications in Japanese

Abe, A. (2008), *Kodomo no hinkon nihon no fukōhei wo kangaeru (Child poverty: considering Japan's inequalities)*. Tokyo: Iwanami Shoten.

Abe, T. (2002), Sangyō kōzō no henka to dokusen (Change of industry structure and monopoly) in *Nihon keizaishi: Vol. 3: ryotaisenkanki* (Japanese economic history: the interwar years), K. Ishii, A. Hara, and H. Takeda, eds. Tokyo: Tokyo University Press, pp. 58–59.

Arano, Y. (1989). *Kinsei Nihon to Higashi Ajia* (Modern Japan and East Asia). Tokyo: Tokyo Daigaku Shuppan-kai, 3–28.

Chin, H., and Hayashi, T. (eds) (1995). *Ajia no gijutsu hatten to gijutsu iten* (Technology development in Asia and technology transfer). Tokyo: Bunshindo.

Fukao K., Nakamura N., and Nakabayashi M. (eds) (2018). *Nihon keizai no rekishi* (History of Japanese economy), *Vol. 6*. Tokyo: Iwanami.

Fujimoto, T. (2004). *Nihon monozukuri tetsugaku* (The philosophy of Japanese manufacturing). Tokyo: Nihonkeizai shimbunsha.

Fukuoka, M. (2008). Chōsen kankoku seni sangyō no seiritsu to hatten (The formation and development of textile industry in Korea), in *Higashi ajia shihonshugishiron* (Capitalism in East Asia), *Vol. II*, K. Hori, ed. Kyoto: Minerva, pp. 190–218.

Hamamatsu, S., and Kishi, Y. (2018). Kaigai seichu shijo no jittai haaku; nihonshu no yushutsu to kaigai seisan no kankei (Understanding the actual situation in the international sake market: the relationship between Japanese sake exports and foreign production). *Seikei daigaku keizaigakubu ronshu*, 49(1): 107–127.

Hashimoto, J., Hasegawa, S., Miyajima, H., and Saito, N. (2019). *Gendai nihon keizai* (Contemporary Japanese economy). Tokyo: Yuhikaku.

Hori, K. (2008). *Hisashi ajia shihonshugishiron* (Capitalism in East Asia), *Vol. II*. Kyoto: Minerva

Horiuchi, Y. (2008). Kindai Taiwan ni okeru chūshō saisho shokōgyō no hatten (The development of small business in modern Taiwan), in *Hisashi ajia shihonshugishiron* (Capitalism in East Asia), *Vol. II*, K. Hori, ed. Kyoto: Minerva, pp. 138–166.

Imaizumi, A. (2008). Sangyō shūseki no kōteiteki kōka to shūsekinai no kōjyō no tokuchō: Meiji koki no Tokyo ni okeru kikai kanren kōgyō to shūseki no ronri wo taishō ni (Positive effects of industrial clusters and their internal characteristics: focus on the machinery-related industries in Tokyo in the late Meiji period). *Rekishi to keizai*, 201: 19–33.

Hayashi, S. (1962). *Ryūtsū kakumei* (The Distribution Revolution). Tokyo: Chūkōshinsho.

Kasuya, M. (2012). *Monozukuri nihon keieishi* (Business History of Japanese Manufacturing). Nagoya: Nagoya University Press.

Kawabe, N. (2011). *Tai Toyota no keieishi* (Business History of Toyota in Thailand). Tokyo: Yuhikaku.

Kawabe, N. (2017). *'Kokuminshoku' kara 'sekaishoku' e- nikkeisokusekimen me-ka-no kokusai tenkai* (From 'National Food' to 'Global Food'—a Japanese Instant Ramen Noodle Maker's Global Expansion). Tokyo: Bunshindo Publishers.

Kikkawa, T. (2019). *Inobeshon no rekishi* (History of innovation). Tokyo: Yuhikaku.

Kikkawa, T., and Takaoka, M. (1997). Sengo nihon no seikatsu yōshiki to ryūtsū no inpakuto (The impact of distribution on postwar lifestyles in Japan), *Shakaikagaku kenkyū*, 48(5): 111–151.

Kikuchi, Y. (2007). *Nihon ni okeru denkyū sangyō no eisei* (The Formation of the Japanese Electric Bulb Industry), *Keieishigaku*, 42(1): 27–57.

Kinouchi, T. (2020). *Nihon no kigyō gabanansu kaikaku* (Japan's Corporate Governance Reform). Tokyo: Nikkei BP.

Kinugawa, M. (2002). *Nihon no baburu* (The Japanese bubble). Tokyo: Nikkeihyo.

Kirin biiru KK (1957). *Kirin biiru gojyū nenshi* (The 50-Year History of Kirin Brewery). Tokyo: Kirin biiru KK, 20 March.

Kitahara, Y. (1983). Waga kuni Kyodai kigyō ni okeru shoyū to kettei no tokuchō: kabushiki mochiai no kōzō to igi (Features of ownership and decisions in Japan's large corporations: the significance of the system of cross share–holding). *Keio Journal of Economics*, 76(1): 71–109.

Kiyonari, T., Nakamura, S., and Hirao, K. (1971). *Bencha Bijinesu zunō wo uru chiisana daikigyō* (Start-ups: the small giants who sell their brains). Tokyo: Nihon Keizai Shinbun-sha.

Koike, K. (1993). *Amerika no howaito karaa nichibei dochira yori 'nōryokushugi'*(America's white–collar workers: Which is more meritocratic, Japan or the United States?). Tokyo: Tōyōkezai Shinpōsha.

Kuwahara, T. (2010). Taigai kankei: zaikabō, naigaimen kaisha no keiei (Foreign relations: Japanese–owned textile firms in China: internal and external management of cotton spinning companies) in *Kōza Nihon keieishi 3: Soshiki to senryaku no jidai, 1914–1937*, S. Sasaki and M. Nakabayashi, eds. Kyoto: Minerva, pp. 267–305.

Maeda, K. (1991). Ryūtsū (Distribution). In *Sengo nihon keieishi* (Postwar Japanese Business III), S. Yonekawa, K. Shimokawa, and H. Yamazaki, eds. Tokyo: Tōyōkeizai shinshosha, pp. 1–74.

Mitsubishi (1956). *Mitsubishi jūkōgyō kabushiki kaisha shi* (History of Mitsubishi Heavy Industries). Tokyo: Mitsubishi jukogyo.

Miwa R., and Hara A. (2007). *Kingendai nihon keizaishi yōran* (A Handbook of Modern Japanese Economic History). Tokyo: Tokyo University Press.

Miyamoto, M., and Kasuya, M. (2009). *Keieishi: Edo no keiken 1600–1882* (Business History: Experiences from Edo 1600–1882). Kyoto: Minerva.

Miyamoto, M., Okabe, K., and Hirano, K. (2014). *Ichi kara keieishi* (The First Step to Business History). Kizu: Sekigakusha.

Miyamoto, M. (ed.) (2016). *Shibusawa Eiichi: nihon kindai no tobira wo hiraita zaikai rīdā (Shibusawa Eiichi, the business leader who opened the door to Japanese modernity)*. Kyoto: PHP.

Moriguchi, C. (2017) *Nihon ha 'kakusa shakai' ni natta noka, hikaku keizaishi ni miru nihon no shotoku kakusa* (Did Japan become an unequal society?: Japan's income disparity in comparative historical perspective). *Keizai Kenkyū*, 68(2): 169–189.

Morinaga (2018). *Morinaga Nyūgyō 100-nenshi* (Centennial history of Morinaga). Tokyo: Morinaga Kabushiki Gaisha.

Nakaoka, T., Suzuki, J., and Miyachi, M. (eds) (2001). *Sangyō gijutsushi* (History of industrial technology). Tokyo: Yamakawa.

NEC (2001). *Nippon denki kabushikikaisha hyakunenshi* (Centennial history of NEC). Tokyo: NEC.

Nihon seikōjo (2008). Nihon seikōjo hyakunenshi: hagane to kikai totomoni (100–year history of Japan Steel Works: together with steel and machinery). Tokyo: Nihon seikōjo.

Nikkei (2000). *Baburu* (The bubble). Tokyo: Nikkei BP.

Okumura, H. (1993). *Nihon no rokudaikigyō shūdan (Japan's six big business groups)*. Tokyo: Asahi bunko.

Okazaki, T. (1997). *Kōgyōka no kiseki*. Tokyo: Yomiuri Shimbun.

Rodokeizai kenkyujo (1948). *Nihon ni okeru gaikoku shihon* (Foreign capital in Japan). Tokyo: Rodokeizai kenkyujo.

Saito, K. (2020). *Ninshinse no 'Shihonron'* ('The Anthropocene of 'Capitalist theory''). Tokyo: Shinsho Shueisha.

Sakamoto F. (1977). *Nihon Koyō-shi, 2 nenkōsei e no nagai michinori* (Japan's Employment History, 2 the Long Road to a Seniority System). Tokyo: Chūō Keizaisha.

Sapporo Biiru KK (1996). *Sapporo Biiru 120 nenshi* (120-Year History of Sapporo Breweries Ltd.). Sapporo Biiru KK, Tokyo: Dainippon.

Sawai, M. (2008). Senchu—sengo Osaka no shinsetsu kōtō kogyō gakkō—kōgyō senmon gakkō (Industrial schools in Osaka during and after the war). *Osaka Economic Papers*, 57(4): 278–296.

Sawai, M. (2012). *Kindai Nihon no kenkyū kaihatsu taisei* (The System for Research and Development in Modern Japan). Nagoya: Nagoya Daigaku Shuppankai.

Sawai, M. (2013). *Kindai Osaka no sangyō hatten: shūseki to tayōsei ga hagukunda mono* (Industrial development in modern Osaka). Tokyo: Yuhikaku.

Sawai, M., and Tanimoto, M. (2016). *Nihon keizaishi: kinsei kara gendai made* (The Economic History of Japan: From the Early Modern Era to the Present). Tokyo: Yuhikaku.

Shibata, Y. (2013). *Chugoku ni okeru Nikkei tabako sangyō, 1905–1945* (Japanese tobacco industry in China, 1905–1945), Tokyo: Suiyosha.

Shimano, T. (1980). *Shōhin seisan yushutsunyu butsuryorui nen tokei hyō (Annual tables for quantity of product production import–export)*. Tokyo: Aritsune.

Shimizu, T. (2021). *Kansenshō to keiei—senzen no nihon kigyō ha 'shinokage' to ikani muki-attaka* (Infection and Business: How Japanese Companies Faced 'the Shadow of Death'). Tokyo: Chuokeizai-sha.

Shinomiya M. (1998). *Nihon no jidōsha sangyō: kigyōsha katsudō to kyōsōryoku, 1918–1970* (The Japanese automobile industry: activities of entrepreneurs and competitiveness, 1918–1970). Tokyo: Nihon Keizai hyoronsha.

Shōchiku (1985). *Shōchiku 90 nen shi (Ninety-year history of Shōchiku)*. Tokyo: Shōchiku.

Sony (2020). Corporate website, https://www.sony.net/SonyInfo/CorporateInfo/History/ (accessed 12 August 2020)

Sugihara J., and Somehara, M. (2017). *Dare ha apareru wo korosu no ka* (Who is killing the apparel industry?). Tokyo: Nikkei BP.

Takatsuki, Y. (2018). *Osaka dojima kome ichiba* (The rice market of Osaka Dojima). Tokyo: Kodansha.

Teikoku Databank Survey Analysis (2016). *Chōju kigyō 28,972 sha o bunseki; Meiji isshinmae no sōgyō wa 3,343 sha; gyōreki 500 nenijyō wa 41 sha (Analysis of 28,972 old established firms: 3,343 firms established before the Meiji Restoration; 41 firms with a history of over 500 years)*, internal document retrieved from Teikoku Databank.

Teikoku Databank (2019). Tokubetsu kikaku: shinise kigyō no jittai chōsa (2019). Retrieved 20 May 2021, from https://www.tdb.co.jp/report/watching/press/p190101.html

Tokyo kōgaku (1982). *Tokyo kōgaku 50 nenshi* (Fifty-year history of Topcon). Tokyo: Topcon.

Tsuchiya, M., and Miwa, Y. (eds) (1989). *Nihon no chūshōkigyō* (Japanese SMEs). Tokyo: Tokyo University Press.

Uchida, H. (1985). *Tokei kogyō no hattatsu* (The development of the watch and clock industry). Tokyo: Seiko Institute of Horology.

Udagawa, M. (1987). Senzen nihon no kigyō keiei to gaishikei kigyō (The Management of Prewar Japanese Companies and Foreign Firms), *Keiei Shirin*, 24(1): 15–31 and 24(2): 29–40.

Udagawa, M. (ed.) (2002a). *Nihon no kigyōkashi* (History of Japanese entrepreneurs). Tokyo: Bunshindo.

Udagawa, M. (2002b). *Kesu sutadē sengo Nihon no kigyōka-katsudō* (Case Studies of the Postwar Activities of Japanese Entrepreneurs). Tokyo: Hosei daigaku inobe-shon manejimento kenkyū-sentaa.

Udagawa, M. (2015). *Nissan konzerun keieishi kenkyū* (Business history of Nissan group). Tokyo: Bunshindo.

Udagawa, M., and Shōjima, A. (2011). *Kigyōka ni manabu nihon keieishi* (Introduction to Business History in Japan: Entrepreneurs, Themes, and Cases). Tokyo: Yukikaku.

Ueda, Y. (2007). Nihon no chokusetsu toshi to tai no jidōsha buhin mēkā no keisei (Japanese FDI and the formation of car component makers in Thailand).*Keizaigaku ronso*, 58(4): 87–117.
Uemura, S. (1999). Taiwan seitō no setsuritsu (The Establishment of Taiwan Sugar Manufacturing Corporation). *Keieishigaku*, 34(3): 1–22.
Umemoto, T. (2015). *Nihon sutabakkusu monogatari* (History of Starbucks Japan). Tokyo: Hayakawa Shobo.
Yamazaki, H. (ed.) (2004). *Nihon keieishi no kisochishiki* (Japanese Business History: Basic Facts and Conceptd). Tokyo: Yuhikaku.
Yamazaki, Y. (2004). Nihon ni okeru 1970 nendai 'benchaa bijinesu' no tenkai (The development of venture capital businesses in Japan in the 1970s), *Journal of Innovation Management* (1): 139–154.
Yamazawa, I., and Yamamoto, Y. (1979). *Bōeki to kokusai shūshi (Foreign trade and balance of payments)*. Tokyo: Toyo Keizai Shinposha.
Yanotsuneta Kinenkai (2006). *Sūji de miru nihon no hyakunen (A 100-year history of Japan in figures)*. Tokyo: Tsuneta Kinenkai.
Yonekura, S., and Shimizu, H. (2015). *Open inobeshon no manejimento: takai keiei seika wo umu shikumizukuri* (Open Innovation Management: Challenging for Japanese Firms). Tokyo: Yuhikaku.

Newspapers and magazines

BBC, Diamond, The Economist, Financial Times, The Guardian, Japan Times, Kyodo News, Los Angeles Times, The New York Times, Newsweek, Nikkei Asian Review, Nikkei Newspaper, Reuters, Toyo Keizai.

Annual reports of companies

Fast Retailing, Fuji Film, Panasonic, Rakuten, Sony, Toyota

Official reports and publications

Cabinet Office (Naikakufu) (1967, 1962, 1967, 2004), Tōkeihyō-ichiran, shōhi-dōkōchōsa. Retrieved 31 May 2021 from https://www.esri.cao.go.jp/jp/stat/shouhi/shouhi.html
Government of Japan, Abenomics. Accessed 7 September 2021, https://www.japan.go.jp/abenomics/index.html
International Labour Organization ILOSTAT (2020). Gender equality in the workplace remains elusive. Women, wages, employment, 10 Jan 2020. https://ilostat.ilo.org/gender-equality-in-the-workplace-remains-elusive/
The Japan Institute for Labour Policy and Training, https://www.jil.go.jp/kokunai/statistics/timeseries/html/g0401.html (accessed 20 September 2020).
Japan Society for the Promotion of Science (JSPS) Social Scientific Research Committee on the Great East Japan Earthquake (2015). Lessons for the Social Sciences from the 2011 Great East Japan Earthquake, Tokyo, May.
Ministry of Economy, Trade and Industry, https://www.chusho.meti.go.jp/pamflet/hakusyo/H29/h29/html/b2_1_1_2.html (accessed 22 September 2020).

Ministry of Economy, Trade and Industry (2017). *White Paper on Small Enterprises in Japan*, https://www.chusho.meti.go.jp/pamflet/hakusyo/H29/PDF/2017shohaku_eng.pdf (accessed 22 September 2020).

Ministry of Finance, Statistics, https://www.mof.go.jp/english/statistics/index.html

Ministry of Health, Labour, and Welfare. Accessed on 7 September 2021. https://www.mhlw.go.jp/stf/seisakunitsuite/bunya/hukushi_kaigo/seikatsuhogo/jisatsu/jisatsu_year.html

National Law Review (2018). Japan's labor reform caps overtime in a bid to curb karoshi, 10 December. https://www.natlawreview.com/article/japan-s-labor-reform-caps-overtime-bid-to-curb-karoshi

Prime Minister's Office of Japan (Shushō kantei) (2022). 0.2.mirai o kirihiraku atarashi shihon shugi seichō to haibun no kōjunkan. Accessed 5 May 2022. https://www.kantei.go.jp/jp/headline/seisaku_kishida/newcapitalism.html

Renewable Energy Institute, Asia International Grid Connection Study Group. (2017). Interim report. Accessed on 9 July 2021. https://www.renewable-ei.org/en/asg/

United States General Accounting Office, National Security and International Affairs Division (2015). US-Japan Trade Evaluation of the Market-Oriented, Sector-Selective Talks, July, https://www.gao.gov/assets/nsiad-88-205.pdf

UN Global Compact Japan (2017). SDGs in practice, early actions by Japanese companies. Retrieved 9 July 2021. https://www.ungcjn.org/sdgs/files/elements_file_3032.pdf

US-Japan Structural Impediments (SII) (1990). Hearing before the Sub-committee on International Trade, United States Senate, One-hundred First Congress, Second Session, 5 March, https://www.finance.senate.gov/imo/media/doc/hrg101-5943.pdf

Websites

Bank of Japan, https://www.boj.or.jp/en/statistics/boj/other/discount/discount.htm/

Foreign trade statistics of Japan, https://www.customs.go.jp/toukei/suii/html/nenbet.htm (accessed 18 August 2020).

The Henokiens, International Association of Bicentenary Family Companies, https://www.henokiens.com

JETRO, FDI statistics, https://www.jetro.go.jp/world/japan/stats/fdi.html

OECD, FDI statistics, https://data.oecd.org/fdi/fdi-stocks.htm

OICA, http://www.oica.net

SB Energy, retrieved 9 July 2021, https://www.sbenergy.co.jp/en/info/

Statistics Bureau of Japan, https://www.stat.go.jp/

World Bank, https://wits.worldbank.org/

Index

3M 191
'100-yen shops' 182, 252

Abegglen, J. 1
Abenomics 6, 229–31, 245, 246, 252, 254
Abenomics and end of communitarian capitalism 231–7
  politico-economic context 234–7
  reform, context for 233–4
Abe Shinzō 146, 224, 225f, 229–30, 246
Abe Shinzō and three arrows of economic reform 237–43
  'Englishnization' and teleworking 242–3
  fiscal policy 237
  monetary stimulus 237
  new competitive advantage and harnessing women in workplace 240–2
  structural change in workplace 238
  structural reform 237
  work culture, contextual factors for changing 239–40
adult adoption 17–18, 20–1, 248
AEG (Germany) 93, 94
Aeon Bank 180, 200
agricultural, educational and labour reforms 131–4
agricultural sector 24, 31b, 41, 68, 108–9, 128, 131
Aikawa 119
Aikawa Yoshisuke 115–16, 123
AirAsia 244
airline low-cost carriers (LCCs) 244–5
Air Liquide (France) 90, 117
Aisin Seiki 158
Akio Morita 5
Alexander, J.W. 40, 43
Alibaba 227b
All Nippon Airways (ANA) 244
alternative residence system 13, 248
Aluminium Ltd (Canada) 90
Amable, B. 3
Amada 141

American Federation of Labor 82
American models of business 251
American Oil 98
American Tobacco Company (ATC) 101, 104
Anchordoguy, M. 163, 233
Andō Momofuku 173
anime industry 218–20
Anti-Monopoly Law (1947) 6, 136, 137, 145, 198, 204
Aoki Shūzō 42
API 103
Apple 217
apprenticeship 21–2
Arano Yasunori 11
Argentina 1
Armstrong and Whitworth & Co. (UK) 113
arranged marriages 20
Asahi 45, 149
Asano Sōichirō 43
Ashio Copper Mine 166b
Asia 130–1, 154, 246, 249, 251, 253
  bubble economy and its aftermath 191, 199b, 202
  global competition 203, 211, 215–16, 219
  imperialism and militarization 106–7
  industrial capitalism in changing social and geopolitical environment (1895-1930) 70–1
  Meiji Period (1868-1912): private entrepreneurs 56, 63, 65
  Meiji Period (1868-1912): public sector 34
  MNEs, role of (1895-1930) 88
  see also East Asia; Southeast Asia
Asian financial crisis (1997) 211
Asō Tarō 237
Associated Oil (USA) 58, 97, 98
Association of Japanese Oxygen Producers 117
atomic bombs: Hiroshima and Nagasaki 124

automobile industry 98–100, 104, 119, 139, 145, 155–6, 167b, 209–12
Automobile Manufacturing Industry Law (1936) 118, 119
Awaji Condensed Milk (ARKK) 102–3

baby boom/baby boomers 167–8
Bacchus Marsh 102
Banking Act 1927 75
banking crisis 72–5, 77, 199
banking system deregulation 252
Bank of Japan (BOJ) 54–5, 77, 116, 188–9, 195, 197–8
banks, private 54–5
Bank of Taiwan 75–7
beer excise tax 44
beer industry 30, 34, 39, 40–5, 48–9
Bell, A.G. 91
Bellah, R. 22
Bell Laboratories 153b
'big bang' policy 198, 235
big business restructuring 136–8
blue-collar workers 81, 168, 250
'blue-sky markets' 128
Borden 102
Braudel, F. 4
Bridgestone 191
Brother 162
Brunat, P. 46–7
bubble economy and its aftermath 186–202, 251–2
  collapse of bubble economy 195–201
  formation of financial bubble 187–9
  luxury consumption 192–4
  Nakasone Yasuhirō and privatization of SOEs 198–9b
  outward FDI 189–92
bullet train (Shinkansen) 126–7b
bureaucrats/bureaucracy 12, 52, 79, 83, 143, 156, 198, 240
  career 199b
  central 117
  complex 213
  entrepreneurship 108
  foreign companies and MNEs 88, 97, 104
  imperialism and militarization 108, 122–3
  Meiji 33, 39, 67
  Meiji Period (1868-1912): public sector 29, 30, 40, 48

MITI 1552
Occupation period and SCAP 135, 139, 141–2
business schools 59b
buyer's market 182
'Buy Japan' campaigns 117–18

Canon 113
Capron, H. 41
Carnation 102
Carrefour 185
Carrier Co. 118
Carson, R. 166b
'catch up with and overtake' slogan 125, 142, 163, 168, 239
catch-up phase 143, 150, 156, 163–4, 166b, 199b, 253
CBS 154b
Cerman, M. 23
Charter Oath 33, 35
chemical industry 72, 115, 141, 150–2
China 2, 11, 12, 108, 111, 123, 203, 219–20
  authoritarianism 253
  automobile industry 211
  electronics industry 208–9
  expansion 117
  firms in Japan 213–14
  foreign technicians sent to Japan 161
  growth rate 223
  post 3:11 and rebooting global competitiveness 226b, 245
  'unicorns' 217
  Uniqlo outsourced to 221–2b
Christensen, C.M. 153b
Chrysler 99, 167b
Chuo Industry 113
Churchill, W. 130
class system 12–13
  see also middle class
Clean Air Act (1963) 167b
climate change 228b, 254
Coca-Cola 149, 214
coexistence and co-prosperity 178
colonies, investment in 72, 106–11, 108t
Columbia Pictures 92, 154b, 186
commercial capitalism 23–7
commercial code 50, 157
communism 130–1, 133

communitarian capitalism 4, 6, 147, 163, 178, 196, 233, 251
    see also Abenomics and end of communitarian capitalism
competitive advantage 240–2
Confucianism 12, 19–20, 23, 52
consumerism and business in high and stable growth periods 101–3, 165–85, 249
    consumerist middle class 167–9
    'dark side of capitalism' 165, 166–7*b*
    distribution patterns 175–80
    science, technology and innovation 169–72
    Seven-Eleven Japan and third industrial revolution 180–4
    social change and its consequences 172–4
consumption tax 231
continuity and discontinuity of firms 18, 28
control associations 121
Convention of Kanagawa (aka Japan-US Treaty of Peace and Amity) 34
convoy system, end of 196
Cool Japan 218–20, 223
Cool Japan Bureau 220
Cool Japan Fund 220
cooperation and collaboration 3, 96*b*, 101, 104, 112, 162, 163, 251
    see also technological cooperation agreements
coordinated market economies (CMEs) 3–4, 145
Copeland, W. 43–4
corporate governance 76, 201, 204–6, 232–3, 252
Corporate Social Responsibility (CSR) 228*b*
corporate tax 231
cotton industry 60–2, 60*t*, 65, 111, 122
Covid-19 pandemic 17, 182, 240, 243, 244–5, 246, 247
'creative destruction' 52, 171
Credit Suisse 189
cross-regional trade and competition 7, 27–8
cross-shareholdings 145, 147, 157, 197
cultural barriers/differences 3, 107, 143, 162–3, 214–15, 218–20, 222–3
custom duties 101
Cyanamide Japan 152

Daiei supermarket chain 176–81, 183, 184
Dai-Ichi Bank 77, 145
Dai-Ichi Hotel 196
Daimaru with Christian Dior 193
Dai Nippon Arms 113
Dai-Nippon Beer 137
Dai-Nippon Sugar Co. 109
Daisō 182, 252
'dark side of capitalism' 165, 166–7*b*, 250
Datsun 119
DDI 201
'death by overwork' 239–40
Dejima island 11
Denny's family restaurants 181
Dentsū 239
Department for Arms Production (DAP) of the University of Tokyo 112–13, 114–15
Department of Precision Engineering (DPE) 114–15
department stores 175–6, 192–4
deposit banking 25
deregulation 204, 242–3, 245, 251–2
De Vries, J. 26
digitalization 208, 215, 230, 243
Dispatched Workers Law (1985) 235
disruptive innovation 153*b*
distinctive characteristics of firms 14–18
distribution patterns 175–80
    department stores and supermarkets 175–6
    Nakauchi Isao and Daiei supermarket chain 176–9
    new shopping patterns, rise of 179–80
distribution revolution 168–9
diversification 9*b*, 102, 110*b*, 116, 136, 154*b*, 161, 204, 209
    industrial capitalism (1895-1930) 72, 74, 75–6
    Meiji period (1868-1912): private entrepreneurs 56, 57–8, 62
division of labour 9*b*, 27, 63, 107, 172
Dodge, J. 128
Dodge Line 128–9, 140
domestic sources of entrepreneurship 38–40
Doshima Rice Exchange market 13
Dow Chemicals 151
Dower, J. 124
dualities 67–8, 78–9, 87

Dun, E. 41
DuPont 151
DuPont Japan 151, 152

earthquake bills 77
earthquakes
 Great Kantō (1923) 64, 74, 76–7, 86b, 98, 210
 Great Tōhoku (2011) 224–5
 Hanshin Awaji (1995) 180
East Asia 69, 70, 106, 129, 143, 161, 209, 218–19, 250
Echigoya drapery 7
Economic Stabilization Board subsidies 140
economic stimulus package 237
economy, changes in (1914-1940) 73t
eco-point system 237
Edison, T. 91
Edo Hideo 135–6
Edo period (1603-1868) 1, 6, 7, 8b, 10–11, 13–14, 56, 90, 248
education system 59b, 112, 131–2, 217
EIE International 191, 195
electrical appliances sector 90, 91–6, 104, 105, 153b, 154, 208t
Electrical Laboratory of the Ministry of Communication 112
electronics industry 69, 146, 152–3, 154b, 155, 161–2, 190, 206–9, 217
Elimination of Excessive Concentration of Economic Power Law (1947) 136–7
employers' association 80
employment system, transformation of 206, 217, 223
energy mix ratio 229f
'Englishnization' 242–3
enterprise unions 134, 147, 251
Environmental Agency 167b
environmental damage and pollution 165, 166b, 226–8b, 250, 254
Environmental, Social and Governance (ESG) standards 228b
Equal Employment Opportunity Law (1985) 172
Ericsson 209
Europe 12, 24, 159, 161, 162, 179, 190, 218
 see also Western Europe
exchange rate 73, 129, 202
Ezaki Glico 148

Factory Law (1911) 80, 84
factory system, growth of 66–7
Faculty of Engineering, University of Tokyo 94
Fairchild 153–4
Fairchild Semiconductor Co. 161
fair pricing movement 178
familism 80, 82
Family Mart 180
FANUC 216
Fast Retailing Company 221b
Fillmore, M. 34
financial capitalism 4, 6, 251–2
financial system and private banks 54–5
First National Bank 52–3
food and drink industry 16–17, 101–2, 219–20
 see also beer industry; sake brewing
Ford 98–100, 118, 119–20, 120t, 167b
Ford Japan 99, 119
foreign companies/multinational enterprises (MNEs) (1985-1930) 88–105, 248
 consumer goods 101–3
 electrical appliances sector 91–6
 FDI 88, 90, 91, 101, 104–5
 Ford and General Motors 98–100
 number of companies with foreign capital (1931) 89t
 oil industry 96–8
 Shimadzu and Siemens 95–6b
foreign direct investment (FDI) 36, 65, 118, 129, 145, 151, 207, 236
 inward 55, 88, 90, 157, 212–15, 223
 outward 158–62, 186, 189–92, 201–2, 207, 220
 see also foreign companies/multinational enterprises (MNEs) (1985-1930)
foreign enterprises, control over 117–21
Foreign Exchange and Foreign Trade Control Law (1949) 149, 157, 170
foreign experts 36–8
Foreign Investment Law (1950) 149
foreign sources of business creation 36–8
foreign technology acquisition 148–56
France 37t, 150, 156, 162, 215
free-trade policy 62
Friendly Society 82
Fuji Bank 145, 151
Fuji Electric 92, 94
Fuji Film Corporation 204–5

Fujii Shinichi 214
Fujimoto Takahiro 210
Fujita Den 165
Fujitsu 146, 155, 161
Fujiya 214
Fukuhara Arinobu 84*b*
Fukushima Daiichi 188
Fukushima earthquake, tsunami and nuclear disaster (3:11) 224–5, 228–9
Fukuzawa Yukichi 35, 59*b*, 249
Furikawa 92

gapponshugi capitalism 51
Garon, S. 79
Geisenheimer, F. 46
gender factors 173, 206, 235, 241
    see also women
General Agreement on Tariffs and Trade (GATT) 156, 157
General Electric (GE) 92–3, 95*b*, 117, 137, 155
General Motors (GM) 98–100, 118, 119–20, 120*t*, 167*b*
General Motors (GM) Japan 119
Genroku period (1688-1704) 7, 29
Germany 3, 37*t*, 38, 89, 91, 150, 215
Ghosn, C. 206, 211
Global Energy Interconnection Development and Cooperation Organization 227*b*
global financial crisis (2008) 207, 224, 236
Glover, T.B. 44, 88
Goldman Sachs 189, 191
gold standard 55, 89
good conduct payments 81
Goodrich 118
Gordon, A. 68, 79
Gorham, W.R. 119
Goto Fuundo Manufacturing (GFM) 92, 96*b*
Gotoh, F. 236
Gotō Shinpei 75
Goto Toshio 14, 22
GoTo Travel Campaign 246–7
Great Depression (1932-33) 99
Great Kantō Earthquake (1923) 64, 74, 76–7, 86*b*, 98, 210
Great Tōhoku Earthquake and Tsunami (2011) 224–5
Greyhound Bus Company (USA) 127*b*

Gross Domestic Product (GDP) 50, 69*t*, 144, 197, 201, 207, 212, 220, 237, 238, 246, 250
Grossman, H. 85*b*
Gross National Product (GNP) 69, 70–1
growth periods *see* consumerism and business in high and stable growth periods
gunboat diplomacy 34

Hachirōbe Takatoshi 8–9*b*
Hall, P.A. 3
Hanae Mori 194
Hankyū department store 175
Hanley, S.B. 13–14
han model of industrial development 12, 35, 36, 37, 61
Hanshin Awaji Earthquake (1995) 180
Hara Takashi 83
Hashimoto 230
Hashimoto Ryūtarō 198, 234–5
Hattori 113
Hattori Kintarō 64
Hayashi Shūji 175
heavy industries 37–8, 70, 80, 108, 109–10, 115–17
Heisei Recession *see* 'lost decades' and global competition
Hénokiens 17
Hibiya Anti-Treaty Riot (1905) 78
Hino 161
Hiroshima Stock Exchange 221*b*
Hirschmeier, J. 38, 80
Hisamitsu Pharmaceutical Company 24
history-of-capitalism approach 3–4
Hitachi 94, 137, 154, 155, 160, 205
Hitachi Arms 113
Hitachi Mine 115
Hitotsubashi University 59*b*
Hitotsubashi Yoshinobu 52
Hoden Oil 97
Hokkaido 70, 102
Hokkaido Colliery & Steamship Co. 113
Hokkaido Colonization Office 41–2
Hokkaido Development Commission 70
Hokkaido Takushoku Bank 196
Hokuetsu (Niigata) railway 32*b*
holding companies 58, 76, 111*b*, 115, 137, 198, 204
Honda 141, 146, 156, 167*b*, 171, 190, 209

Honda Motor 159, 164, 165
Honda Sōichirō 159, 227*b*
Hori, K. 107
Hori Kazuo 122
Horiki Kenzō 126*b*
Horioka, C.Y. 203
Horiuchi, Y. 109
Hoshi Ryokan 17
House of Konoike 52
House of Mitsui 8–10*b*, 8*f*, 21, 39, 52
    Hachirōbe Takatoshi 8–9*b*
    innovations and new approaches to governance 10*b*
    novel business practices 9–10*b*
House of Ono 39
House of Shimada 39
House of Sumitomo 39
housing prices 188*t*
human capital 36, 49, 94, 123, 124, 132
Hunter, J.E. 31–2*b*
Hyundai (Korea) 212

IBM 155
IBM Japan 155
Ibuka Masaru 153*b*, 228*b*
Ikeda Hayato 134, 174
Imasen 148
imitation 35, 40–1
imperialism 6, 33, 69
imperialism, war and business development 106–23
    foreign enterprises, control over 117–21
    investment in Japanese colonies 106–11
    military and technological development 111–15
    new industrial *zaibatsu* (*shinkō zaibatsu*) 115–17
    South Manchuria Railway Company (Mantetsu) 110–11*b*
    war economy 121–2
import duties 99, 102
import substitution 65, 67, 70, 72, 88
income-doubling plan 174
Industrial Bank of Japan 110, 115, 116
industrial capitalism 4, 6, 29, 66–87, 88, 249
    geopolitical environment, changing 68–72
    labour movement characteristics 81–3
    labour movement formation 78–81
    Shiseido 84–6*b*
    social changes and rise of women in workforce 83–6
    Suzuki & Co.: rise and fall 75–7
    zaibatsu, rise of and banking crisis (1920s-1930s) 72–5
Industrial Control Law (1931) 118, 121
industrial policy 144, 148–56
industrial production in Tokyo and Osaka 63*t*
industrial revolution 4
    first 88
    second 88, 90, 91, 96, 104, 175
    third 180–4
Industrial Safety and Health Act (ISHA) 238
inflation 54, 128, 143, 198*b*, 237, 246
innovation 35, 40–1, 165, 166–7*b*, 169–72, 184, 216
'insider shareholders' 200–1, 205, 232
Integrated Services Digital Network of POS data 184
intellectual property rights 72
international currency policy 188
international fairs 47
International Labour Organization (ILO) 82, 84
International Monetary Fund (IMF) 157
International Oil 97
international relations 30, 82, 130
    and brewing industry 40–5
International Telephone and Telegraph (ITT) 118
Isetan with Pierre Cardin 193
Ishida Baigan, I. 22–3
Ishikawa 160
Ishikawajima Shipyard 98
Issey Miyake 194
Isuzu 161
Itochū 24
Itō Chūbei 24
Itoh 192
Itō Horobumi 46
Itō Masatoshi 180
Itō-Yōkado 176, 181–2, 184
Iwadare Kunihiko 91, 104
Iwakura Mission 35
Iwasaki family 48
Iwasaki Yatarō 45, 57–8

J. & O. Coats (UK) 104
Jablkowski Brothers Department Store 18

278 Index

Jade Production 219
Japan Airlines (JAL) 199b, 244
Japan Asia Investment Company 216
Japan Brewery 40, 43–5
Japan Communist Party (JCP) 133
Japanese Business System 6, 66, 144–8, 162–3, 200, 201, 205
'Japanese Miracle' 107, 143–64, 250
  industrial policy and foreign technology acquisition 148–56
  keiretsu and Japanese Business System 144–8
  outward FDI 158–62
  trade and capital liberalization 156–8
Japanese mystique 80
Japanese-style management 66, 81, 134, 162
Japan Industrial Club 80
Japan National Railroad (JNR) 126b, 199b
Japan Optical Industry 113
Japan Post Holdings 33b
Japan Productivity Centre (JPC) 170
Japan Railways 198
Japan Renewable Energy Foundation 227b
Japan Revitalization Strategy 2014 232
Japan Steel Works 113
Japan Tobacco 199b
Jardine, Matheson & Co. 44, 88
JetStar 244
Jobs, S. 217
Johnson, C. 1, 143
joint-stock companies 51, 52–3, 54, 59b, 60, 62, 64, 78, 85b, 249
joint ventures 113, 116–18, 151–2, 155, 161, 209, 214–15
  foreign companies and MNEs 90–2, 94, 95b, 98, 101–2, 104
Jusco supermarket 176
'just-in-time' production system 156

Kaishinsha 98
kakun (precept or constitution) 19–20
Kanakin Cotton Weaving 62
Kanebō (Kanegafuchi) 81, 82
Kaneko Naokichi 75–6
Kan Naoto 225
Kansai railway 32b
Kao Corp. 178
Kataoka Naoharu 77
Kawabe with Yves Saint Laurent 193
Kawasaki Steel 134, 140–1

Keio University 59b
keiretsu 137, 144–8, 204, 251
  bubble economy and its aftermath 191, 197, 201
  consumerism in high and stable growth periods 178–9
  end of 200
  horizontal or financial 146–7
  'Japanese Miracle' 157, 164
  vertical 158
Kenzō Takada 194
Kikkawa Takeo 164, 188, 204
Kinokuniya supermarket 177
Kinouchi Toshihisa 232
Kirin 45, 48, 147, 149
Kirkland, M. 44
Kishi 116–17
Kishida Fumio 252
Kishi Nobusuke 116
Kiyonari Tadao 171
knowledge transfer 99, 120, 171
Kobe University 59b
Koizumi 230
Koizumi Jun'ichiro 32b, 235
Kōmei Genjirō 45
Kōnoike 19
Korea 11, 70–1, 72, 107–9, 110b, 115, 122–3, 209, 219–20
Korean Airlines 194
Korean War (1950-3) 131
Kuhara Mining Co. 115
Kuril Islands 70
Kuznets, S. 1, 2
Kwantung army 110–11b, 116–17
Kyōdō Unyu Company 57
Kyōhō period (1717-1736) 19
Kyoritsu 99, 100t
Kyoto Protocol 228b

labour market deregulation 252
labour movement 6, 66, 68, 78–83, 87, 133–4, 249
  see also unions/unionization
labour reforms 79, 80, 131–4, 235
labour relations 166b
Labour Relations Adjustment Laws (1946 and 1948) 133
labour shortages 80–1, 87, 231
Labour Standards Act (LSA) 238
Labour Union Law (1945) 133

Index

Large, G. 82
Large-scale Retail Law (1974) 179
Large Store Law (LSL) (1974) 182–3
lean production system 161
LG (Korea) 208
Liaotung 72
Libbey-Owens (USA) 90
Liberal Democratic Party (LDP) 33b, 198, 235
liberalization 156–8, 198–200, 201, 220
liberal market economies (LMEs) 3–4
licensing agreements 94, 193
lifetime employment 134, 147, 251
light industry 37, 48, 72, 108, 139
Lilienthal, Hècht and Company 46
limited partnership 50–1
Long-Term Credit Bank of Japan (LTCB) 191, 195, 196
'lost decades' and global competition 203–23, 224, 231, 236, 253
   automobile industry, transformation of 209–12
   Cool Japan 218–20
   corporate governance 204–6
   electronics industry, transformation of 206–9
   foreign firms and inward FDI 212–15
   start-ups and problem of entrepreneurship 215–18
   Uniqlo fast fashion brand 221–2b
Lubinski, C. 5
luxury consumption 192–4
LVMH 194

MacArthur, General D. 129, 131, 133
McDonald's 165
McGray, D. 218
Macnaughtan, H. 240–1
Maddison, A. 70
Maejima Hisoka 32–3b
Makoshi Kyōhei 45
Manchukuo 70, 110, 111b, 116
Manchukuo Heavy Industrial Development Co. 111b, 116
Manchuria 70–1, 72, 107–8, 110, 115, 116, 119
manufacturing industry 4, 28, 50, 63, 65–6, 71, 78, 107, 144–7
maritime transportation industry 50, 55, 57

Market-Oriented, Sector-Specific (MOSS) Talks 179
Marubeni 24, 192
Maruwa Food Center 177
mass-production system 53, 95b, 207, 249
   consumerism in high and stable growth periods 166b, 169, 173–5, 178
   imperialism and militarization 112, 119
   'Japanese Miracle' 148, 156
Masuda Takashi 59b
Matsudaira Tadashi 126–7b
Matsui Construction Company 14–15
Matsui, K. 240
Matsukata Deflation (1881-1885) 50, 54–5
Matsukata Matsuyoshi 48
Matsushita 92, 94, 137, 147, 153, 153b, 157, 160, 161, 178, 189, 190
Matsushita Kōnosuke 137, 178
Matsuzakaya with Nina Ricci 193
Mazda 156, 161–2
MCI 117, 121–2
M-curve 241–2
mega banks 200, 204, 216
mega-mergers 199–200
Meiji (food company) 102–3
Meiji government foreign employees 37t
Meiji Holdings 109
Meiji Life Insurance 58
Meiji period (1868-1912) 5, 15, 27, 76, 78, 88, 90, 129, 248
Meiji period (1868-1912): private entrepreneurs 50–65, 248
   Eiichi Shibusawa 51–4
   financial system and private banks 54–5
   Osaka Cotton Spinning Co. 60–2
   small and medium-sized enterprises (SMEs) 62–4
   zaibatsu and transformation into modern corporations 56–9
Meiji period (1868-1912): public sector 29–49, 248
   contextual factors 33–5
   international relations and brewing industry 40–5
      Japan Brewery (later Kirin) 43–5
      Snow Country (now Sapporo Beer) 41–3
   key players in transition from proto-industrial to capitalistic development 35–40

Meiji period (1868-1912): public sector (*Continued*)
   domestic sources of entrepreneurship 38–40
   foreign sources of business creation 36–8
   postal service 30–3*b*
   Tomioka Silk Filature
      image over technological appropriateness 46–7
      zaibatsu capitalism 48
Meiji Restoration 3, 10*b*, 33
Meiji Seika 109
Mendels, F.F. 23
Mercari 216
merchant capitalism or mercantilism 4
merchant houses 12–13, 19–23, 38–9
mergers and acquisitions 62, 75, 115, 138, 199–200, 204
Metzler, M. 11–12
middle class 134, 144, 147, 165, 167–9, 235, 250, 253
Mie Cotton Spinning 62
Mikimoto 193–4
Miki Tadao 126*b*
Mikitani Hiroshi 217, 242–3
militarism 30, 111–15, 116–17, 122
Military Vehicles Subsidy Law 98
Minamata 250, 254
mining sector 73, 74, 81, 83–4, 88
Ministry of Agriculture, Forestry and Fisheries 220
Ministry of Communications 118
Ministry of Economy, Trade and Industry (METI) 220
Ministry of Finance 90, 149, 196
   Reform Office 52
Ministry of Foreign Affairs (MOFA) 220
Ministry of Health, Labour and Welfare 240
Ministry of Industry 35, 36–7
Ministry of International Trade and Industry (MITI) 143, 149, 152, 153*b*, 154–5, 159, 170, 179
Ministry of Justice 44
Minomura Riazemon 10*b*
Mirai Securities 216
Mitsubishi 56, 110, 115, 157, 161–2
   bubble economy and its aftermath 192
   co-founded companies 152

foreign companies and MNEs 88, 90, 97–8, 104
industrial capitalism (1895-1930) 72, 74, 76
'Japanese Miracle' 145
'lost decades' 211
Meiji Period (1868-1912): public sector 32*b*, 44, 48
Mitsubishi Bank 58, 77, 146, 164
Mitsubishi Electric 58, 92, 146, 154
Mitsubishi Heavy Industries 58, 113, 137, 149
Mitsubishi International Corporation 159
Mitsubishi Mining 137
Mitsubishi Oil 58, 98
Mitsubishi Shipbuilding 58
Mitsubishi Shōji 136
Mitsui 8*b*, 48, 56–7, 64, 157–8, 159
   bubble economy and its aftermath 192
   co-founded companies 152
   foreign companies and MNEs 92, 102, 104
   imperialism and militarism 109, 110, 111, 115
   industrial capitalism (1895-1930) 72, 74, 76
   'Japanese Miracle' 145
   Occupation period and SCAP reforms 135
   see also House of Mitsui
Mitsui Bank 10*b*, 54, 59*b*, 77, 146, 158, 164
Mitsui Bussan 62, 72, 136
Mitsui Mining 137
Mitsui Polychemicals 151
Mitsui Sekiyu Kagaku 151
Mitsukoshi 175
   with Guy Laroche 193
Miyamoto, M. 10–11, 19, 21, 52
Mizuho Holdings 199
modernity/modernization 33, 47, 49, 53
moga ('modern girls') 84, 86*b*
Monsanto 151
Monsanto Japan 152
Moriguchi Chiaki 254
Morikawa, H. 135
Morinaga 102–3, 173, 178
Morita Akio 153*b*, 228*b*
Mori Taikichirō 201
Mori Yoshitaka 219
Morris Suzuki, T. 139

M-shaped organization 137
MSK and Suntech Group 214
MUFJ Bank 200
multinational enterprises (MNEs) see foreign companies/multinational enterprises (MNEs) (1985-1930)
Murai Brothers & Co. 101
Murai Kichibei 104
Muskie, E./'Muskie Act' 167b
Mutō Sanji 81–2
My Shop 180

Nagasaki Munitions Works 113
Nagasaki Shipyards 48, 58
Nagoya Aircraft Works 113
Naigaimen 111
Nakagawa Seibei 41–2
Nakai Mitsutake 25
Nakamura Hideichirō 148
Nakamura, T. 128
Nakasone Yasuhirō 198–9b, 227b
Nakauchi Isao 176–9, 228b, 251
Natel, L. 5
National Bank Act 1872 54
National Cash Register Co. 118
National General Mobilization Law (1938) 121
National Innovation System (NIS) 111–12, 249
nationality cloaking 103
nationalization 18, 60, 101, 196
natural disasters 74, 98, 180, 210, 224
NEC 146, 153, 154, 155, 160, 162
neoliberalism 198–9b, 235, 253
Nescafé 214
Nestlé 101–3, 104, 121, 149, 173, 214
Nestlé Japan 214–15, 223
networks 53, 120, 137, 144–5, 147–8, 171, 178, 243, 251
  rural 23–7
  see also keiretsu
New Deal 130
new industrial *zaibatsu* (*shinkō zaibatsu*) 115–17
'new Japan' emergence 229–31
New York Standard Oil Japan 97
New York Stock Exchange 197
Nichie supermarket 176
Nidek 148
Nihon Menka 72

Nihon Optical Industry 112
Nihon Rōdō Sōdōmei 82
Nihon Sangyō 115–16
Nihon Tokushu 160
Nimura Kazuo 134
Nintendo 246
Nippon Animation 219
Nippon Columbia 92
Nippon Construction Materials 104
Nippon Credit Bank (NCB) 196
Nippon Denki 90
Nippon Electric Co. 91–2, 112, 118
Nippon Oil 97, 98
Nippon Sangyō 115
Nippon Steel 137
Nippon Telegraph and Telephone (NTT) 187, 199b, 226b, 243
Nippon Yusen 57
Nishiyama Yatarō 134, 139, 140–1
Nissan 99, 100, 156, 160, 161–2
  bubble economy and its aftermath 190
  imperialism and militarism 115, 116–17, 118, 119, 120
  'lost decades' 209, 211–12, 213
  post-3:11 and rebooting competitiveness 234
Nissho Iwai 192
Nissin 173, 178
Nisso 115
Nitchitsu 115
Nonaka Ikujiro 163
non-bank financial institutions 74
non-regular workers 147, 223, 235–6, 242
non-tariff barriers and quotas 119, 156, 162, 179

occupation period and Supreme Commander of the Allied Forces (SCAP) reforms 6, 124–42, 249–50
  agricultural, educational and labour reforms 131–4
  bullet train (Shinkansen) 126–7b
  demilitarization and democratization 130
  economic situation 127–9
  ideological underpinnings of reforms 129–31
  Kawasaki Steel and Nishiyama Yatarō 140–1

occupation period and Supreme Commander of the Allied Forces (SCAP) reforms (*Continued*)
    'punish Japan' phase (1945-6) 130, 137, 142
    'reverse course' phase (1947-8) 130, 137
    steel industry 138–41
    zaibatsu capitalism, end of and big business restructuring 130, 134–8
Ogilvie, S. 23
Ogura Oil 98
Ohno Ken-ichi 37–8
oil industry 96–8
Oji Paper 53, 137
Oki Electric 118, 146
Ōkubo Toshimitsu 41
Ōkura Trading Company 42–3, 110
old-well-established firms 14, 18–27
Olejniczak, T. 18
'open sky' agreement 244
Organization for Economic Cooperation and Development (OECD) 157
Osaka Beer 43, 45
Osaka Cotton Spinning Co. 60–2
Osaka Shōsen 57
Osaka Stock Exchange 55
Otsuka Foods 173

Panasonic 208, 220
Paramount Pictures 101
Paris Convention for the Protection of Industrial Property 89
Paris Peace Conference 82
patents 52, 72, 89, 91, 93, 150
paternalism 163, 233, 234
Peach 244
Penwalt Japan 152
performance-based career system 81, 206, 234
Perry, M.C. 1, 34
Petroleum Industry Law (1934) 118
Philips 153
Piketty, T. 253–4
pilot plant construction 40
Pioneer 141
Platt Brothers & Co. 61–2
Plaza Agreement 188
point of sales (POS) data 184
Police Regulations (1900) 132–3

population/demographic changes 13–14, 167–8, 203, 220, 231, 252
Porter, M. 163
Portmann, M. 43
post 3:11 and rebooting global competitiveness 224–47, 252
    Abenomics and end of communitarian capitalism 231–7
    Abenomics and 'new Japan' emergence 229–31
    Abe Shinzō and three arrows of economic reform 237–43
    Softbank 226–8*b*
    tourism and Tokyo Olympics 243–6
postal service 30–3*b*
Potsdam Declaration (1945) 129
Pratt, E.E. 25–6
price deflation *see* 'lost decades' and global competition
priority production system 140
private entrepreneurs *see* Meiji period (1868-1912): private entrepreneurs
privatization 54, 57, 198–9*b*, 226*b*
Procter & Gamble 151
professional managers 76, 135, 250
protectionism 64, 89, 156
protests and riots 78, 83, 133–4, 250
proto-industrialization 23–4
public sector *see* Meiji period (1868-1912): public sector
putting-out system 60

Radio Corporation of America (RCA) 155
Railway Technical Research Institute (RTRI) 126*b*
Railway Workers' Union 133
Rakuten 217
    and LinkShare Corp. 218
Rakuten Bank 200
RCA Victor 118
Reagan R. and Reaganomics 198*b*, 235
Reconstruction Finance Bank 18–19, 140
reinvention 165, 166–7*b*
Renault 211
Renault-Nissan BV (Alliance) 211
renewable energy 226, 227*b*
Renewable Energy Institute 227*b*
repressive policies 19–20
research and development (R&D) 91, 111–13, 156, 170, 215

resource-seeking strategy 159–60
retailers: ranking of sales 176t
reverse engineering 88, 91, 120
rice-based taxation system 248
'rich nation, strong army' 70, 106
Riken Institute 115
riots *see* protests and riots
Rising Sun 97, 98
Rockefeller, J.D. 96–7
Roentgen, W. 95b
Roosevelt, F.D. 130
Rowntree (UK) 214
Royal Dutch Shell 96
rural capitalism 4, 24, 27–8, 39, 44, 248
Russel, L. 213
Russo-Japanese War (1904-5) 70
Ryūkū Islands (Okinawa) 70

Saga Domain 88
Saitō Kōhei 254
sake brewing 15, 28, 219–20
Sakhalin 72
Salt Public Corporation 199b
Samsung (Korea) 208
Samuel Samuel & Co. (UK) 97
San Francisco Treaty (1951) 129
Sanwa Bank 145
Sanyo Electric 141, 160, 161
 and Haier 214
Sanyo Securities 196
Sanyo Shōkai with Burberry 193
Sapporo Breweries Company 43, 45, 147, 149
Sawai Minoru 112
SB Energy 227b
scaling up 27–8
Schaede, U. 233–4
Schumpeter, J. 171
science, technology and innovation 169–72
Sears, Roebuck and Co. 181
seclusion policy 2, 4, 6, 11, 34
Seibu department store 175
Seika Mining 137
Seiko 64, 194
Seiyū Store 176, 178, 180
self-expression 78, 86b, 133
self-sufficiency 71, 72, 76
seniority-based pay 81, 134, 147, 241, 251
Seven & i Group 184
Seven Bank 200

Seven-Eleven Japan 180–4, 185
Shanghai Spinning Co. 111
shareholder capitalism 233
Sharp 146, 153b, 155, 162, 208
Shell 97
Shibaura 92, 94, 104
Shibusawa, Eiichi 26, 43, 45, 46, 51–4, 57, 59b, 61–2, 82, 109, 227b, 248–9
Shimadzu 95–6b
Shimano 148
shipbuilding 70, 71, 81
Shipping and Shipping Promotion Law (1896) 70
Shiseido 84–6b, 147
Shiseidō Geppō 86b
Shōchiku 101
Shōjima, A. 171, 179
shopping patterns, rise of 179–80
Shōwa Denko 151
Shōwa Emperor 169
Shōwa Financial Crisis/Depression (1930) 73–4, 135
Shōwa period 134
Siemens 92, 95–6b
silk industry 65
silver standard 55
Siniawer, E.M. 166b
Sino-Japanese Wars 69, 70, 121, 135
Skymark 244–5
small and medium-sized enterprises (SMEs) 51, 62–4, 67, 78, 116, 121, 148, 198–9b
Smith, T. 25
Snow Country Breweries 40–3
social change 6, 26, 56, 63, 68–9, 83–6, 172–4, 201, 215
social contract 233, 251
social entrepreneurship 227b, 228b
social model 230–1
social welfare programmes 81–2
Sockice, D. 3
Socony 97
Socony-Vacuum 98
Softbank 196, 201, 226–8b
Sogo Department Store 196
Son Masayoshi 226–8b, 243
Sony 5, 141, 153–4b, 155, 159, 161, 164, 250
 bubble economy and its aftermath 186, 190

Sony (*Continued*)
  consumerism in high and stable growth periods 170–1
  and Ericsson 209
  'Japanese Miracle' 146
  and Konica-Minolta 209
  'lost decades' 208, 216
  occupation period and SCAP reforms 125
  and Olympus 209
  and PlayStation Network 209
  post 3:11 and rebooting global competitiveness 246
Sony Bank 200
Sony Corporation of America 154*b*
Sony do Brasil 5
Sony Prudential Life Assurance 154*b*
South East Asia 36, 190, 207
Southeast Asia 36, 190, 207, 250
South Korea 161, 203, 208
Southland 181, 185
South Manchuria Railway Company (Mantetsu) 110–11*b*, 116
specialization 27, 63, 148
spousal tax exemption system 172
Spring Valley Brewery 43–4
stagnation *see* 'lost decades' and global competition
Standard Oil 96–7
Starbucks Coffee 214–15
start-ups 36, 128, 141–2, 170, 171–2, 215–18, 250, 252
state capitalism 30
state monopoly 101
steel industry 75, 81, 138–41
strategic alliances 20, 211
Streeck, W. 3
strikes 79, 80, 82, 133, 134
Stringer, H. 206
Structural Impediments Initiative (SSI) 179
structural reforms 237, 238, 250
Subaru 156
succession system 20–1
Suehiro Akira 163
sugar industry 72, 109
Suga Yoshihide 229, 252
Sumitomo 56, 58, 72, 74, 157, 159
  co-founded companies 152
  foreign companies and MNEs 90–1, 104
  imperialism and militarism 110, 115, 118

  'Japanese Miracle' 145
  see also House of Sumitomo
Sumitomo Bank 77, 146, 191
Sumitomo Electric 92
Sumitomo Forestry Company 14
Sumitomo Mitsui Bank 199–200
Sumitomo Mitsui Financial Group (SMFG) 216–17
Sun Maid 101–2
Suntory 45, 147
supermarkets 175–85
Supreme Commander of the Allied Forces (SCAP) *see* occupation period and Supreme Commander of the Allied Forces (SCAP) reforms
Sustainable Development Goals (SDGs) 228*b*
Suzukawa Hiroshi 113
Suzuki 74–5, 156, 183–5
  and Maruti Ltd. (India) 212
  rise and fall 75–7
Suzuki Bunji 82
Suzuki Iwajirō 75
Suzuki Shōten 74–6
Suzuki Tosaburō 109, 123
Suzuki Toshifumi 180–1, 251

Taira, K. 80
Taishō period 6, 76, 86*b*, 102, 109, 134, 249
Taiwan 69, 70–1, 72, 107–9, 123, 129, 203, 208, 209
Taiwan Sugar Manufacturing Co. 109
Takahashi Harunori 201
Takahashi Korekiyo 117
Takahashi Matsuri 239
Takamatsu Kensetsu 17
Takara Shūzō 220
Takashima coal mines 57
Takashimaya department store 175
  with Pierre Cardin 193
Takemura, E. 20
Takenaka Heizō 235–6
Takeuchi Hirotaka 163
Takuma Dan 80
Tanaka Kakuei 32–3*b*, 199*b*
Tanimoto, M. 63
tariffs 34, 67, 72, 97, 99, 156
Tata 212
Tateho Chemicals 197
TCL (China) 208

Index

technological cooperation agreements 94, 150, 152
technological developments 38, 64, 90, 111–15, 117–18, 122, 150, 208, 215
technology transfer 36–8, 39, 47, 49, 93–4, 97, 99, 104, 119, 126b, 248
  'Japanese Miracle' 150, 155, 157
Teijin 160
Teikoku Databank (TDB) 14–17
Tejima Tōan 23
teleworking 242–3
Temporary Capital Adjustment Law (1937) 121
Temporary Export and Import Commodities Law (1937) 121
Temporary Industry Rationality Bureau 121
temporary workers *see* non-regular workers
tertiary industry 60, 65, 68, 69, 72, 80–1, 83–4, 122–3
Texas Instruments (TI) 152, 154–5
textiles industry 40, 65, 67, 69, 72, 81, 108–9, 117, 122, 133, 145
  see also cotton industry; silk industry
Thailand 161, 253
Thatcher, M. 162, 198b, 235
Tidewater 118
Toa Electric 118
tobacco industry 101
Tobata Casting 99
Toei Animation (Korea) 219
Tōhō 134, 141
Tokugawa class system 38–9
Tokugawa Period 7–28, 30b
  distinctive characteristics of firms 14–18
  historical context and implications for business development 12–14
  old-well-established firms 18–27
    merchant houses 19–23
    rural networks and roots of commercial capitalism 23–7
Tokuyo Bank 196
Tokyo Aircraft Instruments 113–14
Tokyo Automobile Industries Co. 119
Tokyo Chamber of Commerce 53, 248
Tokyo Electric 92–3, 95b, 117
Tokyo Gas Electric 98
Tokyo Machine Works 113
Tokyo Marine Insurance Company 58
Tokyo Olympics (2020) 224, 230, 243–6
Tokyo Optical Industry 113

Tokyo Stock Exchange 53, 55, 60, 116, 200, 205, 221b, 248
  JASDAQ Securities Exchange 216, 218
  Nikkei index 187, 195
Tokyo Tsūshin Kōgyō 152, 153–4b
Tōkyū department store 175
Tomioka Silk Filature 31b, 40, 45–8, 49, 61
Toray 151, 160, 222b
Tore 160t
Toshiba 92, 137, 146, 154, 155, 157, 160, 161, 162
  bubble economy and its aftermath 190
  consumerism in high and stable growth periods 170
  'lost decades' 208
Totobo 160t
tourism 224, 230, 243–7, 252
  see also Tokyo Olympics (2020)
Toyo Babcock 104
Tōyōbō 62, 160, 178
Toyoda Automatic Loom Works Co. 99, 119–20
Toyoda Kiichirō 119–20
Toyoda Loom 158
Toyo Industries 146
Tōyō Menka 72
Toyo Otis Elevator 104
Toyota 100, 119, 147, 156–62, 189–90, 205, 209–12, 246, 250
Toyota Motor 99, 120, 147, 158, 197, 210–11, 220
Toyota Sales 158
Toyota Tsūshō 158
TPV (Taiwan) 208
transaction cost theory 56
Trans-Pacific Partnership (TPP) 237
transportation networks 13, 16
Treaty of Shimonoseki 69
Treaty of Versailles (1919) 82
Trump, D. 237

UBS 189
Udagawa, M. 171, 179–80
UFJ Bank 200
unequal treaty system 34–5, 40, 44
  renegotiation 65, 67
UNESCO Intangible Cultural Heritage list 220
'unicorns' 217
Union Carbide 151

Union Carbide Japan 152
unions/unionization 80, 82, 83, 133–4
Uniqlo fast fashion brand 201, 221–2*b*, 252
United Artists 101
United Kingdom 3, 37*t*, 38, 61, 67, 89, 217
   'Japanese Miracle' 150, 156, 159, 162
United States 2–3, 41, 50, 175, 252, 253
   bubble economy and its aftermath 190, 198
   consumerism in high and stable growth periods 179, 181
   Department of Commerce 1
   Environmental Protection Agency 167*b*
   foreign companies/multinational enterprises (MNEs) (1985-1930) 89, 91, 96
   'Japanese Miracle' 143, 150–2, 156, 159–61, 163
   'lost decades' 203, 206, 210, 213–14, 215–16, 217, 218, 220, 223
   Meiji government foreign employees 37*t*
   see also occupation period and Supreme Commander of the Allied Forces (SCAP) reforms
Universal 101
Universal Postal Union 32*b*
Uny supermarket 176
urban migration 68, 168

Vacuum Oil 97
varieties-of-capitalism approach 3
venture capital 171, 216–17
Vickers, Sons & Co. (UK) 113
Victor Company of Japan (JVC) 92
Victor Talking Machine (USA) 90, 92
Vision Fund 226–7*b*
Vogel, E.F. 1, 143, 252
Vogel, S. 234
Voluntary Export Restraints (VERs) 162

Wachigai 64
Wacoal 141
Wadhwani, D. 5
wage-bargaining 3
wage controls 122
Walmart 185
war economy 70, 121–2
Warner Brothers 101
wartime capitalism 6, 122
Wartime Industrial Property Law (1917) 72

Watson Tabulating Machines 155
welfare-state model 236
Western Electric (WE) (USA) 91–2, 118, 152
Western Europe 2–3, 4, 96, 198, 203, 216, 223
Westernization of society 33, 35, 40, 101, 165, 174
Wittner, D. 37, 47
women
   advancement of in business 252
   as consumers 87
   harnessing power of 240–2
   role of in social change 172
   in workforce 68–9, 81, 83–6, 87, 241–2, 249
womenomics 172, 240–1
work culture, contextual factors for changing 239–40
worker turnover 80–1
working conditions 66, 78, 79, 81, 84
working hours 238
   see also 'death by overwork'
Work-style Reform Act (2018) 239
work-style reforms 236, 237–8, 252
World Bank 141
World Innovation Lab 216
World War I 70, 75, 83
World War II 124

Yahoo 227*b*
Yamabe Takeo 62
Yamaichi Securities 196
Yamamura, K. 3, 39
Yamazaki Yoshiki 146
Yanagida Fujimatsu 75
Yanai Tadashi 221–2*b*, 242
Yanase Automobile Company 98
Yarrow (UK) 94
Yasuda 56, 58
Yasuda Bank 77
Yasuda Fire and Marine Insurance Company 186
Yawata Ironworks 70
Yokohama Specie Bank (YSB) 55
Yōmeishū Seizō Company 14
Yomiuri newspaper 32*b*
Yonekura Seiichiro 140
Yoshida 160
Yoshida Shigeru 129

Yoshimune 20
Yoshino, M.Y. 75
Yui, T. 38, 80

zaibatsu 3, 10*b*, 249
    capitalism 48, 68, 135
    capitalism, end of and big business restructuring 136–8
    decline and dismantling 130, 134–6, 145, 250
    foreign companies/multinational enterprises (MNEs) (1985-1930) 90, 104
    imperialism and war 110, 122–3
    industrial 108
    industrial capitalism (1895-1930) 67–8, 78, 80, 87
    new 135
    new industrial 115–17
    private sector in Meiji Period (1868-1912) 51, 54
    rise of and banking crisis (1920s-1930s) 72–5
    and transformation into modern corporations 56–9
zaiteku (high-tech financial techniques) 197